Politicized Religion and the Reframing of Fundamental Rights

OXFORD COMPARATIVE CONSTITUTIONALISM

Series Editors
Richard Albert, William Stamps Farish Professor of Law,
The University of Texas at Austin Law School

Robert Schütze, Professor of European and Global Law,
Durham University and College of Europe

Comparative constitutional law has a long and distinguished history in intellectual thought and in the construction of public law. As political actors and the people who create or modify their constitutional orders, they often wish to learn from the experience and learning of others. This cross-fertilization and mutual interaction has only accelerated with the onset of globalization, which has transformed the world into an interconnected web that facilitates dialogue and linkages across international and regional structures. Oxford Comparative Constitutionalism seeks to publish scholarship of the highest quality in constitutional law that deepens our knowledge of local, national, regional, and global phenomena through the lens of comparative public law.

ALSO PUBLISHED IN THIS SERIES

Constitutional Change Under Autocracy
Anna Fruhstorfer

City, State
Constitutionalism and the Megacity
Ran Hirschl

The Politics of Constitutional Rigidity
Unveiling Pathways to Change in Mexico
Mariana Velasco-Rivera

Courts and LGBTQ+ Rights in an Age of Judicial Retrenchment
Rehan Abeyratne

Ex-Ministers as Constitutional Judges
Mathias Möschel

Redefining Comparative Constitutional Law
Essays for Mark Tushnet
Edited by Madhav Khosla and Vicki C. Jackson

Foreign Relations Federalism
The EU in Comparative Perspective
Thomas Verellen

Responsive Judicial Review
Democracy and Dysfunction in the Modern Age
Rosalind Dixon

Outsourcing Rulemaking Powers
Constitutional Limits and National Safeguards
Cedric Jenart

Abusive Constitutional Borrowing
Legal Globalization and the Subversion of Liberal Democracy
Rosalind Dixon and David Landau

A Theory of African Constitutionalism
Berihun Adugna Gebeye

Eternity Clauses in Democratic Constitutionalism
Silvia Suteu

Deliberative Peace Referendums
Ron Levy, Ian O'Flynn, Hoi L. Kong

Scales of Memory Constitutional Justice and Historical Evil
Justin Collings

The Global South and Comparative Constitutional Law
Edited by Philipp Dann, Michael Riegner, and Maxim Bönnemann

Constitutional Change in the Contemporary Socialist World
Ngoc Son Bui

Poland's Constitutional Breakdown
Wojciech Sadurski

Politicized Religion and the Reframing of Fundamental Rights

SUSANNA MANCINI
Full Professor of Comparative Public Law, Department of Legal Studies, University of Bologna, Italy

MICHEL ROSENFELD
University Professor of Law and Comparative Democracy, Justice Sydney L. Robins Professor of Human Rights, Cardozo School of Law, Yeshiva University, USA

OXFORD
UNIVERSITY PRESS

OXFORD
UNIVERSITY PRESS

Great Clarendon Street, Oxford, OX2 6DP,
United Kingdom

Oxford University Press is a department of the University of Oxford.
It furthers the University's objective of excellence in research, scholarship,
and education by publishing worldwide. Oxford is a registered trade mark of
Oxford University Press in the UK and in certain other countries.

Published in the United States of America by Oxford University Press
198 Madison Avenue, New York, NY 10016, United States of America.

British Library Cataloguing in Publication Data
Data available

Library of Congress Control Number: 2025950533

ISBN 9780192888037

DOI: 10.1093/9780191982149.001.0001

Printed and bound by
CPI Group (UK) Ltd., Croydon, CR0 4YY

The manufacturer's authorized representative in the EU for product safety is
Oxford University Press España S.A. of Parque Empresarial San Fernando de Henares,
Avenida de Castilla, 2 – 28830 Madrid (www.oup.es/en or product.safety@oup.com).
OUP España S.A. also acts as importer into Spain of products made by the manufacturer.

MIX
Paper | Supporting responsible forestry
FSC® C013604

Brief Contents

Detailed Contents

Introduction

Throughout much of history, religion and politics have been inextricably intertwined. Religions and the religious have had their own politics. And, for their part, political actors have invoked, used, adapted, and at times reworked religious traditions, symbols, and elements to suit their worldly objectives and agendas. Accordingly, two correlated phenomena have spread side by side: religion's appropriation of politics and the politicization of religion. The first of these seeks to infuse, in part or whole, the dictates of a particular religion into the laws and politics of the relevant polity. Thus, for example, Catholic Church clergy or practicing Catholics may seek to turn their religion's prohibitions against abortion and divorce into the law of the land of their country of citizenship. The second phenomenon, in turn, consists of the appropriation by political actors of religious symbols, creeds, or practices for what are primarily identitarian and cultural purposes. In the most dramatic instances, which will be addressed in the course of the following discussion, secular leaders in countries with scant devotion to religious life have made use of religious symbols or traditions, such as the crucifix, the Islamic veil, or Christian "family values" in order to fuel a divide between those cast as "insiders" who belong and those cast as "the Other" either within or beyond the confines of the relevant polity. For instance, requiring crucifixes or the Ten Commandments to be displayed in state school classrooms in a Christian majority country, and insisting that these figure as traditional and cultural symbols rather than as expressions of the truth of Christianity, may well cause feelings of exclusion among those who belong to minority religions or who embrace atheism or agnosticism. In short, in pluralistic and religiously diverse polities, both religious politics and the politicization of religion, whether operating separately or in tandem, have often been prone to fostering contention and divisiveness (Mancini 2009).

As against this, liberal constitutionalism originating in the eighteenth-century Enlightenment has sought to disentangle religion from politics by institutionalizing secularism (Rosenfeld 2020). On the ashes of the wars of religion that tore through Europe in the sixteenth and seventeenth centuries (Crouzet 2008) emerged a quest to devise a public sphere free from religious controversy through a neutralization or depoliticization of religion. Eventually, this resulted in the advent of the concept of institutional secularism that was to become a pillar of liberal constitutionalism (Rosenfeld 2020). Its essence boils down to the following: ideally, religion ought to be expelled from the state's affairs and from the public sphere in exchange for being granted special protection and a maximum of liberty and autonomy within the private sphere consistent with pluralist inclusion of as many religions (and

Politicized Religion and the Reframing of Fundamental Rights. Susanna Mancini and Michel Rosenfeld, Oxford University Press. DOI: 10.1093/9780191982149.001.0001

non-religious conceptions of the good) as possible as much as possible so long as peaceful coexistence can be maintained throughout the polity.

The conventional narrative surrounding secularism and the Enlightenment has been critically reassessed from multiple perspectives. One of the central critiques targets the assumed clear-cut dichotomy between the private and public spheres, a distinction that has proven to be conceptually and politically unstable. Feminist scholarship, in particular, has underscored the inherently political nature of the private sphere—traditionally associated with familial relations, sexuality, and reproduction. As Pateman (1988) argues, sexual difference constitutes political difference, thereby imbuing the so-called private domain with profound political implications. Consequently, the relegation of religion to the private sphere produced two significant effects: first, it shielded religious practices and institutions from democratic oversight; second, it enabled religious norms to exert regulatory power over matters such as gender roles, family structures, sexuality, and reproductive rights (Stopler, 2025). As illustrated in Chapters 6 and 7, this framework has facilitated nationalist and populist religious movements in targeting sexual and reproductive rights.

Furthermore, the privatization of religion did not lead to a straightforward removal of religious influence from political discourse. On the contrary, it facilitated a process whereby religious thought, particularly Christian traditions, became secularized and universalized, thereby permeating liberal political theory. This entanglement is especially evident when one considers that Western secularism is historically rooted in the separation of the state from Christian institutions specifically, rather than from religion in general. As such, secularism not only accommodates Christian majorities but also contributes to the culturalization of Christianity, embedding its normative frameworks into the broader socio-political fabric. The Enlightenment, therefore, did not eliminate religion from the public sphere but rather transformed and abstracted it. As Talal Asad observes (1992), religion shifted from being a concrete set of practices tied to specific power structures to becoming a universalized and abstract moral framework.

This equation of secularized Christianity with purportedly universal values has underpinned the promotion of the secular state ideal in the West. Yet, models for managing the religion–state relationship differ significantly across Western contexts, reflecting diverse historical and cultural trajectories.

Various instantiations of institutional secularism have yielded six basic models of constitutional ordering of the relationship between religion and the state. As we will discuss in Chapter 1, all of these models aspire to approximate the institutional secularism ideal, and although they all fall short of that objective, each of them emerges as partially successful and keeps the focus on containing religious conflict through depoliticization. This is well exemplified by the US Constitution's First Amendment Establishment and Free Exercise clauses, which require sufficient separation between state and religion to allow for a pluralistic polity in which various religious and non-religious conceptions of the good can be peacefully accommodated. The Establishment Clause prohibits the state from embracing any particular religion or from preferring any of them over others.[1] At the same time, the Free Exercise Clause guarantees freedom of belief and the right of every person to practice the religion of her choice.[2] Other liberal constitutional democracies draw the line somewhat differently, with some like France requiring stricter separation between the state and religion,[3] and others like the United Kingdom enshrining an official state religion that does not operate in any ways that curtail the religious liberties of the religiously diverse citizenry.[4] The key to maintaining a workable arrangement geared toward institutional secularism consists in the state and the public sphere operating, in substance, largely independently from religion, while providing in the private sphere enough room for religions to thrive and to coexist.[5]

Significantly, in the last decades of the twentieth century, there was a dramatic "repoliticization" of religion in various parts of the world (Casanova 1994: 3–6), and this has led to sustained and systematic attacks on institutional secularism. Moreover, as we will amply address in Part II of the book, the repoliticization in question and its consequent assault on institutional secularism have led to concerted efforts to reframe many of the fundamental rights that have stood as one of the fundamental pillars of liberal constitutionalism (Rosenfeld 2022: 1). The

[1] *See Everson v Bd. of Educ.*, 330 U.S. 1, 15–16 (1947); *Bd. of Educ. of Kiryas Joel Vill. Sch. Dist. v Grumet*, 512 U.S. 687, 703 (1998).

[2] US Const amend I ("Congress shall make no law respecting an establishment of religion or prohibiting the free exercise thereof"); *Church of the Lukumi Bablu Aye, Inc. v Hialeah*, 508 U.S. 520, 534 (1993) ("The Free Exercise Clause, like the Establishment Clause, extends beyond facial discrimination. The Clause 'forbids subtle departures from neutrality,' ... and 'covert suppression of particular religious beliefs'" (citations omitted)).

[3] *See* Loi du 9 décembre 1905 concernant la séparation des Églises et de l'État [Law of December 9, 1905 concerning the Separation of Church and State], arts 1–2, *Journal Officiel de la République Française* [*Official Gazette of France*], December 9, 1905 (ensuring both the freedom of conscience and exercise of religion while also holding that the non-recognition, payment, or subsidization of any religion by the state and the abolition of public religious establishments).

[4] The UK codified its constitutional protection for freedom of religious belief and manifestation of that belief in 1998 with the incorporation of the European Convention on Human Rights (ECHR), Article 9 of which upholds the freedom of thought, conscience, and religion. Human Rights Act 1998, c 42, § 1(3), sch 1, incorporating Convention for the Protection of Human Rights and Fundamental Freedoms, art 9, November 4, 1950, Europ.TS No 5; 213 UNTS 221. In fact, the only legal, constitutional vestiges of preference for the Church of England relate to monarchical succession. *See* Act of Settlement 1700, 12 & 13 Will 3 c 2 (officially declaring the Crown as joined "in Communion with the Church of England"); Accession Declaration Act 1910, 10 Edw 7 & 1 Geo 5 c 29 (providing the coronation oath, where the monarch must swear that she or he is a "faithful Protestant" and will act to "secure the Protestant succession to the Throne").

[5] To the extent that freedom of religion is a fundamental constitutional right, religious belief should be inviolable and religious practice protected from majoritarian policies unless the relevant state meets the high thresholds allowing for limited and targeted limitations of fundamental rights under the constitution. *See, e.g.*, ECHR, art 9(2) ("Freedom to manifest one's religion or beliefs shall be subject only to such limitations as are prescribed by law and are necessary in a democratic society in the interests of public safety, for the protection of public order, health or morals, or for the protection of the rights and freedoms of others"); *Lee v Weisman*, 505 U.S. 577, 587 (1992).

late twentieth century repoliticization of religion began in earnest around 1980 in the waning days of the Cold War, which had in effect largely relegated religion to the periphery of the political sphere. Indeed, the Cold War's dominant struggle between capitalism and communism under the sustained fear of nuclear conflagration pitted two secular visions with universal ambitions fiercely against one another. Soviet communism was systematically hostile towards religion, whereas American-led capitalism was essentially ideologically neutral on the subject. Tellingly, to the extent that American capitalism did on occasion align itself with religion, this was through politicization rather than through any concerted commitment to religious dictates. Thus, in the largely secular 1950s Eisenhower era, a reference to God was added to the United States' "Pledge of Allegiance," whereby Americans declare their patriotic commitment to their flag and to their republic. Unmistakably, though, this addition of a divine reference was explicitly made for political purposes, namely, to differentiate American openness to freedom and to religious tolerance from the oppressive state-enforced atheism that prevailed throughout the Soviet-dominated communist world (Stoelting & Stacie 2013). In the midst of the Cold War, therefore, Americans could thrive religiously within the private sphere while not losing sight politically of the ongoing aim to unwaveringly counter what was perceived as the omnipresent threat posed by the polities ensconced within the communist camp.

The novel wave of repoliticization of religion launched around 1980 has proven complex and variegated. In some cases, such as in that of Iran, a secular regime was replaced by a theocratic one;[6] in others, such as that concerning Protestant fundamentalists and conservative Catholics in the United States, religious fervor has motivated strong political organization and deployment with notable policy successes but without thus far altering the basic constitutional order.[7] Furthermore, the repoliticization of religion has taken different forms, ranging from radically progressive to radically conservative ones. One can think of the political praxis of Latin American Liberation Theologians, who integrated Catholic teaching and Marxism to advocate for social justice and the liberation of oppressed people (Araujo 1994–1995: 63, 66–67). In many more recent cases, however, one of the

[6] Greg Bruno, "Religion and politics in Iran," *Council on Foreign Relations*, June 19, 2008, <www.cfr.org/backgrounder/religion-and-politics-iran>, accessed October 2, 2025; Farhad Rezaei, "Theocracy vs. democracy in Iran: A new round in an old conflict," *Atlantic Council*, July 3, 2017, <www.atlanticcouncil.org/blogs/iransource/theocracy-vs-democracy-in-iran-a-new-round-in-an-old-conflict/>, accessed October 2, 2025. *See also* Interview by David Speedie with Dr Mohammad Javad Ardashir Larijani, "Report from Iran," *Carnegie Council*, November 15, 2011, <www.carnegiecouncil.org/studio/multimedia/20111115-report-from-iran>, accessed October 2, 2025 (describing Iran as "a polity which has a democratic structure," but differs from the Western experience in that "[i]t is a democracy based on Islamic rationality").

[7] Clyde Haberman, "Religion and right-wing politics: How Evangelicals shaped elections," *New York Times*, October 28, 2018, <www.nytimes.com/2018/10/28/us/religion-politics-evangelicals.html>, accessed October 2, 2025; Michael Lipka, "Half of Americans say Bible should influence U.S. laws, including 28% who favor it over the will of the people," *Pew Research Center*, April 13, 2020, <https://pewrsr.ch/3eeiiZI>, accessed October 2, 2025.

most salient and far-reaching consequences of the repoliticization of religion has been its starkly anti-pluralist thrust, which is perhaps best exemplified by contemporary deployments of religious nationalism and of religious populism. In both of these cases, what is crucial is not whether or not there is a significant or widespread commitment to religious belief or dogma, but instead the use of religion as the basis for forging identitarian bonds that are strongly exclusionary of those cast as the "Other." In religious nationalism, national identity is defined above all by belonging to a single (usually majoritarian) religion—whether in terms of religious belief and practice or in terms of embracing the cultural mainstays associated with the religion in question. Moreover, this religious belonging implies that commitment to other (usually minoritarian) religions is contrary to, or erosive for, the unity or coherence of the imagined community bound together by its own distinct national identity. For example, by insisting that the United States be regarded above all as a Christian nation, one can readily convey to non-Christians that they do not belong or that, at best, they should be merely tolerated.[8] On the other hand, religious populism—as all populism—consists in projecting a part as the whole when circumscribing "the people."[9] Accordingly, the people may be the ordinary citizens led by their charismatic leader against the "elites"; the native born versus the immigrants; a particular ethnic group against all others; and, in the case of religious populism, those belonging to one religion as opposed to all those who belong to other religions. In addition, in certain cases, populism may aggregate the non-elite, ethnically uniform, and designated co-religionists into a recrafted brand of peoplehood. Thus, for example, in a contemporary populist (and nationalist) regime, such as that of Prime Minister Orban in Hungary, ethnic Hungarians are privileged, and references to the country's Christian heritage are directed against liberal secular cosmopolitan elites cast as internal enemies of the Hungarian people, and against Muslim would-be immigrants who figure as the Hungarians' external enemies.[10]

[8] *See Town of Greece v Galloway*, 572 U.S. 565, 632–33 (2014) (Kagan J, dissenting) (stating that a municipality's invocation of Christian prayer during town hall meetings "infuse[d] a participatory government body with one (and only one) faith, so that month in and month out, the citizens appearing before it become partly defined by their creed—as those who share, and those who do not, the community's majority religious belief").

[9] Albertazzi & McDonnell 2015: 5 (defining populism as "[a] thin-centred ideology which pits a virtuous and homogeneous people against a set of elites and dangerous 'others' who are together depicted as depriving (or attempting to deprive) the sovereign people of their rights, values, prosperity, identity and voice").

[10] *See* Péter Krekó, Bulcsú Hunyadi, & Patrik Szicherle, "Anti-Muslim populism in Hungary: From the margins to the mainstream," *Brookings*, July 24, 2019, <www.brookings.edu/research/anti-muslim-populism-in-hungary-from-the-margins-to-the-mainstream>, accessed October 2, 2025. *See also* ibid. ("In [the Hungarian far-right's] view, the European Union and some member states force the dictatorship of liberal values on their citizens and other countries. Hence, according to their narrative, the 'cosmopolitan' elites in Brussels and some other capitals (e.g., in Berlin) dictate just like Moscow did back in the communist era" (citing "Orbán a rezsicsökkentést hasonlítja március 15-éhez," *Origo*, March 15, 2014, <www.origo.hu/itthon/20140315-orban-viktor-unnepi-beszede-2014-marcius-15-en.html>, accessed October 2, 2025)).

To the extent that nationalism and populism resort to religion to establish markers of inclusion and of exclusion, they seek to turn institutional secularism associated with liberal constitutionalism on its head. However, religious nationalism and populism do not thereby necessarily cast secularism away altogether. Instead, they tend to reposition secularism by replacing *institutional* secularism with *ideological* secularism (Rosenfeld 2014: 79). The dynamic between institutional and ideological secularism is essential both from the standpoint of the perspective of the defenders of institutional secularism and from that of its contemporary detractors. This dynamic will be critically examined in depth in Chapter 4, but for now suffice it to characterize ideological secularism as a conception of the good among many. Accordingly, so long as institutional secularism can be defended as distinct from its ideological counterpart, its aspiration to neutrality can be emulated with a view to placing ideological secularism on a par with all religion-based conceptions of the good equally entitled to freedom and autonomy, so long as they remain depoliticized. On the other hand, if institutional secularism cannot avoid collapsing into its ideological namesake, then the separation of religion from the state preached by liberal constitutionalism is much more likely to smuggle in and enshrine a single conception of the good—and an irreligious or anti-religious one at that—to the detriment of all those who share ways of life carved out by religion.

Contemporary nationalism and populism weigh in on the complex and intricate dynamic between institutional and ideological secularism, and take the position for or against secularism, with the overriding aim to better suit their anti-pluralist inclusionary and exclusionary agendas. Thus, as will be detailed through discussion of many instances below, some nationalists and populists have endeavored to reduce secularism to a selfish, hedonistic, and morally vacuous ideology that has overtaken Western liberal constitutional democracies. To escape this declared dire predicament, nationalist leaders call upon the majority religion in their country to become prominently engrafted or greatly magnified in the national identity. This move has a twofold aim: first, an inclusionary appeal to all fellow religionists coupled with an exclusionary setting apart of all those who adhere to other religions or to a secular outlook; and two, a degradation of institutional into ideological secularism and a rejection of the latter as unworthy and dangerous to the nation and to its self-definition through embrace of its traditional religion (most often primarily treated in identitarian terms, but at times also supplemented with varying links to its genuinely devout adherents). Similarly, populists who appeal to religion set the religious tradition of the part of the polity's population they have renamed as its "people" as a means to rally the latter and to set them against all those meant to be excluded within and those cast as enemies lurking outside the populist nation-state's borders. Where religion functions as the dominant marker within a nationalist or populist project, secularism is altogether likely to be attacked as unworthy of respect or of inclusion. But in other settings with strong secular roots, such as France, the populists belonging to the National Front, now renamed the National Rally, espoused anti-Semitic positions in the past and more recently Islamophobic ones (Fieschi 2019). Perhaps the best way to characterize these singularized anti-religious stances is in terms of a reworking of secularism through erasure of the boundary between its institutional and its ideological iterations. Indeed, taken by itself, institutional secularism would command affording full protection to Islam and to Judaism within the French private sphere. Moreover, because the populists in question do not reject secularism in favor of Catholicism, the country's majority religion, their particular anti-religious stances imply a combination of two separate, albeit misplaced, concerns. The first of these is that the two targeted minority religions are poised to disrupt and undermine the neutrality and integrity of the French public sphere. In contrast, the second concern seems to be squarely grounded in adherence to ideological secularism. This is because this latter populist concern frames the targeted minority religions as contradicting and squarely conflicting with France's secular way of life, whereas Christianity (as it has adapted in response to the institutionalization of *laïcité*) remains largely understood as posing no comparable threat.[11]

Religion-based appropriation of politics and nationalist or populist politicization of religion with a view to pursuing an anti-pluralist illiberal agenda is certainly compatible with doing away with the fundamental rights associated with liberal constitutionalism. And this is all the more so if the illiberalism in question is deployed in the course of a transition to authoritarianism. Notably, however, many anti-liberal polities that have forcefully embarked on a course of repoliticizing religion have insisted on maintaining commitment to human rights and to fundamental constitutional rights, albeit in somewhat different and mostly more limited ways. Illiberal religious nationalist and populist polities tend to reshape and to reinterpret those rights in ways that suit their anti-pluralist agendas. Thus, for instance, Christian nationalists or populists may reinterpret freedom of religion rights in ways that disadvantage or exclude the rights asserted by Muslims.[12] Also, polities dominated by certain religious traditionalists may promote versions of fundamental rights that may well exacerbate discrimination against women and sexual minorities.[13]

Populists and illiberals who do not do away with rights tend to colonize them. Moreover, such colonization typically takes different forms, which will be addressed in detail throughout the book. In the broadest terms, in a number of cases, the content of a right is, quite simply, turned on its head: thus, for example, reproductive rights are presented as the right of women not to have an abortion;

[11] For further discussion of the special accommodation that has developed between French *laïcité* and Catholicism in that country, *see* below at pp. 15–16.

[12] *See* below at pp. 115–116.

[13] *See* below at pp. 122–123.

and the right to self-determination as that of not wearing a face mask during a pandemic. In other instances, the content of the relevant right remains seemingly untouched, but there is a flipping of hierarchy between the victim class entitled to invoke the right and those who figure as belonging to the perpetrator class (Mégret 2022), so that whites become the victims of race-discrimination, and Christians are recharacterized so as to project a narrative that portrays them as vulnerable religious minorities in need of special accommodation in traditionally religiously and culturally Christian polities. Another strategy designed to secure rights colonization consists of blatantly altering the content of a right, so that it becomes applicable only to a selected number of individuals, to the detriment of others. As an example of this, one can think of eco-fascists' anti-immigration claims in order "to protect the environment viewed as essential to White identity."[14] Another strategy seeks to colonize rights by hierarchizing them (De Burca & Young 2023) in ways that privilege the interests of certain groups (whites, Christians, financially powerful segments of society). The neatest example of this strategy is offered by the attempt by the Pompeo Commission during the Trump administration to exclusively single out the rights to private property and to religious freedom (particularly suited to conservative iterations of the Christian way of life) as inalienable while casting social and economic rights as merely partisan political ones and thus undesirable.[15]

Illiberals and populists use various techniques to alter the content of rights. These include the selection of a limited number of documents (the Universal Declaration of Human Rights, the American Declaration of Independence) as the only legitimate sources of rights.[16] Another technique consists of adherence to noncontextualized, literal interpretations of rights provisions (Young 2022); appeals to "natural law" and to other vague pre-political sources, such as common sense and tradition. As a frequently used example, one can cite the assertion that the family has always been made up of a man and a woman.[17] In the latter case, as in many others, one finds that under the pretenses of universalism lurk what amount to sectorial moral and religious conceptions. In addition, several doctrinal mainstays of liberal constitutionalism have been invoked to turn the table on the relatively recent beneficiaries of expanded liberty and equality rights to favor or enhance religion-based rights. In particular, conscientious objection claims have

[14] Alex Amend, "Blood and vanishing topsoil: American ecofascism past, present, and in the coming climate crisis," *Political Research Associates*, July 9, 2020, <https://politicalresearch.org/2020/07/09/blood-and-vanishing-topsoil>, accessed May 26, 2025.

[15] *See* Department of State Commission on Unalienable Rights, 84 Fed. Reg. 25,109 (May 30, 2019).

[16] *See, e.g.*, US Commission on Unalienable Rights, *Draft Report of the Commission on Unalienable Rights*, July 16, 2020, <www.state.gov/wp-content/uploads/2020/07/Draft-Report-of-the-Commission-on-Unalienable-Rights.pdf>, accessed October 2, 2025.

[17] In Hungary's Orban's words, "[f]amily ties shall be based on marriage or the relationship between parent and children. The mother is a woman. The father is a man." Cited in *Rolling Stone*, August 4, 2022, <www.rollingstone.com/politics/politics-news/viktor-orban-cpac-speech-standing-ovation-1392714/>, accessed October 2, 2025.

proliferated for the purpose of obtaining increasingly sweeping exemptions from generally applicable laws on religious grounds (Mancini & Rosenfeld 2018:1–2). Similarly, anti-discrimination constitutional doctrine linked to equality rights has been invoked to turn the table on its relatively recent beneficiaries, such as women and members of the LGBTQ + community. Thus, claims of religious discrimination have been advanced to seek broad and far-reaching exemptions from laws designed to vindicate or to reinforce the equality rights of women or of LGBTQ + persons (Mancini & Rosenfeld 2018: 1).

The book's principal objective is to provide a systematic account of the repoliticization of religion launched in the 1980s and of its consequences, particularly as they inform the dynamic between liberal constitutionalism's conception of fundamental rights and its illiberal counterparts. Moreover, in order to thoroughly assess how the illiberal challenges and refashioning of fundamental rights ultimately impact the liberal constitutionalism project and its reliance on institutional secularism, the book will inquire into the latter's past as well as into its present and plausible futures. This will be done in order both to fully appreciate the import of the current illiberal challenge in its full nationalist, populist, and transnational dimensions, and to assess the potential of liberal fundamental rights to endure or to adapt and evolve in order to overcome the fierce illiberal attacks on institutional secularism. With this in mind, the book will integrate various approaches, drawing on history, political and constitutional theory, and comparative constitutional law in order to provide a comprehensive functional understanding of the post-1980s attacks and of their implications for constitutional secularism.

In terms of organization, the book is divided into two parts. The first part of the book concentrates on the theoretical underpinnings of the advent and deployment of, and attacks on, institutional secularism and its Enlightenment-grounded premises. The second part of the book, in turn, focuses from a comparative constitutional perspective on the various ways in which fundamental rights have been illiberally reframed throughout a vast array of different jurisdictions.

Part I of the book is entitled "The Theoretical, Historical, and Constitutional Context." Chapter 1, "Overcoming the Wars of Religion: The Enlightenment and the Constitutional Enshrinement of Institutional Secularism," explores the historical and theoretical foundations of institutional secularism. The concept of what is now called secularism originated *within* the Christian religion and only evolved toward a conception aiming at neutrality among religions in the aftermath of Europe's wars of religion, culminating in the Enlightenment's endeavor to implant a categorical distinction between Faith and Reason. Institutional secularism aspires to be "areligious" as contrasted with "irreligious" or "anti-religious," and its two principal normative dictates are commitment to religious pluralism and prohibition to base political rule on contested religious (metaphysical) truth. Aspirations to approximate the institutional secularism ideal have yielded six distinct models for handling the constitutional nexus between religion and the state.

After describing the main features of each of these models, the latter's virtues and vices will be critically assessed and compared.

Chapter 2, "Repoliticized Religion and the Dialectic Between Religious Appropriation of Politics and Political Appropriation of Religion," recounts the historical evolution toward the 1980s repoliticization of religion and its grounding in critiques of institutional secularism. Emphasis bears on the differences between: (i) religious appropriation of the constitution—as was the case in Iran; (ii) reinterpreting the constitution through religion—as spearheaded by Protestant fundamentalists in the United States; (iii) the political appropriation of religion—as exemplified by the Solidarity movement in Poland and theological liberation in Latin America; and (iv) the unresolved and ongoing clash between religious and constitutional norms—as it has uniquely unfolded in Israel.

Chapter 3, "Religious Nationalism and Religious Populism: Religious Rule of the Nation and the People Versus National and Popular Acculturation of Religion," traces and critically assesses the key role of religious nationalism and religious pluralism in the ongoing repoliticization of religion for anti-pluralist purposes. The movement toward nationalism emerged as a secular phenomenon, but has evolved in several quarters toward inextricably entwining the relevant nation with a particular (usually majoritarian) religion or religious tradition in order to stand against secularism and other (usually minoritarian) religions traditionally embedded within the polity. Similarly, populism itself need not be conjoined with religion, but like in cases involving its nationalist counterparts, has conjoined with a particular religion to demarcate those included within the more narrowly redefined "people" and those meant to be excluded as the latter's "Other." Whereas both nationalism and populism can embrace religious rule, for the most part, in the context of its repoliticization religion figures primarily as a cultural and identitarian marker politically invoked and adapted for exclusionary purposes. The chapter contrasts attempts at religious appropriation of the nation—as exemplified by the efforts to (re)conceptualize the United States as a fundamentalist Protestant New Jerusalem—with appeals to broadly shared cultural mainstays originating in the dominant religious tradition to propel anti-pluralist designs—as illustrated by European anti-Muslim policies grounded in Christian culture and tradition as well as sometimes in secular ideology internalized as compatible with Christian culture. Although nationalism and populism alone or in combination can similarly incorporate religion, in one key respect, populism's nexus to religion differs from that of nationalism. This stems from the fact that populism itself, even when manifestly secular—as it was in the Venezuela of Hugo Chavez—exudes a religion or religiosity of its own. Indeed, as the chapter will detail, populism links the newly anointed people with its charismatic leader to embark on a messianic mission toward a utopian future or toward recovery of an idealized past, which the pre-populist polity is accused of having forsaken.

Chapter 4, "The Dynamic Between Institutional and Ideological Secularism and Its Uses in Anti-Secular Attacks in the Name of Religion," focuses on the dynamic between institutional and ideological secularism and places that dynamic in its proper historical, theoretical, and political context. From a theoretical standpoint, institutional secularism's aspiration to neutrality must be contrasted to ideological secularism, which amounts to one conception of the good among many and is characterized above all by its rejection of transcendence and its embrace of science. Next, the chapter engages with the relevant history of religion-based attacks on institutional secularism as inherently non-neutral or downright anti-religious. Two specific religion-based attacks that straddle the boundaries between institutional and ideological secularism are particularly revelatory in relation to the major theoretical issues at stake. The first of these concerns religious attacks on science, spanning from intransigent insistence that the earth is flat to the push for eradication of the teaching of the theory of evolution in public school science classes. The second attack, in turn, is one that is more accurately captured in terms of a co-optation of secularism in order to subsume it under religion. This second attack is perhaps best illustrated by Pope Benedict XVI's conflation of Faith and Reason to align the truth revealed by the Catholic religion with the corresponding version of natural law claimed to be equally discoverable through faith or through reason. Finally, the chapter engages with the recent special circumstances, such as the struggle against global terrorism and the management of the COVID-19 pandemic, in relation to which religion has been invoked to undermine established standards of proportionality in fundamental rights constitutional adjudication. To conclude, the chapter poses the key question that animates the book in its proper multifaceted context: Can the two essential prescriptions of institutional secularism, namely the pursuit of pluralism and the banning of purely religious truth from law and politics, be salvaged *independently from* institutional secularism? Although this question cannot be properly answered without reference to the comparative constitutional analysis provided in Part II of the book, its posing usefully circumscribes the consideration of the various instances of fundamental rights reframing that will be dealt with in detail in subsequent chapters.

Part II of the book is entitled "Applications: Illiberal and Anti-Pluralist Recasting of Fundamental Constitutional and Human Rights in the Name of Religion."

Chapter 5, "Secularism as Religious Majoritarianism," tackles two distinct but closely connected phenomena: the reinforcement of the privileges of religious majorities and the marginalization of denominational minorities. Starting in the 1980s, religious majorities have become increasingly politicized in different parts of the world, and majority religions have regained a paramount role in conceptualizing national identities. In this respect, the emphasis is often placed not on the transcendent nature of religion but, rather, on its cultural dimension. Thus, religion undergoes a process of secularization and semantic disarticulation, and becomes an implicit mainstay engrained in the secular nation's tradition and culture. This process leads to two consequences: on the one hand, it fosters the return of the majority religion's culture and tradition in the public sphere, challenging the principle of separation between church and state. The premise is that states must recognize that the predominant national religious inheritance does not just amount to one among many other denominations but, in addition, and perhaps most importantly, provides a key element of civic cohesion. What follows is that the historical national religion should enjoy a preferential treatment, while other denominations should simply be tolerated. On the other hand, the culturalization of religion facilitates the othering and the marginalization of minority religions, on the ground of their incompatibility with the national culture.

The chapter traces the analogies between the secularization of Hinduism in India and of Christianity in Europe, through a comparison of the *rationale* of the "Hindutva cases" decided by the Indian Supreme Court, and of laws and judicial cases regarding the display of Christian symbols in the European public sphere. It then moves to the analysis of two particularly effective strategies through which religious minorities are marginalized in different contexts: the regulation of minority religious attire and religion-based discrimination in immigration and citizenship law. Finally, the chapter focuses on the shifting role of Islam in defining national belonging in Turkey, from the birth of the Kemalist Republic to Prime Minister Erdoğan's Islamist populist project.

Chapter 6, "The War on 'Gender Ideology,'" addresses the reshaping of rights as a consequence of domestic and transnational mobilizations against "gender ideology." The latter term, which emerged in Catholic circles, initially indicated opposition to activism around sexual and reproductive rights, and to the scholarship deconstructing essentialist and naturalistic assumptions about gender and sexuality. With time, however, anti-genderism has gained significant traction across various regions, turning into a "symbolic glue" that brings together a wide range of illiberal and populist actors across political and religious spectrums, serving as a unifying discourse amid otherwise fragmented interests. In this context, the term *gender* has become a battlefield through which broader critiques of liberal democracy, globalization, democratic norms, and human rights frameworks are articulated. The chapter first offers an overview of the emergence and of the global spread of anti-genderism, and of its religious, political, and ideological roots, with a particular focus on the appropriation of "rights talk" by illiberal and populist actors relying on anti-gender arguments. Next, the chapter presents the unique case of the Istanbul Convention, a Council of Europe Treaty aimed at combating violence against women, which was manipulated and misrepresented in several Central and Eastern European countries by illiberal and populist actors claiming that it imposes "gender ideology," promotes LGTBQ+ rights, and threatens state sovereignty.

Chapter 7, "Reinventing Traditions to Subvert Constitutional Law and the International Human Rights Regime," explores the ways in which narratives of tradition are invoked to justify the dismissal of international legal norms, reconfigure international relations, and reinterpret rights frameworks in a manner that legitimizes gender-based discrimination, suppresses freedom of expression, and facilitates the marginalization of minority groups. The chapter focuses on case studies from Russia, the United States, and several African countries, demonstrating how different forms of traditionalism are employed as interpretive frameworks to justify the subordination of international law to imperialist policies and the reconfiguration of rights in conservative and religious terms.

In the Russian context, this phenomenon is shaped by a complex interplay of geopolitical theories, religious doctrines, and historical revisionism, which underscore narratives of national exceptionalism and imperial legacy. In the United States a similar dynamic emerges through the fusion of Christian theological principles—particularly dominion theology—with originalism as a method of constitutional interpretation. In certain African contexts, such as Uganda, US-based Christian organizations exploit local theological traditions and demographic concerns, co-opting political leadership to reinstall colonial-era anti-homosexuality legislation, as a purportedly authentic expression of human rights aligned with African cultural values.

The comparative analysis showcases that, despite these contextual differences, the invocation of traditionalism in all cases does not reflect an organic continuity with indigenous or historical traditions. Rather, it constitutes a deliberately constructed and ideologically driven form of conservatism, selectively engineered to serve authoritarian political and religious agendas.

PART I

THE THEORETICAL, HISTORICAL, AND CONSTITUTIONAL CONTEXT

1

Overcoming the Wars of Religion: The Enlightenment and the Constitutional Enshrinement of Institutional Secularism

The nexus between constitutionalism and secularism traces back to the Enlightenment's delinking Faith from Reason. Viewed from above and in terms of its essentials, liberal secular constitutional democracy is built upon a three-pronged re-conception. This re-conception delimits the polity slated to become the relevant constitutional unit; the relevant collective units—including religious ones—recognized as constitutionally significant within that polity; and the newly valorized singularity that the individual citizen of the relevant polity is meant to project into the realms of the social and the political. The liberal secular constitutional polity is historically rooted in the late eighteenth-century American and French revolutions, and fitted to the nation-state, to the plurality of relevant collective units within the latter, and to the aggregation of individual citizens regarded as equals that comprise that nation-state's people. In this context, the nation-state figures as the community of (relevant) communities and its normative constitutionally enshrined prescriptions as the universal within its precincts.[1] To this universal

[1] Universal norms are generally understood as those that apply to all peoples at all times whereas as used above they are meant to encompass the constitutional unit as a whole as well as the individuals and collective units within the relevant constitutional polity. To avoid confusion, one may differentiate between the "absolute" universal that encompasses all people at all times and the "relative" universal confined to a particular constitutional unit. The latter distinction does not preclude, however, confluences

Politicized Religion and the Reframing of Fundamental Rights. Susanna Mancini and Michel Rosenfeld, Oxford University Press. © Susanna Mancini, Michel Rosenfeld 2026. DOI: 10.1093/9780191982149.003.0002

one must add the plural meant to differentiate among diverse constitutionally relevant national, ethnic, linguistic, cultural, and religious collective units. Finally, standing alongside the above-mentioned universal and plural, is the singular embodied by the individual citizen who is entitled and encouraged to plow into the depths of her own singularity in order to devise and pursue her own personal path to self-realization and self-fulfillment.

The ideal of liberal constitutionalism and its incorporation of secularism derive from the historical and conceptual repudiation of the hierarchical social and political order prevailing throughout Western feudalism. In its heyday, feudalism combined estate-based hierarchy and privileges with a governance based on dependences, alliances, and confrontations among a variegated array of interlaced fiefdoms (Ganshof 1976). This system, which eroded greatly with the rise of Europe's absolute monarchs, eventually gave way to the Westphalian nation-state, which would eventually become the locus of the liberal constitutional unit. At first, as the increasingly centralized and unified state consolidated its foothold in a Western Europe newly divided among Catholics and Protestants, it embraced the slogan *cuius regio, eius religio* also referred to as "one king, one faith, one law," which required weaving together religion, the state, and politics to secure the hegemony of the dominant religion throughout the realm (Lecler 1951: 38). This embrace by the state of the dominant religion within the realm is dramatically illustrated by the fate of Henry IV, king of France from 1589 till 1610, who had fought in his country's fierce sixteenth-century wars of religion as a Protestant, ascended its throne as such, but converted to Catholicism a few years later under relentless pressure from Catholics who insisted that only one of their faith could be the legitimate king of France (Potter 1997: 231). Henry IV converted after having supposedly famously uttered that "*Paris vaut bien une messe*" ("Paris is well worth a mass"), and he ruled for many years until he was assassinated by a Catholic zealot in 1610 (Mousnier 1973: 36–37). Mindful of the predicament of his country's religious minority, Henry IV proclaimed the Edict of Nantes in 1598, which accorded substantial rights to French Protestants and promoted mutual tolerance among the two religious communities that had long been at war with one another. This Edict was revoked, however, by Henry IV's descendant, King Louis XIV, in 1685, prompting France's Protestants to flee in massive numbers (Grandjean & Roussel 1998).

As long as a significant percentage of the population within a polity adhered to minority religions, imposition of the majority religion throughout all confines within the realm was prone to generate conflict, discrimination, and instability. This, as we shall see, eventually led to recourse to secularism in the hope

between these two types of universals. Thus, for instance, from the standpoint of liberal individualism granting the individual rights to freedom of conscience and to freedom of and from religion ought to be the norm in all constitutional regimes regardless of any historical, cultural, or religious differences among them. For a more extended discussion of the contrast between absolute and relative universals in the context of liberal constitutionalism, *see* Rosenfeld 2022.

of reducing or neutralizing religious tensions within the political sphere. Briefly stated, the idea was to facilitate a *modus vivendi* among Catholics and Protestants by fostering a truce in the public sphere and by leaving ample room for each of them to thrive separately in the private sphere. Although the term "secularism" was not used before the mid-nineteenth century, the concept associated with it—contested as it has enduringly proven to be—traces back to antiquity (Holyoake 1896: 51). Within the scope of the dynamic between Catholics and Protestants, optimally secularism would allow devising a public sphere that remained neutral as between these two contending faiths. Moreover, this aspired-to neutrality could be approximated, as best as possible, through the institutionalization both of norms commonly shared by the two religions and of norms that neither embraced but that remained neutral between the two.

Conceptually, finding commonly shared religious norms becomes more elusive the greater the number of competing religions within the same polity. Furthermore, with the spread of non-religious conceptions of the good during the period of the Enlightenment and into the nineteenth and twentieth centuries, the bundle of society-wide commonly shared norms, values, and ways of life would logically dwindle to the point of becoming impervious to stable or meaningful mutual accommodation. Accordingly, the task of secularism would seem increasingly daunting as recourse to neutral norms would be needed to fill the vast space left bare by the continuing serious retreat of commonly shared normative goals and commitments.

Under these conditions, for multi-religious, multi-cultural, Enlightenment-grounded polities, the best conceivable option from the standpoint of liberal constitutional democracy seems to consist in combining a neutral public sphere with a private sphere suited to peacefully accommodate all religious and non-religious conceptions of the good with adherents within the relevant constitutional unit. This, in turn, would require depoliticizing formerly warring or hegemonic religions while at the same time affording robust freedom-of- (and from-) religion constitutional protections spanning throughout the private sphere. Constitutionally, the combination of public depoliticization and private secure and steadfast protection calls for the implementation of what we call "*institutional secularism*," which will be further discussed in Section C of this chapter. Institutional secularism sets an ideal of complete neutrality, which the six principal constitutional models are meant to approximate but have never come close to achieving. That and the repoliticization of religion started around 1980, discussed in Chapter 2, have fueled a wide-ranging set of critiques of secularism as a concept and as an instrument fit for constitutional ordering of the multifaceted relationship between state and religion.

These critiques and the seeming impossibility of ever coming close enough to the ideal of institutional secularism pose a daunting challenge to the central thesis advanced in this book, namely that there are crucial qualitative and normative differences setting apart fundamental rights relating to religion under liberal constitutional regimes from their equivalents deployed under illiberalism or populism. In short, the attack on the possibility of neutrality implies that institutional secularism is a mirage and that there is no way to avoid the dominance of religion or of anti-religious hostility to religion in the public sphere.[2] Also, this latter attack is not only mounted by illiberal and populist political actors, but also by several leading scholars. Thus, for example, the anthropologist Saba Mahmood has argued that secularism in the West as well as beyond—including in Muslim majority countries such as Egypt—instead of inching closer to neutrality does in effect manage to enshrine the dominance of the majority religion to the detriment of the latter's minority counterparts (Mahmood 2016).[3]

Unless these critiques can be countered in a principled manner, the clash between institutional secularism and various religious and anti-religious ideologies would be ultimately reducible to a *Kulturkampf* among proponents of different fundamental values and ways of life. And in that case, *institutional secularism* would collapse into *ideological secularism*, which will be discussed further in Chapter 4, but which in essence amounts to an ideology and a way of life that embraces the secular as against all religion. Accordingly, consistent with Mahmood's thesis, institutional secularism would end up repackaging majority religion dominance while endeavoring to better conceal it. Or, in line with the view that institutional secularism is a mere stand-in for an ideological secularism that amounts to an anti-religious ideology, constitutional adherence to secularism would be properly regarded as inevitably institutionally enshrining hostility against all religions.

Although ideally institutional secularism would carve out a sphere of the *areligious*—namely, one that is completely neutral as between all religious and non-religious conceptions of the good in play—the fact that this has not been achieved to date and will likely never come close to realization does not thereby preclude a cogent and principled defense of the core of institutional secularism.[4] Indeed, the impossibility of the areligious does not force constitutional secularism into an inevitable choice between the *irreligious*—namely, ideologies that set aside religion without harboring any intended hostility toward any of them—and the *anti-religious*—namely, ideologies such as Marx's which regard religion as the "opium of the people" (Marx 1975: 175) or as some other nefarious impediment to pursuit or achievement of the good. What we will aim to demonstrate is that adhering to the core of institutional secularism allows for the preservation of the integrity of liberal constitutionalism and its framing of fundamental rights relating to religion in ways that can be contrasted as a matter of principle to the transformation or

[2] *See* the discussion, p. 74.

[3] *See also*, Assad 2003: 193 (noting that "although religion is regarded as alien to the secular, the latter is also seen to have generated religion").

[4] For a more extended discussion of the "areligious" in the context of the secular, *see* Rosenfeld 2011: 151–54.

distortion of such rights by proponents of populism and of illiberalism. In short, neither the secular nor secularism can be purged of, or purge, all religion, but they are not thereby prevented from dialectically reframing the relationship between state, constitution, and religion in ways that can prove innovative and productive as opposed to a mere repackaging or concealing of a dominant religion or anti-religion. With this in mind, this chapter will set the stage for the full articulation of our theoretical inquiry and proceeds as follows: Section A traces the religious roots of Western secularism and its historical journey into Enlightenment-based constitutionalism; Section B focuses on the core of institutional secularism; and Section C outlines the six principal models seeking to regulate the relationship between state and religion within the scope of institutional secularism and assesses the respective virtues and vices of each of them.

A. Overcoming the Wars of Religion and Dethroning State Religions

If we trace back to its historical origins, what we understand at present, as contested as such understanding may be, to qualify as secularism or as the secular, we discover that the concept in question originates not only in religion, but in a single one, namely Christianity. Indeed, as a concept, secularism traces back to the reference made in the New Testament to Jesus' dictum to render unto Caesar what is Caesar's and to God what is God's (Matthew 22: 21). Augustine further elaborated this distinction through the contrast he drew between the "City of God" and the "City of Man" (Augustine 1958). Later in the medieval era, the term "*secularis*" was used to designate those members of the clergy who worked with people within society, in contrast to their brethren who were exclusively devoted to spiritual pursuits within the confines of monastic life.[5] What is most striking about all three of these historical references is that the secular is wholly encompassed within the Christian religion, and that, from its very beginnings, Christianity sets a divide between the spiritual realm and the arena of politics.[6] Notably, neither such divide nor secularism more generally form part of Judaism or Islam, the two other Abrahamic religions. Judaism has a comprehensive legal system that it posits as divine in origin, thus leaving no room for any division tracking the Christian one between the realm of God and that of Caesar. Moreover, though in the diaspora, Judaism commands obeying the law of the land, that is only so long as the latter remains consistent with the Noachide code, which is the divinely prescribed norms

[5] Augueste Boudinhon, "Secular clergy," *The Catholic Encyclopedia* (1912 edition), Charles G. Herbermann (ed), <www.newadvent.org/cathen/13675a.htm>, accessed May 26, 2025.

[6] Giving to Cesar what is Cesar's does not necessarily derive from any religion but doing so to conform to the Word of Jesus does fully incorporate obedience to a worldly non-Christian ruler within the edicts of Christianity.

applicable to humanity as a whole (Stone 1993: 894). Similarly, Muslims do not embrace internally any concept of secularism and approach non-Muslim states in which they find themselves in a constrained way, delimited by the dictates of Islam (March 2014: 298–306).

Returning to Western Europe, a different conception of secularism became prevalent after the sixteenth-century Protestant Reformation split Western Christianity into two. This occurred after the prolonged series of wars of religion pitting Catholics against Protestants in several European realms made it clear that war would not eradicate the split within Western Christianity. This led to secularism re-entering the scene in a new guise as a buffer *among* religions—albeit only Christian ones. Building on the earlier example set by France's Henry IV, support grew for the idea that there ought to be room for tolerance of the religion that happened to be in the minority within a particular polity by the latter's majority religion. Moreover, for there to be the requisite locus for tolerance without compromising theological truth, it was necessary to effectuate some disentanglement of the realm of politics from that of religion. In this setting, secularism could keep the antagonistic religions at arm's length so long as neither of them could muster a decisive victory over the other. The secularism involved had to remain within Christianity but had to avoid favoring Catholicism or Protestantism, so it could serve as a buffer between them. Furthermore, the instantiation of the kind of secularism under consideration was amenable to being located *within* Christianity in two mutually reinforcing ways. First, the domain of disentangled politics necessary for coexistence could certainly promote Christianity (and that would be fully consistent with the standpoint of the antagonistic Christian religions) so long as it left sufficient room for tolerance of all Christian religions within the realm. And second, this newly minted brand of secularism could build upon the distinction between the sacred and the secular found in the formerly united Christian religion. In other words, even in united Christianity, the spiritual is separated from the political, and therefore, this already entrenched separation can readily be adapted in order to accommodate a plurality of Christian spiritual perspectives coupled with a separate political sphere shared in common by all Christians regardless of their religious differences.[7]

The next important turn in the historical journey of secularism coincided with the deployment of the philosophy of the Enlightenment and the late eighteenth-century launch of modern constitutional democracy in France and the US. Although both countries were imbued by general Enlightenment ideas regarding secularism, they each left a distinct historical imprint on the evolving connotations

[7] It may well be that the Christian divide between the sacred and the secular may be better suited to Protestantism than to Catholicism given the unique institutional and political role played by the Catholic Church since the consolidation of Christianity in medieval Europe. On this last point, *see* Zagrebelsky 2014: 247–68. Be that as it may, the concept of the divide in question, however interpreted or implemented, remains a truly Christian one with no equivalent in the other Abrahamic religions.

of the concept. The French Revolution was strongly anti-clerical rather than anti-religious (Collins & Price 2003: 176ff) and its anti-clericalism, combined with its antagonism against the aristocracy, is to be placed in the context of its struggle to topple feudal privilege to establish rule by the Third Estate (Sieyès 1963 [1789]). Moreover, the French Revolution brought forth a republican ideal inspired by Rousseau's political philosophy, which promoted democratic self-government for a polity of equal citizens bound together by a social contract. Drawing on Rousseau's distinction between the citizen and the *bourgeois* (Rousseau 1968 [1762]: 2–3), the French Revolution's constitutional vision left no room for group-based allegiances or interests in the public sphere. This was dramatically illustrated by the famous dictum of Clermont-Tonnerre in connection with the emancipation of the Jews during the French Revolution: "Everything must be refused to the Jews as a nation, and everything must be accorded to the Jews as individuals … they must be individual citizens … It would be repugnant to have groupings of non-citizens within the state, a nation within the nation" (Birnbaum 1988: 44–45). In short, the two salient features of secularism in the context of the French Revolution were an attack against the political power and privileges of the dominant institutionalized organized majority religion combined with a call to every citizen to suppress the calls of his or her religious allegiance when called upon to fulfill the republican duty of self-government within the political sphere. Although the secularism in question differs from *laïcité*, which originated in the nineteenth century (Birnbaum 2014: 136–45), it certainly prefigures the latter.

The American Revolution—which was above all a war of independence—also rejected the aristocratic ways and the dominant religion, which in this case was (and continues to be) the official state religion of its English colonizer. Beyond that, however, the US Constitution set out a late eighteenth-century secularism that differs markedly from its contemporaneous French counterpart. American constitutional secularism is encapsulated in the First Amendment's "Religion" clauses, namely the "Establishment Clause" and the "Free Exercise Clause."[8] On the surface these two religion clauses may seem to call for a public sphere purged of religion combined with a private sphere constitutionally protected to allow for optimal religious flourishing. But when placed in their historical context and in light of the conflicting interpretations they have fostered throughout American constitutional history, the clauses in question project a rather different image of secularism. It has often been observed that the two clauses are in tension with one another, with the Establishment Clause calling for state disengagement from religion while at the same time the Free Exercise Clause requiring state involvement to provide meaningful sustenance to religious practice and expression (Redlich et al. 2005: 510–29).

[8] The relevant language is: "Congress shall make no law respecting an establishment of religion or prohibiting the free exercise thereof." US Const amend I.

These tensions reflect an ambivalence concerning the optimal relationship between the state and religion, which is traceable to America's colonial period when it became an immigration haven for minority, persecuted, and dissident religions and religious movements. For example, in the seventeenth century, the thirteen American colonies saw significant immigration of Huguenots who fled from persecution in France (Butler 1992) and of Puritans who, as dissenters within the Church of England, felt increasingly socially ostracized at home and therefore opted to resettle across the Ocean (Ahlstrom 1972: 121ff). This pattern of immigration by religious minorities persecuted within their country of origin has continued throughout the history of the United States. Consistent with this, at a minimum, exclusion should prevent the functional equivalent of a state religion, which would recreate conditions similar to those that prompted large waves of immigrants to leave their country of origin. Conversely, given American society's steadfast commitment to religion (Birnbaum 2014), at a maximum, the public sphere should be inclusive of all that the various religions within the country share together. Ideally, therefore, consistent with this vision, American secularism should at once favor religion over irreligion and prohibit discrimination among religions.

As a matter of history and of constitutional jurisprudence, however, the American approach has in fact often promoted rather than eradicated discrimination among religions. Thus, for example, there has been a debate among US Supreme Court Justices concerning the status of religions that do not revere a transcendent Supreme Being, thus potentially fencing off such religions as Buddhism and Hinduism.[9] Moreover, perhaps most notoriously, the US Supreme Court has set a sharp divide between religious faith and acts or practices commanded by religion, in apparent accord with what could be understood as a Christian, if not a downright Protestant, conception of religion. This is reflected in decisions rejecting claims to constitutional protection of acts commanded by religion[10] and has led to the assertion that the religion clauses jurisprudence has been modeled on a Protestant conception of religion (Hamilton 2004).

The preceding brief historical review of the broad outlines of the evolution of the concept of secularism from the Middle Ages until the Enlightenment highlights the latter as being distinctly Christian in nature. Secularism thus emerges as not equally suited to meet the needs of the other two major Western religions, Islam and Judaism. As already noted, these latter religions do not adhere to an internal division akin to the Christian distinction between the sacred and the secular, or between faith and deeds, but instead embrace all-encompassing approaches requiring that religious rule extend over (what in Western constitutional democracies is

[9] *See McCreary Cnty v ACLU* 545 US 844 (2005) (Scalia J, dissenting).

[10] *See Reynolds v United States* 98 US 145 (1878). (Mormons' religious duty to practice polygamy does not require a Free Exercise-based exemption from state law making it a crime to be married to more than one woman.)

apportioned among) the private, the public, and the political spheres (Blech 1992; Wallace 2009).

To the extent that secularism may be inherently biased against non-Christian religions, constitutional secularism would seem vulnerable and at odds with the Enlightenment ideal of equal liberty for all, regardless of their particular religion or their lack thereof. Thus, for example, if Christian religions predominantly valorize faith and worship whereas for Islam and Judaism deeds such as male circumcision rank among the most sacred of religious obligations, then a secularism that accords priority to beliefs over deeds would inherently disadvantage the non-Christian religions involved—a situation bound to be aggravated if the latter religions happen to be minority ones within the relevant polity. Structurally, French constitutional secularism, as dramatically exemplified by the granting of individual rights to Jews during the 1789 Revolution, suppresses to a large extent the collective communal aspects of religion in order to strike a balance between the individual and the universal while sacrificing the plural. Constitutionally, under such a scheme, the communal aspects of religions such as Judaism and Islam seem mainly confined to protection under freedom of association in the private sphere.[11] Similarly, to the extent that the US jurisprudence regarding secularism is principally based on a Protestant conception of religion, it also tends to systematically favor individual creed to the detriment of collectively embedded deeds and practices. Finally, minority religions in Christian majority countries—and for that matter in any country with a dominant religious majority (Mahmood 2016: 12–13)—tend to be doubly vulnerable to the extent that they deviate from mainstream culture and that they are permanently subject to being disadvantaged (unless specifically constitutionally protected) through the democratic lawmaking process.

B. The Ideal of Institutional Secularism and the Two Principles at Its Core

Notwithstanding the Christian imprint that it seemingly cannot transcend, secularism as reshaped by the Enlightenment has become an institutional pillar of modern Western constitutionalism. Notoriously, in spite of its Christian origins and the country's large Catholic majority, French Jews were among the leading promoters of *laïcité* in the nineteenth century (Birnbaum 2014). As already mentioned, the *ideal* of institutional secularism is conceived as being areligious or neutral in relation to all religions and non-religious conceptions of the good.

[11] The current situation in France is complex and somewhat contradictory. On the one hand, as discussed below in Chapter 5, severe new restrictions on wearing the Islamic veil in public schools and the Burka in public spaces have been imposed in the twenty-first century. On the other hand, however, during the same period state financing for Catholic and Jewish schools and to a lesser extent Muslim ones has been vastly expanded. *See* Hennette-Vauchez 2023: 84.

Institutional secularism is supposed to carve out a public sphere with no room for religion, which is to remain distinct from the private sphere, wherein all religions are equally supposed to be granted full protection and equally allowed to thrive. This division between these two realms is exemplified both by the already alluded to contrast envisioned by Rousseau between the citizen who at once governs and serves the republic and the private person (*bourgeois*) who is free to follow the religion of his choice within the ambit of his family and social community; and by the "wall of separation" prescribed by the US Constitution (Levy 1986: 188), which many have understood as requiring a religion-free governmental sphere combined with full protection of religion within the private sphere. Moreover, to the structural ideal of neutrality embedded in institutional secularism must be added a dynamic that presumably secures the passage from secularism as the means toward securing a truce in the context of Christian wars of religion to secularism as an institutional mainstay of Enlightenment-based constitutional democracies. Achievement of the Enlightenment-prescribed conditions calls for all religion to be expelled from the public sphere and made to withdraw from the realm of politics in exchange for acquiring a special status and special protection within the private sphere. In other words, consistent with Enlightenment values, religion must become "depoliticized" in exchange for acquiring special privileges in a private sphere meant to be shielded from politics. Thus, for example, official spokespeople for a pacifist religion would be barred from participating in the name of that religion in the political debate (Levy 1986), culminating in the polity entering a war. But at the same time, practitioners of that religion would be entitled to an exemption from military service, which would allow them to honor their religiously prescribed pacifism.[12] To put it in the language of John Rawls, political discourse should be subjected to the criteria of "public reason" (Rawls 1996: 9). Conversely, propositions of faith, revelation, or other transcendent origin, which remain inaccessible to public reason, should be excluded from the realm of governance and of political argumentation, but afforded special status through constitutional protection of religious faith, practice, and worship within the confines of the private sphere.

Assuming acceptance of the neutrality of the ideal of institutional secularism, the key question posed at the level of constitutional architecture and functioning relates to the proper calibration of the public depoliticization of religion with the corresponding private privileging of it. This question proves vexing, however, because although the ideal of institutional secularism may well remain theoretically clear and coherent, the same seems virtually impossible at the institutional and practical levels. Indeed, the separation between the public and private spheres is often elusive, and even more so in the context of the modern welfare state, where

[12] *See Welsh v United States* 398 US 333 (1970); *Gillette v United States* 401 US 437 (1973).

subsistence, education, and healthcare are largely handled and/or regulated by the state. Thus, for instance, if education were exclusively relegated to the private sphere, each religious group within the polity could set up its own schools and ward off any plausible government interference through vindication of its freedom of religion rights under the country's constitution. But what if public education were mandatory or private education subject to government regulation imposing the teaching of certain subjects, such as science or civics, that may conflict with certain widely held religious precepts?

One possible way to overcome the above difficulties would require embracing a thicker, more substantive conception of secularism. Under that conception, secularism through the use of public reason would educate, sustain, and, to the extent necessary, constrain each person in her capacity as a citizen while at the same time affording complete freedom of religion to every person in her capacity as a private individual engaged in social and non-state communal interaction. This approach has the advantage of circumventing the difficulties posed by the elusiveness of the public/private divide. Indeed, to become a responsible citizen requires, among other things, some basic education in civics, which can be as easily made part of the curriculum of state-run schools as it can be imposed by law on private religious schools.[13]

Expanding the depth and scope of secularism may solve some problems, but only at the expense of raising others. For example, it would seem much more difficult to limit secularism to an institutional role that may be plausibly perceived as neutral if one conceives of the citizen and of democratic governance from a civic republican perspective as opposed to a liberal one. In the broadest terms, civic republicanism requires the citizen to engage in civic virtue in pursuit of the common good of the polity. In contrast, liberalism only calls for mainly procedural tasks to be performed by citizens directly or through their representatives, namely the maintenance of basic political constitutionally enshrined institutions and the guaranteeing of majoritarian rule to allow for an orderly competition among a plurality of constitutionally permissible interests. A secular conception of virtue and of the common good appears to require enshrining a conception of the good that may be, in whole or part, contrary to the particular conceptions of the good respectively espoused by the various religions practiced through the polity. Accordingly, secular civic republicanism is likely to be perceived as institutionalized non- or anti-religion and as definitely non-neutral in sharp distinction to secular liberalism with its mainly procedural institutional apparatus and its lack of explicit embrace of the competing religious and non-religious conceptions of the

[13] As of September 2016, in order to complete the requirements for a high-school diploma in New York, a student must receive instruction and pass final examinations in United States history and government, or in global history and geography (1750 to present), as well as receive instruction and pass one final exam in a different course in social studies or a department-approved alternative. 8 NYCRR § 100.5(a)(4)(i)(c), (e).

good variously espoused within the polity. Indeed, civic republicanism possesses a collective communal dimension that commits it to at least a partial conception of the good that cannot be neutral as to all prevalent competing conceptions of the good. In contrast, at least *prima facie*, purely procedural liberalism looms as purely individual regarding, abstracted from any communal commitment, and thus in principle neutral inasmuch as it prohibits all individuals from appealing to religion in the public sphere while enabling all of them to pursue the religion (or non-religion) of their choice in the private sphere.

As the preceding brief observations suggest, the Enlightenment ideal of a neutral institutional secularism as the constitutional standard to manage the relationship between the state and religion is both theoretically contestable and fraught with numerous difficulties in relation to practical implementation. Consistent with this, the best that can be expected in evaluating actual modern Western constitutional approaches to the relationship between the state and religion is a rough and relative approximation to the ideal of institutional secularism. Because of the complexities noted above, combined with the fact that each country has a different history, tradition, culture, constitution, and quite often a different mix of religions and non-religious ideologies, one thing is clear: there is no single solution to the constitutional challenge facing Western democracies. This becomes obvious upon examination of the principal different constitutional models for handling the relationship between the state and religion within the ambit of Western democracies, which we are about to undertake.

Before doing so, however, as the ideal of institutional secularism itself remains well beyond reach, it is useful to focus on the principles that lie at its core. There are two such principles, and they derive from the institutional secularism ideal's essentially pluralistic orientation. Indeed, the primary objective of the Enlightenment-based constitutionalization of secularism is to secure the peaceful coexistence of all religions and non-religious conceptions of the good with adherents within the confines of the relevant polity. And consistent with this, two principles emerge. The first of these is the principle that the greatest possible number of religions and non-religious conceptions of the good within the polity ought to be constitutionally protected within the constraints of adherence to peaceful coexistence. The second principle, in turn, requires that in the affairs of the state and in public policy, no religion shall be considered or treated as the sole possessor of the truth. In other words, whereas each religion is entitled to comport itself as the exclusive possessor of the truth within its communal life carried out in the private sphere, no religion is entitled to insist within the public sphere on institutionalization of its own truth so long as the latter is contested by proponents of other religions and of non-religious perspectives.

Consistent with the first of these principles, for example, no jihadist or crusading religion could be accommodated to the extent that it proved incompatible with the maintenance of peaceful coexistence with those it casts as infidels. And as to the second principle, assuming, for instance, that Catholicism commands the ban of all abortions, but Judaism, Islam, and many non-religious conceptions of the good do not, then it would be illegitimate to constitutionally enshrine or legislate a ban on all abortions without any plausible public reason-based justification.

Because none of the constitutional models that we are about to discuss comes close to the institutional secularism ideal, we believe that the latter's two core principles become crucial for purposes of drawing cogent qualitative distinctions between approaches to the relationship between religion and the state espoused by liberal constitutional democracies as opposed to their illiberal and populist counterparts. Accordingly, we will bear in mind these two core principles as we discuss the constitutional models and then further rely on the said principles subsequently as we broach illiberal and populist approaches to fundamental rights.

C. The Six Principal Constitutional Models for Handling the Relationship Between the State and Religion

Under current constitutional practice in secular constitutional democracies, there are essentially six different models for managing the relationship between the state and religion. These are (i) the militant secularist model bent on keeping religion completely out of the public sphere; (ii) the agnostic secularist model, which seeks to maintain a neutral stance among religions but which does not shy away from favoring religion over atheism and other non-religious perspectives; (iii) the confessional secular model, which incorporates elements of the polity's mainstream majority religion, primarily for identitarian purposes, and projects them as part of the polity's constitutional secularism rather than as inextricably linked to the country's main religion; (iv) the official state religion with institutionalized tolerance for minority religions model; (v) the *millet*-based model in which high priority is given to collective self-government by each religious community within the polity; and (vi) the conflation model pairing (the majority) religion with secularism as exemplified in the case of the constitutional treatment of Hinduism in India. There are also significant variants in relation to many of these models, the most salient of which will be briefly mentioned in the discussion below.

(i) The Militant Secularist Model

This model, which sets as its ideal the complete separation between the state and religion, is the one that most approximates the Enlightenment's radical distinction between the realm of Faith and that of Reason and its call for Reason to rule the public sphere while allowing Faith freely to spread within the private sphere. Militant secularism is most famously enshrined in the French conception of *laïcité* currently embodied in Article 1 of France's 1958 Constitution.[14] *Laïcité* was institutionalized in France by a law enacted in 1905 to eliminate government subsidy of religion, which was established by Napoleon I to make up for state confiscation of church property during the French Revolution.[15] The 1905 law has been said to be built around three principles: "freedom of conscience, separation of state and churches, and the equal respect of all of all faiths and beliefs" (Weil 2014: 199). What *laïcité* encompasses has evolved from its 1905 legalization to its 1958 constitutionalization, but one of its most striking features is the near complete expulsion of religion from the realm of the state and from most of the public sphere. This has been most vividly exemplified in recent times by the complete ban regarding public school students' wearing of the Islamic veil or other "ostentatious" religious signs (Weil 2014: 201). Moreover, as to the state itself, in the words of a leading French legal scholar, it "presents itself to all, stripped of all metaphysical symbols, distant from any trace of the spiritual" (Weil 2014: 200).

Turkey, like France, has also adopted this militant secularist model, but there are important differences between these two countries. Whereas French *laïcité* was adopted in a social and political setting that was already significantly secularized (Troper 2014: 146–59), its Turkish counterpart was imposed in the 1920s by Kemal Atatürk to trigger a shift toward modernism and secularism in a polity that was overwhelmingly rooted in the Islamic religion (Borovali 2009). As a consequence, as evinced by two countries' bans on Islamic headscarves, French *laïcité* is mainly directed against minority religions, whereas Turkish *laïcité* is squarely turned against the country's dominant majority religion (Mancini 2009). Moreover, an overwhelming majority of French society is currently largely secularized and thus well adapted to the dictates of *laïcité*. Turkish society, in contrast, is still in large part committed to Islam, which explains the large popular support behind Erdoğan's extensive impositions of Islamic norms through his expanded powers, despite the persistence thus far of secularism as a constitutional pillar.[16]

France's constitutional *laïcité* may well come closest to the ideal of institutional secularism, as in principle all manifestations of religion and all endorsements of it are excluded from the public sphere. Accordingly, formally at least, the public sphere looms as truly areligious and neutral, whereas the private sphere seems primed to accommodate all religions within the polity so long as they do not seek to undermine peaceful coexistence among all religious and non-religious groupings

[14] The opening sentence of the first article of France's 1958 Constitution states: "France shall be an indivisible, secular, democratic and social Republic."

[15] *See* Law of 9 December 1905 on the Separation of Church and State, France, <www.legifrance.gouv.fr/loda/id/JORFTEXT000000508749> accessed May 26, 2025; Concordat Watch, "Napoleon's Concordat 1801: text," Concordat Watch, <www.concordatwatch.eu/napoleons-concordat-1801-text--k1496>, accessed May 26, 2025.

[16] *See* Soner Cagaptay, "In long-secular Turkey, sharia is gradually taking over," *The Washington Post*, February 16, 2018, <www.washingtonpost.com/news/democracy-post/wp/2018/02/16/in-long-secular-turkey-sharia-is-gradually-taking-over/>, accessed May 26, 2025.

within the polity. Nevertheless, upon closer consideration, even this most pristine iteration of militant secularism suffers from serious shortcomings. First, although the French state is supposed to be religiously neutral, it can be attacked as being ultimately hostile to religion inasmuch as its institutional apparatus seems much more attuned to the ideological inclinations of those who are irreligious or only nominally associated with religion. Second, for all its irreligious or anti-religious connotations, French *laïcité* is historically rooted in a particular accommodation between the French Catholic Church and the state (Troper 2009: 2568–69). To be sure, the deployment of *laïcité* in France required some restraints on religion, thus somewhat relativizing Catholicism within the polity. But at the same time, *laïcité* was molded so as to render the public space as compatible as possible with the culture associated with Catholicism, if not with the religion itself. This phenomenon is succinctly captured in the French popular term *Catho-laique*, which connotes both a Catholicism adapted to *laïcité* and a *laïcité* fitted for harmonious coexistence with Catholicism.

(ii) The Agnostic Secularist Model

The agnostic secularist model differs markedly from its militant counterpart in its refusal to categorically exclude religion from state affairs and most of the public sphere, and instead purports to maintain an agnostic position between all religions. The agnostic secularist model thus aims to remain neutral among religions by ideally inviting all of them in while barring the state from favoring any one religion over any other. Moreover, there are two principal variants of this model: one that is in principle equally inclusive of all religions, but not of anti-religious or of irreligious ideologies; and the other that is meant to be equally inclusive of all ideologies, whether religious or not. The US embodies the agnostic secularist model and, as its constitutional jurisprudence demonstrates, it variously gives expression to both of its variants.

Although the ideal of non-discrimination among religions has remained a constant in American constitutional jurisprudence, its meaning and scope have fluctuated due to the changing and contested dynamic between inclusion and exclusion framed by the two religion clauses of the US Constitution. Thus, Jefferson's famous proclamation of the need for "a wall of separation" between church and state has been variously interpreted as requiring a complete separation between state and religion (Levy 1986: 188) and as merely banning official state preference of one religion over others (Cord 1982: 213–15). Underlying this divergence were several factors that led to fluctuation of the scope of non-discrimination and to shifting attitudes concerning the ratio of benefits to detriments linked to greater or lesser state involvement or promotion of religion. In the earlier days of the American republic, the country regarded itself by and large as a Protestant one, and constitutional non-discrimination was understood by many as applicable to the various Protestant denominations within the polity, but not necessarily to other (minority) religions (Ahlstrom 1972: 330ff). Although since then Catholicism and Judaism have been explicitly included within the effective non-discrimination purview, as already noted, there still is a current debate among US Supreme Court Justices concerning constitutional protection under the religion clauses of certain other religions or non-religious ideologies. Consistent with this, moreover, those who have advocated strict separation between the state and religion fall generally into three categories: agnostics or atheists whose freedom *from* religion may be trampled by a state endorsed religion;[17] minority religions which feel *de facto* discriminated against by falling outside the scope of non-discrimination or excluded from state endorsement or promotion of what the latter presents as a common denominator among all religions, but is in fact contrary to the precepts of the minority religions involved;[18] and, religions, whether belonging to the majority cluster that fully benefits from constitutional non-discrimination or within the minority, which are convinced that any state involvement, no matter how benign, is bound to result in state meddling that would inevitably lead to unacceptable compromising of sacred religious principles or practices.[19]

American constitutional secularism is by no means anti-religious or even irreligious, as it boils down to state acceptance or even endorsement of what is perceived as shared in common by all protected religions, combined with an ongoing contestation of the proper bounds of the dynamic between inclusion and exclusion. Thus, the inscription "In God We Trust" on official US currency,[20] or the recitation of the Pledge of Allegiance to "one nation under God" by public school children,[21] or official prayers characterized as generic at the opening of parliamentary sessions,[22] are all arguably justifiable as falling within the common religious denominator shared by a vast majority of Americans.[23] At the same time, however,

[17] *See, e.g.*, the opinion of the court and Justice O'Connor's concurring opinion in *McCreary Cnty*, 545 US 844.

[18] *See, e.g.*, *Lynch v Donnelly* 465 US 668 (1984). (Court majority depicts state display of the *crèche* as non-exclusionary notwithstanding that it symbolizes Jesus' divine nature which is rejected by Judaism and Islam).

[19] *See, e.g.*, Testimony of J Brent Walker, General Counsel and Associate Director, Baptist Joint Committee on Public Affairs before the Senate Committee on the Judiciary (Federal Document Clearing House, October 25, 1995).

[20] *See Lynch v Donnelly* 465 US 668.

[21] *See Newdow v US Congress*, 292 F3d 597, 609 (2009). ("[T]he words 'under God' [added to the Pledge of Allegiance in 1954] were intended to recognize a 'Supreme Being,' at a time when the Government was inveighing against atheistic Communism.")

[22] *See Marsh v Chambers* 463 U.S. 783 (1983). (Nebraska legislature prayer by state-paid chaplain held constitutional.)

[23] As the US Supreme Court jurisprudence on the religion clauses has been evolving and as Justices on the Court have generally been divided on many relevant issues, the actual justifications offered for constitutional acceptance of these state endorsements of religion have varied from religious common denominator ones to others based on the argument that these propositions or practices are so widely accepted within the country as to become part of its culture beyond any religious connotation. *See* the

such state endorsements of religion remain contested as objectors charge that what purports to be inclusionary, such as what a majority regards as a generic prayer, is in essence a Christian or a Judeo-Christian prayer, and is thus in fact exclusionary as it effectively casts non-believers and members of other religions as outsiders.[24]

As the above cursory references to American jurisprudence indicate, the agnostic secularist model may seem more inclusive than its militant counterpart, but it does have at least two major shortcomings. The first of these is that it is at times construed as disfavoring agnostics, atheists, and proponents of non-religious ideologies. The second shortcoming stems from actual discrimination among religions under the guise of neutrality. As already noted, American jurisprudence on religious freedom may ultimately depend on a Protestant model of religion. Accordingly, what appears to be formally religiously neutral may turn out in practice to embody a Protestant bias.

(iii) The Confessional Secular Model

The confessional secular model differs from its agnostic counterpart in that it incorporates elements of the polity's majority religion by casting them primarily as cultural and identitarian symbols inherent in the fabric of its citizenry's national identity. Thus, for example, in Germany and Italy, two prime exponents of the present model, the display of the crucifix in state school classrooms has sought to be justified in terms of the country's Christian tradition and as a symbol of the values of universalism and tolerance that Christianity and secular constitutionalism happen to share, thus downplaying the crucifix's profound religious meaning for Christian believers.[25] Moreover, there are significant variants within the confessional secular model, depending, among other things, on whether the polity at stake has one dominant religion, as in the case in Italy, or whether it has more than one traditionally implanted religion, as is the case in Germany, where Catholicism is predominant in some regions and Protestantism in others. Finally, there are also important differences regarding how far the majority religion and its practices and traditions are incorporated into the institutions of the secular state. From a theoretical standpoint, the confessional secular model encompasses the entire spectrum that spans between the agnostic secularist model and model (iv) below, which comprises an official state religion.

various opinions in the cases cited in the preceding three footnotes and some of those discussed in Chapter 4.

[24] *See* pp. 49–50.

[25] *Lautsi v Italy* App no 30815/06 (ECtHR, March 18, 2011).

The German version of the confessional secularist model provides a sparkling example of the combination of history, culture, and constitutional vision. The German Basic Law incorporates the religion-related provisions incorporated in the 1919 Weimar Constitution, which itself traces back to the seventeenth-century end of the wars of religion (Dorsen et al. 2016: 1293). After these wars, each German state adopted the religion of its ruler (Dorsen et al. 2016), and under the current Basic Law, the state incorporates religious education in its public schools, with Protestant Länder providing Protestant religious instruction, and Catholic ones imparting Catechism (Grimm 1999: 3–13). In addition, the state collects taxes from the citizenry for redistribution to churches, this being tantamount to state collection of dues from members of a church for purposes of disbursement to the church in question (Grimm 1999). In short, whereas the above features may insinuate that the Protestant and Catholic religions amount to the state religion in their respective Länder, the Basic Law makes it clear that there is no state religion in Germany (Grimm 1999).

German institutionalization of religion may not itself necessarily trample on the freedom of religion of adherents to minority religions, as parents are allowed to have their children opt out of state school religious instruction (Grimm 1999). The same is often not the case, however, when religion is invoked as a component of tradition and culture as opposed to in its own right. One such telling example is provided by the German Constitutional Court's decision in the *Headscarf Ludin* 2003 case,[26] which upheld certain Länder's prohibition against public school teachers wearing Islamic headscarves while at the same time allowing teachers who happened to be nuns to wear their religiously prescribed habits. As the Court understood it, this difference did not in any way manifest any expression of religious discrimination, but instead reflected the well-established historical and cultural tradition wherein nuns figure as an integral part of Germany's heritage and identity.[27]

Perhaps the most striking example of portraying religion not only as historical tradition but also as largely coextensive with secular values is provided by the Italian public classroom crucifix case, *Lautsi*,[28] which is more extensively discussed in Chapter 5 below. In the words of the Italian Administrative Court, which held that the display of the crucifix in public school classrooms was compatible with Italy's constitutional secularism:

[26] *BVerfGE* 108, 282 (2003).

[27] This trend of excluding the veil was officially embraced by an increasing number of German Länder for over a decade. In 2015, however, the German Constitutional Court held that a "general prohibition" against teachers wearing headscarves in public schools was unconstitutional. Headscarf Ban Case, 1BvR 471/10 (2015).

[28] *Lautsi v Italy* App no 30815/06 (ECtHR, March 18, 2011).

> It is easy to identify in the constant central core of Christian faith, despite the Inquisition... anti- Semitism ... and the crusades, the principles of human dignity, tolerance and freedom, including religious freedom, and therefore, in the last analysis, the foundations of the secular state.[29]

Confessional secularism gives rise to two major problems. First, it can easily be found wanting by most, if not all, religions within the polity and by all those who are genuinely committed toward secularism. Indeed, "confessionalized" secularism is likely to offend both the very religious who would consider their deeply held religious convictions trivialized,[30] and the committed secularists who would feel their position being undermined through saturation of the public space with religious symbols and practices relabeled as secular (Mancini 2009: 2634–35). Second, confessional secularism seems bound to disfavor minority religions as the German headscarf jurisprudence mentioned above illustrates, thus significantly thwarting the equal treatment of all religions within the polity.

(iv) The Official State Religion with Institutionalized Tolerance for Minority Religions Model

This model is characterized by the constitutional adoption of a particular religion as the official state one and thus differs from the confessional secular model in that it incorporates the state religion *qua* religion as opposed to as an element of culture or tradition. Western countries with an official state religion include the United Kingdom (UK), Scandinavian countries, and Greece, and each of these makes for important variants regarding both the relationship between the state and religion and the degree of inclusiveness accorded to minority religions. In general terms, the more the official religion is compatible with the essential tenets of liberalism, the better it is likely to fit within the strictures of constitutional secularism. Thus, for example, liberal interpretations of Christianity that promote equality between the sexes as well as non-discrimination based on sexual orientation seem better adapted to constitutional secularism than Christian fundamentalist interpretations that are widely regarded as discriminatory against women and the LGBTQ community. Moreover, it may be quite important from the standpoint of constitutional secularism whether a country's official religion is promoted mainly in a ceremonial capacity as opposed to through the institutionalization of its substantive precepts and values.

This contrast between a ceremonial and a substantive implementation of the official religion is well illustrated through a comparison between the role of the

[29] Cited in *Lautsi v Italy* App no 30815/06 (ECtHR, March 18, 2011).
[30] Testimony of J Brent Walker, n 19.

Church of England in the UK and that of the Greek Christian Orthodox Church in Greece. The UK is, by and large, a much less religious polity than the US, and the Church of England seems to have little more than a ceremonial presence in the public sphere. Accordingly, the role of the official religion in the UK may impinge less on secularism than several other versions of the confessional secularist model and even than some iterations of the US approach under its agnostic secular model (Greenawalt 2009: 2383, 2386–87). The role and influence of the Eastern Orthodox Church on the Greek polity, on the other hand, is in large measure substantive and often quite intrusive on those who stray from the constitutionally enshrined official national religion. Article 3 of the Greek Constitution establishes the above Orthodox religion as the "dominant" one and prohibits any translation of the Holy Scriptures "without the prior consent of the Greek Church."[31] Moreover, while the Greek Constitution protects freedom of conscience and the right to practice any "known" religion, it prohibits proselytism.[32] As proselytism is an essential obligation for much of Christianity, its prohibition under Greek law was held in violation of the right to freedom of religion under Article 9 of the European Convention on Human Rights.[33] Accordingly, whereas the UK's embrace of an official state religion seems squarely consistent with adherence to constitutional secularism, Greece's pairing of the state with its officially adopted religion seems positioned close to the very boundary between constitutional inclusion and exclusion of religious pluralism.

Besides its greater potential for disadvantaging minority religions, the official state religion model may foster drawbacks for both the state and the official religion. From the standpoint of the state and that of democratic majorities, the official religion may succeed in perpetuating burdensome impediments. Thus, for instance, Catholicism prohibits divorce, and were it to figure as the official state religion, it could thwart the granting of a right that may be deemed fundamental within the ambit of contemporary liberal constitutionalism. From the standpoint of the official religion, on the other hand, state intervention may result in dilution of religious freedom and in contravention or dilution of religious dogma. A good example of this phenomenon is provided by the Egyptian Supreme Court interpretations of Sharia law in ways contrary to those of that country's religious Islamic authorities (March 2014: 298–306). In the last analysis, in the best of cases, adoption of an official religion allows for greater consolidation of the country's majority's way of life with enough room for religious freedom for all while allowing the state to curb those excesses of the official religion that pose a threat to liberal constitutionalism. In the worst of cases, though, the official religion will unduly impinge on religious tolerance for all others, while the state will systematically frustrate,

[31] Constitution of Greece, art 3(1), (3).
[32] Ibid, art 13 (1), (2).
[33] *See Kokkinakis v Greece* (1993) 17 EHRR 397 (ECtHR).

through its processes of institutionalization, the official religion's authorities and true believers.

(v) The *Millet*-Based Model

The *millet* system, which originated in the Ottoman Empire, is premised on collective self-government by each religious community within the polity. More specifically, under this system, in matters of personal law, such as marriage and divorce, each individual is subjected to the laws, courts, and authorities of her religious community. The *millet*-based model is currently in force in Israel, a Western constitutional democracy with a Jewish majority and sizable Christian and Muslim minorities.[34] The *millet*-based model seems particularly attractive to the extent that it is well-suited to accommodate minority religions. Unlike other models in which the individual and collective rights of minority religions and of their adherents are often limited through the projection of majority religion ideology or biases and primary emphasis on individual freedom of religion, the *millet*-based model allows for equal full self-determination within the realm of personal law of each religious community, regardless of its majority or minority status. Thus, as already noted, where the Christian distinction between faith and deeds is pervasive, it may lead to restrictions on the religious practices of minority religions that do not draw such a distinction. In contrast, in Israel, which has adopted the millet-based model, the Muslim imams and the Christian priests have as much power in the lives of their respective religious communities as do the Jewish rabbis, notwithstanding that Jews comprise around 80 percent of the country's population.[35]

As much as the *millet* system strongly reinforces the objectives of the plural by guaranteeing an equivalent measure of self-government to all (recognized) religious communities within the polity, it seems manifestly less well-structured than the previously discussed models for purposes of vindicating individual-regarding religious freedoms. Indeed, individuals who wish to intermarry in Israel, such as a Christian who wishes to marry a Jew, will be unable to find any officially state-empowered priest or rabbi to perform such a wedding. Moreover, because marriage in Israel is delegated to specified religious communities, there is no existing civil marriage option within the country's borders.[36] Similar restrictions arise

[34] Israel does not have a formal constitution but adheres to constitutional rule and respect for fundamental rights secured through Basic laws. *See United Mizrahi Bank Ltd v Migdal Village*, CA 6281/93 (Supreme Court, Israel, 1995).

[35] *See The Jerusalem Post*, "Israel's population nears ten million, Central Bureau of Statistics finds," *The Jerusalem Post* (online), August 26, 2024, <www.jpost.com/israel-news/article-821800>, accessed September 8, 2025.

[36] *See* Sapir & Statman 2014: 269–82. To compensate for this drawback, Israel readily recognizes marriages obtained abroad. This allows Israeli interfaith couples to marry in Cyprus and to have their marriages recognized in Israel upon their return home. Whereas this practical option may minimize

within Egypt's secularism, which is largely congruent with the *millet* approach as exemplified by Coptic Christian individuals being confined to turn to Muslim religious authorities if they wish to obtain a divorce, which is permitted under Islam but prohibited by the Coptic Church (Mahmood 2016: 133).

More generally, the *millet*-based model, however, is also prone to fostering several drawbacks from the standpoint of Western constitutional secularism as attested by its nearly eight-decade implementation in Israel. These drawbacks fall essentially into three distinct categories. The first of these, as we have seen, concerns inter-religious matters or relationships, such as intermarriage; the second, intra-religious matters; and the third, conflicts between religious self-rule and fundamental precepts of constitutional secularism. With respect to the second category relating to intra-religious matters, unless a religious community is unified or hierarchically woven together, the *millet* system seems bound to exacerbate intra-religious splits and divisions. This is well illustrated by the systematic exclusion of Conservative and Reform Judaism from the rabbinate and all relevant Jewish religious authorities with religious legal authority over Israel's Jews (Sapir & Statman 2014: 269–82). Moreover, there are even splits among the officially established and empowered Orthodox Jewish community, with at times contentious disagreements on important legal issues between the Ultra-Orthodox and the Modern Orthodox (Sapir & Statman 2014). Finally, the third category of difficulties arises whenever the dictates of applicable religious law clearly contravene the basic precepts of constitutional secularism. One example of this is provided by the controversy over Jewish divorce law in Israel. Under current rabbinic law that applies to all Jewish divorces in the country, a couple cannot be granted a divorce unless the husband gives his voluntary consent to it, thus not only creating a glaring inequality between the sexes, but often leaving women who are estranged and separated from their husband in a state of limbo with no legal recourse regarding divorce or remarriage (Sapir & Statman 2014).

The above difficulties besetting the *millet*-based model may be mitigated by instituting two kinds of changes. First, one could conceive, and there has been much discussion about this in Israel (Sapir & Statman 2014), of a *millet* system in which a secular civil libertarian alternative is available for those who wish to opt out from the religious community to which they belong. Such a change in Israel would allow for interfaith marriage and for civil divorce, as well as more generally for those committed to secularism and not in accord with any religious communities to live and benefit from fundamental constitutional protections consistent with their ideology and way of life. Second, to lessen intra-religious strife and reduce unfairness among religions and religious denominations, the *millet*-based model could be opened up to become more inclusive. If Israeli Jews could

the harm to the individuals involved, it does not redress the affront against a basic precept of constitutional secularism.

choose among Orthodox, Conservative, and Reform Judaism as well as purely secular alternatives, it would seem that much of the frustrations and felt unfairness regarding the current system could be significantly alleviated. Accommodating more religious identities and communities would improve the *millet*-based model without ever making it fully satisfactory, as it seems impractical to give all religious viewpoints, no matter how isolated and no matter how small in terms of adherents, the ability to promulgate and enforce their own law and, at the same time, to have such law be part of the law of the land.

(vi) The Conflation Model: Equating Secularism with the Majority Religion

The conflation model has emerged over time in India, and it is tied to unique features and interpretations of Hinduism, that country's majority religion. In the preamble to its Constitution, India declares itself to be "a secular socialist democratic republic."[37] The model of secularism enshrined in the Indian Constitution and further developed through its Supreme Court jurisprudence is, however, quite different from those advanced by the preceding models. This is due, in part, to the fact that Hinduism differs very significantly from monotheistic religions in general, and Christianity in particular, and in part due to an increasingly recent pairing of a particular interpretation of Hinduism with a populist vision of Hindu nationalism.[38] As emphasized by one observer, unlike Protestantism which is *internally* tolerant as inclined to enable each of its adherents to engage in her own reading of the Holy Scriptures, "Hinduism . . . does not give much freedom to its own adherents, at least in some respects, but is *externally* tolerant: its grants great latitude to non-Hindus in their religious beliefs and practices" (Spinner-Halev 2005: 30). Moreover, unlike Christianity which primes belief over deeds, Hinduism highly prioritizes practices. As already noted, practices also figure prominently in Judaism and Islam, but unlike the latter, which are intransigent in their commitments to monotheism, Hinduism relates to a large and seemingly flexible number of gods and goddesses. Accordingly, as characterized by India's Supreme Court, "the Hindu religion does not claim any one prophet; it does not worship any one God; it does not subscribe to any one dogma; it does not believe in any one philosophic concept; it does not follow any one set of religious rites or performances; in fact, it does not appear to satisfy the narrow traditional features of any religion or creed. It may broadly be described *as a way of life* and nothing more."[39]

[37] The Constitution of India 1950, Preamble (as amended up to July 2024).

[38] *See* Chapter 5 below for a more extended discussion of the ongoing trend to couple Hinduism and nationalism in the name of Indian secularism.

[39] *Sastri Yagnapurushadji v Muldas Brudardas Vaishya* (1966) 3 SCR 242 (emphasis added).

Given these differences, Indian secularism is not, and need not be, neutral. By its very nature, Hinduism leaves virtually unlimited room for freedom of belief and of conscience. Furthermore, even if the state were to institutionalize Hindu practices, so long as that would leave enough room for other religions to engage in their own practices largely unimpeded, the embrace of Hinduism as a way of life would be consistent with institutional secularism. Indeed, as presented thus far, a Hindu way of life appears largely compatible with the peaceful coexistence of a wide plurality of diverse religious beliefs and with broad tolerance of varied, contrasting religious practices. Moreover, from this perspective, the conflation of, or overlap between, secularism and religion seems quite different from that associated with the confessional secularism model. Unless it impinges on the practices of other religions, the conflation of Hinduism and secularism is prone to leaving all other religions present in India free to believe and practice as they may choose. In contrast, as well illustrated by Italy's *Lautsi* case, turning the crucifix into a secular national cultural symbol is bound to upset both the religious Christian who regards such cultural appropriation as a trivialization of his religion and the non-Christian who considers state imposition of the crucifix in public school classrooms to be an instance of religious coercion.

Ideally, India's conflation model seems to align neatly with the core requirements of institutional secularism. Two developments, however, have over time driven the implementation of that model away from the pluralist requisites commanded by institutional secularism. The first of these developments derives from India's constitutional jurisprudence. Based on a situation in which certain Hindu practices were found to be violative of the constitutional equality rights of women, India's Supreme Court prohibited their implementation.[40] That itself would be unremarkable as, under all previously discussed models, freedom of religion is subject to limitations where it disproportionately impinges on other fundamental rights, such as that to equality. What made the Indian Supreme Court decision very different is its reliance on, and subsequent expansion of, the "essential practices" doctrine. Pursuant to that doctrine, it is the Court that is charged with drawing lines between genuine religious practices and secular practices couched in religion and superstitious beliefs. As the Court specified, it should bear the burden of deciding what counts as an essential practice of religion "because the community might speak with more than one voice and would thus fail to come up with an unequivocal answer."[41] As the arbitrator of essential religious practices, the Indian Supreme Court may not only infringe on the freedom of religion of the country's Hindu majority, but also, more ominously, on that of the country's Muslim and Christian minorities.

[40] *Indian Young Lawyers Association v State of Kerala* (Supreme Court of India, September 28, 2018).
[41] *Durgah Committee v Syed Hussain Ali* 1962 SCC OnLine SC [para 33].

The second development mentioned above, which is extensively discussed in Chapter 5, consists of the redefinition of secularism so as to make it coincide with a version of Hinduism that seamlessly adapts to India's recent turn to nationalist and populist politics. In this context, Hinduism is secularism and this is because:

> [The] Hindu Right has hijacked the dominant understanding of secularism as the equal respect of all religions in order to promote its vision of Hindutva and its agenda of establishing a Hindu State. In its hands, the equal respect of all religions becomes a tool for attacking the rights of minority religious communities. Its emphasis on the formal equal treatment of all religions operates as an unmodified majoritarianism whereby the dominant Hindu community becomes the norm against which all others are to be judged Cossman & Kapur 1997: 115).

To the extent that a particular articulation of Hinduism is wedded to a brand of nationalism and populism that lends itself to systematic discrimination against the country's more than 150 million Muslim minority, India's present-day conflation model obviously fails to meet the most basic requirements set by institutional secularism. In short, the conflation model associated with Hinduism is, in theory, fully compatible with the essential tenets of institutional secularism. In its current iteration, however, the model in question may or may not promote what may qualify as a secular way of life, but it certainly fails to afford the minimum of religious tolerance called for by institutional secularism.

In the last analysis, all six models can satisfactorily, though to be sure imperfectly, adhere to the core requirements mandated by institutional secularism. Also, as noted, each of these models allows for deviations from this core, with some more prone than others to stray too far from an acceptable minimum. All of these models, but the conflation one, are based on at least a partial depoliticization of religion. And although the conflation model does not rely on depoliticization, in its ideal iteration, its politics are largely compatible with pluralism and with the accommodation of a wide array of differing religious truths. As we shall see, the repoliticization of religion, which originated in the last quarter of the twentieth century and which we will examine in Chapter 2, has raised a whole new set of vexing challenges to the maintenance of the core minimum prescribed by institutional secularism.

2

Repoliticized Religion and the Dialectic Between Religious Appropriation of Politics and Political Appropriation of Religion

As detailed in Chapter 1, the ideal of institutional secularism is difficult to approximate even under the most favorable circumstances, and it becomes increasingly problematic as the modern welfare state encroaches on what traditionally pertained to the private sphere. As already noted, a prime example of this is provided by public education, which will displease some whether it includes or excludes religion within the curriculum, thus creating serious doubts about institutional secularism's potential for neutrality.[1] Moreover, whereas the blurring of the boundaries between the public and private spheres has certainly increased the burdens on institutional secularism, a far greater threat to the latter's legitimacy and viability stems from the systemic re-entry of religion within the political sphere of many different countries throughout the world, starting in the 1980s. This new development consists in the "deprivatization" of religion (Casanova

[1] Compare *Sch. Dist. v Schempp*, 374 US 203 (1963) (finding reading of Bible verses and reciting of Lord's prayer by students at public school to violate Establishment Clause) with *Smith v Bd. of Sch. Comm'rs*, 827 F 2d 684 (11th Cir 1987) and *Grove v Mead Sch. Dist.*, No 354, 753 F 2d 1528 (9th Cir 1985) (finding no violation of Establishment Clause after secular education in public school challenged by fundamentalist Protestant parents as amounting to the unconstitutional teaching of the religion of "secular humanism"). *See* the discussion below, at p. 30.

Politicized Religion and the Reframing of Fundamental Rights. Susanna Mancini and Michel Rosenfeld, Oxford University Press. © Susanna Mancini, Michel Rosenfeld 2026. DOI: 10.1093/9780191982149.003.0003

1994) and involves two interrelated processes: the "repoliticization of the private religious and moral spheres" and the "renormativization of the public economic and political spheres" (Casanova 1994: 5–6). As Jose Casanova has noted, religion in the 1980s "went public . . . leaving its assigned place in the private sphere" and thrusting itself "into the public arena of moral and political contestation" (Casanova 1994: 3). This new phenomenon has been complex and variegated. It has involved many different religions that have sought to alter or redefine the constitutional and political landscape in many different ways.

As highlighted in Chapter 1's discussion of the six models associated with institutional secularism, religion has never been fully ousted from the public sphere. Indeed, even in the case of France, where exclusion of religion from the public sphere has been most vigorously and persistently pursued, *laïcité* has not shielded the polity from vestiges of religious preferences as attested by what has been labeled the *Catho-laique* state inclination and what many have cast as the anti-religious measures against wearing the Islamic veil in public schools or the *burka* outside the home or mosque. On further thought, even if the boundary between the private and public spheres could be made formally impenetrable, it would still almost inevitably remain substantively porous. Thus, for example, entire religious communities could commit to vote as their priests, pastors, imams, or rabbis exhorted them to do. This, in turn, raises the question, which proves crucial for our purposes, of whether "deprivatized," "repoliticized" religion post-1980 differs in kind from what prevailed before then in secular constitutional democracies or whether, in the end, the differences involved amount to fluctuations of degree. In other words, does the greater visibility and assertiveness of repoliticized religion boil down to an intensification of a preexisting religious input into politics, or does it mark the onset of a categorical shift bent on uprooting established modes of interplay between state and religion in constitutional democracies?

Based on developments since the 1980s and on the more recent experiences involving religious nationalism and religious populism, we are convinced that the rise and trajectory of repoliticized religion have prompted categorical shifts rather than mere incremental amalgamations. In order to buttress our conclusion and to specify how the categorical changes in question have altered the nexus between state and religion and cleared the way for a reframing of fundamental rights, we examine in the course of the present chapter four different salient instances of attempted or realized uprooting of the status quo to better integrate religion within the life and objectives of the state. In addition, in Chapter 3, we will focus on how religious nationalism and religious populism have made use of repoliticized religion to combat liberalism and to revamp its secular constitutional order.

The present chapter proceeds as follows: Section A briefly addresses the repoliticization of religion in the 1980s and its attacks on institutional secularism. The rest of the chapter recounts four salient cases in which repoliticization plays markedly different roles and is deployed for ostensibly different purposes. Section

B examines how the 1979 revolution in Iran led to religion altogether appropriating the Constitution and the state; Section C traces how Protestant fundamentalists within the US have sought to push for religious interpretation of the Constitution while remaining within its broadly established confines; Section D concentrates on the political appropriation of religion through the examples provided by Latin American liberation theology and Poland's Solidarity movement; finally, Section E focuses on the clash between religion and constitutional norms in the context of Israel and its reliance on the *millet* system.

A. Critiques of Institutional Secularism and Repoliticization of Religion Starting Around 1980

From a bird's eye perspective, the repoliticization of religion that emerged in various parts of the world in the 1980s can be split into two distinct phenomena: the infusion of religion into politics and the political appropriation of religion. The first of these is well illustrated by instances in which believers within a particular religion consider that the creeds and practices of the latter establish the truth and the good of the polity and ought therefore to be imposed on all within the relevant constitutional unit. This is the case of Iran's 1979 Revolution, discussed below, which was headed by a revered Shia Muslim religious leader, the Ayatollah Khomeini, and which turned what had been a largely secular, undemocratic, and illiberal autocratic imperial regime into a constitutional theocracy. In contrast, the second of these phenomena is best typified by cases involving the appropriation for political purposes of religion principally to exploit it as a cultural or identitarian marker used for purposes of separating "insiders" from "outsiders" within the confines and spheres of influence of the relevant polity. The prime case in this category is that of Hungary's prime minister, Viktor Orban, which will be discussed more extensively in Chapter 3. Orban, who has been described as an atheist and rules in one of the least religious countries in Europe, has draped himself in Christianity to bolster his brand of illiberal nationalism and populism.[2] Specifically, Orban has pitted his "insiders," ethnic Hungarians, against various "outsiders," including secular Western Europeans, those he casts as cosmopolitan elites within Hungary, and would-be Muslim immigrants portrayed as threatening the unity and well-being of his nation.[3] Furthermore, whereas it is true that aspects of these two phenomena can blend—out of heartfelt religious convictions, one may be driven to politically promote one's religion as a cultural unifying vehicle for spreading at least some of that religion's values or ethics—conceptually they remain distinct. And in most

[2] *See* below, at p. 64.
[3] Ibid.

cases involving blending, as will become plain in what follows, one of the two phenomena will clearly tend to predominate.

The varied instances of religion's repoliticization in the 1980s do not have any apparent common origin, and in most cases, they were not prompted as a reaction against institutional secularism. Concentrating on the four cases discussed below, in Iran, as mentioned, the repoliticization involved was mustered against an illiberal autocrat; in Poland, Solidarity's politicization of Catholicism arose in the context of their struggle against their country's Soviet-backed communist regime; and in Latin America, liberation theology was mobilized against oppressive and often corrupt, largely dictatorial rulers. On the other hand, as will be detailed below, only in the US was the fundamentalist Protestant-led repoliticization squarely oriented against institutional secularism. Finally, in Israel, the struggle between religious and secular Jews is more difficult to categorize, as we shall see, given the peculiarities of the *millet* system and the country's lack of a formal constitution, combined with its constitutionalization of a set of different basic laws.

Beyond individual cases, such as those of Iran, Poland, and several Latin American countries, where repoliticization was mustered against religious oppression or oppression starkly at odds with professed fundamental religious values, it is difficult to pinpoint any clearly manifest common causes for the repoliticization started in the 1980s and extending to the present. Nevertheless, and keeping in mind the importance of contextual factors in play in every case, one can identify several general trends that singularly or severally impact the impetus toward repoliticization. We can roughly divide these trends into three principal ones, depending on whether they are directed "internally" or "externally" against institutional secularism or else are conceptually independent from the latter but are effectively poised to undermine it. Chief among those critiques that loom as internal are those, already identified in Chapter 1, that claim that applications of institutional secularism are not merely imperfectly areligious but inevitably anti-religious or a means to conceal state preference for the majority religion. Another critique that may be regarded as either internal or external, depending on the background convictions of those who launch it, is that institutional secularism is bound to collapse into ideological secularism. Whereas the relationship between these two forms of secularism will be extensively examined in Chapter 4, for now, it is sufficient to distinguish between the following two claims. The first claim, which can be characterized as an internal critique, is that institutional secularism is bound to favor the secular way of life as opposed to all religions. In contrast to this claim, which in relevant respects mirrors those that attack institutional secularism as anti-religious or pro-majority religion, is the claim that institutional secularism is an empty concept that cannot stand on its own. In this latter view, which can be regarded as an external critique, institutional secularism is nothing more than the institutionalization of a secular way of life tied to a singular conception of the good, namely, ideological secularism. Accordingly, institutional secularism would be the equivalent of institutional Catholicism in the sense that, in both cases, institutionalization would have to be crafted, in whole or in part, to advance the objectives delimited by the relevant singular religious or secular conception of the good sought to be imposed (or self-imposed) throughout the polity.

The trends that are independent of institutional secularism but are nonetheless likely to undermine it are potentially manifold. They range from philosophical attacks against the Enlightenment's categorical dichotomy between Faith and Reason to religion-based admonitions against the supposed evils of contemporary Godless selfishness and hedonism in a decimated "naked public square" (Neuhaus 1984). Moreover, the relevant critiques of Enlightenment understandings have been launched by both secular and religious thinkers. The secular critiques at stake can be broadly traced back to what Max Weber has referred to as the "disenchantment of the world," which highlights that reason is ultimately purely instrumental, thus serving to match means to pre-selected ends without providing any guidance in the choice of ends or of conceptions of the good (Weber 1946: 134–56). The religious critiques, on the other hand, vary from those that are premised on a single religious truth and its accompanying norms and values to those that argue for a confluence between faith and reason. This latter view was defended by Pope Benedict XVI, who argued, as will be more fully discussed in Chapter 4, that Catholicism is a universal religion and that the legal and moral edicts derived from the Catholic faith can equally be deduced through the use of human reason.[4] Leaving aside for now the serious objections that may be leveled against Benedict's confluence of Catholic faith and reason, those who accept the latter would have no (non-trivial) use for institutional secularism. Indeed, in such a case, institutional secularism would be completely superfluous as both universal faith and the logic compelled by human reason would yield the same set of natural laws and fundamental rights.

It is beyond the scope of the present undertaking to get any further into these briefly mentioned theoretical debates or into the links between the latter and various strategic or genuinely religiously motivated repoliticizations of religion. What is crucial, for our purposes, is to determine how different types of repoliticization treat those who do not share the majority or otherwise dominant truth and to what extent the particular type of repoliticization involved allows for a pluralistic inclusion of divergent religious and non-religious conceptions of the good. With this in mind, we now turn to the four different types of repoliticization that we have referred to above.

[4] See Chapter 4, at p. 81.

B. Religious Appropriation of the Constitution—The Case of Iran

Post-1979 Iran provides a prime example of a secular regime being replaced by a theocratic one.[5] As described by an Iranian diplomat and adviser to his country's Chief Justice, Iran is "a polity which has a democratic structure," but differs from the Western experience in that "[i]t is a democracy based on Islamic rationality."[6] Leaving aside ultimate questions of substance, formally Iran is an Islamic constitutional democracy as contrasted with the Kingdom of Saudi Arabia, which is also an Islamic polity (albeit a Sunni Muslim one, whereas Iran is a Shiite Muslim one) but not a democratic one.[7] Consistent with this, Iran's post-1979 repoliticization established what may be characterized as a theocratic constitutional democracy put in place after the revolutionary overthrow of a secular imperial autocracy. As specified in the Preamble to Iran's 1979 Constitution:

> In the view of Islam, government . . . represents . . . the fulfillment of the political ideal of a people who bear a common faith and common outlook, taking an organized form in order to initiate the process of intellectual and ideological evolution towards the final goal, i.e., movement towards Allah. Our nation, in the course of its revolutionary developments, has cleansed itself of the dust and impurities that accumulated during the past and purged itself of foreign ideological influences, returning to authentic intellectual standpoints and the worldview of Islam. It now intends to establish an ideal and model society on the basis of Islamic norms. The mission of the Constitution is . . . to create conditions conducive to the development of man in accordance with the noble and universal values of Islam.[8]

Furthermore, the Iranian Constitution not only enshrines Islam, but it accords constitutional supremacy to a particular interpretation of that religion: "The official religion of Iran is Islam and the Twelver Ja'fari school [in usul al-Dîn and fiqh], and this principle will remain eternally immutable."[9]

[5] Greg Bruno, "Religion and Politics in Iran," *Council on Foreign Relations*, June 19, 2008, <www.cfr.org/backgrounder/religion-and-politics-iran>, accessed June 1, 2025; Farhad Rezaei, "Theocracy vs. Democracy in Iran: A New Round in an Old Conflict," *Atlantic Council*, July 3, 2017, <www.atlanticcouncil.org/blogs/iransource/theocracy-vs-democracy-in-iran-a-new-round-in-an-old-conflict/>, accessed June 1, 2025.

[6] *See* Interview by David Speedie with Dr. Mohammad Javad Ardashir Larijani, "Report from Iran," *Carnegie Council*, November 15, 2011, <www.carnegiecouncil.org/studio/multimedia/20111115-report-from-iran>, accessed June 1, 2025.

[7] Article 1 of the Saudi Constitution provides: "The Kingdom of Saudi Arabia is a sovereign Arab Islamic state with Islam as its religion; God's Book and the Sunnah of His Prophet, God's prayers and peace be upon him, are its constitution . . . ."

[8] Islahat Va Taqyyrati Va Tatmimah Qanuni Assassi [Amendment to the Constitution] 1368 (as amended in 1989) (Iran).

[9] Ibid, art 12.

Notwithstanding the constitutionalization of a particular Shiite understanding of Islam, interpretive disagreements within that perspective have stretched over several centuries. Of particular relevance for present purposes, however, is the consolidation of the "Religious Jurist" as the supreme "religiopolitical leader" of Shiism, which was nationalized and institutionalized under the tenure of the Ayatollah Khomeini, who became the country's first leader after having headed Iran's 1979 Revolution (Abdulaziz 2001: 123–47). Although contemporary Iran holds regular presidential and parliamentary elections,[10] its Religious Jurist is constitutionally empowered to impose his interpretation of Shiite Islamic precepts, values, morals, and laws on the polity as a whole. Accordingly, in spite of its adherence to constitutional democracy, Iran remains a theocracy under the dictates of fundamentalist religion.[11] As understood by Habermas, a fundamentalist religion is one that considers itself the repository of absolute truth and that insists that the state be ruled exclusively in accordance with its truth and the dictates that flow from it.[12] In its purest form, a fundamentalist theocracy imposes its own religious truth on all without exception and leaves no room whatever for religious pluralism. Iran, however, allows for a quite limited religious pluralism as its Constitution provides that "Zoroastrian, Jewish, and Christian Iranians are the only recognized religious minorities, who, within the limits of the law, are free to perform their religious rites and ceremonies, and to act according to their own canon in matters of personal affairs and religious education."[13] In spite of this, and because it allows no plurality of interpretations within Islam and affords no freedom of, or from, religion to its Muslim majority,[14] Iran's fundamentalist constitutional theocracy altogether fails to heed the core two principles inherent in institutional secularism—namely, refraining from imposing a single religious truth on most all who do not share it and allowing for a reasonably workable measure of pluralism among diverse religious and non-religious conceptions of the good.

In terms of the present undertaking and of our subsequent discussion of the reframing of fundamental rights, while Iran formally qualifies as a constitutional democracy, its fundamentalist theocracy provides a marker for the negation of what liberal constitutionalism requires in the context of the relation between state and religion. As such, Iran and any comparable constitutional theocracy provide a

[10] *See* Saeed Ghasseminejad, "Why Does Iran Hold So Many Elections?," *The National Interest*, June 24, 2024, <https://nationalinterest.org/feature/why-does-iran-hold-so-many-elections-211551>.

[11] Ibid.

[12] *See* Habermas 1999b: 224. It bears specifying that Habermas' and our understanding of "fundamentalist" is in relation to the socio-political dimensions of religion as contrasted with its purely internal religious ones. From a religious standpoint, a "fundamentalist" religion is one that purports to interpret sacred texts literally. Unless otherwise noted, we will assume throughout that a religion that is not *religiously* fundamentalist, because it does or can command non-literal interpretations of sacred texts, can nonetheless be *socio-politically* fundamentalist.

[13] Constitution of the Islamic Republic of Iran 1979, art 13.

[14] *See* Fitzroy Lee, "The Status of Religious Freedom in Iran," Human Rights Research Center, November 16, 2023, <www.humanrightsresearch.org/post/the-status-of-religious-freedom-in-iran>.

comparative referent for purposes of testing the limits of repoliticization consistent with approximating the two core principles issued from institutional secularism. Present-day Iran fails the test, but the other three examples, which we are about to examine, may at least *prima facie* fare differently as the repoliticization they espouse is either less comprehensive or less radical.

C. Reinterpreting the Constitution Through Religion—The Case of Protestant Fundamentalism in the USA

The intersection between Protestantism in general, Protestant fundamentalism in particular, and the latter's religious allies on certain specific issues, such as Catholics in the quest to completely outlaw abortion, goes back to the very enactment of the 1787 US Constitution. Moreover, the asserted links between Protestantism and the Constitution have been manifold, ranging from declarations that the Constitution itself emerged, at least in part, as an embodiment of Protestant beliefs and principles;[15] to the perceived latent cultural and identitarian Protestant bias inherent in the jurisprudence of the religion clauses of the First Amendment referred to in Chapter 1. Taken as a whole, the prominent place of Protestantism in US history, national and constitutional identity, politics, and ideology is diverse and ubiquitous. Elites that shepherded the former colonies into a constitutional democracy considered Protestantism as the superior religion (Smith 1997: 125). Several of the founding fathers, including John Jay, who proclaimed that America was a divinely favored people, and James Madison, who claimed divine sanction for the new constitutional system he was coauthoring, were firmly grounded in the Protestant heritage (Smith 1997: 121–22). To be sure, these latter assertions may have been more expressions of national identity and of Enlightenment deistic perspectives rather than theistic ones, but their link to Protestantism is beyond contestation.

Throughout the history of the US, Protestant Christianity has maintained a prominent place. To some, the US is the "city on the hill" or the "New Jerusalem" where Protestantism will be in a position of becoming truly and fully realized. Indeed, in the view of members of the American founding generation, the English monarchy had stood as a major obstacle to Protestantism's unmitigated vindication (Smith 1997: 72–74). To others, perhaps in a purely political vein, Protestantism has been invoked better to entrench capitalism (Smith 1997: 37–39). And finally, while managing to carve out their own distinct path, the Protestant fundamentalists who have repoliticized religion starting in the 1980s fit squarely within the same overall tradition. What is most remarkable for our purposes about these various embraces or invocations of Protestantism is that they all assume or seek conformity with the

[15] *See* Smith 1997: 47 (characterizing eighteenth-century American politics as grounded in an amalgamation of Locke's liberalism, Harrington's republicanism, and British iterations of Protestantism).

US Constitution. As we hope to make plain in the course of the following discussion, unlike in the case of Iran, where religion dictates what the Constitution must contain, American Protestantism, in all its alluded-to manifestations, adjusts to the US Constitution. And that is either because the Constitution is understood as already embodying Protestant values and principles in whole or part, or because the Constitution admits of a plurality of plausible interpretations, including ones consistent with the Protestant conception of the good.

The fundamentalist Protestant repoliticization of religion can be traced back to the Reagan era in the 1980s, but this by no means should be taken to imply that politics or constitutional controversies did not pit Protestantism—and for that matter Christianity more generally and occasionally other religions—against defenders of secularism in preceding eras of American history. One need only mention the celebrated and much publicized early twentieth-century litigation regarding the teaching of the Darwinian theory of evolution in public schools, which will be addressed more fully in Chapter 4, to be reminded of the ubiquity of the nexus between religion, the state, and civil society in the American context. This, in turn, raises the following key question for our purposes: Is the repoliticization launched in the 1980s and still prevalent at present significantly different from previous entanglements and conflicts between state and religion? And if so, what are the most salient contrasts between repoliticization and its historical antecedents?

At bottom, it is impossible to disentangle politics from religion. If a Catholic votes against the death penalty in a referendum because her religion commands opposition to it, she brings religion into politics. And accordingly, our Catholic voter shares this mixing of religion with politics with Iran's Religious Jurist, who figures as the ultimate guardian of theocratic political rule. In view of this, so long as it is not reducible to a purely political invocation of religion as exemplified by Hungary's Orban, repoliticization should be understood in a relational contextual sense rather than in any strictly definitional one. Consistent with this, in the US, which ranks as one of the most religious nations among its Western counterparts,[16] the occasions in which politics can be neatly detached from religion tend to be rare. Nevertheless, repoliticization can be distinguished from other entanglements through comparison of certain paradigmatic examples. These examples, which we are about to discuss, fall into four distinct categories: pre-institutional secularism politicization; implicit religious impulse translatable into secular discourse or, to use Rawls' terminology, into the dictates of "public reason"; the subsuming of the religious within the bounds of the secular; and repoliticization itself.

The 1791 US Bill of Rights, of which the religion clauses form part, could only be invoked against the federal government and not against those of the states prior

[16] *See* Jonathan Evans, et al., "Spirituality and religion: How does the U.S. compare with other countries?," Pew Research Center, June 25, 2025, <www.pewresearch.org/religion/2025/06/25/spirituality-and-religion-us-comparison-to-other-countries/>.

to the Civil War of the 1860s.[17] In the 1850s, some of the US states set up public schools and mandated that these impart the teachings of Protestantism to their students (Smith 1997: 218). This upset Catholic parents who, as members of a minority religion, eventually resorted to the creation of private parochial schools (Smith 1997). In this case, religion was straightforwardly (and one should add constitutionally) politicized in favor of the democratic majority and against a democratic minority. In this context, from a political standpoint the decision to teach Protestantism in public schools is no different than would have been a decision for the state to provide free meals to public school students.

The second category involving wrapping religion in a discourse circumscribed within the bounds of public reason is perhaps best exemplified by the intense and highly divisive doctrinal controversy that followed the US Supreme Court's 1973 constitutional decision in *Roe v Wade*.[18] The doctrinal and political uproar that followed *Roe* has lasted a half a century and shows no signs of abating even after the overruling of *Roe* by *Dobbs* in 2022.[19] The aftermath of *Roe* undoubtedly played an important role in the repoliticization of religion led by Protestant fundamentalists in conjunction with Catholics as confirmed by the direct political center stage upheavals relating to abortion upon the wake of the *Dobbs* decision.[20] However, in the early years after the *Roe* decision, the controversy was centered on issues of constitutional interpretation. Originalists and textualists could muster plausible arguments against a constitutional right to abortion, nowhere explicitly mentioned in the Constitution and not manifestly favored by any of its relevant framers. And those objecting to abortion on religious grounds could certainly translate their opposition into the language of constitutional doctrine. Moreover, even if all opposition to abortion were exclusively based on religious grounds, doctrinal criticisms of *Roe* were uttered by many secularists and even by strong supporters of abortion rights, such as Ruth Bader Ginsburg, who would subsequently endeavor to uphold them as a US Supreme Court justice.[21]

The third category, subsuming the religious within the secular, emerges clearly in the 5–4 decision by the US Supreme Court in *Lynch v Donnelly*, which concerned the display of the Christian *crèche* at Christmas time on municipal government grounds.[22] Rejecting an argument that this display violated the Establishment Clause inasmuch as it amounted to the state preferring and endorsing Christianity over other religions, the Court's majority held the presence of the *crèche* as part of a public display that also included Santa Claus and reindeer to be constitutionally

[17] *See Barron v City of Baltimore* 32 US (7 Pet) 243 (1833).
[18] *Roe v Wade* 410 US 113 (1973).
[19] *Dobbs v Jackson Women's Health Organization* 597 US 215 (2022).
[20] *See* Greenhouse & Siegel 2011: 2060–67 (describing the mobilization of Evangelical Protestants against abortion in the late 1970s).
[21] *See* Ginsburg 1985 (arguing that abortion rights would have been better constitutionally grounded on equality between the sexes grounds and criticizing *Roe*'s broad reliance on privacy rights).
[22] *Lynch v Donnelly* 465 US 668 (1984).

permissible. And that on the grounds that the main purpose of the display as a whole was commercial rather than religious, as the municipality's intent was to entice seasonal shoppers to patronize neighboring stores. This merger of the religious and the commercial may have seemed perfectly amenable to proponents of mainstream Christian faith at the time. But the presence of the *crèche* was poised to be perceived as exclusionary to Jews, Muslims, and atheists; and its judicial designation as commercial was condemned as a trivialization of profoundly revered Christian beliefs and symbols by prominent members of the Protestant clergy.[23]

Turning now to the fourth category, repoliticization itself, examples abound. Thus, in a direct church intervention into politics, US Catholic bishops engaged in much publicized refusals to provide Communion to church-attending Catholic political leaders such as President Biden and 2004 presidential candidate John Kerry because of their official endorsement of the (then) constitutional right to abortion.[24] Another glaring example is provided by the almost messianic and seemingly contradictory close association between White Evangelical Christian clergy and practitioners with President Trump by portraying the latter as an imperfect human agent sent by God to save America.[25] For our purposes, however, perhaps the best typical example is that of the following cases brought by fundamentalist Protestant parents against the public schools in which their children were students in the 1980s.[26] The parents claimed that the assigned reading in their children's literature class of a text that characterized a tsunami as resulting from the mysterious forces of nature amounted to an unconstitutional state imposition of the religion of "secular humanism." In the fundamentalist parents' view, God is the cause behind all natural phenomena, and, therefore, the implication that nature acts by itself amounts to a teaching by a religion that contradicts the truth of the transcendent Christian God. In other words, the school may be pretending to comply with institutional secularism as it is embodied in the Establishment Clause, but it is in fact imposing the religion of "secular humanism," which happens to coincide with ideological secularism, and which contradicts fundamentalist Protestant theology. Although the courts rejected the parents' arguments and found no violations of the Establishment Clause, conceptually, in these cases, the distinction between institutional and ideological secularism seems to depend on an interpretive nuance. If the reference to the force of nature in the relevant literary text is taken as being agnostic on the question of whether or not God is behind every natural

[23] *See, e.g.*, Testimony of J Brent Walker, General Counsel and Associate Director, Baptist Joint Committee on Public Affairs before the Senate Committee on the Judiciary (Federal Document Clearing House, October 25, 1995).

[24] *See* Paul Ellie, "The Catholic bishops' brawl over denying Joe Biden Communion," *The New Yorker*, June 22, 2021.

[25] *See* Jonathan Wilson-Hartgrove, "Why Evangelicals support President Trump, despite his immorality," *Time*, February 16, 2018.

[26] *See Smith v Board of Comm'rs of Mobile County* 827 F2d 684 (11th Cir 1987) and *Grove v Mead School District*, 753 F 2d 1528 (9th Cir 1983).

phenomenon, then the public-school teaching at stake would seem fully consistent with institutional secularism. On the other hand, if the reference in question is understood as implying a negation of divine intervention in natural phenomena, then the text advances an ideological secular perspective. For the suing parents, the mere omission of an attribution of divine agency amounted to a denial of a cardinal Christian truth. More broadly, this provides a telling example of attempting to combine an alteration of a key public institution to better suit one's religious objections while at the same time invoking the Constitution and remaining within the bounds of constitutional discourse.

D. Political Appropriation of Religion—The Cases of Liberation Theology in Latin America and of Solidarity in Poland

The Catholic Church has intervened in and influenced politics throughout its history, but in the context of the repoliticization of religion discussed in this chapter, the advent of liberation theology in Latin America and of Solidarity in Poland occupy a very special place. The combination of religion and politics in this latter context stands in sharp contrast to that prevalent in theocracies or in settings in which a particular religious vision is sought to be integrated within the prevailing constitutional order. The Latin American and Polish cases are similar in that they comprise a joining of those within the church with lay political actors of the Catholic faith or tradition who seek momentous if not revolutionary change within their respective polities. But the two cases also differ. In the Polish case, the church led by the Polish pope was, by and large, united behind Solidarity's challenge to the communist regime of the day.[27] In the Latin American case, on the other hand, internal divisions within the church were frequently correlated to those that set apart vehemently split political antagonists (Andes 2020: 175–93). As detailed below, Catholics and their church were on all sides of the political turmoil that led to an enormous number of deaths and uprootings throughout twentieth-century Latin America (Andes 2020: 175–76). In Poland, though, from the Polish pope to the lay Catholics, there was an overall fruitful cooperation in the efforts to liberate their country from the yoke of Soviet communism and the anti-religious bent of Marxist ideology (Andes 2020).

In twentieth-century Latin America, the entanglements between church, state, and civil society first emerged in the anti-clerical Mexican Revolution of 1910, which resulted in one million deaths (Andes 2020: 175). This was followed by a series of coups, military dictatorships, the Castro Cuban Revolution, the Sandinista Insurrection of 1979 in Nicaragua, and the counter-insurgency that followed it

[27] *See* Stephanie Slade, "The Pope who helped bring down communism," *Reason*, December 2021, <https://reason.com/2021/11/20/the-pope-who-helped-bring-down-communism/>.

in the 1980s, as well as by a series of authoritarian repressive regimes in various Central and South American countries during the same period (Andes 2020). In many instances, where right wing authoritarianism was in place those in the top layers of the national Catholic Church hierarchy tended to side with the regime whereas lower ranking clerics took the side of the oppressed and the poor and deployed the precepts of liberation theology which conjoined Marxism with Catholicism's commitment to attend to the social welfare needs of the poor and the dispossessed (Chaves 2015: 113–28). In support of the often brutal authoritarian regimes, Catholic religious discourse was repeatedly invoked to defend state-sponsored repression, and in some cases even torture (Andes 2020: 176). At the same time, however, Catholicism figured prominently in the quest for human liberation. Thus, in accord with the vision of liberation theology, "Catholics established networks of protest against economic and social inequality, opposed poverty and exclusion, and decried injustice and disenfranchisement" (Andes 2020). In short, the twentieth-century Catholic Church in Latin America is perhaps best encapsulated by its "Janus face" hovering over most matters religious and political (Andes 2020).

From our own perspective and focus on fundamental rights, what is most noteworthy in the legacy of liberation theology is the alliance between religion and politics in a struggle for the deployment and enhancement of fundamental rights. And this was undertaken in difficult and often life-threatening conditions (Garrard-Burnett 2016: 123–57) through the teaming up of religious and political actors relying on a convergence between a faith-based call for political action and a political reliance (based on faith, tradition, or even perhaps in some cases strategic calculation) on the preachings of progressive clergy members. Specifically, whereas proponents of liberation theology were initially prone to call for revolution based on their pairing of Catholicism with Marxism, they subsequently evolved toward fighting for human rights while emphasizing human dignity and the basic welfare needs of the poor and the dispossessed (Garrard-Burnett 2016). Notably, the clergy engaged in this rights-enhancing struggle were often at odds with their church superiors, including Pope John-Paul II and Pope Benedict XVI, who strongly opposed liberation theology and never fully embraced the ensuing turn to human rights. (Garrard-Burnett 2016: 151–52). This papal attitude changed with the advent of Pope Francis, the first Latin American pontiff, who has been described as "conservative on hot button issues such as gay marriage, abortion, contraception, and a married priesthood, but cognizant of the need for a pastoral renewal focused on bettering the lot of the poor, the unemployed, and the victims of economic globalization" (Andes 2020: 190).

As already indicated, in the Polish case of the rise of Solidarity in the 1980s against the country's repressive communist regime, the Catholic Church sided with and lent support to those who stood up to the government and who paved the way to their country's transition to constitutional democracy in 1989. Unlike in other communist countries where the Church was subsumed under, and marginalized by, state authorities, in Poland, the Catholic Church had maintained a sufficient degree of autonomy since the end of the Stalinist period in the mid-1950s to function as an intermediary between the communist government and civil society (Gauthier 1998: 289–317). Traditionally, the Polish Catholic Church had functioned as a nationalist and political bastion of resistance going back to the eighteenth century when the country confronted Protestant Prussia and Orthodox Russia invasions (Tazbir 1977: 29–45). In the 1970s, in the years preceding the rise of Solidarity, the Polish Catholic Church played not only the role of intermediary but also that of spiritual guide and physical sustainer of its country's civil society. As recounted by a Polish historian, "in the 1970s, many young people, hundreds of thousands, started going to church and even to pilgrimages. Some of it was authentic religious feeling. Some was the search for some feeling because of the lack of any other ideology or spiritual system. Some was anti-Communist, and some was nationalistic."[28] Moreover, in the 1980s with the rise of Solidarity, first as a labor movement and then as a more broadly based political movement, and during the repression and detention of many Solidarity members (including its leader, Lech Walesa) after the General Jaruzelski government introduced martial law in 1981, Catholic churches became the only places where dissidents could meet and assemble beyond the reach of the government (Michel 1991). Indeed, even the highly repressive Jaruzelski regime was leery of overly antagonizing the church (Brown 1988: 6–7).

The election of a Polish pope and the triumphant trip of Jean Paul II to his native country in 1979 have been cast as the catalysts for the eventual fall of communism in Poland a decade later (Kraszewski 2012: 27–46). The pope and the top of the Polish church hierarchy remained more cautious than several parish priests for fear of triggering a Soviet military intervention or a government repression of extant church privileges (Brown 1988: 7–8). Nevertheless, the church remained steadfast throughout the entire period in its backing of all those who were united by sharing an anti-communist bond and a dedication to enhancing fundamental rights.

Whereas the Catholic Church has continued to play an important political role throughout Poland's post-communist era, notably for our purposes, as will be further explored in Chapter 3, the Polish Catholic Church's close association with the country's illiberal government led by the Law and Justice political party (PiS) became highly divisive inasmuch as it has been geared to effectuate a glaring shrinkage of fundamental rights. The church and PiS have joined to restrict most abortions, to interfere more generally with women's reproductive rights,

[28] *See* Nina Darnton, "The subtle power of the Polish church," *New York Times Magazine*, June 6, 1982 (quoting Marcin Krol).

and to foster discrimination against the LGBTQ community.[29] When the Polish Constitutional Court, reshaped by PiS, upheld the prohibition of most abortions in 2020, women took to the streets in protests that matched in size those last seen in the era of Solidarity demonstrations.[30] Moreover, as a consequence of PiS's divisiveness and its close association with the church, there has been a dramatic decrease in church attendance by Poland's younger generation.[31] In short, as Poland's example vividly illustrates, depending on the circumstances, politicized religion can be unifying or divisive and enlisted to enhance or to restrict fundamental rights.

E. The Clash Between Religious and Constitutional Norms—The Special Case of Israel

In our discussion of Israel's adoption and implementation of the *millet* system in Chapter 1, we focused on its advantages and disadvantages and suggested changes it could adopt to better approximate the two core requirements associated with institutional secularism. In this section, in contrast, we focus on the ways in which Israel's recourse to the *millet* system has channeled politicizations of religion in relation to the nature and scope of protection of fundamental rights. Some of the politicizations in question arise directly in connection with the implementation of the *millet* system. Thus, for example, as will be further specified below, under Jewish religious law, the *halacha*, divorce favors men and disfavors women. Although the consequent inequalities cannot be remedied as long as divorce itself remains within the exclusive jurisdiction of rabbinical courts, some of its incidents, such as property allocations upon marital dissolution, have been entrusted to state-generated civil law.[32] Whereas this shift does not obviate the greater rights of divorcing men, it is meant to significantly curtail abuses based on the advantages provided by rabbinical law. Arguably, the shift in question is contrary to the strictures of the *millet* system, and it has been decried by rabbinical authorities and by political actors in the Orthodox and ultra-Orthodox communities.[33]

Other instances of politicization are indirectly related to the *millet* system or arise independently from the latter but are significantly affected by the devolution of certain state legal powers to religious authorities. Most of the instances in question concern Israel's Jewish majority, but some involve discrimination against the

[29] *See* Zosia Wanat, "Politics of the Polish church scares off believers," *Politico*, December 18, 2019, <www.politico.eu/article/polish-politics-pis-catholic-church-relationship-scares-off-believers/>.

[30] *See* Kate Korycki, "Polish women reject the Catholic Church's hold on their country," *The Conversation*, November 17, 2020.

[31] *See* Andrew Higgins, "Amid scandals and politics, Poland's youths lose faith in Catholic church," *New York Times*, November 28, 2022.

[32] *See* below, at p. 43.

[33] Ibid.

country's Christian and Muslim minorities. Before addressing pertinent examples of the kinds of politicization at stake, however, it is important to briefly concentrate on Israel's official conjunction of the Jewish people and the Jewish religion, which has resulted in a *sui generis* dynamic between religion and politics.

In Israel, religion became essential to the very definition of peoplehood. Thus, Judaism, the religion of a single people, was proclaimed the national religion in the country's Declaration of Independence, which established Israel as a "Jewish and democratic" state (Stopler 2020: 209). Significantly, throughout the country's history, there has been a heated debate among Israeli Jews over the actual meaning of the term "Jewish" in the Declaration of Independence. For some, the term in question refers to Judaism as a religion and to its institutionalization as the state religion. For others, in contrast, "Jewish" cannot be dissociated from "democratic" to which it is linked in the Declaration, with the consequence that it ought to be understood in a historical and cultural sense as secular and religious Jews alike shared in a long history in exile, in the attempted total annihilation in the Holocaust, and in the realization of statehood in 1948. Specifically, Israeli Jews have remained divided over whether the country ought to officially adopt the religion and the *halachic* laws it prescribes to rule over the entire Jewish population as the ultra-Orthodox, also known as Haredim, would wish;[34] or whether Judaism should be incorporated mainly as culture and tradition while maintaining Western secular and democratic laws and values as Israel's secular Jews prefer.[35] Accordingly, at one end of the spectrum, Israel would be transformed into a theocracy—and in the eyes of many secular Israelis become much like Iran[36]—whereas at the other end of the spectrum, Israel would be turned into a Western constitutional democracy with a robust separation between religion and the state. Be that as it may, what is important for present purposes is that Israel is somewhere between these two extremes and that any perceived or proposed change in either direction becomes inevitably highly politicized.

Israel has been described as having adopted a "partial establishment of the Orthodox Jewish religion" (Stopler 2013: 503), which originated in the "Status Quo" agreement between the secular Zionists and the Orthodox Jewish community around the time of the country's independence (Stopler 2013: 514). Pressures on the "Status Quo" have more recently greatly intensified pursuant to the rise of

[34] *See* Pew Research Center, "Israel's religiously divided society" (2016), <www.pewforum.org/wp-content/uploads/sites/7/2016/03/Israel-Survey-Full-Report.pdf> [https://perma.cc/VL3E-ZHUV], accessed May 26, 2025 (reporting 89% of surveyed Haredim believe *halacha* should be given preference over democratic ideals, and 86% of Haredim would favor *halacha* being made the official law of the land for Jews).

[35] *Id.* (reporting that 89% of secular Jews ("Hilonim") believe that democratic principles should take preference over religious law).

[36] *See* Eran Yashiv, "Israel's future: A Jewish theocracy that resembles Iran," *Haaretz*, April 12, 2024, <www.haaretz.com/opinion/2024-04-12/ty-article-opinion/.premium/israels-future-a-jewish-theocracy-that-resembles-iran/000001>, accessed September 8, 2025.

the radical ultra-Orthodox who currently control the religious establishment, thus exacerbating the secular–religious divide within Israel's Jewish majority (Stopler 2013). From a political standpoint, the conflicts fueled by radicalized religion in Israel bear some affinity with those associated with fundamentalist Protestantism in the US and with the conservative understanding of Catholicism that prevails in present-day Poland. However, the Israeli predicament differs from that of its counterparts in view of the unique impact of the *millet* system on the intra-communal relationships among the country's Jewish population. This is vividly illustrated in the following examples.

Israel's rabbinical courts are highly patriarchal, and their exclusive jurisdiction over marriage and divorce among Jews favors men over women (Stopler 2013: 512), as already noted in the above reference to divorce. Not only divorce itself but division of property among the divorcing spouses favors men in rabbinical courts. In 1994, however, in what has been characterized as a "revolutionary decision," Israel's Supreme Court ordered rabbinical courts to apply civil law to, among other things, property allocations incident to divorce (Sapir & Statman 2019: 175). This allowed men and women to share equally in the property subject to division, but caused an uproar within the rabbinical community and among many of the latter's constituents (Sapir & Statman 2019). Accordingly, this intrusion into the *millet* sphere of religious autonomy provided greater equality for Israeli Jewish women while trampling on the freedom of religion of strict *halacha* followers.

Another intrusion into the religious autonomy meant to be safeguarded by the *millet* system concerned Muslim Sharia courts. Consistent with Islamic law, these courts were willing to marry Muslim men to Jewish women, but not any non-Muslim man to a Muslim woman. Based on a concern over erosion of Israel's Jewish majority, conceived as inextricably linked to the Jewish religion, viewed at a very minimum as requiring not embracing any other religion, the Israeli Ministry of Religious Affairs instructed Sharia courts to refrain from performing intermarriages involving Jewish women (Stopler 2013: 512). Notably, this amounts to a restriction on the religious autonomy of a minority religion's use of its *millet* prerogatives. And this restriction was imposed by the Ministry for purposes of reinforcing the amalgamated national and religious identity of Israel as a Jewish state, thus tying together the country's cultural and religious commitment to Judaism.

Perhaps the most dramatic clash between the cultural and religious dimensions of Judaism, squarely steeped in the political sphere, is that prompted by the Law of Return.[37] According to this law, Jews from all over the world can immigrate and become citizens of Israel. This law, premised on the Zionist ideal of attracting the maximum possible number of Jews living abroad to settle in Israel, has adopted

[37] Law of Return 5710–1950 (Israel), as amended in 1954 and 1970.

a criterion of who qualifies as a Jew that conflicts with its *halachic* counterpart. According to *halacha*, to be a Jew one must be born to a Jewish mother.[38] Under the Law of Return, however, anyone who has at least one Jewish grandparent qualifies as a Jew. Moreover, the reason for this departure from *halacha* was both moral and political. The criterion adopted by the Law of Return was the same as that used by Hitler to determine who would be eligible for extermination as a Jew. And the reasoning that led to adopting Hitler's criterion was that it would be unseemly not to admit to the Jewish homeland someone who could or would have been murdered because of having been designated by the Nazis as a Jew. Politically, this expanded criterion of who is a Jew allowed for immigration into Israel in the 1990s of hundreds of thousands of persons originating in the former Soviet Union (Stopler 2013: 513). As large portions of these immigrants were cultural but not *halachic* Jews, they became Israeli citizens but were ineligible to marry other Jews or even one another, as they did not qualify as Jews in the eyes of the rabbinate (Stopler 2013).

Turning to discrimination against religious minorities under the *millet* system, a striking example is provided by the highly disproportionate state financing of Christian and Muslim cemeteries in comparison with amounts spent on Jewish cemeteries. Cemeteries in Israel are exclusively entrusted to the various religious communities, but although Christian and Muslim Arabs add up to 20% of Israel's population, they only received 2% of the funds allotted by the Ministry of Religious Affairs for their religious needs.[39] This disparity led to what the Israeli Supreme Court characterized as "a dire situation in the Arab cemeteries," thus creating a situation that "honors neither the dead nor the living."[40] Notably, as stressed by Israeli commentators, "the motivation of those Israeli Jews who object to equal funding of all religions (in accordance with their relative size) is much more national than religious" (Sapir & Statman 2019: 270). Moreover, as further specified by the same commentators, the Israeli Jews who object to proportionate funding of minority religions are motivated not by theological concerns but instead by the belief that Israeli Arabs may not be sufficiently loyal to the Jewish state (Sapir & Statman 2019). In short, the discrimination at stake in the cemeteries case is ultimately much more political than religious.

The tensions between secular and religious Jews have been exacerbated to the point that, in 2023, the president of Israel asserted that his country was facing

[38] Whereas conversion of non-Jews into Judaism is permissible, it is strongly discouraged and made very onerous by Israel's Orthodox rabbinate, which holds a monopoly over the subject within Israel. *See* Douglas C. Youvan, "The role and influence of the Chief Rabbinate in Israel: Balancing tradition and modernity," ResearchGate, August 2024. <www.researchgate.net/publication/382968792_The_Role_and_Influence_of_the_Chief_Rabbinate_in_Israel_Balancing_Tradition_and_Modernity>.

[39] *See* HCJ 240/98 *Adalah—The Legal Center for Arab Minority Rights in Israel v Minister of Religious Affairs* 52(5) PD 167, 178 [1998] (SC Israel) (Cheshin J, para 17).

[40] CJ 1113/99 *Adalah—The Legal Center for Arab Minority Rights in Israel v Minister of Religious Affairs* IsrLR 133 [2000] (SC Israel) (Zamir J, para 14).

a national state of emergency due to mounting division and polarization.[41] President Herzog's ominous observation and call for greater tolerance came after a virulent clash in the center of Tel Aviv over a Yom Kippur prayer service on municipal grounds that was held in violation of a municipal order prohibiting gender-segregated events on a public square.[42] This clash was regarded as an extension of the nearly daily nine-month-long pro and con demonstrations regarding the judicial overhaul initiative launched by the most extreme right-wing nationalist and ultra-Orthodox government that Israel has known throughout its history.[43] Dramatically, the latter demonstrations and the bitter animosities they fostered were abruptly interrupted in the aftermath of the October 7, 2023 terrorist attack by Hamas that resulted in the killing of around 1,200 Israeli civilians and that led to swift unification of Israelis to confront the life-threatening attacks launched by foreign enemies.[44] Nevertheless, the underlying conflicts that led to divisions within Israel and that concentrated on efforts to curtail the nature and scope of certain fundamental rights—and especially those of women[45]—seem temporarily partially defused but by no means thereby resolved or prone to remaining quiescent once Israel emerges from its present wartime preoccupations.

In conclusion, the various instances of religious appropriations of politics and of political recourse to religion that we detailed in this chapter resulted at times in the protection and expansion of fundamental rights and at other times in the suppression or shrinkage of certain key fundamental rights. Moreover, in some cases, such as that of Israel, the protection of certain rights, such as those of women by state courts, has been obtained at the expense of limiting the freedom *of* religion of the Orthodox rabbinate and of its followers. Also, in the case of Poland, we highlighted a historical trajectory that made use of the same religion, Catholicism, first to promote human rights, as was the case in the Solidarity days, and then to curtail the rights of women and LGBTQ individuals under the more recent rule by PiS.

Perhaps the single most outstanding feature emerging from the varied interpenetrations between religion and politics since the 1980s is the palpable increase in the intensity of tensions and in confrontations pitting secularists against proponents of strong or fundamentalist religion. This, as we have seen, is the case in the US where fundamentalist Protestants and conservative Catholics have pushed for a redefinition of fundamental rights and paved the way to the elimination for the first time in American history of a previously guaranteed right—namely, that

[41] *See* "Herzog: 50 years after Yom Kippur War, Israel facing 'state of emergency,'" *The Times of Israel*, September 28, 2023.

[42] Ibid.

[43] Ibid.

[44] *See* Bill Hutchinson, "Israel-Hamas conflict: Timeline and key developments," *ABC News*, October 19, 2023, <https://abcnews.go.com/International/timeline-surprise-rocket-attack-hamas-israel/story?id=103816006> accessed June 1, 2025.

[45] *See* "Herzog: 50 years after Yom Kippur War, Israel facing 'state of emergency,'" *The Times of Israel*, September 28, 2023.

to abortion, which took place when *Dobbs* overruled *Roe*—thus reducing the constitutional liberty, privacy, and equality rights of women while fueling the bitter divisiveness between abortion proponents and abortion foes. Similarly, the conjunction between Poland's conservative Catholic Church and the illiberal PiS has resulted in the erosion of fundamental rights mentioned above and given rise to massive protests against the newly imposed restrictions on rights.[46] Finally, the same much-increased intensity has fueled the just-described recent standoff between the secular and the ultra-Orthodox in Israel. As we shall make clear in the next chapter, acute tensions fostered by the intermingling of religion and politics also prevail in contemporary polities that have veered to populism and to more exclusive iterations of nationalism. What remains to be seen is to what extent nationalist and populist politicizations of religion differ from those dealt with in this chapter.

[46] *See* Antonia Mortensen and Laura Smith-Spark, "Poland's biggest protests in decades stand against abortion ban," *CNN*, October 31, 2020, <www.cnn.com/2020/10/31/europe/poland-abortion-protests-scli-intl/index.html>, accessed June 1, 2025.

3

Religious Nationalism and Religious Populism: Religious Rule of the Nation and the People Versus National and Popular Acculturation of Religion

In the twenty-first century, the repoliticization of religion has been repurposed in many instances in the pursuit of starkly anti-pluralist agendas. Frequently, this has been accomplished through the implantation or spread of religious nationalism and religious populism. In both of these cases, what is crucial is not whether or not there is a significant or widespread commitment to religious belief or dogma, but instead the use of religion as the basis for forging identitarian bonds that are strongly exclusionary of those cast as the "other." In terms of the distinction drawn in Chapter 2, whereas nationalism and populism may at times involve the infusion of religion into politics, for the most part, they rely on what amounts to an appropriation of religion for purely political purposes. In religious nationalism, national identity is defined above all by belonging to a single (usually majoritarian) religion, whether in terms of religious belief and practice or of embracing the cultural mainstays associated with the religion in question. Moreover, this religious belonging implies that commitment to other (usually minoritarian) religions is contrary to, or erosive for, the unity or coherence of the imagined community bound together by its own distinct national identity. For example, by insisting that the United States be regarded above all as a Christian nation, one can readily convey to non-Christians that they do not belong or that, at best, they should be merely

Politicized Religion and the Reframing of Fundamental Rights. Susanna Mancini and Michel Rosenfeld, Oxford University Press. © Susanna Mancini, Michel Rosenfeld 2026. DOI: 10.1093/9780191982149.003.0004

tolerated.[1] On the other hand, religious populism—as all populism—consists in projecting a part as the whole when circumscribing "the people."[2] Accordingly, the people may be the ordinary citizens led by their charismatic leader against the "elites"; the native born versus the immigrants; a particular ethnic group against all others; and, in the case of religious populism, those belonging to one religion as opposed to all those who belong to other religions. Thus, for example, in a contemporary populist regime, such as that of Orban in Hungary, as already noted, references to the country's Christian heritage are directed against liberal elites in the country and Western Europe and against would-be Muslim immigrants.[3]

To the extent that nationalism and populism resort to religion to establish markers of inclusion and of exclusion, they pose serious threats to institutional secularism without necessarily thereby casting away secular ways of life. Furthermore, numerous religious nationalist and populist polities, though clearly illiberal and anti-pluralist in tendency, are at least officially committed to honoring human rights and fundamental constitutional rights in somewhat different and mostly more limited ways. Illiberal religious nationalist and populist polities tend to reinterpret and reframe those rights, however, in ways that suit their anti-pluralist agendas. Thus, for instance, as will be extensively examined in Part II of this book, Christian nationalists or populists may reinterpret freedom of religion rights in ways that disadvantage or exclude the rights asserted by Muslims.[4] Also, polities dominated by those who appeal to religious traditions often promote versions of fundamental rights that rekindle or exacerbate discrimination against women and sexual minorities.[5]

[1] *See Town of Greece v Galloway*, 572 US 565, 632–33 (2014) (Kagan J, dissenting) (stating that a municipality's invocation of Christian prayer during town hall meetings "infuse[d] a participatory government body with one (and only one) faith, so that month in and month out, the citizens appearing before it become partly defined by their creed—as those who share, and those who do not, the community's majority religious belief"). This case is further discussed in Chapter 4.

[2] Albertazzi & McDonnell 2015: 5 (defining populism as "[a] thin-centered ideology which pits a virtuous and homogeneous people against a set of elites and dangerous 'others' who are together depicted as depriving (or attempting to deprive) the sovereign people of their rights, values, prosperity, identity and voice").

[3] Péter Krekó, Bulcsú Hunyadi, and Patrik Szicherle, "Anti-Muslim populism in Hungary: From the margins to the mainstream," *Brookings*, July 24, 2019, <www.brookings.edu/research/anti-muslim-populism-in-hungary-from-the-margins-to-the-mainstream> [https://perma.cc/B5QX-M6XJ], accessed June 8, 2025 ("In [the Hungarian far-right's] view, the European Union and some member states force the dictatorship of liberal values on their citizens and other countries. Hence, according to their narrative, the 'cosmopolitan' elites in Brussels and some other capitals (e.g., in Berlin) dictate just like Moscow did back in the communist era." (citing "Orbán a rezsicsökkentést hasonlítja március 15-éhez," *Origo*, March 15, 2014, <www.origo.hu/itthon/20140315-orban-viktor-unnepi-beszede-2014-marcius-15-en.html> [https://perma.cc/69SY-TJZN], accessed June 8, 2025)).

[4] *See* Chapter 5.

[5] *See* Chapter 6 and p. 203 below.

A. Nationalism and Populism as Inherently Independent from Religion

Nationalism and populism are not inherently tied to religion. To the contrary, since the Enlightenment, nationalism has been mainly correlated with secularism. As a consequence of the decline of religiosity among European intellectuals during the nineteenth century, nationalism came to replace religion as the main binding force within a political community (Smith 1981). The nation as a source of identity, solidarity, and common political purpose may be based on a shared history, ethnicity, culture, or language without any particular religion playing any defining role.[6] Similarly, populism, with its characteristic embrace of a part of the whole population within the relevant polity as the People, need not invoke religion as it sets its divide between those it includes and those it excludes. Some populisms are thus ethnically based,[7] and others pit the common person against the elites and the expert class.[8] Moreover, even when a particular religion may be tied to an instance of nationalism or populism, this may be largely incidental and have little influence on the shaping and executing of the common project within the polity involved. For example, contemporary France is a secular society where a vast majority of the citizenry is Catholic, but only 5% of the population would be interested in a Catholic political agenda.[9] In contrast, Poland widely regards itself as a Catholic nation. As emphasized by a past prime minister, "Christianity is part of our national identity, the [Catholic] Church was and is the preacher and holder of the only commonly held system of values in Poland."[10]

[6] Anderson 2006: 12, 22, 197 (national identity based on delimiting an imagined community).

[7] For example, Hungarian populism, as exemplified by the policy positions of the right-wing governing party Fidesz and the far right-wing party Jobbik, is ethnic in nature. *See Magyarország Alaptörvénye* [The Fundamental Law of Hungary] (2011) (Fidesz redrafted the Hungarian constitution after taking power in 2010. The current constitution now differentiates between the "Hungarian nation" or "people" and "nationalities living with us . . . [as] constituent parts of the State"); Carol Schaeffer, "How Hungary became a haven for the alt-right," *Atlantic*, May 28, 2017, <www.theatlantic.com/international/archive/2017/05/how-hungary-became-a-haven-for-the-alt-right/527178> [https://perma.cc/8ZKD-3D2N], accessed June 8, 2025 (describing Jobbik's platform for preserving an ethnically pure state); Geneviève Zubrzycki 2001: 629, 638 (stating that "[t]he nation, in Poland, is primarily understood in ethnic terms" and that "the Polish ethno-national identity is based at least partly on religious affiliation"). In countries that are more ethnically homogenous, elites are sometimes declared to be "multicultural 'ethnic traitors.'" *See* Stanley 2008: 104–5.

[8] Müller 2016: 10–11; McDonnell & Cabrera 2019: 485 (discussing who the Bharatiya Janata Party (BJP), or Indian People's Party, determines to be "elites"); Devesh Kapur, "Modi's India is aspirational, assertive—and anti-elite," *Washington Post*, May 29, 2019, <www.washingtonpost.com/opinions/2019/05/29/modis-india-is-aspirational-assertive-anti-elite> [https://perma.cc/QAB3-8XPN], accessed June 8, 2025 (discussing a significant portion of the BJP's support coming from stark class divides between lesser-educated and non-English proficient rural populations and richer, more-educated urban populations).

[9] Catherine Fieschi, Muslims and the Secular City: How Right-Wing Populists Shape the French Debate over Islam, *Brookings Institute*, February 28, 2020, <www.brookings.edu/research/muslims-and-the-secular-city-how-right-wing populists-shape-the-french-debate-over-islam/>.

[10] *See* Rob Schmitz, "As an election nears in Poland, church and state are a popular combination," *National Public Radio*, October 12, 2019, <www.npr.org/2019/10/12/768537341/as-an-election-nears-in-poland-church-and-state-are-a-popular-combination> [https://perma.cc/M55E-S9DY], accessed

To better understand the principal characteristics of the type of contemporary religious nationalism and religious populism that insists on adherence to fundamental human and constitutional rights, while purporting to redefine them, it is necessary to briefly focus on the confluence of key factors that account for the implantation of the phenomenon under consideration. In essence, three developments have converged to bring about the current predicament: the expansion or adaptation of the revitalization and "repoliticization" of religion discussed in Chapter 2; the resurgence of nationalism after the fall of the Soviet Union;[11] and further recourse to nationalism coupled with the widespread embrace of populism as a reaction against transnational governance regarded as a major threat to democratic rule, and against globalization with its propensity to exacerbate huge inequalities in wealth and to threaten traditional values and cultural bonds.[12]

B. Secular Disenchantment and Nationalism's Turn to Religion

Nationalism, in Ernest Gellner's notable definition, is the "principle which holds that the political and the national unit should be congruent" (Gellner 1983: 1). Moreover, in the context of modern constitutional democracies, it is the people that gives itself a constitution meant to be implemented within a nation-state.[13] Although in the vernacular the "people" and the "nation" are often invoked interchangeably, the two are conceptually distinct even when their respective referents are fully coextensive. The people is the aggregate of persons that gives itself a constitution, by which it agrees to be governed within a specified state.[14] The nation, on the other hand, in the words of Benedict Anderson, is an imagined community (Anderson 2006: 5–6) that, as mentioned above, is meant to provide a common identity, a common heritage, and a common basis for the maintenance of bonds of solidarity (Anderson 2006: 5–7). Unlike a family or a tribe that functions collectively on the basis of individual acquaintance and personal relationships, the

June 8, 2025 (reporting that nine in ten Poles are Catholic and quoting former Polish prime minister, Jarosław Kaczyński).

[11] Beissinger 2009; Randall D. Law, "Soviet nationalism is still driving Russian politics," *The Atlantic*, December 22, 2011, <www.theatlantic.com/international/archive/2011/12/soviet-nationalism-is-still-driving-russian-politics/250391> [https://perma.cc/GL54-L8ER], accessed June 8, 2025.

[12] *See* Arts & Halman 2005: 71 ("Many European citizens are afraid 'of being "invaded" by foreign cultures.' Not only foreign cultures from outside Europe are considered a threat, many Europeans of different nationalities also see the further unification of Europe as posing a danger to the survival of national cultures and identities." (quoting Touraine 1994: 13)).

[13] The US Constitution's Preamble much celebrated "We the People" is thus an emblematic iteration of similar pronouncements throughout the world. *See* US Const pmbl; India 1950 Const pmbl; South Africa 1996 Const pmbl.

[14] It is often asserted that, in a democracy, the people engage in self-government. *See, e.g.*, Rousseau 1968. As the focus here is on the state's role in the governing of the people, whether the state acting *for* the people is also run *by* the people need not be addressed any further.

modern nation-state creates a political order in which members of the polity primarily relate to one another as strangers (Anderson 2006: 6). Accordingly, what binds together these strangers is an imagined construct around which they can all rally. Nationalism is thus intrinsically linked to national identity and consists of affirmation and internalization of and commitment to the latter.

Nationalism has both an inclusive and an exclusive facet. Each nation has a distinct national identity, and solidarity within one's own nation requires subscribing to the relevant identity to the exclusion of all others. Singular national identities must remain distinct from one another, but this does not mean that composite or overlapping elements cannot successfully coexist. For example, Irish Americans and Italian Americans can certainly continue partaking in important elements of the national identity of their respective countries of origin without being less loyal to the United States. Nevertheless, in certain circumstances, solidarity with one national identity must exclude given shared allegiances. Thus, to the extent that German and Japanese nationalism fueled those countries' war against the United States during the Second World War, German Americans and Japanese Americans could not be legitimately at once loyal to the political community of their country of citizenship and to that of their country of origin.

There is, however, an important distinction between inclusive and inclusionary, on the one hand, and exclusive and exclusionary, on the other. For example, to the extent that American national identity requires adherence to, and respect for, the US Constitution, it is inclusionary. It leaves the door open for any legal immigrant to eventually obtain citizenship and to become absorbed into the American nation by swearing allegiance to the country's constitution.[15] In contrast, a national identity that relies exclusively on ethnic belonging, such that members of any other ethnic group cannot be included within the nation, no matter how long or deeply rooted they may be within the relevant polity, would plainly be thoroughly exclusionary.[16]

[15] 8 USC § 1448(a) (2012) (stating that a public ceremony for naturalization must include "an oath to support the Constitution"); 8 USC § 1101(a)(22) (2012) (defining a US "national" as a citizen of the United States or a non-citizen that "owes personal allegiance to the United States"); 8 CFR § 337.1(a) (2020) (providing the oath of allegiance for naturalization processes, which states, "I hereby declare . . . that I will support and defend the Constitution and laws of the United States of America . . .").

[16] Compare the Preamble to the 1989 amended version of the 1949 Hungarian Constitution, *Magyarország Alaptörvénye* [The Fundamental Law of Hungary], pmbl. (amended 1989) (which speaks in the name of "the Republic of Hungary"), with the Preamble to the 2011 Hungarian Constitution, *Magyarország Alaptörvénye* [The Fundamental Law of Hungary], pmbl. (2011) ("We, the Members of the Hungarian Nation . . . promise to preserve the intellectual and spiritual unity of our nation torn apart in the storms of the last century."). The latter promise alludes to the dismantling of the vast territory inhabited by Hungarian nationals within the Austro-Hungarian Empire at the end of the First World War upon the adoption of the Treaty of Trianon in 1920. This treaty has been regarded as a national tragedy within Hungary. *See* Alasdair Sandford and Ádám Magyar, "Trianon trauma: Why is the peace treaty signed 100 years ago seen as a national tragedy for Hungary?," *Euronews*, June 4, 2020, <www.euronews.com/2020/06/04/trianon-trauma-why-is-the-peace-treaty-signed-100-years-ago-seen-as-a-national-tragedy> [https://perma.cc/856W-9BYY], accessed June 8, 2025. Additionally, certain Hungarian politicians have toyed with the idea of incorporating ethnic Hungarians living in bordering contemporary countries—such as Romania, Serbia, and Slovakia—into a "greater Hungary."

Religious nationalism seems at first paradoxical, given that, as noted above, nationalism has historically been associated with secularism. In the wake of the Enlightenment, secularism dethroned religion to delimit and sustain the relevant community that could be marshaled into a political unit. Accordingly, the nation, as an imagined community that provides a common identity, shared values, and a congruent set of objectives, loomed as well-poised to fill the growing void stemming from the disenchantment with religion.[17] Although secular nationalism may flourish by occupying a space left open by the retreat of religion, it is nonetheless unlikely that this would result in a complete purge of religion from its former sphere of influence. Indeed, for all its mythical and imaginary dimensions, national identity must incorporate—albeit in an idealized, transformed, or redeployed iteration[18]—aspects of the history, tradition, and culture of those it seeks to rally into a political unit. Almost inevitably, within the history, tradition, and culture at stake, aspects of the relevant religion will remain embedded. Examples abound, extending from Sunday being the day of rest in the most secular of traditionally Christian countries to Weber's linking the "spirit" of capitalism to Protestant ethics.[19] However, religious symbols, elements, or fragments that are embedded in secular national identity typically figure as displaced, detached, or reframed in relation to their position in their religion of origin. Because of this, the religious-based materials in question may be regarded on par with non-religious components of the pertinent imagined community. Thus, for example, Vercingetorix, the pre-Christian Gallic king, is as much part of French national identity as is Joan of Arc, who was reported to have been directed by God to lead the French in battle against the English on the way to the decisive victory that put an end to the Hundred Years War.[20] In short, in the

See Marcel Gascón Barberá and Anja Vladisavljevic, "Orban's 'greater Hungary' map creates waves in neighborhood," *Balkan Insight*, May 7, 2020, <https://balkaninsight.com/2020/05/07/orbans-greater-hungary-map-creates-waves-in-neighbourhood/> [https://perma.cc/9YVY-VJQJ], accessed June 8, 2025. As for non-Hungarian nationals within Hungary, the 2011 preamble states: "The nationalities living with us form part of the Hungarian political community and are constituent parts of the State." *Magyarország Alaptörvénye* [The Fundamental Law of Hungary], pmbl. (2011). Accordingly, non-ethnic Hungarians are excluded from the Hungarian nation but included in their country's political sphere and count as citizens of the Hungarian state.

[17] *See* Anna Grzymala-Busse, "Religious nationalism and religious influence," in *Oxford Research Encyclopedia of Politics*, March 2019, <https://oxfordre.com/politics/view/10.1093/acrefore/9780190228637.001.0001/acrefore-9780190228637-e-813?rskey = 27lUve&result = 2> [https://perma.cc/3JSR-BRLK], accessed June 8, 2025 (stating that this belief derives from the tradition of Emile Durkheim). There is no consensus among scholars over whether modern nationalism was originally grounded in religion or in a secular movement away from religion. *See, e.g.*, Brubaker 1996: 39 (arguing that national and religious projects were consolidated in European countries starting in the sixteenth century). For present purposes, however, it suffices to establish the nineteenth century's largely secular nationalism as our starting point.

[18] *See* Rosenfeld 2010: 45–64 (discussing the role of negation, metaphor, and metonymy in the construction of constitutional identity, which is distinct from, but analogous in its elaboration to, national identity).

[19] *See generally* Weber 2002.

[20] *See* Dietler 1994: 584, 593 (demonstrating various and ideologically opposed French politicians and political movements—such as François Mitterand, Giscard d'Estaing, Jacques Chirac, and the

context of the present analysis, the mere fact that an element or aspect of a secular national identity is issued from religion ought not weigh against any otherwise-reasoned conclusion that a particular imagined community is representative of secular nationalism.

Twentieth- and twenty-first-century religious nationalism emerged because of disappointment with secular nationalism, combined with the repoliticization of religion and the spread of fundamentalism.[21] Instances of contemporary religious nationalism have arisen in the context of various religions, including Christianity, Islam, Judaism, and Hinduism.[22] From a functional standpoint, the religious

Front National—utilizing imagery of Vercingetorix at Bibracte, and also noting a contemporary survey of French schoolchildren between the ages of eight and eleven, in which Vercingetorix was ranked three places ahead of Joan of Arc).

[21] *See* Grzymala-Busse, n 17 (citing these arguments from Juergensmeyer 2008). *See generally* Ajami 1993 (recounting the trajectory from the failure of secular Arab nationalism to the religious Islamist nationalism propounded by the Muslim Brotherhood).

[22] In countries with majority Christian populations, nationalism is often framed predominantly in terms of Christian religious, symbolic, and cultural identity. Regarding US-based Christian nationalism, *see* Whitehead & Scheitle 2018: 161–62, 165 (demonstrating a large wave of Christian nationalism in the United States in 2004 and that heightened sentiments of Christian symbolic boundary in the United States are usually part of a larger wave of exclusionary attitudes); Goldberg 2006 (discussing the rise in bellicose Christian fundamentalism in the United States). In the case of Poland, see Pankowski & Kormak 2013: 157–58 (quoting the "father of modern Polish nationalism," Roman Dmowski, who states that, "Catholicism is not an addition to Polishness . . . but . . . in large measure it defines its essence. Any attempt to separate Catholicism from Polishness . . . threatens to destroy the nation's very essence."). Within Islam, Islamic nationalist movements historically rose in opposition to secular nationalist movements in the Arab world and other Muslim-majority countries in the twentieth century, with an eye to center national governments either around the pan-Islamist idea of the *ummah* or to inject Islamic theology into the constitutional and legal structures of government. *See* Khatab 2004: 219–21 (discussing the belief of the intellectual founder of the Egyptian Muslim Brotherhood, Sayyid Quṭb, that secular nationalism was regional and *jahiliyyah* (i.e., government related to power of humans over other humans rather than submission to God), and that the Islamic view of a nation was centered on that of one nation ("*ummah wahidah*") bound together by belief). Relating to Jewish religious nationalism in Israel, see "Far right lawmaker calls for Israel to follow Biblical law," *Haaretz*, June 3, 2019, <www.haaretz.com/israel-news/elections/.premium-far-right-israeli-lawmaker-calls-for-israel-to-operate-according-to-biblical-law-1.7316580> [https://perma.cc/MB3A-RXCQ], accessed June 8, 2025 (Bezalel Smotrich, a member of the far-right orthodox party Tkuma and Knesset member for the right-wing alliance Yamina, stated, "I want the State of Israel to operate according to the Torah in the long run. That's how it should be, it's a Jewish state . . . "); Allison Kaplan Sommer, "Meet the Israeli political party waging a holy war against the LGBTQ community," *Haaretz*, August 30, 2019, <www.haaretz.com/israel-news/elections/.premium-meet-the-israeli-political-party-waging-a-holy-war-against-the-lgbtq-community-1.7767670?v = 1595949392571> [https://perma.cc/E9GS-FT22], accessed June 8, 2025 (stating that the ultimate goal of the intellectual leader of the Noam party, Rabbi Tzvi Tau, is "that Israel should be an ultra-Orthodox state."); Matthew Wagner, "Religious affairs: Who's afraid of a Halachic state?," *Jerusalem Post*, December 10, 2009, <www.jpost.com/Features/Religious-Affairs-Whos-afraid-of-a-halachic-state> [https://perma.cc/358S-J75L], accessed June 8, 2025 (reporting on then-Justice Minister Yaakov Neeman's remark that "step by step, Torah law will become the binding law in the State of Israel. We have to reinstate the traditions of our forefathers, the teaching of the rabbis of the ages . . ."). In India, the Hindutva, or Hindu-nationalist, movement has been championed by current Prime Minister Narendra Modi and is notorious for being violently anti-Islam. *See* McDonnell & Cabrera 2019: 485 (explaining that the Bharatiya Janata Party (BJP) translates "Hindutva" as "cultural nationalism," or "public culture for a united Hindu people"). *See generally* Juergensmeyer 2008 (providing a general survey of the rise in religious nationalism around the globe).

component of religious nationalism differs, at times quite substantially, from one setting to the next. Nevertheless, in a key departure from secular nationalism, religious nationalism imagines and incorporates religion (or any of the latter's attributes it highlights) qua religion. For example, certain Christian conservatives envision the United States as a Christian nation founded by God and granted a privileged position in the world's history (Goldberg 2006), and, as already noted, some Christian denominations have even portrayed the United States as the New Jerusalem.[23] Although this particular brand of American nationalism is highly contested, if it were to become predominant, it would require combating pluralism and regarding secularists as sacrilegious and therefore, in essence, un-American.[24]

How religion fits within religious nationalism—and what it calls for in terms of the constitution, the laws, policies, civil society, and the state—varies in terms of both the religion (or one among many interpretations of that religion) and of those among its particular elements that figure in the pertinent national identity and in the life of the corresponding polity. Where the religion itself becomes all-encompassing, as is the case in theocracies, then, as pointed out above in discussing contemporary Iran,[25] it does not allow for any rights to interpret that religion save those interpretations that happen to be sanctioned by the national religion as understood by the clergy in power. Where religious nationalism incorporates the ruling religion in a less comprehensive or less unified manner, religion is bound to have an important impact on the polity, but how much and how contested that impact might be will depend on several variables. The case of Israel is instructive in this regard. Israel is a Jewish nation-state, but what "Jewish" means to Israelis is a hotly disputed matter. As discussed in Chapter 2, ultra-Orthodox Jews want the country to be ruled according to religious law, the *halacha*, and argue that since *halacha* provides a comprehensive legal system, the country does not need a constitution.[26] Secular Israeli Jews, in contrast, are likely to acknowledge the biblical origin of the connection between Jews and the land of Israel, celebrate certain religious

[23] The scripture of the Church of Jesus Christ of Latter-Day Saints holds, as a tenant of its faith, the belief in the "literal gathering of Israel and in the restoration of the Ten Tribes; that Zion (the New Jerusalem) will be built upon the American continent." Articles of Faith of the Church of Jesus Christ of Latter-Day Saints 1:10.

[24] *See* William Barr, "Remarks to the Law School and the de Nicola Center for Ethics and Culture at the University of Notre Dame," October 11, 2019, <www.justice.gov/opa/speech/attorney-general-william-p-barr-delivers-remarks-law-school-and-de-nicola-center-ethics> [https://perma.cc/C3WZ-C8GU], accessed May 26, 2025. (asserting that the framers of the Constitution believed that "religion was indispensable to sustaining our free system of government," and that "militant secularists" are a threat to the US's "Judeo-Christian" values); *see also* Assaf Sharon, "Counter-secularism and religious revival," *Reset Dialogues on Civilizations*, October 31, 2017, <www.resetdoc.org/story/counter-secularism-religious-revival/> [https://perma.cc/473U-GX4C], accessed June 8, 2025 (remarking that American conservatives often dismiss secular urban liberals as un-American).

[25] *See* nn 32–33 and accompanying text.

[26] *See* Dorsen 2022: 60–61; *see also* Pew Research Center, *Israel's Religiously Divided Society* (2016) 14, <www.pewforum.org/wp-content/uploads/sites/7/2016/03/Israel-Survey-Full-Report.pdf> [https://perma.cc/VL3E-ZHUV], accessed 26 May 2025.

holidays like Passover marking the exodus of the Jews from slavery in Ancient Egypt in a more nationalistic and cultural, rather than religious, way, but otherwise aspire to enjoy the way of life and the rights typical of Western liberal constitutional democracies.[27] At present, the conflict among these two conceptions of "Jewish" is unresolved, but some of the country's laws, such as the 1961 law against farming pork or various laws against public transportation on the Sabbath,[28] only make sense in reference to the religious proscriptions of Judaism. In addition to the religion component in religious nationalism being often contested and imprecisely delimited, there are many cases in which the content of a religious prescription internalized within the operating national identity happens to be virtually indistinguishable from a similar prescription issued from a secular standpoint. Thus, for example, Catholic social solidarity principles commanding concern for the welfare of the poor correspond to those espoused by secular liberal egalitarians (Rawls 2005: 451–52). In the latter case, whether the asserted principle issues from a religious rather than a secular perspective depends on context. In a Catholic nation, relating the welfare of the poor to the teachings of Jesus would seem much more natural than in a secular nation with a vast array of different religious traditions.[29]

In examining what fuels religious nationalism and what it projects onto the polity it targets, a basic distinction can be drawn between cases where religion seeks to frame nationalism and cases where nationalism aims to appropriate, and in some measure, incorporate religion. US Christian fundamentalists, Islamist adherents to the Muslim Brotherhood, and ultra-Orthodox Jews in Israel all draw on their religiosity and their paramount commitment to religious observance and practice in their struggle to get their respective nation to embrace their religion, its precepts, and its values, and to impose them on the polity as a whole.[30] In contrast,

[27] *See* Pew Research Center, *Israel's Religiously Divided Society* (n 26) 14–15 (reporting that 90% of Hilonim, or secular Jews, oppose the imposition of *halacha* as the state's law, 94% oppose shutting down all public transit for Sabbath observance, and 93% oppose gender segregation on public transit).

[28] Pig-Raising Prohibition Law, 5722–1962, 16 LSI 93 (1961–62) (Israel) (exempting certain communities in the northern part of the country with a large Christian-Arab population, at sch § 2(1)); Shuki Friedman, "The Shabbat wars: A guide for the perplexed on the 'Status Quo' . . . and a possible solution," *Isreal Democracy Institute*, March 2, 2017, <https://en.idi.org.il/articles/14015> [https://perma.cc/5XWY-QRP4], accessed June 8, 2025 (discussing a 1991 Transportation Ordinance prohibiting "[operation of] public bus routes on rest days"). *But see* Oliver Holmes and Quique Kierszenbaum, "'A blessed initiative': Secular Israel rejoices over Sabbath buses," *The Guardian*, December 28, 2019, <www.theguardian.com/cities/2019/dec/28/secular-israel-sabbath-buses> [https://perma.cc/D2A2-NN8R], accessed June 8, 2025.

[29] In this regard, it is instructive to refer to the statement made by US Catholic bishops against the Reagan Administration's policies adversely impacting the welfare of the poor. *See, e.g.*, US Conference of Catholic Bishops, *Economic Justice for All: Pastoral Letter on Catholic Social Teaching and the US Economy* (1986) <www.usccb.org/upload/economic_justice_for_all.pdf> [https://perma.cc/XM7E-XVV4], accessed May 26, 2025. The bishops were clearly weighing in as proponents of moral norms prescribed by Catholicism and not as representatives of the American political left that also decried Reagan's policies adversely affecting the social welfare net previously set in place to protect the poor.

[30] For Christianity in the United States, see Pew Research Center, *White Evangelicals See Trump as Fighting for Their Beliefs, Though Many Have Mixed Feelings About His Personal Conduct* (2020) 16 <www.pewforum.org/wp-content/uploads/sites/7/2020/03/PF.03.12.20_religion.politics_report.pdf> [https://perma.cc/ZLF5-JVWJ], accessed June 8, 2025 (showing that, amongst White Evangelical

in a country such as communist Poland in the 1980s, it was principally nationalism standing against anti-nationalist and anti-religious Soviet domination that enlisted the country's Catholic heritage to forge a path toward an autonomous post-communist future (Zubrzycki 2001: 638–40). And whereas contemporary Poland harbors a large majority of practicing Catholics,[31] several other former communist countries—such as Russia, Bulgaria, and Hungary—emerge as clear examples of nationalism appropriating religion in polities lacking widespread religious fervor.[32]

Protestants, 58% want the Bible to influence US law "a great deal," and 31% saying the Bible should influence it "some"; this figure is 47% and 29%, respectively, for Black Protestants. Additionally, 68% of White Protestants believe that the Bible should have more influence than the will of the people if the two conflict; that figure is 50% for Black Protestants); Paul Rosenberg, "Secrets of the extreme religious right: Inside the frightening world of Christian reconstructionism," *Salon*, July 31, 2015, <www.salon.com/2015/07/31/secrets_of_the_extreme_religious_right_inside_the_frightening_world_of_christian_reconstructionism/> [https://perma.cc/R7HX-6XHS], accessed June 8, 2025 (describing Christian reconstructionism as a pre-conceptualist, post-millennialist, and theonomist movement driven to "reconstruct[] the Kingdom of God as it was intended to be"); Michelle Goldberg, "Dominionism: Michele Bachmann and Rick Perry's dangerous bond," *Daily Beast*, August 14, 2011, <www.thedailybeast.com/dominionism-michele-bachmann-and-rick-perrys-dangerous-religious-bond?ref = scroll> [https://perma.cc/38EC-PNVR], accessed June 8, 2025 (describing the Dominionism movement as one that seeks to have Christians lead national governments and sees "rule by non-Christians [as] a sort of sacrilege . . . [because] 'Christians have an obligation . . . a holy responsibility to reclaim the land for Jesus Christ—to have dominion in civil structures, just as in every other aspect of life and godliness.'"). For Islam, *see, e.g.*, Olivier Guitta, *Policy Brief: Muslim Brotherhood Parties in the Middle East and North Africa (MENA) Region* (Centre for European Studies 2010) <https://martenscentre.eu/sites/default/files/publication-files/muslim_brotherhood_parties_1.pdf> [https://perma.cc/YF83-TRGK], accessed June 8, 2025 (the Egyptian Brotherhood's Reform Initiative proposed that only a Muslim man may become president of Egypt, effectively barring women and Coptic Christians from the presidency); *cf.* Asli Aydintasbas, "Erdogan the nationalist v Erdogan the Islamist," *Caravan*, December 13, 2018, <www.hoover.org/research/erdogan-nationalist-vs-erdogan-islamist> [https://perma.cc/CF5C-73RM], accessed June 8, 2025 (describing Erdogan's "promotion of 'imam-hatip' schools within the Turkish education system . . . [to create] a 'pious generation'" as indicative of a specific brand of Islamism that is geared more to inject philo-AKP conservatism into Turkish society, and to act as an accessory to the nation state, rather than a challenge to it). In Israel there is a highly publicized debate over how appropriate consideration of religious law should be in daily public life. *See* Moshe Feiglin, "The real coercion in Israel," *Israel National News*, December 29, 2011, <www.israelnationalnews.com/Articles/Article.aspx/11066> [https://perma.cc/J9LE-TP55], accessed June 8, 2025 (ex-Knesset member stating that "[t]he entire Israeli reality has become a platform for the multi-faceted tyranny of the secular minority . . . over the traditional/religious/ultra-Orthodox majority"); Ruth Margalit, "How the religious right transformed Israeli education," *New Yorker*, August 23, 2019, <www.newyorker.com/news/letter-from-jerusalem/how-the-religious-right-transformed-israeli-education> [https://perma.cc/L8FX-QE6F], accessed June 8, 2025 (discussing "*hadata*," or "religionization," as a phenomenon of the Netanyahu era over areas of civic life that had normally enjoyed a clear division between religion and state, such as public education).

[31] Centrum Badania Opinii Społecznej (CBOS), *Co Łączy Polaków z Parafią? [What Connects Poles with the Parish?]* (March 2005) 2–3 (study reporting that 58% of respondents take part in Catholic religious practices at least once a week and state that they follow the instructions of the Catholic Church).

[32] *See* Grzymala-Busse, n 17, 60 (referring to Russia and Bulgaria); *Magyarország Alaptörvénye* [The Fundamental Law of Hungary], pmbl. (2011) ("We recognise the role of Christianity in preserving nationhood"); Pew Research Center, *Religious Belief and National Belonging in Central and Eastern Europe* (2017) 70, <https://assets.pewresearch.org/wp-content/uploads/sites/11/2017/05/15120244/CEUP-FULL-REPORT.pdf> [https://perma.cc/3GNC-LRDN], accessed June 8, 2025 (reporting only 9% of Hungarians attending weekly religious services, 26% attending monthly or yearly, and 64% attending seldom or never).

It seems obvious that issues of religiosity, religious practice, and observance are much more likely to arise when religion turns to nationalism than when nationalism embraces religion. From our perspective, what is crucial is to focus on the distinct ways in which religious nationalism promotes anti-pluralistic and exclusionary agendas. Even where religion is sought to be nationalized, the result would not have to be necessarily exclusionary. Indeed, for a nationalized religion not to be exclusionary, it would have to be, on the whole, compatible with freedom of and from religion for all within the polity. Nevertheless, in a large number of cases, the nationalist turn to religion goes hand in hand with an anti-pluralist agenda. Typically, from the internal perspective of a particular religion, that religion is the true one and the right one. Accordingly, by turning to religion qua religion as opposed to religion qua (one among many components of) culture, the nationalist is better positioned to tout her appropriated religion as hierarchically privileged and beyond discussion.[33]

Besides religiosity, religious practice, and observance, some of the other most salient aspects of religion that have been incorporated into nationalism include religious morals, religious values and ways of life, religious customs, religious symbols, and various religious cultural attributes. Both the religious who turn to nationalism and the nationalists who appeal to religion are bound to be selective. Short of a theocracy, the former would have to aim for the most religious situation possible within constitutional limitations. Thus, consistent with the discussion in Chapter 2, if fundamentalist Protestants became the political majority in the United States while lacking the means to amend the US Constitution, they could enact part, but not all, of their agenda on their way to their version of a Christian America. Because of the freedom of speech and freedom of religion rights enshrined in the First Amendment, the fundamentalists would thus have to tolerate views and religious beliefs and practices that their religion might instruct them to ban. On the other hand, the nationalists who turn to religion are most likely to be selective in their appropriations, as some aspects of religion would bolster their nationalist aims while others would be indifferent or even at times counterproductive. For example, a nationalist with libertarian capitalist and patriarchal tendencies may turn to Catholicism to nationalize his campaign against abortion and immigration to bolster the traditional patriarchal family, while at the same time systematically ignoring Catholic social welfare principles.

Although both kinds of religious nationalism may have to be selective to adapt to political realities, they are otherwise likely to differ. The religious who turn to

[33] This suggested contrast between religious tradition and cultural tradition is usefully illustrated by reference to the US constitutional jurisprudence on sexual orientation. *Compare Bowers v Hardwick*, 478 US 186, 196–97 (1986) *overruled by Lawrence v Texas*, 539 US 558 (2003) (Burger, CJ concurring) (invoking Judeo-Christian condemnation of homosexual sex), *with Lawrence*, 539 US at 571–72 (2003) (viewing same-sex intimacy between two consenting adults as belonging within the same evolving long-held tradition originally focused on the heterosexual married couple).

nationalism would most logically seem prompted to exercise selectivity consistent with their religion's demands. Thus, they may prioritize what is more important within their religion over what might be less so. For example, a religion that prescribes an absolute ban on abortion while deeming contraception as sinful, but a lesser evil, might well endorse a national law that criminalizes abortion but affords legal protection to contraception. In marked contrast, the nationalists who seek to incorporate religion are most likely to choose religious morals or symbols or cultural mainstays and to appropriate within each of these those elements that better fit within their nationalistic vision and that are most likely to advance its aims. In other words, nationalists who appeal to religion are prone to being opportunistic.

This kind of opportunism is well illustrated by Hungary's official embrace of Christianity as put forth in the Preamble of its 2012 Constitution, in spite of it being among the least religious countries in present-day Europe.[34] As will be more fully addressed in Section D below, this identitarian adherence to Christianity has been systematically paired by Orban with a xenophobic animus against Muslims. Moreover, this latter anti-Muslim nationalist tendency became notoriously manifest in the course of Hungary blocking and harshly treating Syrian refugees who were seeking entry into the country. Although Orban's stance against Syrian refugees ran counter to EU policy, he justified his anti-European initiative by invoking deeply historically rooted nationalist grounds. Specifically, Orban reminded Hungarians of the centuries-old Ottoman invasion of their country to justify the systematic exclusion of present-day Muslims.[35]

Matteo Salvini, the former Italian defense minister and leader of the right-wing, xenophobic League party, provides another telling example of the mobilization of the majority religion in the service of an anti-pluralist agenda. Arguing for harsh anti-immigration measures, Salvini has systematically portrayed himself as the last bastion of Christianity against the "Islamization of the West."[36] Ironically, in doing so Salvini has been directly challenging the church's social doctrine and the pope's strong and well-publicized humanitarian stance vis-à-vis migrants.[37] The

[34] "Church attendance is pretty low in Hungary . . . . According to the latest study, 'Beliefs about God across Time and Countries' by Tom W. Smith (University of Chicago), only 9.6% of the population has a strong belief in God as opposed to 35% in the United States and 25.8% in Ireland. Hungary is closer to Great Britain, Sweden, and the Czech Republic as far as religious devotion is concerned. At the same time the percentage of atheists is relatively high: 23.1%" ("Church and State in Hungary," *Hungarian Spectrum*, April 21, 2012, <https://hungarianspectrum.org/2012/04/21/church-and-state-in-hungary> [https://perma.cc/2VPW-GZZY], accessed June 8, 2025).

[35] *See* Ishaan Tharoor, "Hungary's Orban invokes Ottoman invasion to justify keeping refugees out," *Washington Post*, September 4, 2015, <www.washingtonpost.com/news/worldviews/wp/2015/09/04/hungarys-orban-invokes-ottoman-invasion-to-justify-keeping-refugees-out> [https://perma.cc/4L54-QUMT], accessed June 8, 2025.

[36] "Salvini alla guerra santa: Sto con Trump perché difende i valori cristiani," *Globalist*, January 4, 2020, <www.globalist.it/politics/2020/01/04/salvini-alla-guerra-santa-sto-con-trump-perche-difende-i-valori-cristiani-2051196.html> (It.) [https://perma.cc/GD7R-YHH9], accessed June 8, 2025.

[37] Gerard O'Connell, "Pope Francis reminds Christians that migrants and refugees should be welcomed around the world," *America*, September 29, 2019, <www.americamagazine.org/faith/2019/

Italian Conference of Bishops has repeatedly accused him of instrumentally using religion to pursue an openly un-Catholic agenda.[38] Salvini, a self-proclaimed devout Catholic despite openly ignoring Catholic teachings in his personal life, has not only consistently exhibited Catholic religious symbols—such as crucifixes and rosaries—during political rallies but also associated religion with his political victories.[39] Thus, for example, after the approval by the Italian parliament of one of the harshest anti-immigration measures adopted upon his initiative, he tweeted his thanks to the Virgin Mary.[40] And, after his party's success in the European elections of 2019, he reiterated his thanks to "the immaculate heart of Mary," for "helping Italy and Europe to find again hope, pride, roots, jobs and security."[41]

Nationalism can unify a political community by cementing strong bonds of solidarity fueled by intense emotional sentiments, leading to patriotic fervor. Patriotism, like nationalism, can be inclusionary or exclusionary, and both can be intensified and further consolidated by linking themselves with religion and religious elements. As discussed above, not all linkages between nationalism and religion are alike. For our purposes, the combinations between nationalism and religion that aim at exclusionary and anti-pluralistic attitudes and policies are the ones that deserve further attention because of their potential in the struggle against secularism and Enlightenment-based understandings of fundamental rights.

Nationalism is conceptually distinct from populism, although, as will be further explored in Section D below, the two can figure side by side in animating the public life of contemporary polities. Moreover, populism, like nationalism, can link itself to religion. In order to be in a better position to understand how these respective links to religion compare, we now turn to an examination of the conditions that result in a nexus between populism and religion.

09/29/pope-francis-reminds-christians-migrants-and-refugees-should-be-welcomed-around> [https://perma.cc/33LU-8NVM], accessed June 8, 2025; Leonardo Salutati, "Immigrazione: Cosa dice la dottrina della Chiesa?," *Toscana Oggi*, September 2, 2018, <www.toscanaoggi.it/Rubriche/Risponde-il-teologo/Immigrazione-cosa-dice-la-dottrina-della-Chiesa> [https://perma.cc/TY2G-Y59Y], accessed June 8, 2025.

[38] The most influential Catholic press has also systematically denounced Salvini's instrumental use of religion. *See* "'Vade retro Salvini,' La Chiesa reagisce a certi toni sprezzanti," *Famiglia Cristiana*, July 26, 2018, <www.famigliacristiana.it/articolo/migranti-vade-retro-salvini-la-chiesa-reagisce-ai-toni-sprezzanti.aspx> [https://perma.cc/W45G-QRDM], accessed June 8, 2025; *see also* Davide Re, "Salvini brandisce il rosario durante il comizio e ribadisce: porti chiusi," *L'Avvenire*, May 18, 2019, <www.avvenire.it/attualita/pagine/salvini-a-milano> [https://perma.cc/NAH7-TS69], accessed June 8, 2025.

[39] *See* Gabriella Cerami, "Salvini trionfa, bacia il rosario e ringrasia la Madonna. Non vole poltrone ma l'agenda di governo la detta lui," *Huffington Post*, May 27, 2019, <www.huffingtonpost.it/entry/salvini-vince-non-vuole-poltrone-ma-lagenda-di-governo-la-detta-lui_it_5ceb232be4b00e036570be00> [https://perma.cc/R6MP-9V9V], accessed June 8, 2025.

[40] Matteo Salvini (@matteosalvinimi), *Twitter*, August 2019, 2:30pm, <https://twitter.com/matteosalvinimi/status/1158445073278885889> [https://perma.cc/A5E4-GHMS], accessed June 8, 2025.

[41] "Politica e religione: quando Salvini cerca la benedizione dall'alto," *Il Sole 24 Ore*, August 6, 2019, <www.ilsole24ore.com/art/politica-e-religione-quando-salvini-cerca-benedizione-dall-alto-ACoZKUd> [https://perma.cc/9KQY-GFCU], accessed June 8, 2025 (translation by author).

C. Religious Populism Versus Populism as Religion

Populism, like nationalism, is not inherently religious. Moreover, populism is conceptually distinct from nationalism, although the two can coexist and overlap within the same polity. As already mentioned, populism is characterized by its conception of politics as dedicated to the realization of the will of the people, and by its designation of "the people" as including only a part of the whole within the relevant political unit. Most often, populism pits the average citizens whom it enshrines as "the people" against the elites whom it casts as the (internal) enemies of the people.[42] In some instances, these internal enemies are linked with, or aggregated to, external enemies regarded as threatening the well-being or the political agenda of those recognized as the people within their polity.[43] According to the populist ideal, the people are led by a charismatic leader who embodies their political will and with whom they fully identify (Zúquete 2017: 453). Together with their leader, the people are supposed to form a moral community with the collective goal of fighting those cast as their enemies in order to redeem the polity in a messianic-type enterprise, leading either to the recovery of some lost golden past or to the removal of extrinsic obstacles that block the path toward an exalted forthcoming destiny (Zúquete 2017).

There is an important distinction between right-wing and left-wing populism (Tushnet 2018: 639–40). The latter typically tracks a class struggle model, figuring the working class as "the people" pitted against political and economic elites cast as the enemies (Tushnet 2018: 640–41). Accordingly, left-wing populism may well not be nationalistic, and it may readily promote transnational coordination between various similarly situated peoples fighting against various groups regarded as comparatively oppressive elites. Right-wing populism, on the other hand, whether ethnically or religiously grounded, is very likely to be conjoined to nationalism. But even if most right-wing populism tends to be nationalist, not all nationalism need be populist. Indeed, some instances of nationalism may be inclusive of all within the polity, whether they be elites or part of the common citizenry. Thus, for example, French republican nationalism is not populist, as it includes all French citizens as part of an undivided nation within a united polity.[44] In contrast, in deploying his populist vision of American nationalism, Donald Trump has repeatedly attacked those he portrays as internal enemies. These attacks have

42 *See* Müller 2016: 4, 10–11.

43 Rachel Donadio, "The new populist playbook," *The Atlantic*, September 5, 2019, <www.theatlantic.com/international/archive/2019/09/matteo-salvini-italy-populist-playbook/597298> [https://perma.cc/9AKF-YCE6], accessed June 8, 2025 (reporting that Italy's Matteo Salvini has accused "elites" like Angela Merkel, Emmanuel Macron, and George Soros of "betraying Europe"); Krekó, Hunyadi, & Szicherle, n 3, fn 47.

44 *See* Constitution of the French Republic 1958, arts 1–2.

included calling most of the US press the "enemies of the people,"[45] and Democrats as "un-American."[46]

The contemporary nexus between populism and religion is essentially twofold and based on a distinction between "politicized religion" and "sacralized politics" (Zúquete 2017: 445–54). In the first of these situations, the identity, agenda, and objectives of the people are informed by religion. Religion may be invoked to delimit religious insiders versus religious outsiders within the same polity. Thus, on some views, Jews are the people of Israel, Hindus the people of India, and Muslim Malays the people of Malaysia (Hirschl & Shachar 2018: 517). Religion may also be called upon to sever the people who may belong to diverse religions and non-religious ideologies from internal and/or external outsiders identified with a particular religion regarded as inimical to the relevant populist project. The prime example here is that of populists in Europe, who regard Muslims within their borders as well as would-be Muslim immigrants as threatening outsiders (Hirschl & Shachar 2018). Finally, within a religiously homogeneous polity, religion can be used as a wedge between more conforming religious insiders and less conforming (or non-conforming) internal outsiders. An example of this is provided by the populist rhetoric of a patriarch of the Greek Orthodox Church who linked Greek nationalism to those who adhered to Orthodoxy and Hellenism against those he identified as supporters of the contemporaneous ruling Greek government, which he chastised as being "atheist, modernizing, intellectualist and repressive" (Zúquete 2017: 447).

Unlike in politicized religion, where religion infuses politics, in sacralized politics the key feature is an analogy or resemblance between politics and religion (Zúquete 2017: 451–52). In this modern phenomenon, the people represents the good, its enemies personify evil, and the charismatic leader figures as a pastor leading his flock to salvation in a to-be-recovered or yet-to-be-reached promised land (Zúquete 2017).[47] Moreover, although sacralized politics may be practiced much like a religion, it may well operate without reference to religion and without incorporation of any religious symbols or attributes. Hugo Chavez was thus a consummate practitioner of sacralized populism in Venezuela, but his fight was a secular one against those he called the oligarchs, while his inspiration came from the great nineteenth-century liberator of the Americas, Simon Bolivar (Zúquete

[45] Donald Trump (@realDonaldTrump), *Twitter*, April 5, 2019, 1:41pm, <https://twitter.com/realDonaldTrump/status/1114221533461790721> [https://perma.cc/HK2M-E7QY], accessed June 8, 2025 ("The press is doing everything within their power to fight the magnificence of the phrase, MAKE AMERICA GREAT AGAIN! . . . They are truly the ENEMY OF THE PEOPLE!").

[46] Jessica Taylor, "Trump: Democrats 'un-American,' 'treasonous' during State of the Union," *National Public Radio*, February 5, 2018, <www.npr.org/2018/02/05/583447413/trump-democrats-un-american-treasonous-during-state-of-the-union> [https://perma.cc/5WLL-CJN6], accessed June 8, 2025.

[47] For a seminal account of modern politics as secularized religion, see generally Schmitt 2005. For present purposes, suffice it to characterize populism as a special kind of sacralized politics.

2017: 458). In other cases, however, sacralized politics can invoke religion or religious elements in support of its political aims. This is the case in Orban's populist and nationalist agenda in Hungary, as he invokes Christianity both against the external outsider enemies, the Muslims, and against the internal enemies, the secular Hungarian elites.[48]

Sacralized politics frames populism as a religious pursuit, but to the extent that it is separated from religion itself, as it was in the case of Venezuela under Chavez, it remains peripheral to the book's principal aims. Purely secular populism is most likely illiberal and anti-pluralist, but it does not resort to religion itself in its dealings with fundamental rights. In contrast, populism as politicized religion, as well as the subset of populism as sacralized politics that happens to turn to religion do have recourse to the latter in their approach to fundamental rights. Moreover, the nature and scope of uses of religion in relation to populism are potentially equivalent to those we have identified in relation to nationalism. For present purposes, the principal difference between religion within nationalism and that within populism is linked to the fact that populism, by its nature, is prone to being more vehemently inclusionary and exclusionary than nationalism. Indeed, all populisms rise against both internal and external enemies, whereas certain nationalisms may be internally inclusive and, for the most part, aspirational. Additionally, although nationalism must nurture the differentiation between nations, it need not treat foreign nations as enemies.

As already highlighted, nationalism and populism often go hand in hand. A prime example of that is provided by the conjunction of the two in Orban's Hungary. This example is important for our purposes, as we shall now see, insofar as it makes diverse and intertwined uses of mainly politicized, identitarian, symbolic, and cultural aspects of religion to weave together a Hungarian nation that overflows the current boundaries of Hungary and an exclusionary vision of the Hungarian people that happens to be ethnically and religiously set apart from those cast as enemies within and without.

D. Orban's Hungary: Uses of Religion to Conjoin Nationalism and Populism

Orban's Hungary provides a propitious case study of the uses of religion for identitarian purposes in the coordinated furtherance of nationalism and populism. Hungary's populism is mainly ethnic based, but Orban has also very deliberately embraced the Christian religion against what he has characterized as the

[48] *See* Krekó, Hunyadi, & Szicherle, n 3, fn 47.

evils of Western European liberalism.[49] Furthermore, Orban has sided with the common Hungarian everyday citizen against the cosmopolitan elites, whom he has personalized by demonizing George Soros, an American philanthropist who happens to be a Jewish Holocaust survivor of Hungarian origin.[50]

The identitarian particulars of Orban's nationalist and populist constitution are clearly framed by the Preamble to his 2012 Constitution. This new constitution, meant to replace the extant liberal one that prevailed in the country since its transition from communism,[51] was tellingly undertaken in the name of "the Hungarian nation" instead of "the people of Hungary."[52] Consistent with this, the Preamble's first proclamation states: "We are proud that our king Saint Stephen built the Hungarian State on solid ground and made our country a part of Christian Europe one thousand years ago."[53] To this, the Preamble adds that "We recognize the role of Christianity in preserving nationhood" and that "we honour the Holy Crown, which embodies the constitutional continuity of Hungary's statehood and the unity of the nation. We do not recognize the suspension of our historical constitution due to foreign occupations."[54] Pointedly, this embrace of Christianity as a constitutional foundation seems difficult to take at face value as, contrary to neighboring populist Poland, where religious belief has a profound imprint, Hungary, as already noted, is one of the least religious countries in all of Europe.[55] Also, as one commentator put it, "Orban's embrace of Christian nationalism is a relatively recent turn for a once-avowed atheist."[56]

The constitutionally relevant identitarian consequences of the combined references to the Hungarian nation, Christianity, and the rejection of the periods of foreign occupation can be interpretively accounted for in terms of a transformation of Hungary's imagined community into a populist one. Starting with religion, negation, metaphor, and metonymy as discursive devices in the construction of inclusionary and exclusionary constitutional narratives[57] are enlisted to achieve

[49] Amanda Coakley, "Hungary's Orban tries to snatch mantle of Christian democracy," *Foreign Policy*, August 3, 2021, https://foreignpolicy.com/2021/08/03/hungary-orban-fidesz-christian-democracy-right/>, accessed June 8, 2025; see also Brubaker 2017.

[50] Franklin Foer, "Viktor Orban's war on intellect," *The Atlantic*, June 2019, <www.theatlantic.com/magazine/archive/2019/06/george-soros-viktor-orban-ceu/588070> [https://perma.cc/TX76-AFNW], accessed June 8, 2025.

[51] Ironically, the constitution in question was the 1949 socialist one which became a liberal democratic one through radical use of the amendment process. *See* Kovács & Tóth 2011: 183–203.

[52] *See* European Commission for Democracy Through Law (Venice Commission) Opinion 720/2013.

[53] *Magyarország Alaptörvénye* [The Fundamental Law of Hungary], pmbl. (2011).

[54] Ibid.

[55] *See* n 34.

[56] *See* Ishaan Tharoor, "Hungary's Orban invokes Ottoman invasion to justify keeping refugees out," *The Washington Post*, September 4, 2015, <www.washingtonpost.com/news/worldviews/wp/2015/09/04/hungarys-orban-invokes-ottoman-invasion-to-justify-keeping-refugees-out> [https://perma.cc/4L54-QUMT], accessed June 8, 2025.

[57] *See* Rosenfeld 2010 (discussing the role of negation, metaphor, and metonymy in the construction of constitutional identity).

an uprooting from liberal constitutionalism to launch a reorientation toward populism and a restrictive vision of nationalism. Grounding the new constitution in Christianity negates the non-religious Hungarian people's immediately preceding liberal secular constitutional tradition. Christianity, moreover, is used metaphorically to link together Saint Stephen, the first king of Hungary in 1000, the Ottoman—and hence anti-Christian—invasion and occupation of Hungarian territory starting in 1521 and ending in in 1699,[58] the Soviet-imposed (atheist) communist era from 1949 till 1989, and the post-communist threat to Christianity posed by secular cosmopolitan elites, including those at the helm of the EU. Finally, Christianity is used metonymically in that it is not the religion itself but its appeal as a principal token of cultural identity that unifies the narrative of ethnic Hungarians, projected as a unified and continuous nation (though one in captivity during the Ottoman and Soviet periods) from 1000 till 2012, the year of the constitutional turn to populism. Continuing with emphasis on the Hungarian *nation*, in addition to its crucial linkage to (cultural) Christianity, it serves to distinguish between the ethnic Hungarians who are *the* people of the 2012 Constitution and other Hungarian citizens, such as the country's Jews and Roma who, pursuant to the new constitution's Preamble, are "The nationalities living with us [who] form part of the Hungarian political community and are constituent parts of the State."[59] Accordingly, non-ethnic Hungarians excluded from the Hungarian nation, but included in their country's political sphere and counted as citizens of the Hungarian state, become akin to second-class citizens deprived of full membership within the Hungarian people. Finally, the reference to explicit (constitutional) negation of foreign occupations has both a positive and a negative connotation: positively, it strengthens the image of a strong, free, continuously united nation and people bound together by ethnicity, religion, culture, and tradition; negatively, it is invoked to justify militance against Muslim immigration and to use the image of Soviet oppression against all enemies internal and external whom a populist may cast as posing threats to the indissoluble link that unites Hungarian nationhood and peoplehood.

Constitutional identity narratives tend to be overdetermined and hence the above account is certainly subject to further elaboration and nuancing. To illustrate this, suffice it to briefly expand on the seeming paradox, inscribed in the 2012 Preamble, of at once investing Christianity with an ethno-national cultural valence that separates the Hungarians as descendants of King Stephen and with a pan-European unifying bond that links Hungary to the rest of the continent. The paradox involved is highlighted by Orban's rejection of Western European secular

[58] Brubaker 2017; Celestine Bohlen, "Glimpsing Hungary's Ottoman past," *New York Times*, March 10, 1991, <www.nytimes.com/1991/03/10/travel/glimpsing-hungary-s-ottoman-past.html> [https://perma.cc/5Q29-76KC], accessed June 8, 2025.

[59] Magyarország Alaptörvénye [The Fundamental Law of Hungary], pmbl. (2011).

liberalism, and its "ruthless capitalism and selfish individualism," in favor of a national populist illiberal ethnocentric democracy.[60] Does that not stand against emphasizing whatever links together virtually the whole of Europe as Christian along a metaphoric axis that incorporates Eastern Orthodox and Western Catholic and Protestant Christianity as well as the attenuated, mainly cultural Christian heritage prevalent in certain highly secularized countries, such as France or the UK? Upon closer consideration, the juxtaposition of Hungarian and European Christianity does bind together several facets of Orban's nationalist populist project from an identitarian standpoint. Hungary as part of Christian Europe performs an important identitarian nexus given the Hapsburg military victory that resulted in the end of Ottoman occupation of Hungarian territory;[61] the Austro-Hungarian Empire that gave Hungary its most glorious golden age both because of its unification with one of Europe's greatest powers and civilizations and because it gave Hungary sovereignty over the greatest proportion of ethnic Hungarians—such as those who at present are citizens of other countries such as Romania, Serbia, or Slovakia—that it ever had under its jurisdiction;[62] and the EU that provides Hungary financial support that Orban needs to maintain his popularity among "his" people.[63] These European-wide connections may appear to pull Hungary away from populism, but Orban has used them to bolster his populist project. Indeed, he has used the Ottoman invasion image to promote not only a Hungarian anti-Muslim front, but also to counter the EU's pro-immigration and asylum accommodating policies. Reminiscing the glory days of the Austro-Hungarian empire abruptly dismembered by the 1920 Trianon Treaty, Orban and (even more so) his extreme right parliamentary allies have suggested that ideally Hungary and its new constitution should unify not only Hungarian nationals within the country's present borders, but also ethnic Hungarians who are currently citizens of neighboring countries, such as Romania, Serbia, and Slovakia. The Trianon Treaty has been characterized as a national tragedy for Hungary,[64] and some Hungarian politicians have toyed with the idea of incorporating ethnic Hungarians living in

[60] *See* Jan-Werner Mueller, "Moscow's trojan horse: In Europe's ideological war, Hungary picks Putinism," *Foreign Affairs*, August 14, 2014.

[61] The Ottomans ceded Hungarian territory to Austria pursuant to the Carlowitz Treaty in 1699 ("Treaty of Carlowitz (1699)," *Encyclopaedia Britannica*, <www.britannica.com/event/Treaty-of-Carlowitz>, accessed May 26, 2025).

[62] *See* Marcel Gascón Barberá and Anja Vladisavljevic, "Orban's 'greater Hungary' map creates waves in neighborhood," *Balkan Insight*, May 7, 2020, <https:// balkaninsight.com/2020/05/07/orbans-greater-hungary-map-creates-waves-in-neighbourhood/> [https://perma.cc/9YVY-VJQJ], accessed June 8, 2025.

[63] *See* Timothy Garton Ash, "Europe must stop this disgrace: Viktor Orbán is dismantling democracy," *The Guardian*, June 20, 2019.

[64] *See* Alasdair Sandford and Ádám Magyar, "Trianon trauma: Why is the peace treaty signed 100 years ago seen as a national tragedy for Hungary?," *Euronews*, June 4, 2020, <www.euronews.com/2020/06/04/trianon-trauma-why-is-the-peace-treaty-signed-100-years-ago-seen-as-a-national-tragedy> [https://perma.cc/856W-9BYY], accessed June 8, 2025.

bordering contemporary countries into a "greater Hungary."[65] Finally, Hungary's projection as being at once pro- and anti-EU definitely appears to serve Orban's nationalist and populist objectives. As a populist anti-European, Orban protects the Hungarian nation against transnational cosmopolitanism. At the same time, by remaining within the EU and avoiding any Brexit-like movement, Orban secures EU money for *his* people and those powerful "friends" that bolster his illiberal populist rule.

Taken out of its overall context, Hungary's nationalist and populist constitutional identity-building project differs little from that of its typical liberal counterparts insofar as they both proceed through a series of demarcations involving an interplay between inclusions and exclusions. It is important to emphasize, however, that taken as a whole, the Hungarian project is above all exclusionary. And this is true of even its most far-reaching aspiration (which for now is nothing but a distant dream for some) of including all the ethnic Hungarians living beyond its current borders within a reconstituted "greater Hungary." On its face, that aspiration seems overwhelmingly inclusionary, but its realization seems inconceivable without some prior wars to annex now foreign-held territory with large clusters of ethnic Hungarians and without disenfranchizing the non-ethnic Hungarian Serbs, Slovaks, or Romanians who would assume second-class citizenship status in a newly formed greater Hungary.[66]

In the end, how inclusionary or exclusionary a particular religious nationalism or religious populism may happen to be can only be assessed when placing the relevant polity in context. We will be in a position to illustrate this in the course of discussing the cases and initiatives that will be the focus of Part II below. Before turning to these particulars, however, it is necessary to briefly examine the dynamic between institutional and ideological secularism, which figures prominently in the illiberal and anti-pluralistic agenda launched by religious nationalists and religious pluralists.

[65] *See* Marcel Gascón Barberá and Anja Vladisavljevic, "Orban's 'greater Hungary' map creates waves in neighborhood," *Balkan Insight*, May 7, 2020, <https://balkaninsight.com/2020/05/07/orbans-greater-hungary-map-creates-waves-in-neighbourhood/> [https://perma.cc/9YVY-VJQJ], accessed June 8, 2025.

[66] It should also be pointed out that a large proportion of ethnic Hungarians living in neighboring countries have little desire to give up their current country of citizenship in order to become part of a greater Hungary. *See, e.g.*, Michaela Terenzani, Nina Hrabovska Francelova, and Radka Minarechova, "Slovak election to test Orban's clout among ethnic Hungarians," *Reporting Democracy*, February 12, 2020, <https://balkaninsight.com/2020/02/12/slovak-election-to-test-orbans-clout-among-ethnic-hungarians/>, accessed June 8, 2025.

4

The Dynamic Between Institutional and Ideological Secularism and Its Uses in Anti-Secular Attacks in the Name of Religion

As discussed in the preceding chapters, the attacks on the Enlightenment-based constitutional ideal of institutional secularism have been varied and wide-ranging. In certain contemporary constitutional theocracies, such as Iran, secularism is altogether officially repudiated. In contrast, in most settings comprising repoliticized religion and religious nationalists and populists operating within constitutional democracies, the political and institutional interplay between invocations of religion and attitudes toward secularism can be complex, murky, and even at times contradictory. In many instances in which aspects of religion have been constitutionalized or prioritized within evolving iterations of the polity's collective identity, secular approaches and ways of life retain an important, if not predominant, role. Thus, in Hungary, Viktor Orban's illiberal regime embraces Christianity both against the secularism of the domestic "cosmopolitan"

Politicized Religion and the Reframing of Fundamental Rights. Susanna Mancini and Michel Rosenfeld, Oxford University Press. © Susanna Mancini, Michel Rosenfeld 2026. DOI: 10.1093/9780191982149.003.0005

elites and against a much-decried putative foreign Muslim threat all while, as already noted, the country's population continues ranking as one of Europe's least religious ones. In secular France the far-right National Front (now National Rally) party's anti-Semitism of the 1980s seems to lack coherent meaning unless linked to the country's Christian heritage. Yet in a seeming direct contradiction, that same party's more recent anti-Muslim stance—marking a shift in focus from assimilated French Jews to more religiously ubiquitous Muslims—has been clearly and explicitly launched in the name of *laïcité*.[1] More generally, the ideal of institutional secularism, widely associated with the deployment of a liberal and pluralist array of fundamental rights, has been attacked by proponents of illiberalism who make constitutional and political uses of religion. Moreover, these attacks have been at times coupled with broader assaults on secular ways of life or, somewhat paradoxically, with invocations of the latter for purposes of denigrating or excluding particular (usually minority) religions. This is done, as will be detailed below, to narrow or to recast liberal constitutional rights into illiberal and less inclusive ones. Although secularism always figures in these efforts, it is often unclear how or what those pursuing an illiberal agenda mean by the term. In particular, it is often difficult to determine whether a particular illiberal project is set against secularism as a constitutional principle or ideal, namely institutional secularism, or against secularism as a way of life or an attitude toward certain aspects of the life of the polity, namely ideological secularism. Indeed, not only do atheists and agnostics engage in secular ways of life, but also believers who systematically rely on science even when the latter is in direct conflict with religion, and politicians or judges who side with secular constitutional precepts even when these clash with their personal religious beliefs. Thus, for example, practicing Catholic US judges and executive officials have actively safeguarded constitutional rights to abortion and same-sex marriage in spite of any commitment in their private lives to their church's prohibitions against both.[2]

The distinction between institutional and ideological secularism is often hard to draw in practice as both attacks against secularism and defenses of it confound, overlap, or mix the two. It is nevertheless important to distinguish the two conceptually in order to obtain a better grasp on the attacks launched against secularism both from within religion itself—as in the case of Pope Benedict XVI equating Catholicism with universal morality and natural law discussed in Section D below—and from constitutional perspectives that rely on religion as a symbol of culture, or as a mainstay of tradition or national identity. Also, the focus on the

[1] *See* Catherine Fieschi, "Muslims and the secular city: How right-wing populists shape the French debate over Islam," *Brookings*, February 28, 2020, <www.brookings.edu/articles/muslims-and-the-secular-city-how-right-wing-populists-shape-the-french-debate-over-islam/#muslims>.

[2] *See* Alex Gangitano, "Biden says as Catholic he's 'not big on abortion' but thinks Roe 'got it right,'" *The Hill*, June 27, 2023, <https://thehill.com/homenews/administration/4070735-biden-says-as-catholic-hes-not-big-on-abortion-but-thinks-roe-got-it-right/>.

conceptual distinction between institutional and ideological secularism is particularly relevant to assessing the place of secularism in securing liberal and pluralist constitutional rights in light of the strong contemporary critiques of institutional secularism's aspirations to neutrality in its constitutional mediations of the interface between state and religion.

A. Institutional Secularism's Claim to Neutrality Contrasted with Ideological Secularism's Rejection of Transcendence and Embrace of Science

As previously noted in Chapter 1, institutional secularism is an ideal of constitutional neutrality among religions that can at best be roughly approximated in liberal constitutional settings. Because of this, it is necessary to briefly examine some of the most salient features of the dynamic between the latter and ideological secularism in order more cogently to sort out *internal* critiques within the ambit of secular constitutionalism from their *external* counterparts based on invocations of religious perspectives, including those launched by nationalists and populists. Moreover, the task of systematically distinguishing between internal and external critiques is made all the more difficult as religion-based contestations against secular laws or institutions are often couched in the language of liberal constitutional rights, such as freedom of speech and anti-discrimination rights (Mancini & Rosenfeld 2018a). Thus, for example, a religious US commercial wedding cake maker sought to justify his refusal to sell a cake for use at a same-sex wedding as a constitutionally protected expression of his views in opposition to such weddings.[3] For her part, a practicing Christian UK government official who was dismissed for her failure to register the civil partnership of a same-sex couple claimed she was the victim of religious discrimination. In her estimation, she was forced to choose between her religion and her job while her secular colleagues, and even her religious ones, without a similar conflict were not (McCrudden 2018: 414–45). With this in mind, we will first briefly address how the ideal of institutional secularism—which, as detailed in Chapter 1, is deployed to varying degrees in all the major models of liberal pluralist constitutional ordering—compares to ideological secularism. Second, even assuming, for the sake of argument, that institutional secularism became hard to defend in light of the constant and unrelenting attacks to which it has been subjected in the age of repoliticized religion, ideological secularism would, in all likelihood, still retain a strong following among a significant portion of the citizenry in most constitutional democracies (Rosenfeld 2014: 107–8). Accordingly, short of disenfranchizing all proponents of secular values, fundamental rights

[3] *See Masterpiece Cakeshop, Ltd. v Colorado Civil Rights Commission*, 584 US 617 (2018).

conceptions and interpretations in present-day constitutional polities would still have to account for the claims of secularists alongside those of proponents of various religious perspectives. This, in turn, calls for exploring to what extent it would be possible to maintain a principled distinction between liberal and religiously oriented illiberal iterations of fundamental rights by drawing on ideological secularism rather than by attempting to reconceive institutional neutrality.

As already noted, the ideal of institutional secularism requires depoliticizing religion by expelling it from the public sphere while privileging it in the private sphere. As detailed in Chapter 1, institutional secularism has been deployed in various modern constitutional democracies and has yielded different models of regulation of the relation between religion and the state. What is crucial for present purposes is that none of these models comes close to meeting the ideal, but all are compatible with the two principal aspirations embedded within it. These aspirations are a commitment to religious pluralism (understood as inclusive of non-religious conceptions of the good) and to the related principle that, in the affairs of the state and in public policy, no religion shall be considered or treated as the sole possessor of the truth.

As contrasted to institutional secularism, which aspires to being *areligious*—neither in favor nor against any religious or irreligious perspective—ideological secularism figures as one conception of the good among many others. In the broadest terms, ideological secularism is grounded in an immanent world view that rejects all transcendence from an epistemological, ontological, moral, and political standpoint (Taylor 2007: 18–20). As noted, ideological secularism is certainly congruent with atheism and agnosticism, but it is also compatible with certain forms of religion, provided they are exercised in a compartmentalized fashion. Thus, a person who is committed to the social and political spheres being ruled by humanistic values, human rights, science, and public reason, but at the same time believes in, and worships, a transcendent being individually or within a like-minded religious community operating within the private sphere, would satisfy in all relevant respects the dictates of ideological secularism as a way of life extending to all areas of constitutional concern. Contrary to institutional secularism, ideological secularism does not aspire to neutrality and thus, for example, prioritizes science and humanistic values over inconsistent or contradictory religion-based values and imperatives.

Even under this minimal definition, institutional secularism's rejection of any possibility for transcendent religious truths to prevail within the public sphere is largely compatible with one of the fundamental tenets of ideological secularism, namely the exclusion of religious rule in the public sphere. On the other hand, ideological secularism does not necessarily require adherence to pluralism. Thus, for example, anti-religious ideological secularism may conceivably be intolerant of all religion. In addition, certain non-transcendent ideologies, such as fascism or Soviet-style communism, have characteristically lacked any tolerance toward all non-conforming perspectives. However, because liberal constitutionalism requires commitment to pluralism through its freedom of speech, freedom of religion, and freedom of conscience provisions, all ideological secularists who embrace such a vision of constitutionalism are bound to incorporate commitment to pluralism within their own secular conception of the good. Conversely, any constitution that aspires to institutional secularism and that adheres to pluralism and to the prohibition against life in the public sphere being under the sway of any singular contested religious truth must perforce incorporate some of the key tenets of ideological secularism.

Attacks against constitutional instantiations of institutional secularism are essentially twofold. The first of these assails institutional secularism's very aspiration to neutrality by claiming that any attempt at implementation is bound to yield an anti-religious outcome. Thus, for instance, for the French authorities, the prohibition against wearing the Islamic veil in public schools may be entirely consistent with *laïcité*'s aspiration to neutrality, but to those who feel obligated to wear the veil and to their families the said prohibition may naturally be taken as an official stance against their religion.[4] Furthermore, even if expelling religion from the public sphere may not be in and of itself anti-religious, as already noted, some critics have railed against it on the grounds that it leads to an utter impoverishment of social interaction within the polity by herding the citizenry into a "naked public square" (Neuhaus 1984). The second major line of attack against institutional secularism is premised on the claim that the latter amounts to a convenient screen for statewide impositions of ideological secularism. One striking example of this kind of attack, which we discussed in Chapter 2, is the lawsuits brought by US fundamentalist Protestant parents against their children's public schools, alleging violations of the Establishment Clause.[5]

Both of these kinds of attacks have figured in illiberal attacks on constitutional secularism and will be further examined in Sections B and C below. A different kind of attack, which denies the gap between faith and reason and asserts that true reason corresponds to true faith, will be discussed in Section D. In Section E, we will address the special illiberal invocation of religion in cases of prolonged societal stress, such as those that arose in the wake of global terrorism or of the more recent COVID-19 pandemic. Finally, in Section F, we will assume, for the sake of argument, that all these attacks may end up delegitimizing institutional secularism, and we will explore whether reliance on ideological secularism without pretense of neutrality could suffice to defend the integrity of liberal constitutional secularism against the illiberal assaults being currently waged against it.

[4] *See* Rim-Sarah AlouaneAlouane "The Weaponization of Laïcité," *Berkeley Forum*, October 7, 2020, <https://berkleycenter.georgetown.edu/posts/the-weaponization-of-laicite>.

[5] *See Smith v Board of Comm'rs of Mobile County*, 827 F 2d 684 (11th Cir 1987) and *Grove v Mead School District*, 753 F 2d 1528 (9th Cir 1983).

B. Religious Attacks on Secularism as Non-Neutral and Anti-Religious

Attacks on institutional secularism as non-neutral or anti-religious do not dwell upon inevitable imperfections but instead concentrate on what are regarded as unwarranted biases. Moreover, the claimed biases at stake are not all anti-religious, as some focus on constitutionally anchored preference for one (usually majority) religion to the detriment of (usually minority) others. French *laïcité* is especially remarkable in this context, for it stands as the most logical and pristine expression of institutional secularist aspiration to areligious neutrality, and yet it has been accused both of being anti-religious and of favoring Catholicism over the other religions present in France. France's above-mentioned prohibition against wearing the Muslim veil in public schools is thus arguably anti-religious as well as religiously discriminatory. On the one hand, the Muslim veil does not interfere with public education as demonstrated by its tolerance in many other constitutionally secular democracies, such as Italy and the US.[6] In view of this, the French prohibition looms as anti-pluralist, if not downright anti-religious. On the other hand, as Catholic girls have no religious obligation to wear a veil to school, the government's anti-veil policy can be criticized as being religiously discriminatory. More generally, France's proscription of religion in public schools and throughout the public sphere seemingly leaves nothing but what qualifies as ideological secularism as the only viable alternative beyond the confines of the private sphere. And this makes the French public sphere anti-religious for believers in a transcendent realm primed to permeate all facets of life. Whereas French *laïcité* is firmly constitutionally entrenched and continues to be lived and defended with great vigor, it is noteworthy that there have been recent discussions from within concerning some loosening of its hermetic closure to the public display of religion.[7] Finally, for all its areligious or anti-religious connotations, French *laïcité* is historically rooted in a particular accommodation between the French Catholic Church and the state (Troper 2009: 2568–69). To be sure, the deployment of *laïcité* in France required some restraints on religion, thus somewhat relativizing Catholicism within the polity. But at the same time, *laïcité* was molded so as to render the public space as compatible as possible with the culture associated with Catholicism, if not with the religion itself. This phenomenon is succinctly captured, as already underscored, in the French popular term *Catho-laique*.

[6] *See* R. Vance Eaton, "Veiled: Institutional messages in the language of secularism in public schools in France and the United States" (2010) 6(2) *South Carolina Journal of International Law and Business*, <https://scholarcommons.sc.edu/scjilb/vol6/iss2/5>; Ennio Codini, "The Veil at School in Italy and in France" [2019] *Italian Law Journal* 76, <https://theitalianlawjournal.it/data/uploads/5-italj-1-2019/71-codini.pdf>.

[7] *See* Elizabeth Winkler, "Is it Time for France to Abandon Laïcité?," *The New Republic*, January 7, 2016, <https://newrepublic.com/article/127179/c>.

Institutional secularism is supposed to safeguard freedom *of* as well as freedom *from* religion and, as already noted in Chapter 1, the second of these protections is as important to religious believers who wish to remain free from impositions coming from all religions but their own as it is to non-believers who wish to keep all religions at bay. As all instantiations of institutional secularism are admittedly imperfect, they are all subject to fair criticism and calls for improvement from an internal perspective. Thus, *laïcité*'s veering on anti-religious stances and better accommodation, though not endorsement, of Catholicism than of other religions may well be addressed within the ambit of French secularism. Similarly, whereas US constitutional secularism is more open to public manifestations of religion than its French counterpart, it still prohibits state preference for one religion over others. In spite of this, as already mentioned, the US Supreme Court has developed a jurisprudence of the religion clauses that has been characterized as favoring a Protestant conception of religion. This bias is implicit and it consists in drawing a firm line between religious belief and religious practice that does not hold in other religions, such as Judaism or Islam.

Whereas this latter bias is subject to internal critique and better accommodation of minority religions through doctrinal adjustments, the same cannot be said for some more recent cases that are better understood as contradicting the no-preference constitutional mandate than as merely serving it imperfectly. One notorious such case is *Town of Greece v Galloway*,[8] a 5–4 US Supreme Court decision upholding the constitutionality of starting the monthly board meeting of a New York state town with a prayer recited by a religious chaplain. Whereas US judicial precedents sanctioned generic prayers at the beginning of legislative sessions as part of the culture and tradition of the country and as a symbol of common identity rather than of religiosity (after all, the US dollar contains the inscription "in God we trust"), this case was different in several important respects. First, although all chaplains of all religions were eligible to deliver the prayer, only Christian ones had done so throughout the many years of the practice.[9] Second, unlike a prayer at the beginning of a legislative session where elected parliamentarians are gathered to work among themselves, the town board meetings were opened to members of the public who had business before the board and who might therefore feel pressured to participate in the prayers in the hopes of increasing their chances of obtaining a favorable ruling in the matter for which they were attending the meeting.[10] Third, one of the ministers conducting one of the prayers at stake criticized neighboring towns for not having "God fearing" leaders.[11] And fourth, several of the Christian ministers involved did not confine their invocations to the seeking of guidance

[8] *Town of Greece v Galloway* 572 US 565 (2014).
[9] Ibid.
[10] Ibid.
[11] Ibid.

from a generic Supreme Being, but made statements appealing to Jesus Christ and the Holy Trinity to provide leadership and inspiration to the about-to-commence official proceedings.[12]

The Court's majority held that the prayers at stake did not violate the Establishment Clause's prohibition against giving preference to one religion over others because the law authorizing such prayers was non-discriminatory and would have allowed for non-Christian prayers and even for nontheistic invocations.[13] When placed in context, however, as Justice Kagan's dissent emphasized, the prayers involved were both palpably anti-secular and religiously objectionable to non-Christian believers. Indeed, such prayers turn every non-Christian into an outsider and amount to an external repudiation of institutional secularism as opposed to a mere internal inconsistency or a tolerable borderline imperfection within the scope of the latter. Also, to the extent the official prayers included criticism of those not deemed "God fearing," they squarely qualified as explicitly hostile toward ideological secularism.

Cases such as *Town of Greece* are cast in the language of institutional secularism while transgressing its spirit. There are, in addition, many initiatives and endeavors at redefining fundamental rights in the US and elsewhere—several of which will be more fully broached in Chapter 5—below—that attack secularism head-on. Some of these initiatives focus their attacks on ideological secularism and object implicitly or explicitly to institutional secularism as boosting or perpetuating its ideological counterpart. Thus, for example, secularism has been accused of being morally relativistic if not downright immoral; of making its adherents untrustworthy due to their lack of the fear of God; and of being the source of many other evils perceived as conspiring to deprive human life of all meaning and to reduce human beings to depraved hedonism or to mere calculating mutual exploitation.[14]

The above condemnations of secularism have been issued both by religious authorities, such as Catholic popes, and by illiberal political figures, such as the reputedly atheistic autocrat Viktor Orban, who has appealed to Christian values to steer Hungary away from the expansive conception of fundamental rights prevalent in Western Europe. Whether based on genuine religious beliefs or on an opportunistic recourse to religion to bolster illiberal nationalism or populism, such attacks can open the way to a realignment of rights along two principal alternative courses. One possibility is to brand secularism as anti-religious and hence anti-pluralist in its supposed denigration of all religions. Consistent with this, the state

[12] Ibid, at 588 (Kagan J, dissenting).

[13] Ibid.

[14] *See, e.g.*, McCann & Bradlaugh 1881; Garcia & King 2009; Joseph Ratzinger, *Homily for the Mass "Pro Eligendo Romano Pontific"* (Saint Peter's Basilica, April 18, 2005) <www.vatican.va/gpII/documents/homily-pro-eligendo-pontifice_20050418_en.html>, accessed June 22, 2025; John Paul II, *Evangelium vitae* (March 1995), para 22–23, <www.vatican.va/holy_father/john_paul_ii/encyclicals/documents/hf_jp-ii_enc_25031995_evangeliumvitae_en.html>, accessed June 22, 2025; Bhargava 2007; Kennedy 2006.

should privilege religion against secularism while remaining tolerant of religious diversity. This latter position was embraced by Justice Scalia in dissenting opinions that objected to the prevailing US jurisprudence according to which the state's non-preference must extend to all religions and to non-religion.[15] In Scalia's view, not only can government prefer religion over non-religion,[16] but it can also promote theistic religion predicated on a belief "in a benevolent, omnipotent Creator and Ruler of the world" so long as it does not enter into sectarian disputes such as that which divides Jews and Christians regarding the divinity of Jesus.[17] Accordingly, had Scalia's position prevailed in the US, presumably the state could have constitutionally promoted Abrahamic religions to the exclusion of other major world religions such as Buddhism and Hinduism to the extent that the latter do not comply with all the strictures of the theistic canon.

The other alternative to remedy the claimed vacuous and detrimental legacy of secularism consists in aligning the constitution with a single religion and to do so either on the basis of religiosity or of cultural and nationalist religion-based identitarian considerations. An initiative that combines both religiosity and nationalism is that of the Pompeo Commission, more fully discussed in Chapter 7, which sought to redefine American exceptionalism and Christian heritage to narrow the scope of US constitutional rights generally while vastly expanding two specific ones among them.[18] Active during the first Trump presidency, the Pompeo Commission railed against what it characterized as the pernicious inflation, and hence devaluation, of rights in American constitutional jurisprudence, and instead advocated priming private property and freedom of religion rights. The upshot of the Commission's project, which faded from public view upon the advent of the Biden presidency, would have been to foster a Christian vision of religious freedom that would have led to the curtailment of rights deemed offensive to many Christians, such as those to abortion and to same-sex marriage. Moreover, coupled with that would have been an expansion of private property rights, making them explicitly inimical to the institution and expansion of social welfare rights. Ironically, this latter objective may have been consistent with the views of certain Protestant denominations but is squarely contrary to long-standing Catholic commitments eloquently promoted by Pope Francis.[19]

[15] *See McCreary County v ACLU of Ky*, 545 US 844, 860 (2005).

[16] Ibid, at 885 (Scalia J, dissenting).

[17] *See Lee v Weisman*, 505 US 577, 641 (1992) (Scalia J, dissenting).

[18] Department of State, *Report of the Commission on Unalienable Rights*, <https://2017-2021.state.gov/wp-content/uploads/2020/08/Report-of-the-Commission-on-Unalienable-Rights.pdf>, accessed January 24, 2026.

[19] *See* Whitney Eulich, et al., "Pope Francis focused on 'this world.' He angered some, and inspired many others," *The Christian Science Monitor*, April 24, 2025, <www.csmonitor.com/World/Americas/2025/0424/pope-francis-catholic-church-social-justice>.

C. Religious-Based Attacks on Science: The US Cases Against Teaching Evolution Theory and for Teaching Creationism in Science Classes

The clash between religion and science has a long history, as the Renaissance cases of Copernicus and Galileo have vividly illustrated for centuries. In the sixteenth century the religious authorities had the uncontested upper hand, but, with the firm implantation of institutional secularism embodied in the two late eighteenth-century religion clauses contained in the US First Amendment, it may seem surprising that in twentieth-century America religion has been invoked by state authorities and by certain religious groups to suppress or to blunt science. The twentieth-century villain was not the scientific refutation of the thesis that the Earth was flat but the theory of evolution in biology. Freedom of scientific inquiry is without doubt a centerpiece of the spirit of the Enlightenment, and an attack on science in the context of institutional secularism cannot be equated with disputes in the realm of morals and human values discussed in the preceding section. Religions differ among themselves and with ideological secularism over what constitutes a good and valuable life. Notably, there are no fair, universally applicable criteria to credibly determine whether a life devoted to Christ is superior to one following the precepts of Buddhism or to one consecrated to fighting hunger and disease throughout the world on the basis of humanistic rather than religious beliefs. In contrast, science, while far from infallible, has its own methodology, approach to facts, and criteria of verification and falsification, which are common and open to orderly challenge to the entire worldwide community of scientists. Because of this, from the standpoint of constitutionally enshrined secularism, the attack on science looms as much more radical than those on moral or ideological grounds.

The most famous American case against the teaching of the theory of evolution in public school science classes is the 1925 *Scopes* trial (also referred to as the "Scopes Monkey Trial").[20] The case concerned a Tennessee law, lobbied for by a Christian fundamentalist association, that prohibited the teaching of the theory of evolution in any state-funded school. The defendant Scopes, a teacher in such a school, admitted to presenting the prohibited theory, which he claimed was protected by his academic freedom right under the First Amendment's Free Speech Clause. The trial itself, one of the most publicized in American history, was argued by two of the most celebrated lawyers of the time and was replete with ironies and anecdotes—one of them being the bemoaning by defenders of the challenged law that evolution theory asserted that men were the descendants of monkeys, and not even American monkeys at that. The trial court found Scopes guilty and imposed

[20] *See The State of Tennessee v Scopes* 152 Tenn 424 (1925).

a relatively small fine. Its decision was later reversed by the Tennessee Supreme Court, but on purely technical grounds relating to a flaw in the procedure used to determine the amount of the fine.[21] Several decades later, the US Supreme Court held that an Arkansas law similar to the Tennessee one amounted to an unconstitutional violation of the Establishment Clause in that it had a purely religious purpose.[22]

After the prohibitions against teaching evolutionism were decisively repudiated as unconstitutional, the disappointed Christian groups and the state legislators who had lent them support coalesced around the theory of creationism and embarked on a mission of having the latter taught alongside the theory of evolution in public school science classes (Numbers 1992). Notably, whereas the anti-evolution prohibitionist movement had openly called upon religion to justify its position, the creationism advocates presented their demands as being based on science. Creationism was closely tied to a literal interpretation of the biblical narrative in Genesis, according to which God created the world within one week and man and woman in his own image on the sixth day, and thus contemporaneously but entirely separate from all other animals.[23] This notwithstanding, the creationists hid or downplayed their religious convictions and presented creationism as an alternative scientific hypothesis that competed with evolutionism. In other words, scientific questioning of evolutionism is certainly within the purview of scientific inquiry, and the creationism advocates characterized their view as an alternative scientific explanation that should be regarded as equally plausible and subject to falsification as evolutionism. Furthermore, insisting that creationism amounted to an alternative scientific theory, its proponents argued that it ought to be taught alongside evolutionism on free speech grounds (Brownfield 2007: 146). Thus, to Scopes' unsuccessful free speech argument used as a potential shield to protect him from criminal liability for teaching evolutionism, the creationists opposed a (also ultimately unsuccessful) free speech argument meant as a sword in order to force pairing creationism with evolutionism in the classroom, lest students in science classes would end up with deficient instruction in science due to what amounted to government-mandated censorship.

The US Supreme Court's *Edwards v Aguillard* held in 1987 that a Louisiana law requiring the teaching of creationism in science classes was unconstitutional under the Establishment Clause.[24] The Court justified its conclusion upon a finding that creationism was not a scientific theory but instead a religious one that was not in any way subject to evaluation under scientific criteria such as empirical validation or commonly accepted standards of falsification. Pointedly, the Court

[21] *John Thomas Scopes v The State* (Tenn S Ct 1927).
[22] *See Epperson v Arkansas* 393 US 97 (1968).
[23] *See* Old Testament, Book of Genesis 1:24-26.
[24] 482 U.S. 578 (1987).

endorsed the validity of Louisiana's asserted purpose for its law, namely, furthering academic freedom, but it characterized creationism as a particular religious vision predicated on the belief that a transcendent supernatural being created human beings.[25] It is also noteworthy that the Court made it a point to specify that when a state is not intent on promoting particular religious views:

> We do not imply that a legislature could never require that scientific critiques of prevailing scientific theories be taught.... Teaching a variety of scientific theories about the origins of humankind to schoolchildren might be validly done with the clear secular intent of enhancing the effectiveness of science instruction.[26]

After their defeat in this case, the creationists did not give up, but they replaced their terminology to distance their project from direct biblical connotations. Accordingly, creationism was replaced by "intelligent design" (Petto 2015: 15–27). Under this new rubric, the message became that evolutionism, cast as the theory that the progression from a single molecule to a fully developed human being was achieved through some unconscious self-propelling process, is hard to believe from a rational standpoint. And therefore, it is much more logical to hypothesize that our contemporary world, whether or not the product of evolution, is the product of an intelligent design. However, in spite of its more hidden and somewhat more diluted guise, imposing the teaching of intelligent design alongside evolutionism in science classes was deemed an impermissible promotion of religion by a lower federal court in 2005.[27]

Paradoxically, although in both cases science is treated by certain proponents of Christianity as an integral part of a secularist ideology to which they are hostile, from the standpoint of constitutional secularism, the propagation of creationism and intelligent design as scientific seems more pernicious than outright open religious interference against science.[28] The disruptions caused by such propagation are also exacerbated by the misuse of the constitutional concepts of academic freedom and of free speech. And such misuse is not confined to the average citizen but has extended, on occasion, to high court judges. Thus, the decision in the *Aguillard* case above was a 7–2 one, and Justice Scalia wrote in dissent that he found the teaching of creationism constitutionally permissible to allow students "to decide for themselves how life began, based upon a fair and balanced presentation of the scientific evidence."[29]

[25] Ibid, at 582.
[26] Ibid, at 593.
[27] *Kitzmiller v Dover Area School District*, 400 F Supp 2d 707 (MD Pa 2005).
[28] Besides the logic involved, there is an important technical legal point concerning the *Scopes* case. As of 1925, the Supreme Court had not yet declared that the rights protected against the US federal government by the Establishment Clause were also applicable against the US states. Nevertheless, secularist arguments were extensively used by the defense in the course of the trial.
[29] *Edwards v Aguillard* 482 US 578, 610 (1987) (Scalia J, dissenting).

Modern education in primary and secondary schools is typically divided by subject matter for pedagogical reasons throughout constitutional democracies. Students receive instruction in history, mathematics, biology, literature, foreign languages, etc. It is therefore absurd to pretend that a teacher hired to teach mathematics in a state school has the academic freedom and free speech right to teach her students the plays of Shakespeare instead of her assigned subject. Moreover, whereas these mentioned rights give teachers a fair measure of freedom within their own field, the latter is by no means unlimited. For example, imagine that a history teacher giving a course on World War Two and its aftermath assigns to his twelve-year-old students some standard historical material and a novel premised on the fiction that the Nazis won the war and ruled the world for several decades thereafter. As this may lead to unwarranted confusion, it seems reasonable and not in violation of any freedom rights for the school authorities to ask the teacher in question to refrain from assigning the counter-historical novel in the future. The same novel may therefore be at once a perfectly suitable choice in a literature class but not in certain history classes. Similarly, science and religion are distinct subjects that may be taught separately in schools, just as history and literature are. In fact, as noted in Chapter 1, in certain secular democracies such as Germany, religion is taught by members of the clergy as a separate subject. Also, in countries with a stricter separation between state and religion, the subject may nonetheless be taught constitutionally in public schools so long as this is done from a historical or sociological perspective rather than for sectarian purposes. Finally, scientific vindication of the theory of evolution is by no means incompatible with metaphysical commitment to creationism or intelligent design. Indeed, only if one subscribes to a literal interpretation of the biblical account of God's creation of the world within a week does the theory of evolution appear to be in direct contradiction with biblical teachings. In sum, institutional secularism and the protection it accords to the teaching of science are by no means incompatible with belief in creationism, but only with a very narrowly confined version of the latter.

D. Envisioning Religion as Fostering a Universal Merger of Faith and Reason, thus Preempting Secularism: Pope Benedict's Theory of Natural Law

Secular political theorists have argued for the exclusion of public arguments solely based on religion, such as the assertion that abortion should be made a crime because it is contrary to God's will. Thus, as already mentioned, Rawls has proposed that the discourse within the political sphere ought to be limited to that which may be subject to evaluation through the use of "public reason" (Rawls 1996: 9). For his part, Habermas has insisted that in matters of morals, politics, and law, legitimacy is based on reaching a consensus after a fair and thorough discussion of all relevant arguments relating to the matter at hand, but has specified that admissible arguments should be limited to those that are "post metaphysical" (Habermas 1992). These liberal positions align particularly well with institutional secularism, but have been open to attack as anti-religious or as privileging ideological secularism over all religion-based perspectives. More recently, Habermas has become more inclusive of religious views without thereby abandoning his fundamental commitment to secular Enlightenment values. In a dialogue he had with Cardinal Ratzinger, the then-future Pope Benedict XVI, Habermas acknowledged an analogy between the religious belief of "man in the image of God" and the secular belief in the equal dignity of all humans (Habermas & Ratzinger 2006: 45).

Consistent with institutional secularism, some may act in the public sphere out of religious belief and others out of secular ones, so long as there are justifications open to evaluation under a "public reason" standard. Also, whereas some have argued that public officials, legislators, and judges ought to confine official pronouncements to language that can be justified or contested within the constraints of public reason, there seems to be no categorical impediment to the linking of religious and secular justifications so long as the latter are in themselves sufficient to legitimate the official action taken. However, the linkage in question may be appropriate in certain contexts but not in others, depending on the degree of harmony and conviviality among religions and among the latter and ideological secularism. Thus, in a polity where a high level of mutual tolerance prevails among all groups, religious and not, it would seem entirely acceptable to endorse fundamental liberty and equality rights both because of a widely shared belief that God created human beings in her own image and because of another widely disseminated conviction that all human beings inherently possess equal dignity due to their capacities as moral agents. In contrast, in a polity beset by contentious religious divisions and by open antagonism between secularists and the rest, limiting official pronouncements to those subject to public reason-based evaluation seems critical and worthy of constitutional backing in order to preserve the integrity of institutional secularism.

There have been a wide range of views on the relationship between faith and reason, ranging from the *credo quia absurdum* (I believe because it is absurd)—once attributed to Augustine and more recently further elaborated in substance by the nineteenth-century Christian existentialist philosopher Kierkegaard (Kierkegaard 1992)—to largely equating the two. One of the most remarkable proponents of a version of the latter position is the systematically rationalist seventeenth-century philosopher Spinoza. According to him, reason is equated with truth and reality,[30] and virtue with acting according to reason.[31] Moreover,

[30] "It is in the nature of reason to perceive things truly . . . namely . . . as they are in themselves . . . Reason perceives this necessity of things . . . truly—that is . . . as it is in itself" (Spinoza 1951: 116–17).

[31] "To act virtuously is to act in obedience with reason" (Spinoza 1951: 211).

Spinoza draws a sharp distinction between faith and reason. In his own words, "between Faith or Theology, and philosophy, there is no connection, no affinity... Philosophy has no end in view save truth: faith... looks for nothing but obedience and piety" (Spinoza 1951: 189) Yet in spite of this, Spinoza does not simply align himself with a philosophy of reason that casts matters of faith as purely irrational or that regards religion as a mere projection of human hope and fear. A philosophy of reason is necessary to unmask the evils produced by a theology that results in mass-induced superstition and intolerance, but to the extent that such a philosophy thinks that it can do away with faith and religion, it ultimately becomes yet another theology (Balibar 1998: 7). In other words, for Spinoza, lest philosophy become "an anti-religious discourse" (Balibar 1998: 8), it must not set aside *true* religion and faith, but rather account for them from the standpoint of reason.[32]

There may seem to be a superficial affinity between the illiberal view of secularism as yet one more religion and Spinoza's subsuming "true" religion within the realm of reason. However, there is a key difference between the two, as Spinoza equates the precepts and virtues of true religion with those derived from reason. In other words, whereas Spinoza regards "false" religion as fostering dangerous irrationality and prejudice, he suggests that "true" religion and reason use two different languages that lead to the same universally valid normative truths.

Spinoza's approach may seem promising from the standpoint of expanding pluralism and compatibility within the scope of institutional secularism, but more importantly for our purposes, it provides a valuable springboard to our brief examination of Pope Benedict XVI's linking the precepts of natural law derived from reason with the dictates emanating from Catholic faith. The pope, in contrast to Spinoza, starts from faith and finds that reason, when properly applied, yields the same moral and legal precepts as those revealed through faith. According to Pope Benedict, the faith involved is Catholicism, which considers itself the universal religion, and the law discovered through a proper use of universal reason is natural law (Cartabia & Simoncini 2015: 3–9). There is a long tradition, going back to the Middle-Ages philosopher Thomas Aquinas, of linking Christian faith with natural law discoverable through reason. In this light, the proper use of reason in legal discourse leads to the same conclusions as theological reasoning within the language of true (Catholic) faith. Moreover, given the pope's assertion that Catholic faith and reason coincide in affirming universally valid morality and law (Cartabia & Simoncini 2015), all law should be consistent with Catholic faith, and those who do not share that faith should recognize the law in question as legitimate through a consistent use of reason. Thus, murder and theft are prohibited by the Ten Commandments, and presumably it would stand against reason to contend that any decent, viable society could thrive without legally prohibiting murder or theft.

[32] *See* Spinoza 1951: 9 (nothing in "universal religion" is repugnant to reason).

In short, assuming for the sake of argument that legitimate law must conform to the dictates of universal reason—a proposition highly disputed by postmodernists and many others (Rosenfeld 1998: Ch. 1)—then in principle all humanity, including those of all different faiths and those with no faith, ought to, consistent with Pope Benedict's vision, agree on which laws ought to be accepted as normatively legitimate and which not. Needless to say, under those conditions, any legal regime consistent with Catholic faith and universal reason would be fully compatible with institutional secularism.

In spite of Pope Benedict's aspirations, his equation of the normative implications of Catholicism and of universal reason is upon further analysis deeply flawed on two crucial grounds: Catholic-based morality and law differ irreconcilably with many prescriptions in full accord with Enlightenment-based conceptions of reason; and Catholic claims to universal validity on the level of faith-based morals and law clash, on important matters, with their faith-based counterparts in other Abrahamic religions, let alone with those reflected within the full gamut of all other currently practiced religions. Also, before pursuing these matters any further, it bears emphasizing that there is a strong disanalogy between Spinoza's joining of faith and reason and Pope Benedict's. Whereas one may disagree with Spinoza's strict correlation between reason and truth, for any persuaded rationalist along Spinoza's line, use of reason suffices to discover all of the truth and to leave all else aside accordingly. Consistent with this, religion does not add anything of its own, but in an *inclusionary* gesture, Spinoza welcomes it within the normative fold provided it reaches the right normative conclusions, albeit through non-rational means. In sharp contrast, Pope Benedict starts from Catholic faith (presumably other faiths correspond to Spinoza's "false" religion to the extent that they are inconsistent with Catholicism), which occupies the position that reason holds for Spinoza, but invokes reason in an *exclusionary* way. Indeed, as we shall detail in what follows, Benedict limits what counts as reason for him as a proponent of his faith in ways that directly counter what ought to generate a reason-based consensus or at least a principled debate within the bounds of public reason.

To begin with, Pope Benedict and his predecessor have condemned secularism as amounting to a "dictatorship of relativism."[33] On this papal view, secularism's relativism is linked to a multitude of evils that conspire to deprive human life of all meaning and to reduce human beings to depraved hedonism or to mere calculating mutual exploitation.[34] Besides this view being false and prejudicial, as there are many secular moralities, ranging from Kantian to utilitarian-based ones, that are not relativistic and a fair number of atheists who devote their lives to the public

[33] *See* Joseph Ratzinger, *Homily for the Mass "Pro Eligendo Romano Pontifice"* (St. Peter's Basilica, April 18, 2005) <www.vatican.va/gpII/documents/homily-pro-eligendo-pontifice_20050418_en.html>, accessed June 22, 2025.

[34] *See, e.g.*, Pope John Paul II, *Evangelium Vitae*, para 22–23, <www.vatican.va/content/john-paul-ii/en/encyclicals/documents/hf_jp-ii_enc_25031995_evangelium-vitae.html>, accessed June 22, 2025.

good while foregoing lucrative mutual exploitation opportunities, it cannot stand under any plausible public reason criterion. The dispute between the secularists and the Catholics is precisely one that cannot be resolved through the use of public reason, as Catholic faith is premised on a transcendent metaphysical creed, as is, incidentally, atheism (as the negation without possible testable proof of transcendent divinity).

Pope Benedict's undue shrinkage of what should be included within the purview of reason goes much farther than his condemnation of ideological secularism. As one prominent Catholic legal scholar has pointed out, there are several tensions between the Catholic Church's positions and those prevalent within contemporary human rights jurisprudence (McCrudden 2015: 164–65). Moreover, the disagreements at stake are by no means limited to the contentious issue of abortion, but extend to many others, such as contraception, non-marital sex, same-sex marriage, divorce, euthanasia, and embryonic research. To take but one example, to argue that universal reason categorically condemns euthanasia is manifestly counterintuitive. Are there not weighty public reason arguments in favor of injecting a lethal dose of morphine into a terminal patient in excruciating pain who, at best, has but a couple of weeks of life left? Universal reason may not have a definitive answer on many of the above questions, but no recourse to reason justifies extending the Catholic Church's univocal answers beyond those who have accepted to be bound by the dictates of Catholic faith.

Finally, as already mentioned, Catholicism does not align with other Abrahamic faiths on several important matters of religious morals and law. One area of clear disagreement is divorce, which is permitted both under Jewish *halachic* law (Deuteronomy 24:1) and under Muslim Sharia law.[35] Accordingly, if a country adopted a legal system that conformed with Benedict's imperatives, its Jewish and Muslim citizens would be legally barred from obtaining divorces fully authorized by their respective religions. In addition, Judaism and Islam do not ban all contraception and all abortions. In short, in a jurisdiction subject to Benedict's understanding of natural law, Catholics, but not Jews or Muslims, would find harmony between their faith and the law in square contravention to the imaginable bounds of institutional secularism.

In view of the preceding observations, Benedict's amalgamation of Catholic faith and universal reason boils down, wittingly or not, to a recipe for imposing the morals and laws prescribed by Catholicism under the false and misleading guise that these would conform to any plausible iteration of Enlightenment-based reason. As Catholic positions on many of the relevant rights, including the specifically mentioned ones above, are illiberal, any regime of fundamental rights

[35] *See* "Talaq, Khula, Faskh and Tafweedh: The different methods of Islamic separation—Part 1," *Family Law* (LexisNexis, November 10, 2014) <www.familylaw.co.uk/news_and_comment/talaq-khula-faskh-tafweedh-the-different-methods-of-islamic-separation-part-1>.

aligning with Benedict's Catholic vision of universalism seems bound to be much more restrictive than those prevailing under liberal pluralistic contemporary democracies.

E. Appeals to Religion in Times of Stress to Undermine Proportionality in the Constitutional and Political Realms: The Cases of Global Islamic Fundamentalist Terrorism and of the Covid-19 Pandemic

Even if, under ordinary conditions, a country's constitutional freedom-of-religion rights fit squarely within the purview of institutional secularism, these rights can be curtailed or distorted under extraordinary circumstances, such as national emergencies and persistent conditions of stress. Whereas in national emergencies, rights are often constitutionally curtailed or suspended, logically and pragmatically, religion-related rights ought not to fare differently than other rights. Under conditions of stress,[36] such as those produced by the advent of global terrorism or by the spread of the COVID-19 pandemic, in contrast, religion-based rights, as we shall see, are susceptible to being targeted or enlisted for manifestly illiberal purposes.

Times of crisis occur when the common identity of the polity or its very life is in imminent peril. The cause of the peril may be external, as in the case of a foreign war, or internal, as in the case of a civil war. Emergencies may also be triggered by natural causes as opposed to direct human agency, as exemplified by devastating earthquakes or hurricanes. In times of crisis, there may be a rallying toward unity and acceptance of the suspension of rights. Thus, for example, in the context of repealing a foreign invasion, citizens may be as willing to accept limitations on their freedom of movement, in general, as on their right to gather for prayer at sacred places of worship, in particular. Unless religion itself figures as a major factor in the crisis, as was the case in the 1990s civil war pitting Christians against Muslims in Bosnia (Abazović 2015), restrictions on religion-based rights should, in principle, be set pursuant to the same criteria as corresponding restrictions on other relevant rights. Furthermore, emergencies are supposed to be relatively short-lived and to have sharp boundaries (leaving aside, for present purposes, the important problem posed by abuses of constitutionally provided emergency powers). Accordingly, under the scrupulous watch of a conscientious head of government, a brief foreign invasion culminating in the withdrawal of all enemy forces should yield unmistakable signs that the crisis has subsided and that emergency powers are no longer justifiable.

[36] For a detailed discussion of the contrasts between ordinary times, times of crisis, and times of stress, *see* Rosenfeld 2006.

Unlike crisis conditions, those involving stress do not typically have as readily ascertainable boundaries. Times of stress span the spectrum between ordinary times and times of crisis. In times of stress, there is less extensive and less successful accommodation and integration of politically relevant competing conceptions of the good than in ordinary times. The identity or unity of the national community that is supposed to bind together the citizenry is not disintegrating, but it is destabilized and under various pressures. Whereas conventional wars tend to cause crises, terrorism and the "war on terror" seem more prone to generate stress. Indeed, unlike a military invasion, terrorist acts are likely to be sporadic and widespread, causing more psychological than physical harm. Having terrorists hidden within the polity's population is undoubtedly unnerving and can easily lead to overreactions, undue suppression of fundamental rights, or exacerbation of ethnic, racial, or religious prejudice such that certain minorities and the conceptions of the good they endorse may become increasingly unhinged. For example, terrorist acts in the name of a radical fundamentalist religious ideology by individuals coming from distant foreign lands, such as the Al Qaeda attacks on 9/11, or by one's neighbors, such as the ISIS attacks in Paris in November 2015, have aroused intense anti-Muslim sentiments.[37] This has led to mounting hostility against peaceful, law-abiding Muslim minorities living in countries that have been attacked or that fear that they will be.

Unlike global terrorism, which pits humans against one another, the COVID-19 pandemic emerged as a destructive natural phenomenon that inflicts death, disease, incapacity, and destruction much in the way that natural disasters such as earthquakes or hurricanes do. In places such as Bergamo, Italy, or New York City in the spring of 2020, where hospitals were overwhelmed and the victims so numerous that their bodies could not be buried in a timely fashion, the pandemic had all the trappings of an emergency.[38] But as the pandemic spread throughout 2020 and into 2021, with some surges, various peaks and valleys, and the gradual deployment of vaccines, this settled into conditions of stress. This stress was fueled by a combination of disruptions, exacerbations, retreats, vacillations, and, most notably for our purposes, significant erosions in maintaining accord on workable standards of proportionality.

[37] *See* Nicholas Brooklier, "Islamophobia: The stereotyping and prejudice towards Muslims since 9/11," *Law and Justice in Real Time*, December 17, 2015, <https://hub.wsu.edu/law-justice-realtime/2015/12/17/islamophobia-the-stereotyping-and-prejudice-towards-muslims-since-911/>; Cécile Guerin and Zoé Fourel, "A snapshot analysis of anti-Muslim mobilisation in France after terror attacks," April 20, 2021, <www.isdglobal.org/digital_dispatches/a-snapshot-analysis-of-anti-muslim-mobilisation-in-france-after-terror-attacks/>.

[38] *See* "Surge in deaths overwhelms New York's morgues, hospitals," *PBS News*, March 31, 2020. <www.pbs.org/newshour/health/surge-in-deaths-overwhelms-new-yorks-morgues-hospitals>; Jason Horowitz, "The lost days that made Bergamo a coronavirus tragedy," *New York Times*, November 29, 2020, <www.nytimes.com/2020/11/29/world/europe/coronavirus-bergamo-italy.html>.

In spite of their obvious differences, when measured in terms of the multiplication of disproportionate responses that they give rise to, the reactions to the pandemic share much in common with those to global terrorism. Because of ongoing anxiety, unmastered danger, and fear, they both similarly contribute to the fostering of conditions of stress. Moreover, reactions to the pandemic contribute to conditions of stress through regression in the handling of the standard of proportionality in two different ways. First, much like the war on terror has trouble finding an equilibrium between freedom and security—leading among other things to religious discrimination in the name of security—the fight against the virus has difficulty in finding the proper balance between restraining and vanquishing the disease and safeguarding the dignity and economic well-being of the citizenry. This has magnified political and societal rifts fueled by certain brands of nationalism and populism, at times wedded to certain religious or quasi-religious perspectives. In particular, the rifts in question have focused on pitting science and the rule of experts against the "common" person and the latter's charismatic political or religious leaders.

The challenge to implementing proportional responses to the pandemic arises in the context of the culture wars that are highlighted and intensified within the confines of populist rule. This challenge builds on the typical populist tendency to pit the ordinary person against the experts, and it is well illustrated by the struggle that arose in the US between Trump and his followers against scientists and public health experts. This struggle led to the politicization of the wearing of masks and of other mitigating policies and practices, thus contributing to the country's several glaring failures in its handling of the virus.[39] Trump's followers' rejection of science and their defiant resistance against the wearing of masks were not only highly political but also imbued with a quasi-religious fervor. Moreover, some religious groups, including some US fundamentalist Protestants and some ultra-Orthodox Hasidic Jewish communities both in Israel and the US, have openly defied the law and congregated in large numbers, without abiding by officially mandated health precautions.[40] Was this defiance predicated on a belief in special divine protection?[41] Or was it based on the belief that congregating for religious purposes

[39] *See* C. Scoville, A. McCumber, R. Amironesei, and J. Jeon, "Mask refusal backlash: The politicization of face masks in the American public sphere during the early stages of the COVID-19 pandemic" (2022) *Socius* 8, <https://doi.org/10.1177/23780231221093158>.

[40] *See* John P. Bartkowski, et al., "Fear God, not COVID-19: Is conservative Protestantism associated with risky pandemic lifestyles?", *NIH Healthcare*, February 15, 2023, <https://pmc.ncbi.nlm.nih.gov/articles/PMC9957345/>; Justin Elliott and Agnel Philip, "As coronavirus cases rise, members of some ultra-Orthodox Jewish communities continue to congregate", *Propublica*, March 18, 2020, <www.propublica.org/article/as-coronavirus-cases-rise-members-of-some-ultra-orthodox-jewish-communities-continue-to-congregate>.

[41] In some cases, members of these religious communities justified their refusal to take precautions or to seek hospitalization upon being severely sickened by the virus upon the fatalistic ground that the timing of every human being's death is exclusively in the hands of God. *See* "Israel's Orthodox and Haredi Jews navigate the new normal," *The New York Times*, February 17, 2021, <www.nytimes.

commanded priority over protection against the virus? In any event, once quasi-religious or religious objections lead to resistance to the best that science has to offer; and because defiant behavior is likely to afflict many outside the resisting group as well as many inside it; the relevant constitutional unit seems prone to lacking a common basis upon which proportionate polity-wide responses to the pandemic could be grounded.

In the end, what the different conditions of stress, sustained respectively by the war on terror and responses to the COVID-19 pandemic, share in common is their propensity to block plausible paths to proportionate solutions to major challenges that confront contemporary societies. From our standpoint, what is particularly noteworthy is that these conditions of stress have on repeated occasions led to restrictions on the scope of religion-based rights, pulling the latter out of the bounds of institutional secularism and into illiberalism. To get a better handle on this phenomenon, we now briefly place in context and examine a small sampling of relevant court decisions in the respective contexts of the war on terror and the fight against the pandemic.

Global terrorism in the twenty-first century has been largely unleashed by both Al Qaeda and ISIS in the name of an extreme fundamentalist jihadist version of Islam. The ideology involved, whether an extreme fringe within Islam or an outright heresy, may certainly be officially vigorously countered in a way that is proportionately consistent with the dictates of institutional secularism to the extent that it advocates violence against non-Muslims and certain Muslims it casts as insufficiently religiously conforming.[42] More generally, the war against global terrorism raises two further vexing issues: first, the special problem posed by fundamentalist religion (already in part addressed in relation to Protestant fundamentalism in Section A above) to constitutional regimes governed by institutional secularism; and second, the difficulties posed when religion is, or is perceived to be, correlated to ethnicity.

Fundamentalist religion, as understood here, takes its own truth as both absolute and as applying to the whole polity or the world at large without any room for acceptance or compromise with any other religious or non-religious world view (Habermas 1999b 224). In the present context, three distinctions regarding fundamentalist religion should be kept in mind. Some fundamentalists withdraw within their own religious community, have little to do with the rest of the polity, and are basically law-abiding. Other fundamentalists are not content to stay within their religious community, but seek to impose their views on society as a whole through

com/interactive/2021/02/17/world/middleeast/israel-orthodox-jews-haredim.html>, accessed June 22, 2025.

[42] In the US, advocacy of religious violence as opposed to incitement to it is constitutionally protected, but most other Western constitutional democracies have held criminalization of advocacy of religious hatred to be constitutionally permissible. *See* Rosenfeld 2012.

peaceful means by fighting for legal and constitutional changes, such as those involved in the already discussed cases of the US Christian fundamentalists who sought the prohibition of teaching certain literature texts and of the theory of evolution in state schools. Finally, a third category of fundamentalists is ready to impose their absolute religious truth on everyone throughout the polity or the world as a whole, by force if necessary. The Islamist jihadists belong to this last category, but so do others, such as certain US Christian fundamentalists who, in the name of their faith, have murdered physicians who have performed legal abortions.[43]

Religious positions and projects falling within the just-mentioned third category can be vigorously fought within the ambit of institutional secularism—and even criminalized to the extent that a religious fundamentalist group's calls to violence cannot be disentangled from its overall creeds, commitments, and messages. In times of stress, however, particularly if the violent fundamentalists are part of a minority religion within the relevant polity, the legitimate anti-fundamentalist stance all too easily extends to all those who adhere to non-fundamentalist nonviolent iterations of the same religion. As already noted, this became manifest in many Western countries where terrorist attacks by jihadists fostered general anti-Muslim hostility and repression. Moreover, this tendency becomes exacerbated when a minority religion is equated, rightly or wrongly, with a particular ethnic group. Adherents to Islam belong to a large number of different ethnic groups, but in the aftermath of the 9/11 attacks in the United States, anti-Muslim sentiment zeroed in on those who bore a Middle Eastern appearance and even led to the murder of a Sikh in Texas on the mistaken assumption that he was a Muslim.[44] Anti-ethnic animus need not be tied to religion, as made manifest by the sharp rise in anti-Asian crime in the US after Trump insisted on labeling the COVID-19 virus as "the China virus."[45] The victims of the anti-Asian violence in question could as easily be Korean or Vietnamese as Chinese in origin, and presumably they included members of various religions. At no time did religion seem an issue in anti-Asian animus as it had in its anti-Muslim counterpart. Depending on the circumstances, certain populists can stir anti-religious (or pro-religious against religions cast as the enemy) or anti-ethnic animus. In some cases, such as Trump's Muslim ban, which was addressed in *Trump v Hawaii*,[46] which we are about to

[43] *See* Liam Stack, "A brief history of deadly attacks on abortion providers," *New York Times*, November 29, 2015, <www.nytimes.com/interactive/2015/11/29/us/30abortion-clinic-violence.html>; Chloe Atkins, "The rise of 'abortion abolitionists' targeting women, doctors and Donald Trump," NBC NEWS, May 26, 2024, <www.nbcnews.com/news/us-news/rise-abortion-abolitionists-targeting-women-doctors-donald-trump-rcna147187>.

[44] *See* Tamar Lewin, "Sikh owner of gas station is fatally shot in rampage," *New York Times*, September 17, 2001, <www.nytimes.com/2001/09/17/us/sikh-owner-of-gas-station-is-fatally-shot-in-rampage.htm>.

[45] *See* Deb Reichmann and Terrey Tang, "Trump dubs COVID-19 'Chinese virus' despite hate crime risks," *AP News*, March 18, 2020, <https://apnews.com/article/donald-trump-ap-top-news-asia-crime-virus-outbreak-a7c233f0b3bcdb72c06cca6271ba6713>.

[46] *Trump v Hawaii* 138 S Ct 2392 (2018).

discuss, religion and ethnicity are aggregated, thus adding complexities and potential further constitutional complications. Indeed, there may be undue religious-freedom restrictions because of hostility against the ethnicity of adherents to a particular religion. Conversely, justified or unjustified animus against a religious ideology may unwarrantedly spill over against a particular ethnic group comprised of a large number of members who reject the objectionable tenets of the religious ideology found offensive.

The Trump "Muslim ban" that gave rise to the just-mentioned case refers to one of the first executive orders that he signed upon assuming the US presidency in January 2017, which barred entry into the US of people from seven Muslim-majority countries.[47] The order was extraordinarily sweeping as it not only barred those seeking immigration or visitor visas but also refugees, foreign students admitted or enrolled in US universities, people who had employment in the US but had temporarily returned to their country of citizenship, and even legal immigrants within the US who happened to be in one of the seven targeted countries as the order entered into force.[48] Also, during his presidential campaign, Trump had called for "a total and complete shutdown of Muslims entering the United States"[49] and told an interviewer that "Islam hates us" and that it is difficult to tell Islam apart from the extremists who engage in terror.[50] Trump's Muslim-ban order produced an outcry and multiple lawsuits, which resulted in several adverse court rulings.[51] This led to this order being superseded by another one that removed Iraq from the list of targeted countries and, in turn, added to the latter two non-Muslim countries, North Korea and Venezuela.[52] It is this second order that ended up before the US Supreme Court in *Trump v Hawaii*, based on a claim that it amounted to discrimination on the basis of religion.

The Court's majority upheld the second Trump order, considering it a rational anti-terrorist measure by restricting entry into the US by persons coming from countries, Muslim and non-Muslim, that had inadequate vetting procedures to sort out potential terrorists from the rest of the population. The Court's majority also specified that the long list of Trump's anti-Muslim pronouncements as a presidential candidate and as president had no bearing on the constitutionality of the

[47] *See* Executive Order 13769, January 27, 2017, <https://trumpwhitehouse.archives.gov/presidential-actions/executive-order-protecting-nation-foreign-terrorist-entry-united-states/>.

[48] *See* Amrit Cheng, "The Muslim ban: What just happened?," *ACLU News and Commentary*, December 6, 2017, <www.aclu.org/news/immigrants-rights/muslim-ban-what-just-happened>.

[49] *See* Jill Colvin and Bruce Smith, "Trump calls for 'complete shutdown' on Muslims entering US," AP News, December 7, 2015, <https://apnews.com/united-states-presidential-election-events-b0f4f54bad2843898b8b3b67559588aa>.

[50] John Santucci and Candace Smith, "Trump Says 'I Think Islam Hates Us,'" *ABC News*, March 9, 2016, <https://abcnews.go.com/Politics/donald-trump-islam-hates-us/story?id=37536512>, accessed May 26, 2025.

[51] *See* "Muslim ban timeline", *ACLU Washington*, <www.aclu-wa.org/pages/timeline-muslim-ban>, accessed January 26, 2026.

[52] Ibid.

challenged order, given its independent basis of legitimacy.[53] The four dissenting justices strongly disagreed that the disputed order was not the product of religious discrimination. In her scathing dissenting opinion, Justice Sotomayor denounced the order as an anti-Muslim policy that "masquerades behind a façade of national security concerns."[54] Moreover, Sotomayor characterized Trump's anti-Muslim animus as being based on impermissible ethnic and religious prejudice. Indeed, she noted that Trump had equated his anti-Muslim objective with Roosevelt's Second World War policy of placing Japanese Americans in detention camps.[55] In addition, Sotomayor emphasized that Trump had called for surveillance of mosques in the US, blaming terrorist attacks on, among other things, commitment to "sharia law,"[56] thus clearly placing blame for some of most heinous terrorist attacks of the current generation on a religion followed by several million Americans and a billion and a half adherents throughout the world.

Trump v Hawaii illustrates how conditions of stress linked to terrorism facilitate the shrinkage of fundamental rights in two combined ways. Because of the fear, invisibility, and randomness associated with acts of terrorism, the scope of what is considered rational measures that limit rights to enhance security can be vastly expanded. Moreover, because of the Muslim connection in a large number of attacks by global terrorists, growing prejudice against all those perceived as belonging to an ethnicity associated with Muslims and all those religiously associated with Islam can be exploited for discriminatory curtailments of fundamental rights.

In the case law relating to the governmental restrictions imposed in the fight against the COVID-19 pandemic, on the other hand, the tilt toward illiberalism seems predominantly on the side of an expansive judicial appraisal of religious-freedom rights as against proportionate, if not compelling, governmental regulation designed to control or to mitigate the spread of the pandemic. In these cases, the antagonistic interests are the secular ones embodied in regulations based on medical and public health expertise for purposes of advancing the fight against the virus, stacked against the interests of certain religious groups to congregate in large numbers for prayers or other collective religious pursuits. As we shall see, the contrast between the French Council of State, which adjudicated in favor of the public health regulations, and the US Supreme Court, which upheld the challenges brought by the Catholic Church and an ultra-Orthodox Jewish organization, is rather striking, particularly since the equities among the respective contending parties appear quite similar.

As already noted, some of the contentious political confrontations surrounding pandemic-related regulation in the US did not refer to religion. Because of US

[53] *Trump v Hawaii* 138 S Ct 2392, 2417–18 (2018).
[54] Ibid, at 2433.
[55] Ibid, at 2435–36.
[56] Ibid, at 2437.

federalism, public health regulation is primarily entrusted to the states, with broad powers delegated to the latter's governors. At the same time, federal public health administrative bodies have issued guidance measures, such as the wearing of masks and keeping social distance, during the course of the COVID-19 pandemic. Fairly early in the course of the pandemic, Trump and many Republican governors railed against the prevailing federal health guidelines in the name of freedom and with a view to reopening the economy in spite of the US then experiencing the worst known death toll from the pandemic. Trump was embracing a populist stance that went as far as urging resistance against lockdown policies adopted by Democratic governors, consistent with the then-prevailing federal public health guidance.[57] Within this setting, freedom of religion claims were advanced alongside secular freedom of movement and of association claims, while certain religious groups, as already noted, openly defied mandatory regulations meant to address the ravages caused by the pandemic.

It is in this context that the US Supreme Court considered the freedom of religion claims advanced by the Catholic Church and an ultra-Orthodox Jewish group against the governor of New York, a Democrat, who had restricted attendance at houses of worship to ten or twenty-five people, depending on the prevalence of the virus in the relevant neighborhood. In a 5–4 decision, the Court found the restrictions discriminatory and hence in violation of freedom of religion rights.[58] A few weeks earlier, and on facts for all relevant purposes equivalent, the French Council of State held a total prohibition against holding masses at Catholic churches throughout France in the midst of an acute spread of the pandemic to be consistent with freedom of religion.[59] What accounts for this striking difference was that the US Supreme Court majority found the restrictions involved to be disproportionate, whereas the French adjudicators found very similar restrictions to be entirely proportionate.

Before looking into some key aspects of both decisions, it should be underscored that increases in freedom of religion should be encouraged under institutional secularism unless that would lead to the disproportionate infringement of other fundamental rights or the frustration of important secular government objectives. As we shall now see, the US decision, particularly as set against the populist resistance against public health experts led by Trump, looms as clearly disproportionate and, in an important respect, inconsistent with Supreme Court precedent. In comparison, the French decision evinces a judicial deference to public health authorities that seems entirely appropriate under the circumstances.

[57] *See* Courtney Subramanian, "Trump accuses Democratic governors of keeping lockdowns because of 'politics' as he visits Michigan," *USA Today*, May 21, 2020, <www.usatoday.com/story/news/politics/2020/05/21/coronavirus-trump-blasts-democrats-over-lockdowns-michigan-visit/5235638002/>.

[58] *See Roman Catholic Diocese of Brooklyn v Cuomo* 141 S Ct 63 (2020).

[59] *See Conseil d'Etat*, Judgment 445825 (November 7, 2020).

There are two aspects of the conditions of stress associated with the COVID-19 pandemic that were prone to increasing antagonism within the societies involved. The first is fear and uncertainty concerning the virus that is compounded by the various reversals and adjustments of public health policies as the science on the novel virus evolved over time.[60] The second condition, in turn, which is exacerbated by the first, is the heavy psychological and economic toll that prolonged confinement and drastic curtailment of socializing inflict on the citizenry. Furthermore, these two conditions taken together add challenges of their own to the sense of proportionality throughout the affected society's public and private spheres.

Even with these caveats, the US Supreme Court's decision is remarkable to the extent that the Court's majority substitutes its evaluation of the pertinence of the challenged restrictions for that of the medical and public health experts. Moreover, the Court's finding of religious discrimination was based on a very skewed reading of the major precedent on the subject. On the factual plane, the majority of justices found that New York had a discriminatory animus against churches and synagogues because it did not limit the number of individuals in secular places such as grocery or liquor stores.[61] In the dissenting justices' estimation, the latter analogy was inapt as the congregation in close proximity in confined spaces and the singing associated with religious services is more akin to lectures, concerts, movie showings, spectator sports, and theatrical performances, where large groups of people gather next to one another for extended periods of time.[62] And as stressed by the dissenters, these latter activities were as much or more restricted by New York state than religious services.[63] On the precedential plane, on the other hand, the Court majority relies on *Church of Lukumi Babalu Aye, Inc. v Hialeah*,[64] a case that held that a law that prohibited animal sacrifices by the members of the very small group that practiced the Afro-Cuban Santeria religion was discriminatory as almost all other animal killings were permitted. By being thus singled out, the Santeria religion was uniquely burdened in a way that no other religious or secular group had to endure. As there is no reasonable medical or public health argument that virus spread is less likely at a crowded church service than at a comparably attended lecture or concert, it is clear that there was no religious singling out in *Cuomo*, in sharp contrast to the facts in *Lukumi*.

[60] *See* Alec J. Kacew, et al., "Cross-sectional evaluation of medical reversals among National Institute of Health guideline practices implemented during the COVID-19 pandemic: How often did experts err in a time of crisis?," *BMJ Open*, December 20, 2024, <https://pmc.ncbi.nlm.nih.gov/articles/PMC11667299/>.

[61] *Roman Catholic Diocese of Brooklyn v Cuomo* 141 S Ct 63, 66 (2020) (per curiam).

[62] Ibid, at 79 (Sotomayor J, dissenting).

[63] Ibid.

[64] *Church of Lukumi Babalu Aye, Inc. v Hialeah* 508 US 520 (1993).

As indicated, the equities in the French case are, for the most part, analogous to those in the US case. Two differences, however, are worthy of mention. The first is that French regulation included a fairly strict confinement at home imposition, with no equivalent in New York. The second difference is that the French regulation allowed for the opening of libraries and schools that seem more akin to lectures and concerts than to grocery and liquor stores. In terms of proportionality, the confinement requirement weighs in favor of the government as church attendance requires travel away from home. In contrast, the opening of schools and libraries pulls in the opposite direction. Nevertheless, the Council of State specified that the French government had developed specific regulations for limiting the spread of the virus in schools and libraries. In view of that, and of allowing churches, in spite of the mass prohibition, to conduct funeral services and marriages for a limited number of people, the Council found the government's public health-based regulations to be overall proportionate.

F. Can Institutional Secularism's Two Essentials, Pluralism and Independence from Purely Religious Truth, Be Constitutionally Salvaged Standing on Their Own?

As illustrated above, scores of illiberal attacks have cast institutional secularism as non-neutral, anti-religious, favoring some religions over others, or covering for ideological secularism to hide its dominance in the war of ideologies. Accordingly, one may wonder whether the combination of repoliticized religion and the post-modern "disenchantment of reason"—which casts reason as purely instrumental and thus without any persuasive normative force—has made portentous dents against one of the Enlightenment's principal mainstays. Leaving that question aside as beyond the scope of our present inquiry, we will assume, for the sake of argument, that the critics are right and that institutional secularism ought to be set aside as the constitutional gold standard. In that case, the fight against illiberalism and its reframing of fundamental rights in general, and religion-based rights in particular, depends on finding alternative grounds of justification for the constitutional protection of pluralism combined with the prohibition of imposition of a particular religion's truth on those who contest it.

Upon reflection, the alternative grounds in question can be found through reliance on ideological secularism—understood here as committed to public reason in the realm of politics—and reliance on science to further society's health and material welfare objectives—as one conception of the good among many that are deserving of protection under freedom of religion constitutional rights. Indeed, although, as already mentioned, ideological secularism has come under sharp attack from certain religious perspectives, for the foreseeable future, secularism seems bound to comprise a large contingent of adherents in most contemporary constitutional democracies. And because of this, secularism would have to be constitutionally contended with. Secularism would therefore lose its role as a constitutional marker, but it would instead prominently figure as a major conception of the good competing against many others within the same polity (Rosenfeld 2014: 81–83).

In this scenario, ideological secularism would require freedom *of* religion as well as freedom *from* religion (Rosenfeld 2014: 82). The latter is necessary even within the ambit of institutional secularism, but the former only comes into play when secularism is treated as if it were one religion among many. Furthermore, from a substantive standpoint, ideological secularism aims for the achievement of the greatest possible freedom to pursue all avenues that may lead to the amelioration of human life and well-being on this earth. This requires extensive freedoms of conscience, speech, expression, and scientific inquiry and experimentation that are only subject to limitations that would be constitutionally warranted if they could be justified under a public-reason standard that disregards arguments based on transcendent, metaphysical, or religious reasons. Thus, from an ideological secularist perspective, religion-based objections to abortion, stem cell experimentation, in vitro fertilization, cloning, assisted suicide or euthanasia, and the like should not be entitled to become constitutionally enshrined. Similarly, all religion-based arguments relating to sexual mores, gender differentiation, and sexual orientation ought not enjoy any privilege in official constitutional discourse, deliberation, or decision-making.

Consistent with its commitment to pluralism and to its rejection of rule based on the truth of any one among competing religions and non-religious ideologies, liberal democratic constitutionalism should accord ideological secularism the same right of inclusion and accommodation as it does competing conceptions of the good. In one area, however, ideological secularism should enjoy priority over some of its religious counterparts. That area encompasses the freedom of scientific research and the teaching of science in state-operated schools. Moreover, the reason for this priority is that in the bulk of contemporary constitutional democracies, the vast majority of proponents of religious world views rely on scientific research and on the practical applications of the latter. Therefore, opposition to science on religious grounds would not defy logic but would amount to what philosophers call a "performative contradiction" (Habermas 1990: 80). A religion that accepts and makes use of science in the areas of health, communications, transportation, etc. engages in a performative contradiction when it seeks to prevent, or to interfere with, the pursuit of science by proponents of other conceptions of the good, such as secularism. In other words, the proponent of the religion that wishes to suppress science in part ought to realize that he cannot have it both ways—e.g., prohibit the teaching of evolution theory in public schools while benefiting from the latest medical advances in public hospitals—once he understands that the realm of scientific discovery and application has a unity and integrity of its own and, in a large number of cases, that his own religion requires recourse to some or all available medical means to save or prolong life.[65] As a consequence of this, secularism's pro-science and religion's partially anti-science stances are not equivalent, and the latter ought to give way to the former.[66]

In sum, as one conception of the good among many, ideological secularism requires equal consideration in the fashioning and interpretation of constitutional norms in order to satisfy the requirement of pluralism inherent in democratic constitutionalism. Also, to the extent that religions partially accept and benefit from science, the constitutional pluralist ethos requires giving priority to freedom of scientific inquiry in all its multifaceted dimensions. Moreover, these two fundamental requirements regarding secularism, namely equal consideration and freedom of scientific inquiry, should furnish criteria to determine whether or not any particular reframing of fundamental rights from any illiberal standpoint, including those deriving from religious nationalism or pluralism, is consistent with the minimum requirements of contemporary liberal democratic constitutionalism. In other words, any religious understanding or reformulation of a fundamental right that fails to give equal consideration due to secularism or to the integrity of science would exceed the acceptable bounds within contemporary liberal democratic constitutionalism, regardless of whether the latter adheres to institutional secularism or properly accounts for ideological secularism.

[65] Orthodox Judaism, for example, requires that all available means be used to save or prolong life. *See* Robinson 2001: 200.

[66] A religion that rejected science in whole and that forbade the use or benefit of any of the products of science could well avoid all inconsistency and hence all vulnerability to the secular claim under consideration. However, the most populous religions in Western constitutional democracies, Christianity, Islam, and Judaism, all accept many important benefits of modern science in areas such as health, communications, or transportation.

PART II

APPLICATIONS: ILLIBERAL AND ANTI-PLURALIST RECASTING OF FUNDAMENTAL CONSTITUTIONAL AND HUMAN RIGHTS IN THE NAME OF RELIGION

5
Secularism as Religious Majoritarianism

This chapter tackles two distinct but closely connected phenomena: the reinforcement of the privileges of religious majorities and the marginalization of denominational minorities. The fact that a country's religious majority enjoys a position of privilege does not necessarily translate into a disadvantage for minority religions. Indeed, some commentators have argued that minorities are often better off in countries, such as Italy, where the majority denomination enjoys a privileged position than in strictly secular constitutional systems, such as France (Cole Durham 2013). As we have seen in the previous chapters, however, in recent decades religious majorities have become increasingly politicized in different parts of the world, and majority religions have regained a paramount role in conceptualizing national identities. In this respect, as we have seen, the emphasis is often placed not on the transcendent nature of religion but rather on its cultural dimension. Thus, religion undergoes a process of secularization and semantic disarticulation, and becomes an implicit mainstay engrained in the secular nation's tradition and culture. This process leads to two consequences: on the one hand, it fosters the return of majority religion culture and tradition in the public sphere, challenging the principle of separation between church and state. The premise is that states must recognize that the national religious inheritance is not just one among other denominations, but rather an element of civic cohesion. What follows is that the historical national religion should enjoy preferential treatment, while other denominations should simply be tolerated. On the other hand, the culturalization

Politicized Religion and the Reframing of Fundamental Rights. Susanna Mancini and Michel Rosenfeld, Oxford University Press. DOI: 10.1093/9780191982149.003.0007

of religion facilitates the othering and the marginalization of minority religions, on the grounds of their incompatibility with the national culture.

In Section A, the chapter traces the analogies between the secularization of Hinduism in India and of Christianity in Europe, through a comparison of the *rationale* of the "*Hindutva* cases" decided by the Indian Supreme Court, and of laws and judicial cases regarding the display of Christian symbols in the European public sphere.

Section B moves to the analysis of two particularly effective strategies through which religious minorities are marginalized in different contexts: the regulation of minority religious attire and religion-based discrimination in immigration and citizenship law.

Finally, Section C focuses on the shifting role of Islam in defining national belonging in Turkey, from the birth of the Kemalist Republic to Prime Minister Erdoğan's Islamist populist project.

A. Reinforcing the Privileges of Religious Majorities

(i) The Secularization of Hinduism: The Hindutva Cases in India

India constitutes an example of a system where constitutional secularism has undergone a systematic attack by a nationalist party, the Hindu Right, which has sought to redefine its significance to suit its majoritarian political agenda—that is, the installation of religion and culture as primary attributes of nationalism and citizenship identity.[1]

Indian secularism differs from its Western counterparts in two fundamental ways. First, it does not pursue the ideal of strict separation and neutrality but, rather, a "principled distance" between religion and the state, which entitles the latter to robustly intervene in religious matters, particularly in the affairs of the country's majority religion. Second, Indian secularism, by striking a balance between individual religious rights and the claims of religious communities, does not entail the absolute confinement of religion in the private sphere.[2] This resonates with Hinduism's emphasis on religious practices rather than on religious belief. Because practices have a fundamental collective dimension, their preeminence naturally entails the valorization of religious communities (Bhargava 2007: 20).

[1] Sharma 2011; Jaffrelot 1998 (discussing that India, as conceived by Vinayak Damodar Savarkar (one of the intellectual founders of the *Hindutva* movement), "cannot be dissociated from Hindu culture and the Hindu people").

[2] Article 25 of the Indian Constitution protects all persons' freedom of conscience and religion but also confers to the state the power to regulate and even restrict "any economic, financial, political or other secular activity which may be associated with religious practice," as well as an exclusive entitlement for the "social welfare and reform or the throwing open of Hindu religious institutions of a public character to all classes and sections of Hindus." India Constitution, art 25(1)–(2)(b).

While the distinctive characters of Indian secularism are crucial to understand its implementations and applications, they should not obscure the fact that the country adopted a secular constitution for reasons that are fully comparable to those that prompted Western countries, such as France and the United States, to also enshrine secularism in their constitutions. As Rajeev Bhargava explains, "secularism, anywhere in the world, means a separation of organized religion from organized political power inspired by a specific set of values". As we have seen in the preceding pages, these values boil down to protecting individuals from religious oppression, ensuring that they enjoy freedom of religion and conscience, as well as setting the conditions for the peaceful coexistence of different conceptions of the good within the polity. Different systems may "select different elements from the stock of values that give separation its point . . . [or] place different weights on the same values" (Bhargava 2007). In all cases, however, the aim is to ensure the freedom and equality of all citizens in a pluralistic polity.

The Hindu Right, which emerged in the nineteenth century as a nationalist force relying on Hindu culture to oppose colonialism, has systematically pushed to "redefine the meaning and parameters of the various components of secularism" (Kapur 2020: 43). To this end, the Hindu Right has put forward three lines of reasoning. First, it challenges the special protection provided to religious minorities on the ground that this protection contravenes the principle of equality. This constitutes a direct blow to two fundamental tenets of the Indian Constitution: "contextual secularism," which rejects the notion of strict neutrality and equidistance; and a substantive notion of equality. The Hindu Right argues that the traditional accommodation of religious minorities (including through personal laws) violates formal equality and the "true spirit" of secularism, pushing, as Ratna Kapur explains, to establish "an unmodified majoritarianism whereby the majority Hindu community becomes the norm against which all others are to be judged and treated" (Kapur 2020). The second line of argument put forward by the Hindu Right relies on the construction of Hinduism as the only religion that is compatible with secularism. Unlike universal religions, such as Islam and Christianity, that rely on proselytism, Hinduism is supposedly committed to secular values, such as religious freedom and tolerance. Hence, "only Hindus are truly secular [citizens]" (Kapur 2020).

Finally, the Hindu Right has sought to redefine the content of Hinduism in order to expand its protection under the right of freedom of religion to the detriment of religious minorities. Specifically, it has put forward the notion that among the thousands of Hindu gods, Lord Ram holds a superior status. While this view is highly contested by historians in India (Udayakumar 1997: 23), it has allowed the Hindu Right to justify the destruction of a sixteenth-century mosque by a large mob comprised of members from various Hindu organizations on the ground that it had been built on Lord Ram's birthplace (Ayodhya), and that worship at this particular spot constitutes a fundamental tenet of Hinduism, and is therefore protected by the right to religious freedom (Kapur 2014: 306–09). This incident occasioned a series of cases that were litigated before the Supreme Court and that marked a shift in its jurisprudence.[3] The Indian government acquired the land where the mosque had been destroyed with the purpose of building a Hindu temple alongside a new mosque. The land acquisition was challenged by a Muslim petitioner on the ground that it violated the principle of secularism and the right of religious freedom of Indian Muslims. The Court, however, rejected both claims and concluded that a mosque is not an essential part of the practice of the religion of Islam,[4] and that prayer by Muslims could be offered anywhere, even in the open.[5]

Indeed, for many years, the Supreme Court had upheld the traditional significance of Indian "contextual secularism." As the Ayodhya cases show, however, starting in the mid-1990s, its case law progressively absorbed the agenda of the Hindu Right, ultimately altering the significance of equality, tolerance, and freedom of religion in India, as well as the conceptualization of citizenship (Kapur 2020: 43–46). The Supreme Court expanded the scope of Hinduism, conceptualizing it not just as a religion but as the "way of life" of the entire country,[6] while concurrently dealing restrictively with Islam. The shift in the Court's case law is also clearly noticeable in a series of cases concerning the legitimacy of speeches appealing to *Hindutva* (an ideology that seeks to define Indian culture in terms of Hindu values) in the context of political elections. The Supreme Court held that speeches appealing to Hinduism and *Hindutva* during election campaigns do not breach election laws or the Constitution. The speeches were constitutionally challenged not only on the grounds of appealing to voters on the basis of the candidate's Hindu religion but also for their extremely vituperative and derogatory character, and, therefore, for having the propensity to incite hatred and enmity between religious

[3] *See* Jaffrelot 2007: 287–88 (citing Vazirani 1991, an interview with Lal Krishna Advani—the seventh Deputy Prime Minister of India and a co-founder of the BJP—in which Advani opines that the Court's jurisprudence over the Ayodhya controversy is not sufficient settlement from the Hindu Right's perspective).

[4] "The essential practices test has been used by the court to decide a variety of cases. These can broadly be classified under a few heads. First, the court has taken recourse to this test to decide which religious practices are eligible for constitutional protection. Second, the court has used the test to adjudicate the legitimacy of legislation for managing religious institutions. Finally, the court has employed this doctrine to judge the extent of independence that can be enjoyed by religious denominations." Sen 2020: 226.

[5] *Dr. M. Ismail Faruqui v Union of India* AIR 1995 SC 605.

[6] In *Sastri Yagnapurushadji v Muldas Brudardas Vaishya*—the first decision where the Supreme Court held that Hinduism is not a religion but merely a way of life: "[w]hen we think of the Hindu religion, we find it difficult, if not impossible, to define Hindu religion or even adequately describe it. Unlike other religions in the world, the Hindu religion does not claim any one prophet; it does not worship any one God; it does not subscribe to any one dogma; it does not believe in any one philosophic concept; it does not follow any one set of religious rites or performances; in fact, it does not appear to satisfy the narrow traditional features of any religion or creed. It may broadly be described *as a way of life* and nothing more." *Sastri Yagnapurushadji v Muldas Brudardas Vaishya* 3 SCR 242 (1966) (emphasis added). This pronouncement also paved the way for the Supreme Court to later hold that not only Hinduism, but even *Hindutva*, is merely a way of life of the entire subcontinent.

communities. Yet, the Court gave a broad and expansive meaning to "Hinduism" and "*Hindutva*," and asserted that the appeals to *Hindutva* merely refer to "the way of life of people in the subcontinent [rather than] an attitude hostile to [] persons practi[c]ing [] other [religions or an appeal to religion]," and that it was "difficult to appreciate how . . . [the right wing's position could] be assumed to . . . be equated with narrow fundamentalist Hindu religious bigotry."[7] According to the Court, the appeals to *Hindutva* "promote secularism or emphasise the way of life of the Indian people and the Indian culture."[8] This assertion not only drastically reduces the rich tradition of Hinduism to its interpretation by the Hindu Right, but it also leaves "no room for other non-Hindu ways of being Indian" (Kapur 2020: 45).

(ii) The Secularization of Christianity: Icons and Crucifixes in the European Public Sphere

Attacks on constitutional secularism often involve struggles over the presence of the majority religion's symbols in public institutions, such as courtrooms and state schools.

Indeed, religious symbols play a key role in identity-related dynamics. Thanks to their capacity of evoking unquestioned belongings, they allow for the construction of simplified and artificial identities, and thus provide clear-cut dividing lines by building unity within the "people" and the nation while strengthening divisions with those who do not belong. Religious symbols often play into the hands of nationalists and populists as catalyzers of aggression because they are capable of expressing and generating a primitive intellectual and relational level of human development at the level of blind fixations and belongings (Lombardi Vallauri 2005: 14). Religious symbols also visibly "mark" the public sphere. Their presence—or their banning—symbolizes the prevailing power relations between different cultures and identities. Thus, for example, the display of Christian symbols, such as icons or the crucifix, in state schools or courtrooms identifies the "official" state culture with that of the majority religion. By the same token, the exclusion of minority symbols—such as Muslim traditional attire—marks the marginalization of the culture that such symbols are assumed to represent.

A particularly salient example of the use of religion as a divisive marker of national identity was the controversy over the display of Orthodox icons in Romanian public schools, which occurred between 2006 and 2008. In 2006, petitioner Emil Moise challenged the display of religious icons in his child's public school before the Romanian National Council for Combating Discrimination. The Council agreed that the massive display of icons in state schools violated the principle of

[7] *Dr. Ramesh Yeshwant Prabhoo v Shri Prabhakar Kashinath Kunte* AIR 1996 SC 1113, 1129.
[8] Ibid.

state neutrality and was potentially discriminatory. It thus advised the Ministry of Education to restrictively regulate the presence of icons in public schools, enabling their display only during the teaching of religion.[9] The Bucharest Court of Justice rejected the Ministry's challenge of the Council's decision on the ground that the latter was consistent with human rights standards and religious pluralism.[10] In 2008, however, the Romanian Supreme Court of Justice quashed the Bucharest Court's decision and confirmed the legitimacy of the display of icons in public schools.[11] The case triggered a heated controversy, exposing a deep division within Romanian society concerning the role of Orthodox Christianity in defining the country's national identity. Romanian media widely covered the icons issue and the debate reached an almost apocalyptic dimension, as attested by a series of headlines issued between 2006 and 2008, such as "The War of Icons," "The Scandal of Icons Exiled from Schools," "The Trial of Icons—Part of a Plan to Destroy Faith," and "The Renaissance of Iconoclasm, the First Step to the Pursuit of Christianity in Romania" (Horváth & Bakó 2009: 189). Unsurprisingly, the Orthodox Church, which has become an important ally of the political class as well as one of the most respected institutions in Romania since the fall of the communist regime (Horváth & Bakó 2009: 190–92), vocally advocated for the presence of icons in public schools. Civil society became deeply involved in the controversy, and a special Coalition for the Observance of Religious Faith was put together by hundreds of non-governmental organizations for the purpose of advocating for the presence of icons in state schools (Horváth & Bakó 2009: 191). According to Gizela Horváth and Rozália Bakó, who undertook an empirical analysis of the arguments, the rhetoric, and the language used in the context of the icons debate, there were some key differences between the factions supporting the icons and those opposing them. The latter relied mainly on human rights arguments—specifically, on equality rights, religious freedom, minority protection, and children's rights—and on the secular character of the state.[12] To the contrary, pro-icon advocates tended to put forward either moral arguments—equating the Orthodox religion with morality—or, more often, arguments based on the overlapping of religion and national identity

[9] Consiliul Național pentru Combaterea Discriminării (CNCD) [National Council for Combating Discrimination] Decision No 323 (2006) (Romania).

[10] Curtea de Apel București (CA București) [Bucharest Court of Appeals] Civil Sentence No 1685, File No 1327/2/2007 (Romania).

[11] Înalta Curte de Casație și Justiție (ICCJ) [High Court of Cassation and Justice] Decision No 2398/2008, File No 1327/2/2007 (2008) (Romania).

[12] While the Romanian Constitution does not explicitly state the secular character of the state, it implicitly affirms the principle of separation of church and state. Indeed, Article 29 (on "freedom of conscience") protects the individual's rights to freedom of conscience and to the manifestation of religious belief, as well as the autonomy of religious denominations. The Constitution does not grant the Orthodox Church, by far the country's largest, any special status. It guarantees non-discrimination based on religious belief or membership, as well as the protection of the confessional component of the identity of national minorities. *See* Constituția României [Constitution] art 29 (Rom.). Moreover, Law 489/2006 on Religious Freedom and Denomination declares that the state is neutral. *See* Andreescu 2008: 147.

(Horváth & Bakó 2009: 200–201). Icons were "presented as constitutive parts of the soul of the Romanians . . . [using] 'organicist metaphors': icons cannot be torn out of the soul of Romanians" (Horváth & Bakó 2009: 202). The controversy was often presented as the result of a conspiracy against the Romanian church and the Romanian people, led by foreign forces loyal to George Soros (Horváth & Bakó 2009: 201), and involved personal attacks on public figures such as journalists and civil rights activists, who were portrayed as Bolsheviks, extremists, or even Taliban (Horváth & Bakó 2009: 202).

The high-profile *Lautsi* case, decided by the European Court of Human Rights (ECtHR) in 2011, and briefly discussed in Chapter 1, also sparked controversy over the display of Christian symbols in state schools. The case concerned the legitimacy of the display of crucifixes in Italian public schools under the European Convention on Human Rights (ECHR). Prior to reaching the ECtHR, the case had been litigated before the Italian administrative courts, which, in order to justify the presence of crucifixes against the backdrop of a secular constitution, had relied on similar arguments to those put forward by the Indian Supreme Court in its jurisprudence analyzed above.[13] The crucifix was declared to embody social and cultural values shared by believers and non-believers, and to evoke the fundamental principles of the Italian legal order, including the principle of secularism. Indeed, according to the Italian courts, inherent in Christianity are the ideas of tolerance and freedom, which constitute the basis of a secular state. Therefore, it would be a paradox to exclude a Christian symbol from the public domain in the name of a principle such as secularism, which is actually rooted in, and wholly compatible with, the Christian religion. Just as in India, where Hinduism has been interpreted extensively by the courts as the way of life of the entire secular subcontinent, Italian courts have envisioned Christianity as representing "the principles of dignity, tolerance and religious freedom and therefore . . . the very foundation of a secular state."[14] Specifically, Italian courts have characterized the crucifix as "the symbol of our history and our culture and, consequently, of our identity . . . and also of the principle of state secularism."[15] Conversely, akin to the Indian courts, Italian judges have cast doubts on the compatibility of Islam with the secular state, alluding to "the problematic relationship between certain states and the *Islamic* religion,"[16] as well as to "the need to reaffirm, even symbolically, our identity," in order to "avoid a clash of civilizations."[17] Finally, Italian judges have emphasized the importance of displaying crucifixes in state schools to teach "*non-European*

[13] Tribunale Amministrativo Regionale per il Veneto, Sez III, Sentenza, March 22, 2005, No. 1110, para 16 (*Vittorino da Feltre* crucifix case).

[14] Ibid at para 11.6 (translation by authors); Cons. Stato, 15 febbraio 2006, Decisione Sez. 4575/03-2482/04 (It.).

[15] *Vittorino da Feltre* crucifix case, n 13, at para 12.4 (translation by authors).

[16] Ibid at para 10.1.

[17] Ibid at para 12.6.

pupils . . . to reject all forms of *fundamentalism*."[18] In sum, in both the Indian and Italian cases, the country's majority religion is assumed to be naturally inclusive and encompassing of the ideas of tolerance and freedom, which constitute the basis of a secular state.[19]

The Italian case echoes an earlier decision by the Bavarian Supreme Court, which, in 1991, had similarly separated the religious from the cultural significance of the crucifix, holding that its display in a public school was "not the expression of a conviction of a belief bound to a specific confession," but, rather, "an essential object of the general Christian-occidental tradition and common property of the Christian-occidental cultural circle."[20]

In both the Italian and the Bavarian cases, the crucifix loses its specific (religious) value and becomes a general symbol of civilization and culture, apt to be freely used by the state to meet the needs of the political community. This results in the definitive blurring of the line between secularism and religion. On the one hand, secularism is interpreted in a way that makes it compatible with granting privileges to Christianity, and with the overlap between the religious and the temporal spheres; that is to say, this interpretation denies the very possibility of a clear-cut distinction between the realm of faith and that of reason, and of ruling the public sphere according to the dictates of reason. On the other hand, the use of the crucifix by state authorities produces government interference in Church matters, which is contrary to the principle of separation. This last point was actually stressed in the German Federal Constitutional Court in its 1995 judgment striking down the relevant Bavarian law on the grounds that the pressure to learn 'under the cross' is in conflict with the neutrality of the state in religious matters.[21] Moreover, according to the Court, not considering the crucifix as a religious symbol connected with a specific religion violates the religious autonomy of Christians and actually produces a desecration of the crucifix itself.[22] A similar argument was put forward by the late US Supreme Court Justice Brennan in his dissenting opinion in *Lynch v Donnelly*.[23] In *Lynch*, the Court's majority concluded that the city of Pawtucket, RI, had not violated the Establishment Clause by including a crèche in its annual Christmas display, located in a public park within the downtown shopping district. In Brennan's view, however, "The crèche has been relegated to the role of a neutral harbinger of the holiday season, useful for commercial purposes, but devoid of any inherent meaning and incapable of enhancing the religious tenor of a display of which it is an integral part. The importance of the Court's decision is to encourage

[18] Ibid (emphasis added).
[19] Bhargava 2007.
[20] Bayerischer Verwaltungsgerichtshof (BAYVGH) [Bavarian Higher Administrative Court] June 3, 1991, 122 Bayerische Verwaltungsblatter (BAYVBL) 751, 751–54 (Ger.).
[21] Bundesverfassungsgericht (BVerfG) [Federal Constitutional Court] May 16, 1995 (Kruzifix-Urteil), 93 Entscheidungen des Bundesverfassungsgerichts (BVerfGE) 1 (FRG).
[22] Ibid.
[23] *Lynch v Donnelly* 465 US 668, 728 (1984).

the use of the crèche in a municipally sponsored display, a setting where Christians feel constrained in acknowledging its symbolic meaning and non-Christians feel alienated by its presence."[24]

The *Lautsi* case acquired a European dimension after Ms. Lautsi challenged the display of the crucifix before the ECtHR. The Court first condemned Italy on the ground that such a display violated freedom of religion and the rights of parents to educate children according to their beliefs.[25] This decision immediately became highly controversial, turning the Court into the target of virulent attacks. The mobilization that followed exposed a deep division among the Member States of the Council of Europe concerning the role of Christianity in the European public sphere and in defining European identity. It also showcased a versatile use of the rhetoric of religious nationalism, which applies to single countries as well as to Europe as a political unit. Thus, the crucifix went from symbolizing Italian national identity to representing European identity, the two coinciding as challenged by immigration and secularization. Accordingly, both Italy and Europe became envisioned as somehow projecting the ethos of the same religious identity on the scale of the nation-state as well as on that of Europe's distinct transnational culture, as overlapping political units that are framed as Christian imagined communities (Anderson 1983).

The ten most deeply confessional Member States of the Council of Europe intervened in the case supporting Italy's request to overturn the decision,[26] including the countries most often condemned by the ECtHR for discriminating against religious minorities (Russia, Greece, Bulgaria, and Cyprus). This led a commentator to stress how "Italy . . . has defended the Central-Eastern Europe of traditions against the Western Europe of pluralistic neutrality."[27] The *Lautsi* case also attests to the emergence of a network of right-wing actors and lobbies that work to defend and expand the privileges of Christian majorities in Europe (McCrudden 2015). The ECtHR's Chamber decision was reversed by its Grand Chamber,[28] thanks to the combined effort of a "variegated coalition of actors" ranging from the Vatican to Russia, as well as to American Conservative Evangelicals, whose experience in religious litigation served as a model for their European counterparts (Annicchino 2011: 213). Mr Puppinck, the Director of the European Center for Law and Justice,[29] which submitted a brief advocating for reversing the Chamber

[24] Ibid.

[25] *Lautsi v Italy* [GC] App No 30814/06 (ECtHR, March 18, 2011) 2011-III ECHR 66, paras 4, 32.

[26] The intervening countries were Armenia, Bulgaria, Cyprus, Greece, Lithuania, Malta, Monaco, Romania, the Russian Federation, and San Marino.

[27] Marco Ventura, "La Tradizione come Diritto," *Corriere Della Sera*, March 19, 2011, 19 (translation by the authors).

[28] *Lautsi*, 2011-III ECHR 97, para. 77.

[29] The Strasburg-based European Center for Law and Justice (ECLJ) is the European branch of the American Center for Law and Justice (ACLJ), founded in 1990 by fundamentalist Evangelical Pat Robertson. It is funded by the ACLJ and it pursues a similar agenda, mainly focused on opposing reproductive rights and LGTBQ equality, and on expanding the privileges of Christian majorities. *See*

decision, openly called for an "Alliance against secularism"[30] to wage a "battle of cultural identity."[31] In his opinion: "*Lautsi* is a symbol of the current conflict regarding the future of Europe's religious and cultural identity. The conflict contains on one side, proponents of the complete secularization of Europe, and on the other, those who desire an open Europe, one that is faithful to its true identity and historical roots. Proponents of secularization see secularism, however, as a solution to managing religious pluralism. Moreover, they perceive pluralism as an argument that justifies the imposition of secularism. The so-called 'religious neutrality of society' ('secularization') is nothing but, concretely, the 'de-Christianization' of European culture and society."[32]

Puppinck accused the European institutions of "promot[ing] a cultural model in which the absence of values (neutrality) and relativism (pluralism) are values in themselves. These institutions thus support a policy that wishes to be post-religious and post-identity, in short, postmodern; this policy seeks to exclude all other systems, claiming, in essence, to be a philosophical monopoly."[33]

In order to counter this scenario, he stressed the importance of joining forces with the Russian Orthodox authorities, who had been very vocal concerning the importance of reversing the first *Lautsi* judgment,[34] and, more generally, of pursuing a "strategic alliance between Catholics and Orthodox" Christians to join in defense of the tradition "against secularism, liberalism and relativism prevailing in modern Europe."[35]

About Us (European Centre for Law and Justice) <https://eclj.org/about-us> [https://perma.cc/LA58-3C2W], accessed 26 May 2025.

[30] Grégor Puppinck, "Lautsi v. Italy: An alliance against secularism," *L'Osservatore Romano*, July 28, 2010, <www.eclj.org/pdf/ECLJ-LautsivItaly-crucifix-case-20110315.pdf> [https://perma.cc/A9LR-NTFN], accessed June 22, 2025.

[31] Grégor Puppinck, *Lautsi v. Italy: The Leading Case on Majority Religions in European Secular States* (unpublished manuscript, October 3–6, 2010) 1.

[32] Puppinck, n 30, at 2.

[33] Ibid at 2–3.

[34] Patriarch Kyril of Moscow had written to the then-Prime Minister of Italy, Silvio Berlusconi, offering his support in the *Lautsi* affair: "The Christian heritage in Italy and other countries in Europe should not become a matter to be considered by European human rights institutions. Christian religious symbols present in the public space in Europe are part of the common European identity without which neither the past nor the present or the future of this continent are thinkable. The pretext of ensuring the secular nature of a state should not be used to assert an anti-religious ideology, which apparently violates peace in the community, discriminating against the religious majority in Europe which is Christian." Annicchino 2011: 217 (citing "Italy's ambassador to Moscow thanks Moscow patriarchate for support in getting the case of Lautsi reviewed," *Russian Orthodox Church Department for External Church Relations*, June 23, 2011, <https://mospat.ru/en/2011/06/23/news43653/> [https://perma.cc/KW4N-YQUL], accessed June 26, 2025.

[35] Puppinck, n 31, 6 (citing Robert Moynihan, "Letter #47, from Moscow, Hilarion," *Inside the Vatican*, November 11, 2009, <https://insidethevatican.com/news/newsflash/letter-47-from-moscow-hilarion/> [https://perma.cc/7NXY-64BY], accessed June 26, 2025 (quoting an interview conducted with Metropolitan of Volokolamsk, Hilarion Alfeyev).

B. The Politics of Marginalization

(i) The Regulation of Muslim Clothing in Europe

Since the late 1980s, when a handful of schoolgirls were suspended for wearing their headscarves in a French state school, Muslim women's traditional attire has become a contentious issue throughout Europe, resulting in laws and judicial decisions banning or limiting the right of Muslim women to wear the *hijab*, the *jibab*, and the *niqab*.

These controversies were initially presented as the result of the need for the liberal state to strike a balance between the competing rights of women belonging to minority groups. But while the right to manifest one's religion, including through the wearing of religious clothes, is certainly protected by the constitutions of European states and by the ECHR, it is unclear which other equally protected rights could be violated by the practice of wearing a veil.

The first generation of bills, laws, and judicial cases banning or limiting this right in various European jurisdictions relied on the inherent anti-feminist nature of Muslim clothing. This clothing—or particular types of it—has been judged as colliding with gender equality, with women's equal value, with their autonomy, dignity, and freedom. Pieces of fabric, however, cannot per se violate these rights. In these cases, the balance is struck not among competing rights but rather between religious freedom and the veil's symbolic dimension, that is, the significance attributed to it by Western courts and legislators. When the effect of this balancing exercise results in bans and limitations on the right to wear religious attire, this produces a particular kind of discrimination, in which gender, religion, and ethnicity intersect, affecting the equality of Muslim women and girls in crucial sectors, such as education, the workplace, access to the public sphere, and obtaining citizenship.

Two cases decided by the ECtHR provide paradigmatic examples of the structure of the balancing tests and their paradoxical effects. In these decisions the Court upheld, respectively, the dismissal of a teacher in Switzerland[36] and the expulsion of a medical school student in Turkey[37] for wearing the *hijab*, on the ground that wearing headscarves "[a]ppears to be imposed on women by a precept which is laid down in the Koran and . . . is hard to square with the principle of gender equality,"[38] and that it "[a]ppears difficult to reconcile the wearing of an Islamic headscarf with the message of tolerance, respect for others and, above all, equality and non-discrimination."[39]

[36] *Dahlab v Switzerland* App No 42393/98 (ECtHR, February 15, 2001).
[37] *Sahin v Turkey* App No 44774/98 (ECtHR, November 10, 2005).
[38] *Dahlab*, n 36, 1.
[39] Ibid.

The (assumedly) inherently anti-feminist nature of Muslim clothing also provided the rationale for two French laws that heavily limited the right of girls and women to wear Muslim traditional attire. The French Stasi commission, which set the ground for the enactment of the 2004 law that prohibits the display of religious symbols in state schools, asserted (without supporting this assertion with any data) that Muslim women are pressured by men from their community into wearing "modest and asexual clothes" and are stigmatized as "whores" if they do not conform.[40] Similarly, the preliminary parliamentary resolution to the 2010 law, which criminalized the full-face veil in all public spaces, refers to the veil as a "degrading garment [which] goes hand in hand with the submission of women to their spouses, to the men in their family, with the denial of their citizenship."[41] French courts have also denied citizenship to a woman, who otherwise satisfied all requirements and was married to a French national, on the ground that her practice of Islam (manifested in her wearing the *niqab* and asserting an obligation to obey her husband) was incompatible with basic French values, particularly with the principle of gender equality.[42]

To properly understand the implications of the systematic targeting of women in the proliferation of anti-Muslim measures, one has to bear in mind that the construction of Muslim women as an emblem of their backward civilization and the veil as an obstacle to cultural surrender dates back to colonial times. In colonial times, Muslim women played the role of a Trojan horse that could help the colonizers gain access to the heart and mind of the colonized subject. As the Orientalist tradition shows, veiled women occupied a special place in Western imaginaries, evoking desire, pleasure, and perdition. Then, from the early 1930s, France focused on the veil as an emblem of Algerian resistance against the colonizing power. The rhetoric of the submissive, humiliated, veiled Algerian woman became part and parcel of the official French narrative, together with the specular narrative of the backward, barbarian, despotic Muslim man. Such talk soon morphed into a specific political doctrine, which foregrounded the significance of "conquering" Muslim women: "If we want to destroy the structure of Algerian society, its capacity for resistance, we must first of all conquer the women; we must go and find them behind the veil where they hide themselves and in the houses where the men keep them out of sight" (Fanon 1965: 38). These two visions soon mingled, with Muslim women becoming simultaneously politicized as tools of resistance and objects of desire.

In this light, the significance of the contemporary attack on Muslim women's clothes cannot be disentangled from what Robin Cohen has defined as a

[40] Commission de réflexion sur l'application du principe de laïcité dans la République, *Rapport au Président de la République* ("The Stasi Commission Report") (December 11, 2003) 46.
[41] Assemblée Nationale, *Rapport d'information no. 2262, Au nom de la mission d'information sur la pratique du port du voile intégral sur le territoire national* (January 26, 2010) 14.
[42] *Conseil d'Etat*, Decision No 286798 (June 27, 2008).

"civilization panic,"[43] that is, a profound anxiety regarding the meaning of citizenship and belonging in multicultural societies. "Veiled" women are perceived as a challenge to the traditional representation of national identity, because they disrupt the mythical construction of the latter as uniform and homogeneous. Anti-veil measures target women in the workforce and, in the case of full veil bans, in all public spaces, that is, women who claim a space in the European public sphere. However, the claims to wear a veil and to be part of the European public sphere are viewed as mutually incompatible, as if people of European ancestry had a monopoly in establishing how "Europeanness" and "European tradition" should, literally, look.

"Women protective" rationales for veil bans have been the target of much criticism, which has exposed their imperialistic and patronizing nature. As an initial matter, these rationales conflate the different cultures of Eastern societies and the complex traditions of European Muslims into a homogeneous backward, misogynous, and undemocratic Oriental paradigm, which is pitted against European modernity. In this light, the claims to wear a veil and to be part of the European public sphere are deemed as mutually exclusive, and the regulation of Muslim women's bodies serves to assert Western cultural supremacy, as well as to fuel the narrative of the clash of civilizations (Mancini 2012: 411).

Women-protective rationales for veil bans have also been enforced without allowing Muslim women's voices into this debate concerning their bodies and status. The dissenting judge in the ECtHR case of *Sahin v Turkey*, cited above, stressed that while "[w]earing the headscarf is considered [by the Court] . . . to be synonymous with the alienation of women," "what is lacking in this debate is the opinion of women, both those who wear the headscarf and those who choose not to."[44] Lastly, numerous empirical studies have contradicted the assumptions behind women-protective anti-veil justifications, showcasing the manifold significances of different veiling practices from the perspective of European Muslim women (Brems 2014).

The notion that Muslim women have agency and might actually choose to wear headscarves and face veils has slowly made its way into the public debate. This, however, has not resulted in the lifting of veil bans. Rather, it has resulted in the shifting of their rationale from women-protective to society-protective, which turned religious Muslim women from victims to enemies. In other words, while the first generation of veil bans proceeded from the assumption that Muslim women needed to be protected from a religious practice that negates their equality, the new bans assume that Muslim women wear religious attire out of their own will, and

[43] Robin Cohen, "The burkini as a 'civilization panic,'" *Kellogg College, University of Oxford* (blog), September 26, 2016, <www.academia.edu/28722763/The_burkini_ban_as_a_civilizational_panic>, accessed September 29, 2025.

[44] *Sahin v Turkey*, n 37, para 11 (Tulkens J, dissenting).

cast them as emblems of an irreconcilable, anti-democratic Islamic other, which threatens European fundamental values. This shift is particularly evident in the recent case law of both the ECtHR and the European Court of Justice (ECJ).

Between 2010 and 2011, France and Belgium adopted laws criminalizing the wearing of facial veils in all public places.[45] These laws were upheld, respectively, by the French Constitutional Council and the Belgian Constitutional Court, on the ground that wearing facial veils might jeopardize public safety and fail to comply with the minimum requirements of life in society. The two courts also found that women who conceal their faces, voluntarily or otherwise, are objectively placed in a situation of exclusion and inferiority that is patently incompatible with the constitutional principles of liberty and equality.[46]

Both the French and the Belgian laws were tested before the ECtHR. In *S.A.S. v France*,[47] the Court characterized the full-face veil as "the expression of a *cultural identity*" (§ 120). It then moved on to explain that fulfilling the minimum conditions of "living together" is a legitimate aim for the criminalization of such an expression. "Living together" is not listed in the European Convention among the legitimate grounds for limiting fundamental rights; yet, the Court accepted it as part of the "protection of the rights and freedoms of others" (§ 121), holding that "the barrier raised against others by a veil concealing the face is perceived . . . as breaching the right of others to live in a space of socialization which makes living together easier" (§ 122). In other words, the mere sight of a fully veiled woman can objectively jeopardize the standards of civility in a pluralistic society, and thus justify her criminalization and erasure from the liberal public sphere.

The use of criminal law against fully veiled women constitutes a particularly worrisome turn. Indeed, criminalization carries a strong stigmatizing power. Even if the sanction is light, the symbolic nature of criminal law suffices to attach a particular stigma to a religious practice, constructing women who adhere to it as pernicious outcasts. In the liberal state, criminal punishment should be used as a last resort. Most importantly, criminal law should not adhere to a logic of subjectivity: it should target behaviors, not categories of people. Yet, in this case, fully veiled women are punished for what they wear, not for any act they perform. This is an example of what Günther Jakobs defines as the criminal law of the enemy, whereby some individuals lose the protection of their rights and freedoms and are turned by the law into a source of danger (Jakobs 1985: 751-85).

[45] Law 2010-1192 of October 11, 2010 (France) and Law of June 1, 2011 (Belgium).

[46] Conseil Constitutionnel, Decision No 2010-613 DC (October 7, 2010) (France); Constitutional Court, Judgment No 145/2012 of December 6, 2012 (Belgium).

[47] *S.A.S. v France* App No 43835/11 (ECtHR, July 1, 2014). The Court essentially reiterated its reasoning in *S.A.S. v France* in the Belgian case of *Belcacemi*, holding that by criminalizing facial veils, Belgium had legitimately sought to respond to a practice that it considered to be incompatible with social communication and with the establishment of human relations, which were indispensable for life in democratic society: *Belcacemi and Oussar v Belgium* App No 37798/13 (ECtHR, July 11, 2017) (in French).

Most importantly, the conceptualization of the pre-conditions of democracy provided by the ECtHR in these two cases seems to indicate that legal responses to perceived "cultural clashes" generated by the presence of Islam often deviate from the pluralistic model of democracy that post-WWII Western European countries identify with. Indeed, the construction of a racialized public enemy that needs to be kept out of the public sphere, or even expelled, is a central feature of the identitarian model of democracy theorized by Carl Schmitt. Schmitt argued that political communities are based on a constitutive polarity of friend and enemy (Schmitt 2006 [1927]: 27). Identifying and fighting the enemy is crucial in order to preserve the principles and the values of democracy, which requires "[f]irst homogeneity and second [if the need arises] elimination or eradication" (Schmitt 1985 [1923]: 9).

Two decisions by the ECJ similarly testify to the shift in the rationale of veil bans. The cases of *Achbita* and *Bougnaoui*[48] were referred to the Court by the Belgian and the French supreme administrative courts. In both cases, a woman was dismissed by her private employer on the grounds of wearing a headscarf, which was against the company's dress policy. The Court concluded that such dismissals do not violate European Union law, as long as the employer adopts a general neutrality policy, that is, a ban on all religious signs. The Court thus constructs the principle of neutrality as a legitimate aim that justifies the discrimination against minority religion employees. "Neutrality," however, is not listed among the aims that may justify discrimination in any of the laws applicable to this case. In this respect, the use of "neutrality" by the ECJ is analogous to that of "living together" by the ECtHR. Both are unenumerated grounds for limiting fundamental rights and are vague, culturally loaded, slippery concepts. Being bare-headed is not more nor less neutral than covering one's head, unless one equates neutrality with contemporary Western mainstream attitudes. Moreover, the ECJ, like the ECtHR, did not engage in any victimization narrative. To the contrary, it worked from the assumption that wearing a headscarf is a woman's choice, and it proceeded to give ammunition to the private sector against women who make this choice, in the name of a one-sided and oppressive notion of neutrality.

(ii) Citizenship and Muslim Immigration

The reinforcement of religious homogeneity at the expense of minority denominations also takes place through immigration and citizenship law. Indeed, both fields of law are crucial tools in setting the boundaries of a political community and the key mechanisms for inclusion and exclusion, distinguishing insiders

[48] Case C-157/15 *Achbita v G4S Secure Solutions NV* and Case C-188/15 *Bougnaoui v Micropole SA* [2017] ECLI:EU:C:2017:203; ECLI:EU:C:2017:204 (CJEU).

from outsiders. As Michael Walzer points out, membership was the first social good that needs to be distributed, in that the distribution of all other goods, such as income, positions, benefits, and opportunities depend upon individuals being recognized as members of a polity who would subsequently be entitled to these (Walzer 1983: 50). In a world of deep disparities and mass migration, however, political membership also becomes a fundamental question of domestic and international justice (Benhabib 2002: 439). When confronted with mass migration, refugees, and asylum seekers, populist and nationalist actors push for reinforcing states' boundaries and accentuating the need to preserve their national traits. Religion is often co-opted in this dynamic, as in the rhetoric put forward by Hungarian Prime Minister Viktor Orban, who justified his hardline policies in the refugee crisis on the ground that "[t]hose arriving have been raised in another religion, and represent a radically different culture. Most of them are not Christians, but Muslims. This is an important question because Europe and European identity are rooted in Christianity. Is it not worrying in itself that European Christianity is now barely able to keep Europe Christian? There is no alternative, and we have no option but to defend our borders."[49]

In India, the conflation of secularism and religious majoritarianism is clearly perceivable in the country's increasing "culturalization" of citizenship. In December 2019, India adopted the Citizenship Amendment Act, which provides a fast-track for the acquisition of citizenship for illegal immigrants from Afghanistan, Bangladesh, or Pakistan who arrived in India before 2014, and who are Hindu, Sikh, Buddhist, Jain, Parsi, or Christian.[50] While the amendment was presented by the Bharatiya Janata Party (BJP), or Indian People's Party, as a tool of protection for individuals who belong to persecuted minorities, it is just the latest chapter of a long history of discrimination against Muslim migrants.[51] This is consistent with the Hindu Right's channeling of the immigration issue in essentially religious terms, "as a tension between the Hindu insider and the Muslim outsider" (Kapur 2020: 49).

As Ratna Kapur explains, "[t]he forging of Indian citizenship along the lines of cultural and religious identity finds its origins in the colonial past, where the 'divide and rule' policy of the colonial power produced and perpetuated religious divides. Persons who reside outside of India can register as Indian citizens if they or either of their parents or grandparents was born in India. However, no person is entitled

[49] Robert Mackey, "Hungarian leader rebuked for saying Muslim migrants must be blocked 'to keep Europe Christian,'" *The New York Times*, September 4, 2015, <www.nytimes.com/2015/09/04/world/europe/hungarian-leader-rebuked-for-saying-muslim-migrants-must-be-blocked-to-keep-europe-christian.html>, accessed June 26, 2025.

[50] Citizenship Act, 1955, No 57 of 1955, s 2, as amended by Citizenship (Amendment) Act 2019, No 47.

[51] *See* Francesca Raimondo, "The 'religion of citizenship': The Indian Citizenship Amendment Act 2019," *IACL-AIDC Blog*, July 2, 2020, <https://blog-iacl-aidc.org/2020-posts/2020/7/2/the-religion-of-citizenship-the-indian-citizenship-amendment-act-2019>, accessed September 2, 2025.

to become a citizen of India if he or she has voluntarily acquired citizenship in a foreign state. The courts have also held that a person who migrated to Pakistan after March 1, 1947, and acquired Pakistani nationality could not subsequently claim Indian citizenship" (Kapur 2007: 544). In the 1990s, with the rise of the Hindu Right's aggressive nationalistic project, the role of religion in the culturalization of citizenship became increasingly important. In a case decided in 2005, for example, the Supreme Court had characterized Muslim immigration from Bangladesh as a form of "external aggression," warning that it would have "dangerous consequences . . . for the Nation as a whole . . . [and that n]o misconceived and mistaken notions of secularism should be allowed to come in the way of [recognizing this reality]."[52]

The 2019 Act takes a further step in constructing Muslims as threatening, irreconcilable outsiders. Indeed, the UN High Commissioner for Human Rights has opined that the Act is "fundamentally discriminatory in nature,"[53] as it violates Article 14 of the Indian Constitution, which guarantees to all persons the equal protection of the laws within the territory of India, and has filed an application to the Supreme Court of India. The European Parliament has also drafted a joint resolution that characterizes the Act as "dangerously divisive."[54]

The role of religion in the culturalization of citizenship is clearly perceivable also in Europe. Likewise, in India, Islam has been constructed as an insurmountable obstacle to integration into the liberal state, as in a 2008 case decided by the French *Conseil d'Etat*. The case concerned a rejection of a naturalization application by "Ms M", a Moroccan national, married to a French citizen and the mother of their three French-born children. The applicant had been refused French citizenship on the ground that she was not sufficiently assimilated, based on her dress (a full-face veil), virtual seclusion, and submission to her husband. Ms M claimed that, while she did practice Salafism, a rigorous interpretation of Islam, according to which she rarely left her home and felt obliged to fully submit to her husband, she did not question French republican values and had never given French authorities cause for concern or complaint since arriving in France in 2000. She alleged that the decision to reject her application violated her freedom of religion. The *Conseil d'Etat*, however, upheld the decision of the lower court, on the ground that: "Despite having a good command of French, the applicant has nevertheless adopted a radical practice of her religion, which is incompatible with the essential values of the French community and particularly with the principle of sex equality."[55]

[52] *Sarbananda Sonowal v Union of India* AIR 2005 SC 2920, paras 22, 32.

[53] UN Office of the High Commissioner for Human Rights, "Press briefing on India," December 13, 2019, <www.ohchr.org/EN/NewsEvents/Pages/DisplayNews.aspx?NewsID = 25425&LangID = E> [https://perma.cc/FFN4-FEW2], accessed June 26, 2025.

[54] European Parliament, "Joint Motion for a Resolution Pursuant to Rule 132(2) and (4) of the Rules of Procedure Replacing Scattered Motions on India's Citizenship (Amendment) Act, 2019," para 1, January 28, 2020, <www.europarl.europa.eu/doceo/document/RC-9-2020-0077_EN.pdf> [https://perma.cc/4AEV-ABPX], accessed June 26, 2025.

[55] *Conseil d'État*, Decision No 286798 (June 27, 2008).

In 2006, the German Land of Baden-Wurttemberg proposed to introduce, as part of the citizenship test, a questionnaire that was later retracted and replaced by a federal citizenship test. The questionnaire did not address the practice of Islam as a religion, but rather, it covered virtually all perceived sources of cultural clashes with the Muslim community: homosexuality, terrorism, forced marriage, polygamy, honor killing, etc. Assuming that being Muslim automatically positioned the prospective citizen on the illiberal side of the spectrum, it included questions such as: "How would you react if your adult daughter wanted to dress as any German woman? And if your brother or son was insulted?" This kind of question does not aim to evaluate the prospective citizen's knowledge of the receiving system and society. In this respect, Christian Joppke distinguishes between citizenship tests and cognitive ones and tests that scrutinize the prospective citizens' inner behavior. Examples of the first type are questions that are routinely included in the US citizenship test, such as "What is one right or freedom from the First Amendment?" or "How many justices are on the Supreme Court?" To the contrary, "a citizenship test that scrutinizes a candidate's 'inner disposition' [transgresses] the thin line that separates the regulation of behavior from the control of beliefs . . . Whenever the new citizenship tests are informed by the notion that the liberal state is one only for liberal people, the threshold of the illiberal is passed" (Joppke 2010).

C. Islamic Populism and Authoritarianism: The Case of Turkey

(i) The Ottoman Roots of Erdogan's Populist Project

A common misconception is that, prior to the authoritarian turn of the "Erdogan era," Turkey was a secular, democratic state (Kuru 2008: 101–10). The Constitution does indeed proclaim that "The Republic of Turkey is a democratic, secular and social state governed by the rule of law, respecting human rights."[56] Even at first glance, however, a number of constitutional provisions suggest that the Turkish notions of democracy and secularism diverge substantially from Western ones. Various provisions, for example, limit fundamental rights to protect the democratic and secular character of the state.[57] Furthermore, while freedom of conscience is guaranteed under Article 24 of the Constitution, the state retains "supervision and control" over "religious and moral education." Relying on the self-representation of Kemalism as modern, Western, and secular (Parla & Davison 2004: 5), these anomalies have traditionally been deemed as militant democracy clauses, necessary to guard the Constitution against backward, undemocratic religious forces. In this light, Turkey has often been conceptualized as a "tutelary

[56] Constitution of the Republic of Turkey, art 2.
[57] Constitution of the Republic of Turkey, arts 13–15.

democracy," a definition which legitimizes the role of the military as guardians of the constitutional order, thus downplaying the authoritarian elements of Atatürk's project (Parla & Davison 2004: 2). Another traditional, and equally misleading, narrative is that Turkish secularism is the equivalent of French *laïcité*, on the ground that both are militantly anti-religious (Parla & Davison 2004: 6). Unlike French *laïcité*, however, Turkish secularism does not stem from the ideals of the Enlightenment project: the separation of state and religion and the confinement of the latter in the private sphere. In fact, Turkish secularism is at odds with such principles. Kemalism has undoubtedly succeeded in repressing certain forms of political Islam, but it has done so through the institutionalization of a particular stream of Sunni Islam (Parla & Davison 2004: 50). It suffices to mention, in this respect, that the Directorate of Religious Affairs (*Dyanet*), which is controlled by the executive branch, has traditionally been entrusted, inter alia, with the power to appoint and dismiss all mosque personnel, including imams. Religion is thus fully integrated into the Turkish structure of government (Parla & Davison 2004: 51).

The peculiar role of religion in the Turkish constitutional system mirrors the complex relationship between nationalism and Islam that characterized the birth of the Turkish state. Islam was not traditionally the religion of a people. The collapse of the Ottoman Empire thus "led to unprecedented tension between Islamic belonging and national belonging, hence making the nationalization of Islam a major political issue" (Cesari 2018: 2) Indeed, Atatürk carried on a project aimed at reforming and westernizing Islam, to adapt it to the newly born Turkish nation. In Turkey, state-building preceded the formation of the Turkish nation. As Jocelyn Cesari stresses, there was, arguably, "no Turkish nation before the collapse of the Caliphate" (Cesari 2018). State-building went hand in hand with a process of homogenization of a vastly diverse population,[58] through a comprehensive set of policies. In the 1930s, an official program was set up to rewrite Turkish history, tracing back the ethnic origin of the people to the Turkic tribes of central Asia, thus "marking the ascend of the notion of race in Turkish nationalism."[59] A "Speak Turkish" campaign was launched, making Turkish the only official language, and turning it into yet another articulation of Turkish national identity (Cesari 2018: 9). Subsequently, when mandatory teaching of religion in all state schools was introduced, it only presented the Hanafi school of Sunni

[58] At the time of its birth as a republic, Turkey had a highly diverse population, including Jews, Christians, and Shia Muslims, as well as many non-Turkish Muslims, including Kurds, Arabs, Tartars, and Serbs and Bosniaks: *see* Cagaptay 2004: 86–101.

[59] In 1930, Atatürk instructed a committee to produce studies on Turkish history to be disseminated throughout the country. The resulting "Turkish History Thesis" contended that "the Turks were a bracycephalic people, whose roots went back to central Asia, where they had lived thousands of years ago. In central Asia, they had created a bright civilization around an inner sea. When this inner sea dried up due to climatic changes, they left their original home and moved in all directions to civilize the rest of the world. They went to China in the east; to India in the south; to Egypt, Mesopotamia, Persia, Anatolia, and Greece, and Italy in the west," thus marked the ascent of race under Turkish nationalism: *see* Cagaptay 2004: 87.

Islam (Bâli 2016: 244, n. 28). Assimilation thus took place through the conflation of racial/ethnic (Turkic) and religious (Sunni Hanafi) identities, to provide a "homogenous basis of national loyalty to the state" (Bâli 2016). In this process, Islam became a crucial tool at the service of nation-building (Cesari 2018). In this light, the elimination of religious provisions from family law and the suppression of the visibility of Islam (e.g., by banning Muslim symbols and rituals in the public sphere) in Atatürk's Turkey did not produce the separation of religion/or its privatization. While religious rituals and practices were not deemed useful to the building of Turkish identity, the Republic legitimized a particular stream of Sunni Islam, with which it became closely intertwined, as a structural element of national identity (Cesari 2018: 6). By the same token, the entanglement between church and state, which took place, inter alia, through the appointment of laymen to positions previously held by clerics, and the integration of clerics into the state's administrative structure, produced a profound transformation of Islam and Islamic institutions.[60]

The building of a homogeneous Turkish nation entailed the suppression and marginalization of ethnic, religious, and political minorities that did not fit "the prototype of the Kemalist desired citizen" (Yilmaz 2021: 55). The largest among such groups were practicing Muslims and Islamists, who were labeled as reactionary fanatics, disloyal to the Republic, and nostalgic for the Empire. Throughout the history of the Turkish Republic, countless members of religious communities and Islamist groups were imprisoned, their political parties disbanded, their religious symbols banned from public places and institutions, culminating in the 1997 coup, which further "traumatized millions of practicing Muslims and solidified their victimhood mentality" (Yilmaz 2021: 75).

Eight decades of victimization resulted in the rise and spread of "resentful counter-narratives" (Cagaptay 2004: 87), on which Erdoğan has widely capitalized. The political and constitutional crises that hit Turkey under Erdoğan "are [thus] a consequence of tensions institutionalized within the Turkish Republic's constitutional order from the outset" (Bâli 2016: 243).

The Turkish Justice and Development Party (AKP), led by Recep Tayyip Erdoğan, has dramatically impacted the Turkish political system, turning it, as Ihsan Yilmaz puts it, from an "oppressive Kemalist state to an aggressive autocratic and vindictive Islamist" one.[61] Erdoğan's narrative perfectly fits within the populist

[60] "Generally speaking, the grafting of Islam onto state institutions and national identities has primarily taken place through three mechanisms: nationalization of Islamic institutions and clerics, incorporation of Islam into the legal system, and inclusion of Islam into the national narrative taught in schools. The outcome of these three processes is what I have called hegemonic Islam." Cesari 2018: 7.

[61] Ihsan Yilmaz, "Erdogan's political journey: From victimised Muslim democrat to authoritarian, Islamist populist," European Center for Populism Studies, February 2021, 2, <www.researchgate.net/profile/Ihsan-Yilmaz-3/publication/351119116_Erdogan's_Political_Journey_From_Victimised_Muslim_Democrat_to_Authoritarian_Islamist_Populist/links/6088be632fb9097c0c1322e0/Erdogans-Political-Journey-From-Victimised-Muslim-Democrat-to-Authoritarian-Islamist-Populist.pdf>, accessed May 20, 2021.

frame: it characterizes practicing Muslim Turks as the authentic, morally superior people, who have been deprived of the right to rule their own country by the secular elites, backed by the West.[62] Under Erdoğan, the AKT launched a neo-conservative Muslim political doctrine, as an alternative modernization project (Çinar 2005). Central to this is the use of religion to (re)define Turkish national identity, by recreating Turkish society through a romanticized version of the Ottoman past, as intertwined with Islam. In a reversal of Edward Said's *Orientalism*, Islamic civilization is pitted against the secular West, and Islam is enlisted to consolidate the bounds of Turkish identity.[63] As a consequence, the education system, judiciary, police, and military schools have undergone a deep Islamization process (Yavuz & Öztürk 2019: 1–9), and Islam has become a "re-born element of the new Turkey and has been transforming many areas such as: the Kurdish issue, implementation of the rule of law, foreign policy and gender issues" (Yavuz & Öztürk 2019), and the media, from which critical content has been banned and "replaced with more 'Islamist' or pro-Ottoman oriented content."[64]

The use of religion is key in characterizing Erdoğan's specific form of populism. In a particularly revealing statement, he defined himself as "Istanbul's imam,"[65] thus implying at once that his legitimacy has a transcendent dimension and that Islam is part and parcel of his role in Turkey's democracy, and the two actually intertwine for the welfare of the people.[66]

Religion has also become the protagonist of Erdoğan's model of foreign policy. "In countries from Latin America to sub-Saharan Africa, Turkey is building mosques, financing religious education, restoring Ottoman heritage—and advertising its unique brand of Islamic leadership along the way."[67] Conflating Sunni Islam with national identity, Turkish institutions engage in the international promotion of their language and culture alongside religious curricula, portraying Turkey as the "heir to the Ottoman Empire, [being] Islam's last fortress and the natural leader of a revival of Muslim civilization."[68]

[62] Ibid at 4.
[63] M. Hakan Yavuz, "Erdogan's Ottomania," *Boston Review*, August 8, 2018, <http://bostonreview.net/politics/m-hakan-yavuz-erdogan-ottomanophilia>, accessed June 26, 2025.
[64] Yilmaz, n 61.
[65] Genc 2019 quoted by Yilmaz, n 61.
[66] Yilmaz, n 61.
[67] Gonul Tol, "Turkey's bid for religious leadership: How the AKP uses Islamic soft power," *Foreign Affairs*, January 2019, <www.foreignaffairs.com/articles/turkey/2019-01-10/turkeys-bid-religious-leadership>, accessed June 26, 2025.
[68] Ibid.

(ii) The Deterioration of Women's Rights

As we have seen, the resurgence of political Islam in Turkey must be placed in the broader context of the rise of counter-narratives concerning the country's process of nation-building. While the authoritarian elements of Atatürk's Turkey have often been downplayed, it is undeniable that one of the effects of the Kemalist modernization project was to set the premises for the advancement of gender equality. However, as gender equality has advanced domestically and internationally, becoming a fundamental principle of international human rights law and of democratic constitutionalism, it has increasingly become the target of the AKP's action, wishing to reinstate traditional gender roles. Indeed, issues of gender, sexuality, and reproduction constitute one of the crucial preoccupations of illiberal and right-wing populist actors in contexts as diverse as Poland, Hungary, Brazil, India, and the United States under the Trump administration. These issues increasingly intersect with debates over citizenship, national identity, and culture (Mancini & Palazzo 2021). Illiberal narratives equate the breakdown of traditional gender roles with the breakdown of the nation. Among the many building blocks of this narrative, "family" is central. The collapse of the (heteronormative) family is tantamount to the collapse of the nation, which is founded on a natural (heterosexual, nuclear, dyadic, cohabitant, for-life) conception of family (Palazzo 2021: 3). The breakdown of the natural family is considered the inevitable consequence of denying both the "complementarity" of women and men within it and their different positions in the social hierarchy.

In this respect, one should bear in mind that in all societies, women embody cultural, biological, and reproductive aspects, as the widespread use of female figures, such as Marianne or Germania, to embody the nation shows. Women represent the cultural norms and the values that define a certain group in a given historical moment, and the possibility to pass on such norms and values to the next generation. This explains the great importance that all societies, and all legal systems, place on women's reproductive role: who women can marry, with whom women are permitted to have children. These rules are of key importance in defining the identity of a group, drawing the boundaries between insiders and outsiders, and explaining why women's status and bodies often become political and cultural battlefields. All nations' results depend on particular constructions of gender (McClintock 1993: 62). Thus, nationalistic and feminist claims may be at odds with one another. In nation-building processes and in times of profound political change, women are often co-opted as national emblems to represent the new state's ideals or the return to a mythical, authentic tradition. In the building of modern Turkey, as we have seen, Islam was constructed as an obstacle to the country's road to modernization. Under Erdoğan, it is used to reject the notion that modernity is possible exclusively in European forms, and to assert the possibility of alternative forms of modernity that build on the country's traditional culture.

As Nira Yuval-Davis puts it, "deveiling women in Atatürk Turkey's revolution in Turkey of 1917," to bring about a modern nation-state, "was as important as veiling them has been to Muslim fundamentalists" (Yuval-Davis 1997: 98). Indeed, in Turkey, women have become the target of symbolic and substantial action by the AKP in its effort to distance the new regime from the modern state established in 1920 by Kemal Atatürk. Atatürk's modern Turkey explicitly recognized gender equality under the law. The Turkish Civil Code of 1926 prohibited polygamy, subjected marriage to secular law, outlawed unilateral divorce, and recognized gender equality in inheritance and guardianship of children (Arat 2010: 869). Against this backdrop, Erdoğan's party (AKP) launched a supposedly moderate, neo-conservative Muslim political doctrine, as an alternative modernization project (Çinar 2005).

Yet the AKP's doctrine has consistently undermined the equality of women, relying on the centrality of the family grounded on traditional gender roles. As Tutku Ayan explains, "[i]n this heteronormative approach, family, imagined as a 'prototype of the nation', consists of individuals who share the same values, have different responsibilities based on their age and gender, and do not hesitate to put the familial unity before their own well-being."[69] Traditional gender roles and family values are pitted against "Western" individualism and acquire an almost salvific essence. For example, in 2016, Erdoğan called on Muslim women to reject contraception to ensure the continuing growth of the Turkish population.[70]

The systematic propagation of Islamist norms by the AKP has been made possible thanks to the recruitment of politicians and civil servants who adhere to patriarchal visions of religion, especially regarding the position of women. This has resulted in the lifting of the ban on headscarves in political, educational, and public institutions, a measure purported as a means of liberation from the oppressive secular philosophy that dominated the pre-Erdoğan era and as a triumph of religious freedom (Arat 2010: 872). In our previous critique of European bans on Muslim female traditional clothing in Europe, we have demonstrated how secularism and gender equality are invoked to violate Muslim women's rights, including religious freedom. In the context of Turkey, however, the implications of regulating the veil are much more complex, "due first to the elements of the history of the Turkish Republic, second to the emergence of new state–society relations, and third to the accelerated developments in the conflict between Islamists and secularists" (Saktanber & Çorbacioğlu 2008: 514). While the analysis of such complexities goes beyond the scope of this chapter, lifting the ban has resulted in new forms of pressure that limit women's freedoms and opportunities. Indeed,

[69] Tutku Ayan, "KADEM's 'gender justice' or the momentum of anti-genderism in Turkey," *Engenderings*, April 29, 2019, <https://blogs.lse.ac.uk/gender/2019/04/29/kadems-gender-justice-in-turkey/>, accessed June 26, 2025.

[70] "Turkey's Erdogan warns Muslims against birth control," *BBC News*, May 30, 2016,<www.bbc.com/news/world-europe-36413097>, accessed June 26, 2025.

"[f]eminist researchers argue that women administrators feel AKP bureaucrats and politicians are uncomfortable working with women in the public service and resent the presence of women without headscarves in public places" (Saktanber & Çorbacioğlu 2008).

Action by the AKP has also led to the transformation of the structure of welfare in ways that push women into the role of caregivers and increase their economic dependence and discourage their presence in the workforce,[71] and has infused the educational system with traditional (patriarchal) religious values (Arat 2010: 874). Moreover, under the AKP, the Department of Religious Affairs (the highest religious authority in Turkey and part of the state apparatus tied to the Prime Minister) has consistently upheld patriarchal interpretations of Islam, for example by prompting women to cover themselves, not wear perfume, and not remain alone with men outside of their family (Arat 2010: 875). In sum, as Yesim Arat notes, "the more liberal interpretations of Islam, which do not expect women to cover their heads and which the founding fathers assumed, are being replaced [and propagated by government-controlled bodies] by another interpretation increasing patriarchal control over women's bodies" (Arat 2010).

The crusade against women's equality reached its peak in March 2021, when a Presidential Decree announced the withdrawal of Turkey from the Council of Europe Convention on preventing and combating violence against women and domestic violence ("Istanbul Convention").[72] As it will be analyzed in depth in Chapter 6, the treaty—which covers not only domestic violence but other forms of gender-specific violence including psychological and physical abuse, sexual harassment, rape, "honor" crimes, stalking, and forced marriage—had been systematically targeted by the AKP since 2020, on the ground that it had been instrumentalized by social forces "attempting to normalize homosexuality, which is incompatible with Turkey's social and family values."[73]

D. Concluding Remarks

The cases analyzed in this chapter vastly differ in terms of geography, religious tradition, and form of government. Yet, a red thread runs through all of them. Indeed, in India, Europe, and Turkey, the interplay between secularism and religion has become fundamental in shaping notions of identity and political

[71] Ayan, n 69.

[72] *See* Presidential Decree No 9 (Turkey, March 20, 2021). The Convention had been codified in Turkey via the Law to Protect Family and Prevent Violence against Woman, colloquially referred to as Law No 6284.

[73] Presidency of the Republic of Turkey, Directorate of Communications, "Statement Regarding Turkey's Withdrawal from the Istanbul Convention," March 21, 2021, available at <www.iletisim.gov.tr/english/haberler/detay/statement-regarding-turkeys-withdrawal-from-the-istanbul-convention>, last accessed 30, 2021.

belonging. In all cases, the relevant actors (constitution framers, courts, legislators, and policymakers) have simultaneously constructed secularism as an articulation of the majority religion, and the latter as a cultural construct that serves nationalistic and/or populist goals. By the same token, minority religions have been conceptualized as value systems that are at odds with the shared identity of the majority. Both majority and minority religions have thus been turned from systems of beliefs to systems of values, and measured against the yardstick of national identity. This has allowed for a distortion of secularism, from institutional to ideological. In the context of the European cases regulating Muslim dress, as well as in the Indian *Hindutva* cases, the invocation of secular universalism is, by and large, analogous to that of "Christian traditional values" by illiberal rulers such as Viktor Orbán. Indeed, in both cases, a cultural tradition is turned into an ideological fence that marks the borders between insiders and outsiders and allows for the construction of internal and external enemies.

6

The War on "Gender Ideology"

This chapter addresses the reshaping of rights as a consequence of domestic and transnational mobilizations against "gender ideology." The latter term, which emerged in Catholic circles, initially indicated opposition to "women's and LGBT rights activism as well as the scholarship deconstructing essentialist and naturalistic assumptions about gender and sexuality" (Kuhar and Paternotte 2017: 5). With time, however, anti-genderism has gained significant traction across various regions, turning into a "symbolic glue" that brings together a wide range of illiberal and populist actors across political and religious spectrums, serving as a unifying discourse amid otherwise fragmented interests.[1] In this context, the term *gender* has become a battlefield through which broader critiques of liberal democracy, globalization, democratic norms, and human rights frameworks are articulated.

[1] Weronika Grzebalska, Eszter Kováts, and Andrea Pető, "Gender as symbolic glue: How 'gender' became an umbrella term for the rejection of the (neo)liberal order," *Political Critique*, January 13, 2017, <https://politicalcritique.org/long-read/2017/gender-as-symbolic-glue-how-gender-became-an-umbrella-term-for-the-rejection-of-the-neoliberal-order/>, accessed October 1, 2025.

Politicized Religion and the Reframing of Fundamental Rights. Susanna Mancini and Michel Rosenfeld, Oxford University Press. © Susanna Mancini, Michel Rosenfeld 2026. DOI: 10.1093/9780191982149.003.0008

The chapter first offers an overview of the emergence and of the global spread of anti-genderism, and of its religious, political, and ideological roots, with a particular focus on the appropriation of "rights talk" by illiberal and populist actors relying on anti-gender arguments. Next, the chapter presents the unique case of the Istanbul Convention, a Council of Europe Treaty aimed at combating violence against women, which was manipulated and misrepresented in several Central and Eastern European countries (CEE) by illiberal and populist actors claiming that it imposes "gender ideology," promotes LGBTQ+ rights, and threatens state sovereignty.

A. Religion, Populism, and "Anti-genderism"

(i) The Vatican Roots of Anti-genderism: Sexual Complementarity, the Civilization of Death, and the Culture of Disposal

The seeds of the Vatican's war of gender were laid under the pontificates of John Paul II and Benedict XVI. Both popes theorized a vision of sexuality strictly tied to reproduction and the institution of marriage, the defense of which they elevated as a central political priority. The Vatican's view rested on two pillars: sexual complementarity and the opposition between the "culture (or the civilization) of life" and that "of death." Cardinal Ratzinger had already articulated these principles in the mid 1980s, taking issue with feminist epistemologies and queer theories that advocated for freedom from gender-based societal expectations.[2] If, Ratzinger reasoned, "everything is only a culturally and historically conditioned 'role,' and not a natural specificity inscribed in the depth of being," then "motherhood is a mere accidental function," procreation can occur "at will, and the state must honor the right to be male or female at one's will or pleasure."[3] Ratzinger built on the theology of Pope John Paul II, who upheld the idea of essentialized and unchangeable binary sexual identities: "[w]omen—he cautioned—must not appropriate to themselves male characteristics contrary to their own feminine 'originality'" (John Paul II, 1988: 91). The latter is inescapably intertwined with the physical and spiritual dimensions of motherhood: "[w]omen can find themselves only by giving love to others." Sexual complementarity[4] postulates that women and men are equal in dignity but have intrinsically different biological and psychological characteristics that are unchangeable and should determine their roles in society and in the family. Complementarity is strictly connected with the rejection of the "culture of death," which John Paul II characterized as a "non-reproductive mentality"

[2] Butler 1990.
[3] Case 2019: 640–45ff.
[4] *See also* Chapter 5 on Turkey.

(John Paul II 1995), stemming from a "selfish concept of freedom which sees procreation as an obstacle to the development of one's own personality" (John Paul II 1995: 13). In this light, sexual and reproductive rights are irremediably flawed claims, not because they contradict religion but because they depart from nature and pursue a suicidal model of civilization (Vaggione 2012). Secular law, in Ratzinger's thought, plays a crucial role in upholding these ontological truths, coherently with his position that the church intervenes in political discourses not in the name of religious dogmas but on the authority of reason. Christianity, in Ratzinger's thought, unlike other religions, is not revelation but "reason and nature in their interrelation that form the universally valid form of law"' (Cartabia & Simoncini 2015: 4). What follows is that religion ought to be an essential part of the foundation and infrastructure of the modern constitutional and human rights regime. Secular law should not be divorced from cultural and moral considerations, and it should not endorse a relativistic worldview that contradicts natural law and undermines the church's teachings on human nature and sexuality. Artificial interventions like contraception and abortion, and acceptance of homosexuality and diverse family structures, disrupt the natural order and reflect a non-reproductive mentality. They should thus be resisted and characterized not just as immoral but also as inherently non-legal.

The Vatican's anti-gender war intensified as the concept of gender began to take central stage at the United Nations (UN). This intensification is reflected in a change in the Holy See's use of sexual and reproductive rights-related language within the UN context: "a general shift away from doctrinal arguments towards the use of more secular rhetoric, using sophisticated technical evidence and strategic interpretations of international human rights standards." This shift did not indicate a change of the "doctrinal underpinnings of the Holy See's position . . . , rather, the Holy See has selectively appropriated and accepted UN language to bolster its own influence" (Coates et al. 2014).

A particularly acute irritant for the Vatican was the 1995 UN women's conference in Beijing, which called for the adoption of a gender perspective in addressing women's inequality.[5] Reacting to the UN "gender turn," in 1997 Ratzinger put forward the idea of gender as an *ideology*, in a text where he frontally attacked feminist ideals. Ratzinger wrote:

> Women are currently considered to be oppressed; thus women's liberation serves as a nuclear center for any activity of liberation, both political and anthropological with the objective of liberating the human being from her biology.

[5] The conference recognized that the inequality of women is a structural problem and can only be addressed from an integral perspective of gender and established that "[a]ll economic policies and institutions as well as those responsible for resource allocation should adopt a gender perspective" (Beijing Declaration and Platform for Action, 1995: Article 233).

> Distinction is thus made between the biological phenomenon of sexuality from its historic forms, which they denominate "gender," but the intended revolution against the historic forms of sexuality culminates in a revolution against biological presumptions. It is no longer admitted that "nature" has something to say, it is better that man can shape himself to his taste, must be liberated from any presumption of his being: the human being must make himself as he wishes, only in this way would he be "free" and liberated. All of this, deep down, disguises an insurrection of men against the limits that they carry with them as biological beings. It is opposed, in the final extreme, to the creator. The human being must be their own creator, a modern version of that, "I will be like Gods:" they must be like God.[6]

The Beijing Conference had, indeed, been a frustrating experience for the Vatican. The head of the latter's delegation, Harvard professor Mary Ann Glendon, had strenuously fought to counter "population control lobbyists and old-line, hard-line feminist groups," who pushed for sexual and reproductive rights, at the expenses of religion and freedom of conscience.[7] Glendon was particularly disturbed by the coalition among EU members, Canada, and some Global South states, and their effort to adopt a pluralistic definition of the family "intended to place a range of alternative lifestyles on the same legal footing as families founded on kinship or marriage." These efforts, she argued, carry "ominous implications for universal human rights."[8] In line with Ratzinger's views concerning the role of secular law in upholding the church's moral position and cultural project, Glendon put forward the notion that claims to sexual and reproductive freedoms are not human rights; to the contrary, they contradict the latter's essence and *rationale*. To this end, she accused her opponents of making a "selective use of rights language to advance an anti-rights agenda," and of trivializing "universally recognized core principles through the attempted addition of new rights."[9] This, she concluded, amounts to the "colonization of the universal language of human rights by an impoverished dialect" that prioritizes individualism at the expense of social responsibility.[10] As examples of such rights' colonization, Glendon quoted "the emphasis on formal equality at the expense of motherhood's special claim to protection,"[11] as well as the "ambiguous rights language in the areas of sexuality and fertility. A paragraph in the health section, for example, speaks of women's right to have control over and decide freely and responsibly on matters related to their

[6] Ratzinger 1997: 142, quoted by Miskolci & Campana 2017: 723.
[7] Mary Ann Glendon, "What Happened at Beijing," *First Things*, January 1, 1996,<https://firstthings.com/what-happened-at-beijing/>, accessed September 29, 2025.
[8] Ibid.
[9] Ibid.
[10] Ibid.
[11] Ibid.

sexuality, including sexual and reproductive health, free of coercion, discrimination, and violence."[12] In other words, Glendon engaged in rights manipulation, presenting formal equality and bodily self-determination as distortions of the authentic significance of gender equality as sexual complementarity, in line with the Vatican's theology concerning women's biology and foremost maternal role.

Another area of concern in the aftermath of Beijing was, from the Vatican's perspective, the influence exercised by liberal Global North countries on Southern, financially dependent areas of the world. "What deals—Glendon wondered—did the affluent nations make with their client states?" "How can one explain that many delegations from poor nations came to sessions involving sexual and reproductive matters with well-prepared position papers, yet were absent or silent when resources and other crucial issues were discussed?"[13] These discourses resonate with the anti-colonial frame that has become a prominent dimension of anti-genderism, which will be discussed in the following section. They also anticipated subsequent developments in the Vatican's position, associating sexual and reproductive rights with the perceived failings of global capitalism. According to this vision, reproductive rights, LGBTQ+ advocacy, and global capitalism are all part of an agenda which will destroy the family and ultimately do away with the essence of humanity itself (Case 2019). From this perspective, the pontificate of Francis I is of particular interest. Compared to his predecessors, Francis expressed stronger criticism of global capitalism and neoliberalism, which he characterized as the "economy of exclusion" (Francis I 2013: 45ff). The latter devastates the environments and produces a "culture of disposal," that is, a power system that goes beyond exploitation and oppression, and affects one's very belonging to the society: "It is not a case of being at the bottom, on the margins, or without power, but of being *outside*. The excluded are not 'exploited' but discarded, 'leftovers'" (Francis I 2013: 46). As Vaggione notes, in Francis's thought, "the 'culture of disposal' seems to include not only the devastating consequences of economic oppression and exclusion but also the cultural and legal changes involved in sexual and reproductive rights" (Vaggione 2017: 306). Francis clearly articulated this connection in a speech delivered at the UN in 2015: "The defense of the environment and the fight against exclusion demand that we recognize a moral law written into human nature itself, one which includes the natural difference between man and woman . . . and absolute respect for life in all its stages and dimensions."[14]

Francis's rigidity concerning "gender theory" can be traced back to his time as President of the Argentinian Episcopal Conference. In this capacity, then Cardinal

[12] Ibid.

[13] Ibid.

[14] Francis I, "Meeting with the Members of the General Assembly of the United Nations Organization: Address of the Holy Father," *The Holy See*, September 25, 2015, <www.vatican.va/content/francesco/en/speeches/2015/september/documents/papa-francesco_20150925_onu-visita.html>, accessed October 2, 2025 quoted by Vaggione 2017: 306.

Bergoglio became a key actor in opposing sex education and gay marriage, which he characterized as a "move by the father of lies who wishes to confuse and deceive the children of God" (Vaggione 2017 quoting a 2010 letter by Bergoglio).[15] As pope, however, Francis displayed a more nuanced attitude. On the one hand, he attacked abortion rights, even more virulently than his predecessors, comparing abortion to Nazi eugenics, and doctors who perform it to hitmen.[16] Conversely, he seemed to soften the church's rhetoric toward gay and trans individuals, whom he embraced, and even blessed, while continuing, however, to condemn their rights claims. His pastoral openness, best expressed in the question "Who am I to judge [if someone is gay]?"[17] thus signaled a shift in tone toward LGBTQ+ individuals within the Catholic Church, but not a change of its official doctrine on homosexuality as "intrinsically disordered," and same-sex marriage as not permissible.

Francis's ambiguity toward sexual minorities further complicates the role of "gender ideology" within contemporary Catholicism. Indeed, under Ratzinger's pontificate, the church had progressively adopted a new strategy of vilifying gender discourse as a means of asserting control over liberal Catholics, especially in the wake of the clergy sexual abuse scandals. Anti-gender rhetoric had become a unifying force for conservative Catholics, while those who challenged traditional views on sexuality and reproduction were portrayed as having strayed from true faith.[18] Under Francis—whom conservative segments of the church considered overly progressive (or even "woke"[19]) in light of his environmentalism, advocacy for social justice and migrants' rights, and pursuit of interfaith dialogue—the backlash against gender ideology signaled continuity and unity within Catholicism, despite internal conflicts and contradictions.

As it will be comprehensively addressed in Chapter 7, moreover, anti-genderism facilitated alliances between conservative Catholics and Evangelicals in the United States, where the Catholic Church has progressively moved to the right, especially in matters of family and sexuality. This alliance is best exemplified by figures such as Robert George—a Catholic professor at Princeton, and one of the most influential conservative intellectuals in the United States. Among his many initiatives, George was responsible for drafting a document signed in 2009 by over 150 religious authorities—Evangelicals, Catholics, Mormons, and Orthodox

[15] "Carta del cardenal Jorge Mario Bergoglio, arzobispo de Buenos Aires a las Monjas Carmelitas de la arquidiócesis de Buenos Aires," *Movilh Chile*, June 22, 2010, <www.aica.org/docs_blanco.php?id = 463>, accessed September 29, 2025.

[16] Courtney Mares, "Respect Life: Pope Francis' 8 Strongest Statements against Abortion," *Catholic News Agency*, October 4, 2021, <www.catholicnewsagency.com/news/249172/pope-francis-abortion-statements>, accessed September 29, 2025.

[17] Joshua J. Mcelwee, "Francis Explains 'Who Am I to Judge?,'" *NCR*, January 10, 2016, <www.ncronline.org/francis-explains-who-am-i-judge> accessed September 29, 2025.

[18] Korolczuk & Graff 2018: 803.

[19] Ben Munster and Hannah Roberts, "The Complex Legacy of Pope Francis," *Politico*, April 21, 2025, <www.politico.eu/article/pope-francis-death-complex-legacy-catholic-church-vatican-city-state/>, accessed September 29, 2025.

Christians—titled the *Manhattan Declaration: A Call of Christian Conscience.*[20] The declaration unifies different Christian denominations by centering on the defense of three principles, which lie at the core of the war on gender: the protection of prenatal life, marriage defined exclusively as heterosexual, and religious freedom, understood as an unconstrained right to conscientious objection.[21]

(ii) The Populist Turn of Anti-genderism

While the Vatican continued its polymorphic war on gender ideology, right-wing illiberal and populist actors became increasingly interested in adopting and amplifying the church's stances to gain political support and advance their agendas. The first to develop a comprehensive articulation of "gender ideology" and to disseminate this narrative in Latin America was Jorge Scala, whose 2010 book *La ideología del género. O el género como herramienta de poder* (*The Ideology of Gender. Gender as a Tool of Power*) begins with these words: "The evil called . . . gender . . . "perspective" is in reality an ideology. Probably the most radical ideology in history, given that—by imposing itself—it would destroy the human being in its most intimate nucleus and simultaneously do away with society."[22] Scala, an obscure professor of bioethics in a pro-life Costa Rican online institution,[23] accused "gender ideologists" of denying the natural differences between the sexes and of proclaiming that sexuality should be free of all constraints, particularly for people who do not conform with the norm of heterosexual marriage. In this light, gender ideology not only denies biological differences but poses a moral and societal danger. He portrayed gender ideology as a totalitarian belief system, which aimed at imposing a new political model. This made it possible to reframe traditional religious opposition against sex education, women's reproductive rights, and LGBTQ+ rights in terms of an epic cultural, political, and ethical struggle to save "the future of peoples."[24]

From Latin America, the myth of a plot orchestrated by left-wing intellectuals with the support of international organizations has spread throughout the world.

[20] *See* the Manhattan Declaration at <www.manhattandeclaration.org/> accessed September 25, 2025.

[21] Mancini & Rosenfeld 2018b.

[22] Scala 2010: 7, quoted by Miskolci & Campana 2017: 728.

[23] The leading Catholic news agency Aciprensa defined Scala's Universidad Libre Internacional de las Américas (ULIA), as "created to disseminate content concerning the defense of human life for free on the internet" <www.aciprensa.com/noticias/84528/universidad-online-gratuita-para-la-defensa-de-la-vida-abre-matricula-para-2021>.

[24] See the discussions of the Latin American Catholic Church in the V General Conference of Latin American Bishops (Celam) of 2007, affirming that the defense of the traditional concept of family must be a priority focus of the struggle, given that it is "threatened by secularism and ethical relativism, by the various domestic and external migratory flows, by poverty, by social instability and by civil laws contrary to matrimony that, by favoring birth control and abortion, threaten the future of peoples" (Celam, 2007: 279, quoted by Miskolci & Campana 2017: 724).

"Anti-genderism" has become a key component of "transnational political mobilization —an alternative illiberal civil society —based on an alliance between the religious fundamentalists and illiberal populists."[25] It has become a powerful political strategy to recruit and organize acolytes worldwide. It has, in effect, become the lingua franca of right-wing populist, nationalist movements throughout Europe, the United States, Africa, and Asia.

Indeed, initially, the term "gender ideology" was mobilized globally by right-wing actors opposing gender mainstreaming, LGBTQ+ rights, sexual and reproductive health policies, sex education, the fights against gender-based violence, and sex education. "Anti-genderism," however, soon intersected with the rise of illiberal and populist nationalism, which uses gender as a symbolic battleground in defining the moral boundaries of the nation. The connection between nationalism and traditional gender norms is at the core of illiberal anti-genderism. Indeed, a crucial preoccupation of the illiberal script is the withering away of national identity. This is attributed at times to the impact of transnational liberal forces, other times to the influence of immigration or unspecified "others." Hungarian Prime Minister Viktor Orban clearly articulated this preoccupation in his opening speech at the World Congress of Families, an ultra-conservative anti-gender organization,[26] in 2017:

> In Europe today there are two distinct views on [population decline]. One of these is held by those who want to address Europe's demographic problems through immigration. And there is another view, held by Central Europe—and, within it, Hungary. Our view is that we must solve our demographic problems by relying on our own resources and mobilizing our own reserves.... In the struggle for the future of Europe, stopping illegal migration is imperative. This struggle—which is rationally justified—is only worthwhile if we are able to combine it with a family policy which restores natural reproduction on the continent.[27]

Orban's assertion also unveiled a seeming paradox of anti-gender talk, namely the reliance on nationalist, anti-globalist language to advance a global (in this case, European) political agenda. Thus, while champions of anti-gender talk appear nationalistic in rhetoric, the infrastructure and logic of the anti-gender movement are fundamentally globalized (Korolczuk & Graff 2018). The anti-gender movement is far from being a spontaneous local reaction; to the contrary, it is shaped by international conservative networks, think tanks, religious organizations, and political

[25] Korolczuk & Graff 2018.
[26] Stoeckl 2020a.
[27] Website of the Hungarian government, Prime Minister Viktor Orban's opening speech at the 2nd Budapest World Congress of Families, Budapest, May 27, 2017, <https://2015-2019.kormany.hu/en/the-prime-minister/the-prime-minister-s-speeches/prime-minister-viktor-orban-s-opening-speech-at-the-2nd-budapest-world-congress-of-families>, accessed September 20, 2025.

alliances. These actors share funding, strategies, and discursive frames. As such, anti-genderism represents a global counter-movement to gender equality, human rights, and pluralist democracy, which showcases a high political adaptability and a capacity to reshape democratic discourses (Kuhar & Paternotte 2017).

According to Kuhar and Paternotte, among the first scholars to comprehensively address this phenomenon, the anti-gender movement is not simply a conservative backlash but a new political phenomenon with global reach and strategic goals. "Gender ideology" does not refer to any specific academic theory or political platform. Rather, it serves as a symbolic threat, a catch-all term for a wide range of progressive reforms related to gender and sexuality (Kuhar & Paternotte 2017). The movement constructs a fictitious "gender agenda" that is both homogenized and demonized, positioning it as antithetical to traditional values, national identity, and religious morality. Korolczuk and Graff build on this analysis by illustrating how anti-gender discourse creates a narrative of resistance, where local cultures are portrayed as defending themselves against corrupt Western liberalism, often embodied in international and European institutions, such as the UN and the EU. Right-wing populists, they argue, have appropriated an "anticolonial frame," which has been dissociated from discussions of actual colonialism to depict "gender ideology"-related initiatives as a form of cultural imperialism imposed by Western elites.[28] This rhetoric portrays gender policies—including, as it will be illustrated in the following section, those against domestic violence—as foreign ideologies threatening national identities and traditional values. External forces, the narrative goes, that do not belong in the nation are seeking to impose their own exotic values on national majorities. Notions of exoticism and "aggressive" minorities thus intertwine to create the perfect storm conducive to sparking public outrage (Mancini & Palazzo 2021). Examples of the mobilization of the anti-colonial frame abound in different regions of the world. Javier Milei, the populist president of Argentina, recently called for the "breaking of the chains" imposed by the "abhorrent [gender] ideology" that has "colonized the world's most important institutions" and "set the tone of the global conversation over the past decades."[29] The most vivid illustration of the anti-colonial frame was probably the infamous banner exhibited during a 2015 rally opposing sex education in Warsaw, equating gender ideology to "Ebola from Brussels," a gruesome, highly contagious and deadly disease spread by the EU (Korolczuk & Graff 2018). This metaphor unveils an apparent paradox: in Poland, indeed, the introduction of sex education was first opposed on grounds that it constituted a legacy of the ("colonial") communist regime. In anti-gender rhetoric, however, the EU has come to embody a continuation of the latter, as clearly articulated by a member of the Slovakian parliament: "So-called liberal democracy is in

[28] Korolczuk & Graff 2018: 809.

[29] *See* the transcript of Milei's address at Davos 2025, <www.weforum.org/stories/2025/01/davos-2025-special-address-javier-milei-president-argentina/>, accessed September 29, 2025.

reality a totalitarian neo-Marxist dictatorship and tyranny by minorities . . . Neo-Marxism represented by its most important part—multiculturalism—became official ideology of the EU who builds upon it a new cultural socialism" (Očenášová 2022: 49).

Similar dynamics, as will be analyzed in Chapter 7, are at play in Africa and Russia. In the former case, local illiberal forces, with strong connections to right-wing US Christian organizations, exploit the sensitivity of local populations to neocolonialism and frame phenomena such as "homosexuality" as an implement of Western projects.

Religious nationalism has also reclaimed a fundamental role in the former Soviet Union, where it has filled the void left by the demise of official communist doctrine. Indeed, in Russia, the Orthodox Church has become the elite's most important ally in the promotion of "traditional values," as the primary source of national identity, as an avenue to the country's autonomous path of modernization and as a way to assert Russia's prominence in the new world order.[30] It is no coincidence that Patriarch Kirill of the Russian Orthodox Church, in a March 6, 2022 sermon, characterized the war in Ukraine as a "metaphysical" conflict, emphasizing a fundamental rejection of Western values. He described gay pride parades that had taken place in Ukraine as a necessary "test of loyalty" to the Western world, and as practices that, if normalized, will ultimately lead to the end of human civilization.[31]

In sum, anti-genderism, from a response to the gains of feminism and LGBTQ+ activism, has turned into "a new populist ideology, one that promises to protect 'ordinary people' from elite-driven social engineering" (Korolczuk & Graff: 2018). This is not to say that all anti-genderism is populist. Critical positions in relation to "gender" can be found in mainstream political parties, academic debates, and social movements, with different nuances and motivations that extend beyond the confines of populist politics, and even beyond social and political conservativism. Some feminists and women's rights activists caution against integrating transgender experiences and perspectives into feminism, and maintain that biological sex should be prioritized over socially constructed gender (Lawford-Smith 2022). Moreover, while anti-genderism unifies right-wing populists and illiberals of different stocks, it is not a unified movement. Even among anti-gender activists, there are hard and soft liners, as showcased by the experience of Turkey with the Women and Democracy Association (KADEM) (Unal 2024). The latter is a government-sponsored NGO, created with the purpose of advancing gender justice in the frame of sexual complementarity, in line with Erdoğan's gender conservativism and authoritarianism. Yet, while KADEM cannot be considered a feminist forum, it advocates for women's formal equality, and it has supported the Council of Europe

[30] *See* Stoeckl 2020b and Curanović 2015.
[31] Horsfjord 2024.

Convention on Gender-Based Violence against governmental attacks (Kütük-Kuriş: 2022).

Having said this, the turn of anti-genderism to illiberalism and populism should not come as a surprise. Indeed, gender conservatism is a key component of most right-wing and illiberal projects. Moreover, anti-gender discourses resonate with populist rhetoric and strategies at many levels. In the first place, these discourses have a strong emotional appeal which allows populist and illiberal actors to generate moral panic and to frame themselves as protectors of societal order. At the deeper level, as Ivan Tranfić points out, the gendered dimensions of populism are particularly salient when considered through the intersecting binary and dichotomous logics that structure both gender and populist discourses. Heteronormative and hierarchical gender relations—frequently underpinned by Catholic conceptions of sexual complementarity—reinforce essentialist gender dichotomies, while simultaneously converging with populist constructions of social antagonism. Within such frameworks, "the people" are normatively valorized yet positioned as politically disenfranchised, ostensibly oppressed by deviant minorities and feminists who are cast as elite actors subverting the traditional gender order. This gender hierarchy, which privileges heterosexual masculinity, is thus both sustained and naturalized through populist rhetoric. Moreover, religious populism tends to sacralize 'the people,' reifying social divisions as immutable and absolute, which sustains the populist construction of the social imaginary as an incontestable reality, prescribing both the meaning and regulation of social life.[32]

(iii) Common Good Constitutionalism, Lawfare, and the Reshaping of Rights

To win the war on gender, the anti-gender movement relies on manifold strategies, the key elements of which are: resistance to the "denaturalizing, deconstructive analysis of gender and sex in critical, feminist, and queer scholarship," which is portrayed as a totalitarian ideology akin to Marxism and Nazism, and reassertion of "dominant essentialized gender and sexual norms," which are presented as "natural" and "rational," with an ostensible conflation of nature and common sense occurring. "Gender ideology" is attached to "denaturalized" notions of family and womanhood that run against common sense and are presented as promoting various abominations such as same-sex marriage and the recognition of a "third sex." Often, these discourses are coupled with "assertions of racial, ethnic, or religious majoritarianism" (Graff, Kapur & Walters 2019: 549) and with advocating for isolationism, nationalism, anti-immigration policies, and cultural protectionism.

[32] Tranfić 2022: 3.

The reshaping of rights is central to anti-genderism. The manifesto of Agenda Europe, an umbrella organization which has become a European gravitational center of the global anti-gender community, recommends, among the strategies to "restore the natural order," the "colonization of human rights," that is, as Neil Datta puts it, "the contortion of religiously inspired positions on sexuality and reproduction to artificially resemble classical human rights language" (Datta 2018: 17).

To this end, law had become key to anti-gender action, as showcased by the home page of Ordo Iuris, a Polish extreme right-wing Catholic think tank, which is a clear declaration of intent: "[w]e are engaged in a civilizational war. At stake is the future of our families, our homeland, our faith, and our entire European and Christian culture—one that affirms the dignity of every human being, one that is full of love for freedom, and stands for truth, goodness, beauty, and justice. Law is one of key instruments of this war."[33] Anti-gender activism engages in "lawfare," that is, the use of law—including litigation and legal mobilization from below as well as enactment and enforcement of legislation—as a political tool to advance or halt contested policy reforms and social change (Gloppen 2021: 6–10). Through the reframing of human rights law, anti-genderism uses the law to promote a vision centered on sexual complementarity, traditional family structures, and national sovereignty. Anti-gender actors challenge established international norms and advocate for novel interpretations of rights that restrict or eliminate rights related to gender and sexuality. They emphasize biological sex as the sole determinant of gender and reject the concept of gender identity as a separate or fluid concept. They oppose access to abortion, comprehensive sex education, and other reproductive healthcare services, often framing these as threats to children's and parents' rights, family values, and religious freedom. They often frame their opposition to gender equality as a defense of national/constitutional identity, sovereignty, and cultural values. To this end, transnational right-wing religious actors actively engage in both domestic and international litigation (McCrudden 2015a). Numerous NGOs and pro bono legal organizations specialize in high impact litigation before national, regional, and international judicial bodies in cases regarding gay marriage, abortion, and religious freedom. Many of these lobbies—such as the American Centre for Law and Justice and Alliance Defending Freedom—are based in the United States and have offices or branches in Europe, Africa, and Asia. Today, anti-gender activists from different continents and countries cooperate both formally and informally, unified by an agenda aimed at influencing domestic and international law-making and litigation, in the sphere of religious freedom and sexual and reproductive rights. Anti-gender organizations have become key players in regional and international policy-making fora, such as the United Nations, as well as in norm-creating national and international contexts, such as

[33] Ordo Iuris Institute for Legal Culture, <https://ordoiuris.pl/kim-jestesmy/>, accessed September 20, 2025.

the European Union, and also, increasingly, in constitutional and human rights litigation (McCrudden 2015b).

This transnational activism has resulted in the circulation of anti-gender arguments and strategies across different countries and legal systems. Clifford Bob has remarked that this proliferation of international conservative religious activism was initially fueled by the engagement of the US Supreme Court with foreign law in landmark decisions, including *Lawrence v Texas*,[34] which declared unconstitutional a Texas sodomy law, quoting, inter alia, the jurisprudence of the ECtHR (Bob 2012, 74ff). In a country where courts have traditionally resisted citing foreign law, and the prevailing narrative has associated its use to "liberal" judges, conservative transnational activism soon became a phenomenon of epic proportions. Indeed, a recent report by Open Democracy revealed that US Christian Right groups, many with close links to the Trump administration, have spent at least $280m in the past decade fueling campaigns against the rights of women and LGBTQI people across five continents, of which $90m in Europe alone to influence foreign laws, policies, and public opinion in order "to stir a backlash" against sexual and reproductive rights.[35]

The exponential growth of right-wing transnational activism raises concerns in various respects. The most obvious one is the limited experience that Europe and other non-US contexts have with strategic litigation, and with aggressive ideological legal campaigning by financially powerful actors (Mancini 2025). This is made more worrisome by the lack of financial transparency and accountability of the major US-based Christian NGOs that are active in Europe (including Alliance Defending Freedom, Billy Graham Evangelist Association, American Center for Law and Justice, Focus on the Family, and Human Life International), none of which "reveals who its donors are, or discloses details of how exactly it spends its money overseas."[36]

At a deeper level, transnational anti-gender mobilization poses a particularly acute challenge to supranational organizations and human rights regimes, such as the European Union, the European Council, and the Organization of American States. This challenge is twofold. On the one hand, transnational anti-gender actors colonize rights, infusing them with conservative religious doctrines, disregarding cultural, political, and traditional nation state connections, which results in free-floating, all-applicable doctrines that supposedly satisfies both faith and reason at the transnational level (Mancini 2023). The religious claim to a particular truth that is applicable to all seems in direct contradiction with supranational constitutionalism and human rights regimes, which must and seeks to

[34] *Lawrence v Texas*, 539 U.S. 558 (2003).

[35] Nandini Naira Archer and Claire Provost, "Revealed: $280m 'dark money' spent by US Christian Right groups globally," *OpenDemocracy*, October 27, 2020, <www.opendemocracy.net/en/5050/trump-us-christian-spending-global-revealed/>, accessed February 22, 2024.

[36] Ibid.

reserve a large space for a pluralism of values, including pluralism within and beyond religious communities (Walker 2023). On the other hand, the success of tendentious interpretations of fundamental rights—such as equality—promoted by anti-gender actors in contexts receptive to their theories can lead to a divergence between national and supranational human rights protection systems. In this regard, Poland serves as a key example. In 2020, the Polish Constitutional Tribunal declared the unconstitutionality of abortion on the grounds of fetal abnormalities, thereby eliminating the legal basis for the vast majority of abortions in Poland,[37] in a case that exemplifies the growing influence of transnational anti-gender actors within domestic legal systems. Among the most prominent of these was the European branch (ECLJ) of a US-based ultra-conservative Christian legal advocacy organization, the American Center for Law and Justice. The ECLJ, which submitted an *amicus curiae* brief supporting the restriction,[38] along with other international networks opposed to gender equality and reproductive rights, has increasingly sought to shape domestic constitutional jurisprudence across Europe by promoting a reinterpretation of fundamental rights grounded in conservative, religiously inspired values. In the Polish case, the receptiveness of the Constitutional Tribunal—whose independence and legitimacy have been widely questioned[39]—facilitated the incorporation of these transnational ideologies into domestic constitutional law, resulting in a violation of European standards. Indeed, in 2023, the European Court of Human Rights (ECtHR) found that the 2020 Polish Constitutional Court's decision violated the right to private and family life under Article 8 of the European Convention on Human Rights (ECHR), and that the interference with women's access to abortion was not "in accordance with the law" because of the irregular composition of the Polish Constitutional Court and the absence of proper safeguards against arbitrariness.[40]

As the Polish abortion case demonstrates, the consequences of the war on gender are tangible at many levels in different regions of the world. In Colombia, anti-gender mobilization has endorsed violence under the guise of protecting the "traditional" family and national values, further complicating the delicate peace negotiations after decades of brutal guerrilla warfare. In 2016, the Colombian government reached a peace agreement with the Revolutionary Armed Forces of Colombia (FARC), which included a gender approach, aiming to ensure that women, LGBTQ+ people, and other marginalized groups would be taken into account in the implementation of the accord. To this end, the agreement recognized

[37] Constitutional Court of Poland, Decision of 22 October 2020 (ref. K 1/20) <https://trybunal.gov.pl/postepowanie-i-orzeczenia/wyroki/art/11300-planowanie-rodziny-ochrona-plodu-ludzkiego-i-warunki-dopuszczalnosci-przerywania-ciazy>, accessed September 30, 2025.

[38] "Amicus curiae brief submitted to the Constitutional Tribunal of Poland in the case K 1/20 by the ECLJ": <http://media.aclj.org/pdf/Amicus-Curiae-Brief-to-the-Con-stitutional-Tribunal-of-Poland-K-1.20-ECLJ-October-2020.pdf>.

[39] Sadursky 2020.

[40] *M.L. v Poland* [First Section] App no 40119/21 (ECtHR, October 18, 2021).

sexual violence as a weapon of war; it enabled the participation of women and LGBTQ+ people in the peace process; and it focused on the differentiated impacts of the conflict on women and sexual minorities.[41] The agreement was immediately attacked by conservative political and religious forces, arguing that it was being used to impose an ideological agenda, especially around issues of sexual orientation and gender identity, which threatened the traditional family structure. This narrative played into the hands of opponents of the peace deal, such as former President Álvaro Uribe, who amplified conservatives' concerns, succeeding in mobilizing ample segments of the population, which ultimately rejected the deal in a referendum.[42]

In several countries, anti-gender rhetoric has translated into policy changes that affect free speech, and particularly academic freedom, including the restriction, defunding, and banning of gender studies programs. Hungary's decision in 2018 to remove gender studies master's and PhD degrees from the list of accredited academic programs is particularly illustrative of this trend.[43] In preparation of the decision, the prime minister's chief of staff, Gergely Gulyas, put forward the notion that "[t]he Hungarian government is of the clear view that people are born either men or women. They lead their lives the way they think best, but beyond this, the Hungarian state does not wish to spend public funds on education in this area." Subsequently, Hungary's deputy prime minister, Zsolt Semjen, said that gender studies programs "ha[ve] no business in universities" as they represent "an ideology, not a science."[44] These policies thus aim to reshape knowledge production and public discourse. They testify to a struggle for epistemological control, where scientific inquiry into gender and sexuality is framed as politically subversive and morally dangerous (Kuhar & Paternotte 2017).

Anti-gender policies typically rely on "familialism," that is, the replacement of gender politics with family politics, which benefit only married, heterosexual couples.[45] These policies, often articulated in terms of women's rights, glorify reproduction and female domestic work, and counter women's empowerment and freedom (including from violence), reproductive rights, and same-sex relations. In Hungary and Poland, for example, maternity leave policies raise concerns about potential gender oppression related to their impact and practical application. These policies, indeed, include weak incentives for fathers and long periods of leave for mothers, which negatively affect women's attachment to the labor market

[41] Datta 2018: 16–21.

[42] "Colombia referendum: Voters reject FARC peace deal," *BBC News*, October 3, 2016, <www.bbc.com/news/world-latin-america-37537252>, accessed September 30, 2025.

[43] Becky Prager, "The Hungarian ban on gender studies and its implication for democratic freedom," *Harvard Journal of Law and Gender*, January 20, 2019, <https://journals.law.harvard.edu/jlg/2019/01/the-hungarian-ban-on-gender-studies-and-its-implications-for-democratic-freedom/>, accessed September 22, 2025.

[44] Ibid.

[45] Petó 2021.

and create disadvantages in terms of career progression and pay. Some benefits are only available to heterosexual, married couples and require both partners to be employed, thus excluding single women, women in same-sex relationships, and women in opposite-sex non-marital relationships.[46]

Another effect of anti-gender mobilization is the shaping of attacks on LGBTQ+ rights as measures to protect children's rights to be shielded from immoral ways of life. In Lithuania, a decade-long tug-of-war occurred on whether the law should protect minors from information regarding non-conventional families and sexualities. During a parliamentary debate, a member of the *Seimas* bluntly put forward the notion that "promoting human values" is incompatible with protecting the rights of sexual minorities to exist in the public sphere: "[r]otten Europe is fighting to the death so that children would not be protected from negative sexual education; the same rotten Europe which talks about, and which should promote, fundamental human values seeks to exploit youth and children, so that perverts may freely promote their lifestyle and recruit more followers . . . !"[47] Another MP emphasized how "a distorted rhetoric of human rights" was at play, given that enacting anti-gay propaganda legislation "is not a question of restricting or violating human rights," while *not enacting it* "would amount to a violation of the right of families to educate young people in accordance with their own values."[48]

On March 18, 2025, right before the thirtieth anniversary of the Gay Pride, the Hungarian parliament enacted Russian-style measures[49] to protect minors from demonstrations that promote homosexuality. The new legislation introduces dramatic limitations to freedom of assembly, widens the use of facial recognition (which can now be used to prevent, hamper, interrupt, investigate, and sanction gay parades), and criminalizes behaviors such as organizing, leading, and participating in events promoting homosexuality. The Hungarian government made it clear that such measures constitute a direct challenge to the "impositions from Brussels," and are necessary to "protect children from aggressive LGBTQ propaganda." In Prime Minister Orban's words: "we must not yield; we must not give up on protecting our children. Dragging us before a court in Luxemburg will be of no use to them" (Uitz 2025).

Ultimately, as all of the examples above showcase, in seeking to reshape human rights, anti-gender actors selectively co-opt progressive language, while relying on "traditional" notions, "constructing a new universalism, an illiberal one, that replaces individual right with rights of the family as a basic societal unit and depicts religious conservatives as an embattled minority" (Korolczuk & Graff 2018). Their attempt is to foster a counternarrative to oppose what is seen as the

[46] Szelewa & Szikra 2022.

[47] Quoted by the ECtHR in *Macatė v Lithuania* [GC] App no 61435/19 (ECtHR January 23, 2023), para 79.

[48] Ibid.

[49] *See* Chapter 5.

restless expansion of Western-style individualism. In so doing, they display a strong penchant for communitarianism, infused with references to natural law and morality (Mancini & Palazzo 2021). This resonates with efforts to build coherent theories of illiberal constitutionalism, such as that put forward by Adrian Vermeule, opposing liberals' "overarching sacramental narrative, and the relentless expansion of individualistic autonomy" (Vermeule 2020). Vermeule proposes a theory of "common-good constitutionalism." The theory is a form of substantive moral constitutionalism that seeks to impose a vision of the conservative Good. This vision is forged outside of the legal order (Dyzenhaus 2020) and is grounded in a natural morality that echoes many preoccupations vis-à-vis gender raised by anti-gender movements. Vermeule invokes inter alia the necessity to provide a moral reading to the ambiguities of the Constitution and to legislate morality, contrary to the (urban-gentry liberals') abomination, according to which each individual may "define one's own concept of existence, of meaning, of the universe, and of the mystery of human life."[50] In the domain of gender and family norms, religion is often key in filling with content communitarian resistance to individualism. Religious values are a handy axiological framework to mobilize and are appealing to the "dominant" majority—with the implied consequence that phenomena such as parenting in non-conventional settings or unchecked abortion must be curbed (Mancini & Palazzo 2021).

B. The Misappropriation of a Treaty: How Fighting Domestic Violence Turned into Imposing "Gender Ideology"

(i) Western Eurocentrism and Eastern Peripheries

One of the most dramatic examples of the misappropriation of rights by anti-gender illiberal and populist forces is that of the Council of Europe Convention on Preventing and Combating Violence against Women and Domestic Violence, colloquially referred to as the Istanbul Convention (IC). In this case, a whole human rights treaty was captured in several Central and Eastern European countries: its scope was blatantly distorted and presented as part and parcel of an attempt by Western European elites to impose "gender ideology" on Central and Easter European societies. The case of the IC constitutes a striking contrast if compared to that of the substantially overlapping Inter-American Convention on the Prevention, Punishment and Eradication of Violence against Women, which

[50] Adrian Vermeule, "Beyond originalism," *The Atlantic*, March 31, 2020 (quoting a passage from the US Supreme Court decision *Planned Parenthood v Casey*, 505 U.S. 833 (1992), which upheld the central holding of *Roe v. Wade*—that women have a constitutional right to an abortion before fetal viability) <www.theatlantic.com/ideas/archive/2020/03/common-good-constitutionalism/609037/>, accessed October 1, 2025.

was adopted in 1994 without opposition. This showcases how recently and yet dramatically has the backslash against women's equality occurred under the pressure of transnational anti-genderism.

To fully grasp how the misappropriation of the IC occurred, and, more generally, what are the reasons for the success of anti-gender discourses in CEE, it is necessary to situate the latter within the broader, uneven dynamics of European integration, historically dominated by Western Eurocentrism. This Western-Eurocentric framing has frequently marginalized the cultural and political specificities of CEE, obscuring their contributions to the European project and engendering a sense of peripheralization and resistance. In this frame, Eszter Kováts points to several factors that negatively influenced the perception of gender equality-related discourses and policies in Central and Eastern Europe.[51]

In the first place, gender equality and anti-discrimination legislation were often adopted in CEE during the process of EU accession under external conditionalities, rather than through endogenous democratic deliberation. The subsequent institutionalization of gender mainstreaming—particularly through its integration into European Social Fund projects, aimed at promoting employment, social inclusion, and education—was similarly top-down. In many contexts, such as Poland, critiques of "gender ideology" have drawn rhetorical parallels with the imposed nature of communism, reinforcing narratives of foreign imposition and cultural disruption.[52]

Secondly, Western Europe's achievements in gender equality—manifest in expanded female labor market participation and increased access to leisure—have depended on the transnational reallocation of care work, which is disproportionately performed by migrant women from Eastern and Central Europe. This dynamic reveals a structural dependency, whereby gender equality in the West is partially sustained through the exploitation of labor from Europe's Eastern peripheries.[53] This discredits Western-centric models of promoting gender equality as neo-colonial, and taints as hypocritical the EU attempts to import it in CEE.

A further dimension of the East–West divide on issues of gender lies in the EU's evolving identity as a "community of values." The promotion of LGBTQ+ rights has increasingly become emblematic of normative "Europeanness," delineating a progressive Western core from an ostensibly regressive Central-Eastern periphery. Within this framework, adherence to LGBTQ+ rights is not merely a policy stance but a symbolic marker of civilizational belonging, reinforcing intra-European hierarchies and relegating CEE states to the status of second-class members.[54]

[51] Kováts 2021: 81.
[52] Ibid, 83.
[53] Ibid, 84.
[54] Ibid, 81ff.

The development of gender studies since the 1990s in East-Central European countries, which had not experienced a "shift in social science to social constructivism" and feminist mobilization,[55] has added fuel to the fire. Gender studies have mainly been shaped by exogenous intellectual and financial frameworks, which coincided with the neoliberal restructuring of academia and the import of Anglo-American models. Western donors and academic paradigms frequently set research agendas, determined methodological orientations, and influenced institutional configurations. Gender studies in CEE have thus often served more as a means of signaling alignment with Western liberal norms than as a site of critical engagement with local gender regimes. These developments underscore the power asymmetries embedded in the institutionalization of gender knowledge in the region. They have contributed to the perception of gender studies as a Western import, disconnected from local epistemologies and socio-political concerns—thereby providing fertile ground for anti-gender mobilizations that frame gender equality as culturally alien.

Against this backdrop, anti-genderism, as Kováts explains,[56] has acquired a particular importance in destabilizing the construction of Central and Eastern Europe as politically and culturally "lagging" in post-Cold War imaginaries. Indeed, actors in this region have become influential reference points for global—and particularly Western European and US—anti-gender movements, challenging Western Eurocentrism and liberal hegemony. This explains how anti-gender discourses have assumed a civilizationalist tone, as defenses of a shared Christian and familial heritage allegedly under siege from liberal Western norms regarding gender and sexuality. This narrative synthesizes opposition to LGBTQ+ rights, pro-natalist and pro-family agendas, and anti-immigration sentiment, constructing a coherent ideological identity that transcends traditional East–West divides. Violence against women holds a special place in this ideology, as the analysis in the following section will showcase.

(ii) Violence Against Women, Complementarity, and Same-Sex Marriage: A Matter of Gender-Based Stereotypes

In 2011, the Convention on Preventing and Combating Violence against Women and Domestic Violence was signed in Istanbul. The treaty recognizes violence against women (VAW) as a violation of human rights and a form of gender-based discrimination (Article 3) and establishes comprehensive legal standards to address it. It contains government obligations, including investing in education. The Istanbul Convention defines "gender" as "the socially constructed roles, behavior's,

[55] Ibid.
[56] Ibid.

activities and attributes that a given society considers appropriate for women and men" (Article 3 (c)). The term is used to highlight the harmful attitudes and perceptions surrounding the roles and behaviors expected of women in society, which contribute to the perpetuation of violence against them. This concept does not replace the biological definition of "sex," nor the definitions of "women" and "men," but it emphasizes that inequalities, stereotypes, and violence stem not from biological differences but from damaging preconceived notions about women's characteristics or roles that restrict their agency. Therefore, the Convention frames the elimination of violence against women and domestic violence within the context of empowering women and advancing equality between women and men.[57]

The Convention was initially welcome as a much-needed, ambitious attempt to tackle VAW through comprehensive domestic and regional instruments and strategies. A decade after its signing, however, it had become highly controversial, particularly in Central and Eastern Europe and in Turkey, where misinformation campaigns orchestrated by illiberal and populist social and political actors turned it into yet another emblem of the spreading of "gender ideology" from European institutions into traditional societies. Anti-Istanbul Convention narratives rely, broadly speaking, on four main arguments. First, the use of "gender" as socially constructed promotes harmful gender ideologies and challenges the binary concept of sex. Second, the use of terms such as "domestic violence," "gender," or "violence against women" to challenge gender stereotypes is a threat to the traditional, religious conceptualization and role of the natural family, which will lead to the introduction of same-sex marriage, pernicious educational models, and new refugee status based on gender identity. Thirdly, in some countries, concerns were raised about the potential impact on national sovereignty of the Convention's monitoring mechanism.[58] Finally, the Convention's call to end discriminatory behavior patterns and traditional practices against women constitutes an infringement of local customs and traditions.[59]

These discourses make, from a legal standpoint, quite simply, no sense. In the first place, the notion that there are stereotyped gender roles that negatively impact gender equality is not a novelty: it was introduced in the Convention on the Elimination of all Forms of Discrimination against Women (CEDAW), adopted by the UN General Assembly in 1979, to which all Council of Europe members are

[57] Council of Europe, "Key facts about the Istanbul Convention," <www.coe.int/en/web/istanbul-convention/key-facts>.

[58] Concerns centered around the role of GREVIO, that is, the body of independent experts responsible for monitoring the implementation by the parties of the IC. GREVIO draws up and publishes reports evaluating legislative and other measures taken by the parties to give effect to the provisions of the Convention. In cases where action is required to prevent a serious, massive, or persistent pattern of any acts of violence covered by the Convention, GREVIO may initiate a special inquiry procedure. GREVIO may also adopt general recommendations on themes and concepts of the Convention.

[59] Annika Vollmer, "The Istanbul Convention: A Framework Crisis," *Transatlantic Take*, <www.gmfus.org/news/istanbul-convention-framework-crisis>, accessed September 29, 2025.

parties. Secondly, the Explanatory Report that accompanies the IC clarifies that "the term gender, *based on the two sexes, male and female*, explains that there are also socially constructed roles, behaviors, activities and attributes that a given society considers appropriate for women and men."[60] In the third place, all EU countries are bound by the EU Charter of Fundamental Rights, which prohibits any discrimination based on, inter alia, genetic features and sexual orientation (Article 21). Moreover, the Council of Europe has repeatedly refuted all distortions of the rationale of the Istanbul Convention. In a 2018 legal opinion on the scope of the latter, the Council clarified that the fact that "the Istanbul Convention calls for a gendered understanding of violence against women and domestic violence," by no means requires "member states . . . to include in formal curricula teaching material specifically on homosexuality and/or transgender." "In the same vein, . . . the Convention does not oblige state parties to recognize the status of refugee for transgender or intersex persons," nor "to provide legal recognition of a third sex under domestic law," or "to allow same-sex marriage."[61]

Despite these clarifications, the absence of any textual support for the reading of the Convention as intended to promote same-sex marriage or trans peoples' rights, illiberals and populists succeeded in turning it into a symbol of the European culture wars,[62] which ultimately impacted political, legal, and judicial decisions in most Central and Eastern European countries.

At first, this generalized furor against a Convention aimed at protecting women from violence may seem difficult to explain, taking into account that many European policies, documents, and decisions support much more obvious anti-gender targets, such as gay and trans rights, abortion, and sexual education. Indeed, it is not a coincidence that in all cases opposition to the Convention went hand in hand with formal commitments to protect women from violence, albeit through different means. The problem of violence against women, however, is deeply intertwined with the issues that lie at the core of anti-genderism.

Feminist scholarship has abundantly recognized violence against women as a fundamental mechanism in the construction and perpetuation of gender inequality. Violence functions both as a driver and a manifestation of gender-based disparities: it contributes to inequality by imposing physical, sexual, psychological, and economic harms that disproportionately affect women, while simultaneously emerging from and being justified by existing unequal gender relations (Kelly 1988). In ancient civilizations, physical punishment within the household

[60] Explanatory Report, CETS 210, para 43.

[61] Council of Europe, "Convention on Preventing and Combating Violence against Women and Domestic Violence (CETS 210) – Scope of Obligations," <www.coe.int/en/web/dlapil/-/legal-opinion-on-istanbul-convention>, accessed September 30, 2025.

[62] Maïa de La Baume, "How the Istanbul Convention became a symbol of Europe's cultural wars," *Politico*, April 12, 2021, <www.politico.eu/article/istanbul-convention-europe-violence-against-women/>, accessed September 27, 2025.

was typically viewed not as an act of violence against women but as a legitimate means of correction, unless it exceeded what was deemed reasonable or just by the standards of the time. Only when such actions were judged to surpass acceptable limits were they labeled as violence, or abuse, or excessive force, and treated accordingly (Alfieri 2010). Marital violence was legitimate in France throughout the Ancien Régime (Cavina 2011). In the United States and England, the common law traditionally protected a husband's right to chastise his wife (Siegel 1996). After authorities, in the nineteenth century, declared that a husband no longer had that right, "men who assaulted their wives were often granted formal and informal immunities from prosecution, in order to protect the privacy of the family and to promote domestic harmony" (Siegel 1996: 2118). In both common and civil law countries, men could not traditionally be prosecuted for spousal rape, under the theory that "the marriage constitute[d] a blanket consent to sexual intimacy."[63] Spousal rape has been criminalized in all US states only since 1993.[64] Many Western countries protected honor killing until recently: the last time an Italian judge applied a provision which excused honor killing was in 1981.[65] The provision had been introduced in the Italian criminal code in 1930, during the fascist regime, together with a rape-marriage law, under which a man who committed rape, sexual assault, abduction, statutory rape, or other similar acts was exonerated—together with his possible accomplices—if he married his female victim.[66]

In sum, the history of the legal treatment of domestic violence is deeply rooted in a proprietary conception of the husband over his wife's body. This conception was not limited to a women's body: in common law countries, for example, the law of coverture established that "the very being or legal existence of the woman [was] suspended . . . or at least [was] incorporated and consolidated into that of the husband" during the marriage.[67] Accordingly, a married woman was incapable, without her husband's consent, of making contracts; she could not sue or be sued without her husband's consent; she could not serve as the legal guardians of her children, and lacked the legal capacity to hold or convey property. Women could not practice law, because, in the words of the US Supreme Court, "[t]he harmony, not to say identity, of interest and views which belong . . . to the family institution is repugnant to the idea of a woman adopting a distinct and independent career from that of her husband."[68]

[63] Hasday 2000: 1376 (quoting Model Penal Code and Commentaries, § 213.1 cmt. 8(c), at 342 (Official Draft and Revised Comments 1980)).

[64] Harless 2003: 318.

[65] Article 587 of the Criminal Code (repealed by Law no. 442 of 5 August 1981) stated: "Whoever causes the death of a spouse, daughter or sister when discovering the latter's illegitimate sexual relations, and in the state of anger determined by the offense caused to his honor or that of his family, shall be punished by imprisonment 3 to 7 years."

[66] Article 544 of the Criminal Code, repealed by Law no. 442 of 5 August 1981.

[67] Blackstone 1884: 441.

[68] *Bradwell v Illinois* 83 U.S. 130, 141 (1872) (Bradley J, concurring).

Traditional marriage, which anti-gender actors strenuously defend, was thus grounded historically in the unequal—and complementary—legal status of women and men, which enabled the latter to exercise authority and violence against the former. In this light, the opposition to instruments fashioned to combat violence against women boils down to the defense of the legacy of this tradition, which explains how it has become so popular in anti-gender circles, beyond Eastern Europe. In Argentina, for example, ultra-right-wing populist President Javier Milei recently announced his intention to repeal the crime of femicide as a product of woke culture.[69] In the United States, the Conference of Catholic Bishops "reversed its prior support for the Violence Against Women Act because the reauthorization of the act . . . contained provisions 'that refer to sexual orientation and gender identity,' which in the bishops' view 'undermine[d] the meaning and importance of sexual difference.'"[70]

As the latter statement showcases, opposition to anti-domestic-violence measures goes hand in hand with condemnation of same-sex unions and non-heterosexual marriage. Both, indeed, constitute fatal blows to complementarity and to the "culture of life." Both challenge the archaic and stereotypic notions about the purportedly distinctive roles and abilities of men and women, which justify the subordination of the latter. For decades, domestic and international courts and human rights bodies have relied on the anti-stereotype approach, which deems measures enforcing stereotypical gender roles illegitimate. The doctrine was most prominently developed by the US Supreme Court in sex discrimination cases, aligning with the anti-subordination principle, which aims to address the power imbalances created by discriminatory laws and practices. In this light, even discriminatory practices that seemingly advantage women can be deemed unconstitutional, because they rely on stereotypical notions that have traditionally justified their subordination, entrenched gendered assumptions, and reinforced inequality. Thus, for example, the US Supreme Court invalidated a state statute which prevented men from enrolling in a school for nurses, because it "tends to perpetuate the stereotyped view of nursing as an exclusively women's job."[71] The ECtHR repeatedly affirmed that references to traditions, general assumptions, or prevailing social attitudes in a particular country are insufficient justification for a difference in treatment on grounds of sex, and that states are prevented from imposing traditions that derive from the man's primordial role and the woman's secondary role in the family.[72] The Supreme Court of India recently invalidated the exclusion of female officers from permanent commission in the armed

[69] Noël James, "Women this week: Crime of femicide may be removed from Argentina's Penal Code," *Council on Foreign Relations*, January 31, 2025 <www.cfr.org/blog/women-week-crime-femicide-may-be-removed-argentinas-penal-code> accessed September 29, 2025.

[70] Case 2019: 655.

[71] *Mississippi Univ. for Women v Hogan*, 458 U.S. 718 (1982).

[72] *Konstantin Marin v Russia* [GC] App no 30078/06 (ECtHR March 22, 2012).

forces, recognizing that the justification—based on perceived 'inherent physical differences' between genders—relied on entrenched gender stereotypes.[73]

The underlying principle in these rulings is that the government cannot enforce gender identities and reinforce normative assumptions about the appropriate roles of men and women, because this dynamic contributes to a broader erosion of personal autonomy, and supports a heteronormative and patriarchal social order (Franklin 2010). This is precisely the basis upon which anti-gender actors oppose same-sex marriage: they, "implicitly and explicitly, draw on archaic and stereotypic notions . . . and communicate the . . . view of what is both 'normal' and preferable with regard to the romantic preferences, relationship roles, and parenting capacities of men and women."[74] Same-sex marriage bans, which anti-gender actors sustain, "enforce the state's view that men and women 'naturally' behave differently from one another in marriage and as parents . . . [that] gender diversity or complementarity among parents . . . provides important benefits to children, because mothers and fathers tend on average to parent differently and thus make unique contributions to the child's overall development."[75] In other words, opposition both to same-sex marriage and to anti-domestic violence measure is rooted in resistance to women's equality, and specifically to the anti-stereotyping doctrine. The monopoly of opposite-sex marriage could be justified in a system in which the legal status of men and women was different and complementary, but not in one where women and men have equal rights and cannot be forced by law into complying with stereotypical notions of masculinity and femininity.

The following section offers a comparative analysis of anti-Istanbul Convention campaigns in CEE, and of the political and judicial decisions that resulted from such mobilization. It highlights how—with the obvious exception of Turkey—Christian churches and conservative Christian lobbies were crucial actors in orchestrating the misappropriation of the Istanbul Convention, irrespective of the religiosity of the different populations, and of whether anti-Convention arguments were presented as religious or as having a predominantly cultural or traditional dimension. Other actors that mobilized against the IC include populist governments and parties, ultra-conservative organizations, men's rights groups, supporters of the traditional family models, and various new grassroots initiatives (Korolczuk & Graff 2018). Many of these actors had well-established connections to government officials and political parties, which allowed them to direct resistance to the IC through official political channels. In all cases, anti-IC arguments conflated common sense, religion, tradition, nature, and nationalism, relied on anti-colonial narratives, and ultimately unveiled a profound uneasiness with the pursuit of women's equal position in society.

[73] *Secretary, Ministry of Defense v Babita Puniya*.

[74] *Latta v Otter*, No. 14-35421 (9th Cir. 2014) (Berzon J, concurring) at 16.

[75] Ibid.

(iii) A Comparative Analysis of the Misappropriation of the Istanbul Convention: Estonia, Croatia, Slovakia, Hungary, the Czech Republic, Turkey, and Poland

Anti-Istanbul Convention campaigns occurred in all CEE, through a combination of internal and transnational mobilization. While the arguments and strategies employed to distort the significance of the treaty, and shape public discourses accordingly, were similar throughout the region, the impact of these campaigns varied significantly.

In Estonia, which signed the Convention in 2014 and ratified it three years later, anti-IC actors were largely unsuccessful in their attempt to present the treaty as a component of a broader assault on traditional gender norms and as posing a fundamental threat to the cultural and societal foundations of Estonia (Meurens et al. 2020: 98). These discourses, compared to what occurred in other countries, had a lesser impact in Estonia, which ranks among the least religious countries worldwide, with only 6% of its population regarding religion as highly important.[76] Anti-gender mobilization was efficiently countered by strong feminist reactions, which ultimately strengthened civil society's solid support of anti-domestic violence measures (Tegler 2024: 19ff).

Similarly, in Croatia, which signed the IC in 2013, anti-gender actors did not prevent ratification; but they did, however, succeed in delaying it until 2018. As one of the most religious nations in Central and Southeastern Europe, and as a post-conflict society, Croatia's public and political landscape is heavily influenced by conservative values, and rigid gender norms often take hold, with demographic concerns framed as matters of national security (Korac 1998). The role of religious nationalism should also not be underestimated. The church, which calls itself "Catholic Church among Croats" and has traditionally advocated for the Croatian people's right to statehood, played a key role in politicizing the Convention, which the Croatian Bishop's Conference characterized as antithetical to "natural law" and national traditions. When ratification finally occurred, it was accompanied by a special interpretative statement, according to which the Convention does not contain an obligation for the state to introduce "gender ideology," nor the obligation to modify the constitutional definition of marriage. Taking into account that the word "gender" already existed in the Croatian legal system,[77] the need for the special statement testifies to the ability of anti-IC actors to distort public discourses concerning human rights and international law.

[76] Jonathan Evans and Chris Baronavski, "How do European countries differ in religious commitment? Use our interactive map to find out," Pew Research Center, December 5, 2018 <www.pewresearch.org/short-reads/2018/12/05/how-do-european-countries-differ-in-religious-commitment/> accessed September 29, 2025.

[77] Tranfić 2022.

In contrast with the previous cases, in Hungary, Slovakia, and the Czech Republic, anti-IC mobilization succeeded in preventing ratification, after the Convention had been signed.

In Slovakia, which signed the IC in 2011, mobilization by conservative NGOs and the church, equating gender ideology to the "culture of death," began in 2013, as ratification approached. The following year, the Slovak civic initiative Alliance for Family launched a referendum on banning same-sex marriage and adoption. The initiative was supported by the Conference of Slovak Bishops, and highly praised by Pope Francis.[78] While the referendum failed, due to insufficient voter participation, it ignited anti-gender mobilization, which soon turned primarily against the IC (Očenášová 2022: 42). The church played a fundamental role in this dynamic. including through the organizations of anti-IC public prayers (Očenášová 2022: 45), making rejection of the Convention a priority of its agenda. The Conference of Bishops worked closely with Alliance for Family, pressuring the parliament against ratification. In 2017, the Catholic Church supported the launching of a campaign labeled "Stop the Evil from Istanbul," which, as a commentator observes, "offered politicians a strong geopolitical narrative," as it resonated both with "anti-Ottoman mythology present in Slovak culture and at the same time with anti-Muslim sentiments raised during the migrant crisis in 2015" (Očenášová 2022: 49). Other useful rhetorical tools employed by anti-IC campaigners were the narrative of endangered children, and the equation of gender ideologists with terrorists (Očenášová 2022: 45). Church members also engaged in another technique of rights misappropriation, i.e. the flipping of hierarchies, suggesting that they "might be jailed or even killed" for their anti-gender activism. Narratives of Christians' victimization are particularly powerful in post-communist countries, where churches and believers suffered actual persecutions during communism, suggesting that gender ideology is just Marxism by another name (Očenášová 2022: 46). In 2020, the Slovakian parliament rejected ratification of the IC with a legally binding formulation (Očenášová 2022: 43). Parliamentary rejection occurred in the context of a dramatic conservative turn, after a number of measures aggressively targeting women and LGBTQ+ people had been introduced through different means. Indeed, "a constitutional amendment established the legal protection of heteronormative marriage (2014), nearly a million people voted against the rights of LGBTI people in the so-called 'referendum on family' (2015), and family mainstreaming was legally introduced and required every bill to assess its potential impact on marriage, parenthood, and family (2018)" (Maďarová & Hardoš 2022: 95).

[78] Elise Harris, "Pope Francis backs traditional marriage as Slovakia vote looms," *Catholic News Agency*, February 6, 2015 <www.catholicnewsagency.com/news/31464/pope-francis-backs-traditional-marriage-as-slovakia-vote-looms> accessed September 29, 2025.

Compared to that of Slovakia, the Hungarian trajectory toward the rejection of the IC ratification was atypical in two respects. In the first place, in Hungary, the IC was not attacked in the context of a generalized "war on gender." To the contrary, the war on gender was ignited by the process which should have led to its ratification. Moreover, this war was not started by anti-gender social movements but was carefully crafted by the populist government led by Viktor Orban, who *de facto* artificially orchestrated the anti-IC campaign. The IC was signed in Hungary 2014, four years after Orban's ascension to power, when public discourses and policies concerning gender (equality) had not yet risen to prominence. In the subsequent years, however, while affirming its intention to comprehensively address VAW, the government blocked all attempts toward ratification, until 2017, when a draft was introduced for consultation. This was a turning point: the Center for Human Dignity, a Christian think tank embedded in an international network of extreme right-wing organizations such as the World Congress of Families and Agenda Europe, and with close connections to Orban, released a report called *The Ratification of the Istanbul Convention May Mean the Trojan Horse of Gender Ideology for Hungary* (Krizsán & Roggeband 2021: 67). Based on these arguments, multiple petitions were initiated, including by men's rights defenders, which denounced the Convention for its alleged discriminatory stance toward men. In the aftermath, numerous reports were published by ultra-conservative groups, all emphasizing the perceived threats posed by the notion of "gender ideology" embedded within the Istanbul Convention. The Hungarian government swiftly embraced this rhetoric and consolidated its critique around two principal objections: (1) the use of the concept of gender in the Convention, which was perceived as advancing social change; and (2) the belief that the Convention would compel Hungary to accept increased levels of migration (Krizsán & Roggeband 2021: 69). In 2020, opposition to the IC became official when the Hungarian Parliament adopted a political statement titled "On the Importance of Protecting Children and Women and on the Non-Accession to the Istanbul Convention." In this statement, the parliament affirmed that the IC would be redundant, as Hungary already protected women's rights; it formally opposed the integration of the term "gender" into Hungarian legal discourse; it claimed that the recognition of gender-based violence as a legitimate ground for asylum would threaten Hungarian culture, laws, traditions, and national values; and it called on the government to reject the ratification of the Convention and to oppose it in all EU forums (Balogh 2020: 12, 13). This put an end to the ratification process and paved the way for the Hungarian anti-Convention international activism.

The Czech Republic, which signed the IC in 2016, has also not ratified it. Unlike in the cases of Hungary and Slovakia, however, in the Czech Republic ratification remains possible. Indeed, in 2024, the Czech Senate narrowly voted against ratifying the IC but did not adopt any anti-Convention statement. As in the other countries of Central and Eastern Europe, conservative forces and the main churches opposed ratification on the ground that the Convention promotes "gender ideology," which challenges traditional gender roles and undermines family values. The Czech case highlights the complex overlapping of religious preoccupations and cultural resistances to patriarchal structures. Indeed, the Czech Republic is one of the most secular countries in the world, with 72% of the population not identifying with any religious group and about 47.8%, declaring itself as irreligious.[79] Yet, the arguments put forward by religious actors appealed to segments of Czech society, which is keen on preserving "family values," in light of the communist legacy. Indeed, the family held a special place during the communist regime, irrespective of religion, as a form of resistance against collectivism, as well as in the turmoil that followed the system's collapse, as a source of safety and stability.[80] The potential impact of the Convention on secular cultural traditions was another preoccupation that resonated with conservative segments of Czech politics and society, and it was voiced in particular by the Civic Democrat, the leading party in the ruling coalition. One of such traditions is the whipping of young women on Easter Monday by men, for luck and fertility.[81] The ritual has been increasingly attacked by women's groups. Recently, deputy speaker Olga Richterová called for a consent-based approach, after a report highlighted that women are often attacked against their will by intoxicated groups of men, leaving them bruised, humiliated, and traumatized.[82] Far from being frivolous, the discussion over the whipping tradition intersected with debates concerning the definition of rape in Czech legislation, which was not traditionally framed according to consent. The definition was finally changed in 2024,[83] under the pressure of women's organizations, who had been campaigning to align Czech legislation on sexual violence with the Istanbul Convention,[84] which defines rape as non-consensual acts of a sexual nature.[85]

[79] US Department of State, "2023 Report on International Religious Freedom: Czech Republic," available at <www.state.gov/reports/2023-report-on-international-religious-freedom/czech-republic/#:~:text = Religious%20Demography,Section%20II>, accessed October 1, 2025.

[80] Daniel Straka "Istanbul Convention as a hostage of populism," *Discussion Report*, <www.iir.cz/istanbul-convention-as-a-victim-of-populism>, accessed September 30, 2025.

[81] Daniela Lazarová, "Why is Czechia reluctant to ratify the Istanbul Convention?," *Radio Prague International*, May 25, 2023, <https://english.radio.cz/why-czechia-reluctant-ratify-istanbul-convention-8784080>, accessed September 30, 2025.

[82] Elizabeth Zahradnicek-Haas, "Politician on Czech whipping tradition: 'No means no even on Easter,'" *Expats* CZ, April 9, 2023, <www.expats.cz/czech-news/article/politician-on-czech-whipping-tradition-no-means-no-even-on-easter>, accessed September 30, 2025.

[83] Aneta Zachová, "Czechia's legal definition now includes 'no means no' principle," *Euractic*, December 21, 2023, <www.euractiv.com/news/czechias-legal-definition-of-rape-now-includes-no-means-no-principle/>, accessed October 2, 2025.

[84] Czech NewsAgency, "Czech women's rights organizations calling for a new definition of rape," *Expats CZ*, February 16, 2022, <www.expats.cz/czech-news/article/legal-definition-of-rape-in-czechia>, accessed October 1, 2025.

[85] Article 36 of the Istanbul Convention, on "Sexual violence, including rape," reads:

> Parties shall take the necessary legislative or other measures to ensure that the following intentional conducts are criminalised: a engaging in non-consensual vaginal, anal or oral penetration of a sexual nature of the body of another person with any bodily part or object; b engaging

In Poland and Turkey contestation of the IC occurred predominantly after it had been ratified, as a result of democratic backsliding. The results of anti-IC campaigns in the two countries, however, were profoundly different. The most dramatic case was that of Turkey, which ended by withdrawing from the Convention.

Turkey was the first country to ratify the Convention in 2012. Initial enthusiasm, however, soon turned into open hostility, as the country spiraled into authoritarian Islamist rule under Prime Minister Erdoğan's AKP Party. As analyzed in Chapter 5, women became the target of symbolic and substantial action by the AKP in its effort to distance the new regime from the modern state established in 1920 by Kemal Atatürk, as well as to gain the support of the more religiously conservative segments of the electorate. As reasserting the centrality of the family grounded in traditional gender roles became a priority of the illiberal regime, the Istanbul Convention began being systematically targeted. On March 23, 2021 a presidential decree announced that Turkey had withdrawn from the treaty.[86] No parliamentary deliberation or approval followed, raising concerns regarding the legitimacy of the government's decision.[87] In line with the observations in the previous section, the government carefully crafted the rationale of this decision to make it appear not as a lack of commitment to counter VAW but as a consequence of the misappropriation of the Convention by obscure forces with ulterior motives. Indeed, the statement regarding Turkey's withdrawal from the Convention strongly affirms the country's commitment to the *protection*—not, however, the *empowerment*—of women: "The decision to withdraw from the Istanbul Convention by no means denotes that the State of the Republic of Türkiye compromises the protection of women. Türkiye will not give up on its fight against domestic violence by quitting the Convention."[88] Withdrawal, however, was deemed necessary because: "[t]he Istanbul Convention, originally intended to promote women's rights, was hijacked by a group of people attempting to normalize homosexuality –which is incompatible with Türkiye's social and family values. Hence the decision to withdraw."[89] The statement also refers to a broader Central and Eastern European *malaise* regarding

in other non-consensual acts of a sexual nature with a person; c causing another person to engage in non-consensual acts of a sexual nature with a third person. 2 Consent must be given voluntarily as the result of the person's free will assessed in the context of the surrounding circumstances. 3 Parties shall take the necessary legislative or other measures to ensure that the provisions of paragraph 1 also apply to acts committed against former or current spouses or partners as recognized by internal law.

86 Available at <www.resmigazete.gov.tr/eskiler/2021/03/20210320-49.pdf>, accessed October 1, 2025.

87 Hamdi Firat Buyul, "Turkish court urged to annul Erdogan's withdrawal from Istanbul Convention," *BalkanInsight*, April 28, 2022, <https://balkaninsight.com/2022/04/28/turkish-court-urged-to-annul-erdogans-withdrawal-from-istanbul-convention/>, accessed October 1, 2025.

88 Presidency of the Republic of Turkey, Directorate of Communications, "Statement regarding Türkiye's withdrawal from the Istanbul Convention," March 22, 2021, <www.iletisim.gov.tr/english/haberler/detay/statement-regarding-turkeys-withdrawal-from-the-istanbul-convention>, accessed October 1, 2025.

89 Ibid.

the imposition of "gender ideology:" "Turkey is not the only country who has serious concerns about the Istanbul Convention. Six members of the European Union . . . did not ratify the Istanbul Convention. Poland has taken steps to withdraw from the Convention, citing an attempt by the LGBT community to impose their ideas about gender on the entire society."[90] This statement, which testifies to the existence of concertized anti-gender transnational counternarratives, constitutes a particularly salient example of the misappropriation of rights. Indeed, this is a case of "double misappropriation," whereby the illiberal mis-appropriator, intending to counter measures fashioned to advance the empowerment of women in a context marked by aggressive backlash against gender equality, accuses liberal actors of capturing a human rights treaty to introduce changes incompatible with normative and moral standards.

Furthermore, Turkey's withdrawal from the IC raises issues concerning the interference of anti-gender action with the proper functioning of human rights regimes. The decision to withdraw was met with deep regret by the Parliamentary Assembly of the Council of Europe, which criticized the lack of parliamentary involvement and uncovered the real motives behind the decision, i.e. the mischaracterization of the IC, and the "politically motivated misconceptions and myths" that distorted its objectives.[91] It was, however, the CEDAW Committee which directly challenged the legitimacy of Turkey's withdrawal vis-à-vis human rights law.[92] First, the Committee highlighted how the decision to withdraw "does not have a valid ground and justification."[93] This statement reaches beyond the Council of Europe's condemnation of the misappropriation of the IC. Indeed, the CEDAW Committee maintains that "hostility towards sexual minorities is no ground for exiting a human rights treaty and the position according to which the rights of LGBT people are inconsistent with the protection of women against violence is directly against the very logic of human rights law."[94] In this respect, the CEDAW Committee recalls the principle of indivisibility and universality of human rights enshrined in the Vienna Declaration, according to which "[w]hile the significance of national and regional particularities and various historical, cultural and religious backgrounds must be borne in mind, it is the duty of States, regardless of their political, economic and cultural systems, to promote and protect

[90] Ibid.

[91] Parliamentary Assembly, "Resolution 2376 (2021): The Functioning of Democratic Institutions in Turkey," April 22, 2021, <https://pace.coe.int/en/files/29189/html>, accessed October 1, 2025.

[92] United Nations Press Release, "UN women's rights committee urges Turke to reconsider withdrawal from Istanbul Convention as decision takes effect," *OHCHR*, July 1, 2021, <www.ohchr.org/en/press-releases/2021/07/un-womens-rights-committee-urges-turkey-reconsider-withdrawal-istanbul>, accessed October 1, 2025.

[93] Ibid.

[94] Committee on the Elimination of Discrimination against Women, "Statement: Turkey's withdrawal from the Istanbul Convention: A retrogressive step back in the protection of women's human rights enshrined in the CEDAW Convention," *OHCHR*, July 1, 2021, <www.ohchr.org/Documents/HRBodies/CEDAW/Statements/Statement_Turkey_30.06.2021.doc>, accessed October 1, 2025.

all human rights and fundamental freedoms." The Committee, moreover, put forward the notion that Turkey's withdrawal was inconsistent with its obligations under CEDAW, as well as under *jus cogens*. Indeed, the CEDAW Convention, to which Turkey is a party, requires states parties to eliminate discrimination against women "by all appropriate means" and "without delay." This obligation is of an immediate nature, under Article 2 of the CEDAW Convention, which does not allow for retrogressive measures. Moreover:

> adherence to regional human rights instruments and standards reinforces the rights enshrined in the CEDAW Convention and is an important element of states parties' implementation of their obligations under the Convention. As a unique regional instrument and the most detailed international standard for protection against gender-based violence and violence against women (GBVAW), the Istanbul Convention is a vital complementary platform to CEDAW at the regional level for the realization of the right of women and girls to be free from violence.

Against this background, the Committee characterized Turkey's withdrawal from the IC as "a deliberately retrogressive measure that reduces the scope of protection of women's human rights and is inconsistent with Turkey's due diligence obligation under the CEDAW Convention to prevent and protect women and girls from GBVAW. By disengaging from its international commitments to fight domestic and other forms of GBVAW, Turkey undermines the recognition of peremptory norms of international law (*jus cogens*) such as the prohibition of torture, femicide, and other grievous forms of GBVAW, as well as the guarantees of substantive equality and non-discrimination."[95] Turkey's withdrawal, concluded the CEDAW Committee, undermines the international human rights system seeking to prevent and protect women and girls from violence.

In Poland, unlike in other Central and Eastern European states, attacks on the IC started immediately after signature, in 2012. The then Minister of Justice Jarosław Gowin characterized the Convention as an "expression of feminist ideology," contrary to Polish family values (Krizsán & Roggeband 2021: 2), thus launching what was soon going to become a generalized anti-gender crusade. The Catholic Church joined forces with conservative NGOs in mobilizing against the IC, but also, increasingly, against policies and legislation advancing sexual and reproductive rights (Krizsán & Roggeband 2021: 2). As steps were taken toward ratification of the IC, opposition escalated dramatically. In January 2014, MP Beata Kempa, a vocal anti-gender advocate, established a parliamentary committee titled Stop Gender Ideology, which emerged as a significant platform for fostering

[95] Ibid.

polarization around gender-related issues and for amplifying the broader anti-gender campaign. The Ordo Iuris Institute for Legal Culture played a key role in countering the Convention. Ordo Iuris (a Latin expression which refers to the comprehensive character of Roman Law) is an extremist religious organization that created a web of reactionary organizations in Poland and beyond (Datta 2020). Ordo Iuris has strong connections with ultra-right-wing actors such as Agenda Europe and the World Congress of Families, which receive funding from US lobbies and Russian oligarchs (Datta 2021). To oppose the IC, Ordo Iuris launched numerous petitions and published an assessment report "which served as the blueprint for formulating arguments against the Convention, problematized the ideological nature of the IC, its incompatibility with the Polish legal system and its inefficiency given the existent laws and the minimal violence that exists in Poland" (Krizsán & Roggeband 2021: 59). These concertized efforts, however, did not prevent ratification of the IC, in 2015, just months before the electoral victory of the Law and Justice party (PiS).

The PiS victory was, however, a game-changer, as opposition to the IC became the official governmental position. In the summer of 2021, the government announced its intention to withdraw from the treaty, claiming that it violated religious freedom and promoted controversial ideologies about gender. Unlike in the other Central and Eastern European countries, however, reactions in Poland against the Convention turned into active efforts to replace it with a different treaty, upholding conservative Christian values. Indeed, in a letter to several governments in the region, the Polish minister of justice, "having regard to the constant threats to the family," proposed "that a convention be drafted together to be forwarded to the possibly wide group of addressees at the international forum."[96] The letter constitutes a neat example of rights colonization. It contains several references to "the natural order of things"[97] and it roots the protection of "life since conception" in the 1948 UN Universal Declaration,[98] which, however, contains reference neither to abortion nor to the beginning of life.[99] It distorts the rationale of combating

[96] Claudia Ciobanu, "Poland begins push in region to replace Istanbul Convention with 'family rights' treaty," *Reporting Democracy*, October 6, 2020, <https://balkaninsight.com/2020/10/06/family-rights-treaty/2020>, accessed October 2, 2025.

[97] Ibid.

[98] "[F]amily is the natural and fundamental group unit of society, which . . . should be particularly protected by the society and the State. This arises directly from Article 16(3) of the Universal Declaration of Human Rights . . . Protection of and support for the family is necessary . . . Such protection should be ensured as soon as possible, namely when the family is formed and throughout its existence. What requires particular support is the protection of the life of a conceived child" (Letter, p. 1).

[99] UDHR, art 16:

> 1. Men and women of full age, without any limitation due to race, nationality or religion, have the right to marry and to found a family. They are entitled to equal rights as to marriage, during marriage and at its dissolution. 2. Marriage shall be entered into only with the free and full consent of the intending spouses. 3. The family is the natural and fundamental group unit of society and is entitled to protection by society and the State.

domestic violence, which is presented as being to protect the *unity and existence of the family* and not women. Importantly, the letter carefully avoids linking domestic violence to gender inequality and gender stereotypes, explicitly excluding "a link between violence and gender,"[100] thus "challenging the human rights logic behind the problem" (Krizsán & Roggeband 2021: 57). To the contrary, the letter indicates that the roots of VAW are "pathological factors, such as alcohol and drug abuse, sex addiction or omnipresent vulgarization and sexualization of the image of women in mass-media."[101] The letter continues by altering the definition of "child" in the UN Convention on the Rights of the Child (UNCRC), as comprising the product of conception ("The understanding of a 'child' should be based on the UN Convention on the Rights of the Child . . . with the lower threshold of childhood being clarified. According to this assumption, a child is a human being from conception until the age of majority"[102]). The UNCRC, however, not only does not mention "unborn children,"[103] but it has been interpreted by the Committee on the Rights of the Child, which is responsible for monitoring the Convention's implementation, to include the right to sexual and reproductive health services, including safe abortion.[104]

Unsurprisingly, the letter echoed a similar proposal by Ordo Juris,[105] which, in the meanwhile, had developed a symbiotic relationship with the governing party, sustaining the latter's efforts to build a narrative of "resistance to the West."[106] The proximity to the government opened up a plenitude of opportunities for Ordo Iuris to channel its ultra-conservative views into binding law in Poland and Europe.[107] This explains why many reactionary initiatives targeted at sexual and reproductive rights gathered so much strength in Poland during the years of democratic backsliding.

It was Ordo Iuris' hope that the proposed convention would be ratified by enough CEE to come into force, thus becoming a regional treaty, which would

[100] Letter, p. 1.

[101] Ibid.

[102] Ibid, 2.

[103] UDRC, art 1: "For the purposes of the present Convention, a child means every human being below the age of eighteen years unless under the law applicable to the child, majority is attained earlier."

[104] Committee on the Rights of the Child, "General Comment No. 20 (2016) on the implementation of the rights of the child during adolescence," UN Doc. CRC/C/GC/20, December 6, 2016.

[105] Ordo Iuris, "International support of the Convention of the Rights of the Family – a press briefing in the parliament," *Ordo Iuris*, March 11, 2019, <https://ordoiuris.pl/en/press-newsdesk/international-support-for-the-convention-on-the-rights-of-the-family-a-press-briefing-in-the-parliament/>, accessed October 11, 2025.

[106] Claudia Ciobanu, "Poland's replacement for Istanbul Convention would ban abortion and gay marriage," *Reporting Democracy*, March 15, 2021, <https://balkaninsight.com/2021/03/15/polands-replacement-for-istanbul-convention-would-ban-abortion-and-gay-marriage/>, accessed October 2, 2025.

[107] European Parliament Forum, "Foundation Ordo Iuris Institute for Legal Culture: Intelligence briefing 24/03/2021," *European Parliamentary Forum*, March 24, 2021, <www.epfweb.org/sites/default/files/2021-03/EPF%20Ordo%20Iuris%20-%20EPF%20Intelligence%20brief.pdf>, accessed October 1, 2025.

counter the progress of the Council of Europe system in protecting individual rights. In the words of the Director of the International Law Center at Ordo Iuris, the initiative started "because we saw that the European Court of Human Rights is, step by step, trying to violate the definition of family and marriage in countries like Poland, Romania, Bulgaria. We also have this new project of an EU LGBT strategy, in which the EU would like to impose the recognition of marriage contracted in countries that do recognize gay marriage, on other countries which don't."[108] This constitutes a particularly troublesome declaration of the intent to reshape international law in a "fundamentalist direction by potentially hollowing out existing protections."[109] CEE, whether they have or have not ratified the IC, are bound to respect EU law and the ECHR. A treaty that does not originate in an international organization, but as the initiative of a fundamentalist NGO in tandem with a populist government, and contradicts established human rights standard, would be incompatible with EU law and with the European Council system. Had this project succeeded, it would have deepened the polarization between Western and Central and Eastern Europe on issues of fundamental values, and further raised tension with the EU, which has been struggling to counter democratic backlashes in CEE. An exclusively Central and Eastern convention rooted in Christian patriarchy would have formalized the existence of two mutually exclusive human rights regimes within the EU. An alternative convention that protects and reinforces control over women's reproduction, and legitimizes the discrimination of sexual minorities, would have further led to non-compliance by its parties with EU fundamental values, further exacerbating the rule of law crises within the EU.

The hope of the Polish populist government to launch an alternative convention came to an end when the Law and Justice party lost its parliamentary majority in 2023, paving the way for a new pro-European coalition government. In January 2024, Prime Minister Donald Tusk announced the decision to retract the previous government's motion to the Constitutional Tribunal to examine the Convention's compatibility with the Polish Constitution, effectively halting the withdrawal process. While not successful, however, the Polish effort to build a regional alliance to counter the IC, through the adoption of an illiberal alternative treaty, constitutes a cautionary tale for the EU because it testifies to an escalation in the illiberal misappropriation of rights. The Polish government/Ordo Iuris project was an explicit tentative to subvert human rights standards *by replacing them*, while simultaneously jeopardizing the unity of European Union law.

[108] Ciobanu, n 106.
[109] Ibid.

(iv) (Re)interpreting a Treaty: Anti-genderism in Constitutional Jurisprudence: Moldova, Romania, Latvia, Lithuania, Bulgaria, and the European Union

In five cases (Lithuania, Latvia, Moldova, Romania, and Bulgaria) anti-IC campaigns resulted in constitutional courts' decisions, which directly engaged with the misappropriation of the treaty by anti-gender actors. The Court of Justice of the European Union (CJEU) also issues an Opinion affirming the ability of the EU to ratify the Istanbul Convention, even without complete agreement among all Member States.

The Romanian case stands out as unique because the relevant Constitutional Court's decision directly reviewed the constitutionality not of the IC but of a bill which resulted from opposition to the IC. In Romania, which signed the IC in 2014, anti-gender movements unsuccessfully opposed its ratification, which occurred two years later. The Orthodox Church was a vocal opponent of the IC, together with several conservative NGOs. They accused the IC of introducing the un-Romanian notion of gender as a social construct and of violating the right of parents to educate their children according to their beliefs, and held that the GREVIO monitoring mechanism violated the national sovereignty of Romania. Anti-gender activism persisted after ratification, despite a failed national referendum in 2018 aiming to constitutionalize opposite-sex marriage only. In June 2020, a bill was adopted under the pressure of anti-gender mobilization, banning all educational institutions from "activities propagating theories and opinions on gender identity according to which gender is a separate concept from biological sex" (Brodeală & Epure 2021: 725). The bill, however, was struck down by the Constitutional Court in a remarkable judgment, which, despite not focusing directly on the IC, had important repercussions concerning the latter. First, the Court clarified that the concepts of "sex" and "gender" do not overlap in Romanian law, in light of the fact that the latter allows for gender reassignment, recognizes that sexual orientation is a dimension of sexual identity, and defines "gender" as a social construct that differs from biological sex. In the second place, the Court held that banning gender studies—which are widely recognized and integrated within the field of social sciences—violates free speech and access to information, as well as the rule of law. In relation to the latter principle, the Court emphasized that the ban would create confusion and inconsistency in the legal definitions of "sex" and "gender," making it unclear for people in Romania which laws to adhere to—those banning discrimination or those restricting actions aimed at combating gender-based discrimination and stereotypes (Brodeală & Epure 2021: 746). Finally, the Court recalled that Romania is under the obligation of respecting and advancing gender equality, in accordance with international human rights law and EU law, which take precedence over national legislation. In this respect, the Court mentioned specifically the ECHR *and the Istanbul Convention*, thus putting an end to the credibility of all characterizations of the latter as inconsistent with domestic law (Brodeală & Epure 2021: 733).

Moldova ratified the IC in 2021, after having long refused to do so, due to a change of regime. The Orthodox Church immediately emerged as a central player in opposing the Convention. In its appeal to the president, parliament, and government, the church expressed the opinion that the text of the Istanbul Convention "denies the reality of the existence of a man and a woman." The church further pointed out that the Istanbul Convention had proven controversial in other countries, which had characterized it as a Trojan Horse, which will introduce a "third sex" and "gay marriage."[110] The church's attacks on the IC prompted two MPs to raise the question of constitutionality of the Law of Ratification, which, they claimed, violated freedom of conscience; the right to education; and the institution of the family (Pūraitė-Andrikienė 2025: 328). Before deciding, the Court requested an *amicus curiae* opinion from the Venice Commission, to evaluate the constitutional ramifications associated with the ratification of the Istanbul Convention.[111] The Venice Commission reiterated that "[b]y defining the term gender in Article 3(c), the Istanbul Convention recognises that violence against women does not only originate from biological differences between men and women, i.e. sex, but mainly from 'socially constructed roles, behaviors and attributes that a given society considers appropriate for women and men. Such stereotyped gender roles contribute to the subordinate status of women in society and may result in making harmful practices and violence against women acceptable in the private and public spheres.' In this respect, the Istanbul Convention reflects Article 16 of the [Moldovan] Constitution concerning equality," and does not seek to "eliminate the differences" between men and women, or to suggest that men and women are, or should be, "the same" (para 14). The Commission further clarified that "the Istanbul Convention does not interfere with the right of parents to educate their children according to their own religious beliefs, because this falls outside the scope of the treaty" (para 43), and that "the different types of family and the matters related to it—such as the definition of marriage and adoption—remain subject to the national laws of the Contracting States. Consequently, if the Republic of Moldova establishes that marriage is between a man and a woman, and that the foundational element of the family excludes same-sex couples from marriage then the Istanbul Convention cannot be considered as foreseeing a different type of family as the one established under domestic Moldovan legislation" (para 32). On these grounds, the Moldovan Constitutional Court rendered its

[110] Venice Commission, Opinion no 1065/2021, "Republic of Moldova - Amicus curiae brief for the Constitutional Court on the constitutional implications of the ratification of the Council of Europe Convention on preventing and combating violence against women and domestic violence (Istanbul Convention)" para 14 (December 14, 2021) <www.venice.coe.int/webforms/documents/default.aspx?pdffile = CDL-AD(2021)044-e>.

[111] Ibid.

decision. Distancing itself from the anti-gender narratives, the Court rejected the "Trojan Horse" theory, and it affirmed that the fundamental objective of the IC is to "fight violence against women and domestic violence," and that achieving gender equality is necessary to this end (Pūraitė-Andrikienė 2025: 231). The Court, moreover, relied on the Explanatory Report to the IC,[112] and affirmed that the introduction of the concept of gender in the latter was intended to emphasize that violence against women and domestic violence stem from gender stereotypes. The Court also concluded that the "Istanbul Convention does not define the concept of family, address relationships between partners or same-sex couples, nor does it promote such relationships in any particular way" (Pūraitė-Andrikienė 2025: 46). Thus, it concluded that the Convention did not conflict with the Constitution, which defines marriage as a union between a man and a woman.[113]

The Istanbul Convention was highly politicized also in Lithuania and Latvia. In both countries, anti-IC campaigns resulted in constitutional courts' rulings, which upheld the constitutionality of the Convention on very similar grounds. However, while in Latvia the Convention was finally ratified following the Court's decision, in Lithuania ratification is still pending. While both Lithuania and Latvia are constitutionally secular states, there are significant differences in the religion landscapes of the two countries. In Lithuania, which is overwhelmingly Catholic, the church played a critical role in forging the country's national identity and in preserving its cultural traditions, as an antagonist to Russia, first, and to the Soviet Union, subsequently (Juchnevičiūte, Ališauskienė & Pocé 2023: 267). Latvia, on the other hand, is more religiously diverse, with Lutheranism, Catholicism, and Russian Orthodox Christianity being its most prominent denominations. While both countries have seen a decline in religious practice since the Soviet era, Lithuania maintains a stronger Catholic identity,[114] while Latvia exhibits a high rate of religious

[112] Definition of "gender" (Explanatory Report, CETS 210, para 43):

As the Convention places the obligation to prevent and combat violence against women within the wider framework of achieving equality between women and men, the drafters considered it important to define the term "gender". In the context of this Convention, the term gender, based on the two sexes, male and female, explains that there are also socially constructed roles, behaviors, activities and attributes that a given society considers appropriate for women and men. Research has shown that certain roles or stereotypes reproduce unwanted and harmful practices and contribute to make violence against women acceptable. To overcome such gender roles, Article 12 (1) frames the eradication of prejudices, customs, traditions and other practices which are based on the idea of the inferiority of women or on stereotyped gender roles as a general obligation to prevent violence. Elsewhere, the Convention calls for a gendered understanding of violence against women and domestic violence as a basis for all measures to protect and support victims. This means that these forms of violence need to be addressed in the context of the prevailing inequality between women and men, existing stereotypes, gender roles and discrimination against women in order to adequately respond to the complexity of the phenomenon. The term "gender" under this definition is not intended as a replacement for the terms "women" and "men" used in the Convention.

[113] Decision on inadmissibility of complaint no 219a/2021 (Constitutional Court of the Republic of Moldova, January 18, 2022).

[114] Evans and Baronavski, n 76.

non-affiliation, ranking as one among the most secular countries in the world.[115] In Lithuania, the public role of the church is reflected in a marked politicization of religion, particularly regarding sensitive fields such as education, the family, and other ethically divisive issues. Christian conservative media and NGOs have been highly influential in shaping public discourses since the year 2000 (Juchnevičiūte, Ališauskienė & Pocé 2023: 272). Importantly, Lithuanian NGOs maintain close connections with similarly minded actors in Central and Eastern Europe, and particularly with the Polish Ordo Iuris Institute.[116] Anti-gender lobbying campaigns had been active long before the IC controversies. In 2008, their pressure succeeded in pushing the parliament to adopt legislation which rigidly defined the family as based exclusively on heterosexual marriage. It was, however, a Pyrrhic victory, as the law was declared unconstitutional by the Constitutional Court.[117]

Lithuania signed the Istanbul Convention in 2013, followed by Latvia in 2016. In both countries, the IC was met with hostility by churches and conservative NGOs, on the ground that it constituted a menace against "the natural rights of men and women, their natural roles and traditional and Christian values."[118] Anti-Convention propaganda was absorbed in populist discourses against globalization and the European Union "corrupted liberal elites" imposing foreign conceptions on traditional family models, local values, and ways of life that pertain to the ordinary people (Pocé & Skulte 2023). Consistently with the dynamics of rights colonization, religious actors' arguments relied predominantly on the incompatibility of the Convention not with religion but, rather, with constitutional law and human rights, interpreted through the lenses of secularized Christian traditional values. An open letter by the leaders of the four leading Latvian churches—Evangelical Lutheran, Roman Catholic, Russian Orthodox, and Baptist—warned that "the [Istanbul] Convention is not calling to fight with the real causes of violence, but opens up the opportunity to impose on Latvia a project of transformation of society based on social sex [gender] ideology, which would be contrary to the Constitution of the Republic of Latvia."[119] Similarly, a 2018 letter by the bishops of the Lithuanian Catholic Church warned that the Convention's reference to gender imposed a distorted view of sex in society: "[i]n the noble aim of preventing violence against women, ideological attitudes incompatible with the natural concept of human rights are imposed on society, and an attempt is made to construct an artificial view of women and men."[120] Pocé and Skulte have also showcased how

[115] Ibid.

[116] Juchnevičiūte, Ališauskienė & Pocé 2023: 269–70.

[117] In its ruling of 28 September 2011, the Constitutional Court assessed the state family policy concept, approved by the *Seimas*, which defined family as arising exclusively from marriage. The Constitutional Court held: "15.1 . . . [T]he constitutional concept of family may not be derived solely from the institution of marriage."

[118] Pocé & Skulte 2023.

[119] Ibid.

[120] Ibid.

religious actors in Lithuania and Latvia have resorted to another strategy, which is often used to misappropriate rights, namely the reliance on the notion of "nature" as a foundation for normative arguments about human rights. Biological sexes are portrayed as "natural," whereas "genders"—often poorly translated in the local languages as "social sexes"—are framed as artificially constructed: the differing social roles of men and women are rooted in nature, and any attempt by equal rights discourse to override them is deemed an "artificial" imposition.[121]

In Latvia, the Convention was finally ratified in 2023, with opposition parties largely abstaining from the vote, and with an accompanying Declaration affirming that the Convention would be implemented in accordance with Latvia's constitutional values, particularly concerning human rights, gender equality, and the protection of marriage and family, and that the term "gender" as defined in the Convention does not involve the obligation to introduce a new understanding of sex in Latvian legal and education systems.[122] The ratification followed a 2021 ruling by the Latvian Constitutional Court,[123] which directly engaged with anti-gender arguments. Indeed, the Court rejected all distortions of the *rationale* of the Convention. First, the Court clarified that all the obligations placed on the member states by the Istanbul Convention apply solely as far as the issues pertaining to the elimination of violence against women and domestic violence are concerned and that they do not mandate the acceptance or introduction of any specific form of marriage or family. The Court also found that the Convention does not restrict the freedom of thought, conscience, and religious beliefs, as it does not force particular views upon individuals.[124] The Court also addressed the constitutionality of para 4 of Article 4 of the Convention, which provides that special measures that are necessary to prevent and protect women against gender-based violence are not considered discrimination. The Latvian justices recalled that in Latvian constitutional law, the state may have the obligation to take special measures to decrease circumstances that promote inequality, as long as they are rational, objective, and proportional, a standard which clearly applies to gender-based violence, which not only affects women disproportionally but continues to plague Latvian society. The Court also engaged with a particularly delicate issue, namely the claim by

[121] Ibid, 50.

[122] Parliament of the Latvian Republic, "Saeima ratifies Convention on Preventing and Combating Violence Against Women and Domestic Violence," November 30, 2023, <www.saeima.lv/en/news/saeima-news/32945-saeima-ratifies-convention-on-preventing-and-combating-violence-against-women-and-domestic-violence>, accessed October 1, 2025.

[123] Constitutional Court of Latvia, Case no 2020-39-02, decided on June 4, 2021, <www.satv.tiesa.gov.lv/wp-content/uploads/2020/08/2020-39-02_Judgement.pdf>, accessed October 1, 2025.

[124] Constitutional Court of the Republic of Latvia. Information regarding the judgment of the Constitutional Court of the Republic of Latvia in case no 2020-39-02, on the compliance of the Istanbul Convention with the Constitution of Latvia, is available at <www.satv.tiesa.gov.lv/en/press-release/information-regarding-the-judgment-of-the-constitutional-court-of-the-republic-of-latvia-in-case-no-2020-39-02-on-the-compliance-of-the-istanbul-convention-with-the-constitution-of-latvia/>, accessed October 1, 2025.

anti-gender actors that the IC is incompatible with Latvian constitutional identity. The Court considered that, while both Christian values and the assertion that the family is the foundation of a cohesive society are part of the Latvian constitutional identity, the mention of Christian values in the preamble of the Constitution is essentially a reference not to religion but to being part of the European or Western civilization; and the reference to family denotes that this form of social life is to be recognized morally and legally. According to the Court, these elements are extra-legal factors and cannot be considered binding legal norms in their own right. As a consequence, the constitutionality of the Convention cannot be tested against them.

On October 30, 2025, however, the Latvian Parliament (Saeima) approved a bill, put forward by the far-right party *Latvia First*, initiating the country's withdrawal from the Istanbul Convention. Following widespread mobilization against withdrawal, President Edgars Rinkēvičs referred the bill back to parliament. In doing so, he raised concerns that the decision could undermine the Baltic state's credibility within the European Union, its commitment to complying with international obligations, and the shared architecture of the rule of law in Europe. Consequently, the Saeima decided not to reapprove the text and instead postponed the issue until November 2026, one month after the next parliamentary elections.[125] The October vote shed light on the emergence of a new and troubling political dynamic in Latvia, stemming from Russia's increasingly significant interference in the political processes of the Baltic states.[126] Traditionally, political polarization in Latvia has been characterized by cooperation among so-called "Latvian parties"—ranging from nationalists to liberals, despite ideological differences—against parties representing the Russian-speaking minority. In contrast, the vote in favor of withdrawal from the Istanbul Convention brought together Latvian nationalists and populists with the party representing the Russian minority, demonstrating that, despite deep internal divisions, socially conservative and anti-European forces are now motivated to act collectively.[127]

In Lithuania, on the other hand, anti-Convention propaganda has so far succeeded in freezing ratification, despite a ruling by the Constitutional Court that confirmed that the Convention is compatible with the Constitution.[128] Likewise

[125] Paul Kirby, Latvian vote to pull out of treaty on protecting women from violence prompts outcry, *BBC News*, October 31, 2025, <www.bbc.com/news/articles/cn09x7jpvw7o>, accessed October 25, 2025.

[126] Iryna Matsiuk, The Kremlin Shadow: Strategies and Tactics of Russian Interference in the Baltic States Election, *Blue Europe*, 3 September 2025, www.blue-europe.eu/analysis-en/full-reports/the-kremlins-shadow-strategy-and-tactics-of-russian-interference-in-the-baltic-states-elections/, accessed October 25, 2025.

[127] Bartosz Chmielewski, Latvia's governing coalition is falling apart: a dispute over the Istanbul Convention, *OSW Center for Eastern Studies*, www.osw.waw.pl/en/publikacje/analyses/2025-11-06/latvias. governing-coalition-falling-apart-a-dispute-over-istanbul, accessed October 25, 2025.

[128] Constitutional Court of Lithuania, Case no 18/2023, decided on March 14, 2024, No KT24-I1/2024, <https://lrkt.lt/lt/teismo-aktai/paieska/135/ta2975/content>, accessed October 1, 2025.

in Latvia, the Court was requested by parliament to assess the constitutionality of the "gender-related" provisions of the IC. Specifically, the applicant argued that "the inherent differences between men and women are a given on which the family and society are based," and that the provisions of the Convention therefore negate the notion of the family, according to which only men or women are considered to be members of the family, and that marriage is only between a man and a woman in the biological, but not in the social, aspect. Furthermore, according to the applicant, the Convention's obligation to introduce teaching on non-stereotypical gender roles in the curricula of all levels of formal education would deny a section of the population the right to be guided by their concept of gender and to bring up their children according to that concept, while a different worldview would be taught in education institutions, where education is compulsory under the Constitution.

Remarkably, in the Lithuanian case, the parliament also raised the question of whether the IC threatened the Lithuanian language, in the light of the fact that the IC was assumed to impose the use of gender-neutral language in the public sphere, while Lithuanian is not sex-neutral. To capture the *rationale* of this seemingly nonsensical claim, one must take into account how profound the implications of language policies still are in the Baltic region. During the Soviet era, the Baltic states experienced massive Russian immigration, due to policies aimed at Russification, which included deportations of native populations and resettlement of ethnic Russians and other Soviet citizens. This resulted in a substantial Russian-speaking population in the Baltics, which became a point of contention after the collapse of the Soviet Union. A first generation of aggressive language policies were implemented in the aftermath of independence from the USSR (Alijeva 2017), turning languages into articulations of constitutional and national identity, and language proficiency into a litmus test of loyalty.[129] Traditional fear and suspicion of Russophones have been revived in connection to the invasion of the Ukraine, prompting new initiatives targeting Russian. In Lithuania, for example, the Ministry of Education recently proposed to follow the example of Estonia and Latvia in abandoning Russian-language education, and to limit schools' teaching to official EU languages or those of countries "friendly to Lithuania."[130] These anxieties were easily channeled by anti-gender actors into narratives of neocolonialism, portraying the imposition of gender ideology by the IC as a challenge to

[129] Peters Vecrumba, "Fear and suspicion and Russophones in Latvia," *Balticum*, January 31, 2024, <https://latvians.com/blog/2024/01/31/fear-and-suspicion-and-russophones-in-latvia/>, accessed October 1, 2025.

[130] "Lithuania's minorities department slams proposals to phase out Russian-language education," *Laikas Zinoti Viska*, October 1, 2024, <www.lrt.lt/en/news-in-english/19/2167764/lithuania-s-minorities-department-slams-proposals-to-phase-out-russian-language-education?srsltid=AfmBOoosv6P1mlukKnW2bMTsGZjRX_2YMTdihwJZWMsVJUduJcA_Iisy>, accessed October 1, 2025.

national and constitutional identity, of which official languages constitute a core dimension.

The Court, unsurprisingly, rejected the argument that the Convention entails the introduction of new linguistic rules. The dispute nevertheless highlights the schizophrenic nature of the arguments and political dynamics of anti-gender actors, who, on the one hand, invoke the specter of a renewed Russification, while, on the other hand, politically align with the Russian minority against the European Union in the name of a shared defense of "traditional values," as evidenced by the Latvian Parliament's vote to denounce the IC. In assessing the other claims raised by parliament, the Lithuanian Court borrowed from its Latvian and Moldovan counterparts[131] and relied on the *amicus curiae* of the Venice Commission (para 16.2), which had been requested in the Moldovan case. The Court thus affirmed that the objective of the Convention is to comprehensively counter VAW, and that all of its provisions must be interpreted accordingly. In this light, the Court pointed out that the Convention's use of "gender" refers to stereotypes, but does not negate the binary (female and male) concept of gender (sex), and does not impose an obligation on the state to recognize families other than those provided for in the Constitution or to change the constitutional concept of marriage. The Court further stressed that the state has a duty to take measures to reduce gender-based violence, and that the purpose of education is to reduce society's tolerance of violence, which does not violate the right of parents to educate their children at home in accordance with their beliefs. The Court also noted that gender-based violence not only violates the constitutionally protected right to dignity but is also a form of discrimination based on sex and thus prohibited by the Constitution. Both the Convention, which is aimed at combating VAW by promoting full gender equality, and the Constitution thus pursue the same objectives. In the light of this analysis, the Court concluded that the Convention does not contain any provisions which are contrary to the Constitution.

In Bulgaria, in stark contrast with Latvia, Lithuania, and Moldova, the mischaracterization of the Istanbul Convention by anti-gender social actors ultimately provided the *rationale* to a 2018 Constitutional Court decision declaring its unconstitutionality. When Bulgaria signed the Istanbul Convention in 2016, discussions about gender in Bulgaria were largely confined to specific contexts like women's rights groups, academic research on gender studies, and broader human rights discourse. As in in Hungary, therefore, the Convention in Bulgaria acted as a catalyst for the politicization of gender in the public sphere. Pending ratification, indeed, a "coordinated moral panic campaign was staged by several actors," including the ruling parties' coalition, with the support of the Bulgarian Orthodox Church, the Muslim community, the Evangelical churches, and other religious

[131] Constitutional Court of Lithuania, n 128, para 18ff.

groups, with the aim to undermine simultaneously the rights of women and sexual minorities, and European institutions.[132] The campaign mischaracterized the Istanbul Convention as purporting to protect women from violence, but in fact introducing "gender ideology" and advancing the agenda of the "LGBTQ+ lobby."[133] Various religious organizations and NGOs testified and submitted opinions before the Bulgarian Parliament, emphasizing the utterly un-Bulgarian nature of the concept of "gender," which, they held, is inconsistent with that of sex, and thus challenges traditional notions of masculinity and femininity, and makes it possible for individuals to "choose their own sex." "Instead of highlighting the socially constructed differences between the sexes, the transliterated word 'gender' came to mean the blurring of the distinction. 'Gender' came to denote a gay or trans person, or someone with a fluid identity, a 'third sex', and sometimes even a liberal supporting gender equality and LGBT rights, having a strong pro-European orientation and threatening the traditional family."[134] Opposition to ratification also centered on Article 14 of the Convention, which focuses on preventing VAW through education and awareness-raising. Teaching gender equality and non-stereotyped gender roles was presented as contrary to the belief that marriage is only between a man and a woman, as well as a form of "psychological violence" toward children, as an affront to the right of parents to educate their children according to their beliefs, and as a violation of religious freedom, given that "gender ideology" contradicts the theology of the most widespread denominations.[135] Anti-Convention propaganda also trivialized and misrepresented gender-based violence, putting forward the argument that women are only one among the various groups impacted by violence, and there is no need to address this phenomenon through a comprehensive human rights instrument.[136] Finally, the monitoring mechanism was accused of undermining state sovereignty, suggesting that the new anthropology that will be imposed by gender ideology will do away not only with moral standards but also with fundamental political structures.

Public opinion in Bulgaria was markedly affected by the alarmist and emotionally charged narratives surrounding the Istanbul Convention. An analysis of media coverage revealed that the initial reporting—during a period critical for shaping public opinion—was predominantly characterized by sensationalism, scandal-focused narratives, and propagandistic discourse. The dissemination of manipulative content and the intentional amplification of societal anxieties significantly contributed to the development of a negative public response. In this increasingly

[132] Emilia Slavova, "Notes from the gender republic: The curious case of translating gender in Bulgarian," *Gender Campus*, December 2020, <www.gendercampus.ch/en/blog/post/notes-from-the-gender-republic-the-curious-case-of-translating-gender-in-bulgarian>, accessed October 1, 2025.

[133] Ilcheva 2020.

[134] Slavova, n 132.

[135] Ilcheva 2020.

[136] Ibid.

antagonistic climate, the government, despite having the parliamentary majority required for ratification, refrained from proceeding with the process, due to concerns over potential political fallout and declining public support (Smilova 2020: 186).

As tensions over ratification intensified, a majority of seventy-five members of parliament requested the Constitutional Court to evaluate the constitutionality of the Convention. In 2018 the latter was pronounced unconstitutional.[137] The eight to four decision heavily relied on the "gender ideology" arguments mounted against the Convention by the anti-ratification propaganda. In a nutshell, the Court held that the Convention is self-contradictory and has a broader scope than its title suggests, and can thus compromise the rule of law, which requires legal certainty and predictability, and does not allow the existence of the two parallel, "mutually excluding" concepts of sex and gender. In particular, Article 3(c) and Article 4(3) of the Convention were deemed not compatible with Bulgaria's Constitution. The former provision defines gender as socially constructed;[138] the latter lists gender, sexual orientation, and gender identity among the grounds upon which discrimination is prohibited in the implementation of the Convention by state parties.[139]

The Convention, the Court held, did not provide a definition of the term "gender identity." After reviewing unrelated resolutions by the Council of Europe, aimed at promoting LGBTQ+ rights, the Court asserted that there was "a link between the Council of Europe's policy on the prevention and combating of violence against women, such as discrimination against women based on gender, and the protection of certain rights of transgender people." The majority held that the notion of gender enshrined in Articles 3(c) and 4(3) of the Convention was not compatible with Bulgaria's Constitution. It underlined that "the Constitution and Bulgaria's legislation as a whole were built on the understanding of the binary existence of human species." Traditionally, human society is built on binarism, or the existence of two opposite sexes, each of which has specific biological and social functions and responsibilities. In particular, the Court it referred to Article 47(2) of Bulgaria's Constitution and came to a conclusion which caused lively reactions, namely that "the female biological sex was related to the following social roles – 'mother', 'giving birth', and 'midwifery'" (Smilova 2020: 193).

The majority also held that the IC contradicts Article 6(2) of Bulgaria's Constitution, which forbids limitations of rights based on various factors,

[137] Constitutional Court of the Republic of Bulgaria (2018). Decision No 13, Sofia, July 27, 2018, promulgated SG issue 65/7 August 2018.

[138] Article 3 (c): "'gender' shall mean the socially constructed roles, behaviors, activities and attributes that a given society considers appropriate for women and men."

[139] Article 4 (3): "by the Parties, in particular measures to protect the rights of victims, shall be secured without discrimination on any ground such as sex, gender, race, color, language, religion, political or other opinion, national or social origin, association with a national minority, property, birth, sexual orientation, gender identity, age, state of health, disability, marital status, migrant or refugee status, or other status."

including the sex of a person: "The biological sex is determined by birth and is the basis of civilian sex." Clarity in this matter is essential also in relation to the related regulation of marriage and parenthood: "the understanding that marriage is a relationship between a man and a woman is deeply rooted in Bulgarian legal consciousness."[140] In this light, it was "obvious" that the Istanbul Convention was self-contradictory, because its title referred to the protection of women—which is fully compatible with the Bulgarian legal system—but most of its provisions used the term "gender." The Court, as Smilova explains, based its reasoning on the *formal dimension* of the rule of law, which mandates legal certainty and prohibits the incorporation of vague or ambiguously defined concepts into the legal framework. It held that ratifying the Istanbul Convention would introduce the terms "gender" *and* "gender identity" into Bulgarian law—concepts the Court deemed insufficiently clear and legally indeterminate. Such an introduction, the Court argued, would contravene the requirement for clarity inherent in the formal aspect of the rule of law. This would create grounds for inconsistent interpretations, which compromised the idea of the rule of law. The majority also emphasized that "the meaning implied in the terms, which were used, not only did not promote equality between the sexes, but blurred the differences between them, thus depriving the principle of equality of any meaning": "[i]f society lost its ability to differentiate between a woman and a man, combating violence against women would remain a formal commitment, which was impossible to fulfill" (Smilova 2020: 194). Given that the rule of law constitutes a foundational and structuring value of Bulgaria's constitutional system, the adoption of a core concept of the Convention—*gender*—was found to be incompatible with the Constitution. Consequently, the Court concluded that the Convention, in its entirety, conflicted with the Constitution, thereby precluding its ratification (Smilova 2020: 195).

The reasons for the stark contrast between the other courts in CEE, which deemed the IC constitutional, and the Bulgarian court, which adhered to the anti-gender Trojan Horse narrative, are complex and multifaceted. As a general observation, the Bulgarian Constitutional Court has traditionally struggled to adhere to European human rights standards (Smilova 2020). This can help explain the Court's reluctance to interpret the IC according to its accompanying Explanatory Report, which explicitly builds the socially constructed roles (gender) on the two biological "sexes." Linguistic challenges also contributed to the flawed Court's decision. The Court was not presented with an official translation of the Istanbul Convention and instead based its assessment on an inaccurate Bulgarian rendition. This mistranslation opened the door to "speculations that the Istanbul Convention is introducing a 'third sex' along with male and female sexes" even though an accepted translation of "gender" as "the social role of the sexes" had

[140] Vassileva (2018).

already been incorporated into existing Bulgarian anti-discrimination legislation (Smilova 2020: 189–90). The primary factor influencing the ideological stance of the Constitutional Court's decision was, however, the atmosphere of heightened public anxiety surrounding the ratification process set in motion by anti-gender actors. Notably, the dissenting judges criticized the majority for basing its decision on political and ideological considerations rather than on a thorough and objective legal interpretation. They further alleged that the majority had become entangled in the broader struggle for public approval and had allowed their reasoning to be swayed by the prevailing negative emotional responses toward the Convention expressed by certain segments of society.[141]

The Court's ruling carries far-reaching and detrimental implications that extend well beyond the non-ratification of the Convention. The decision has indeed impeded initiatives aimed at combating gender-based violence and promoting gender equality; has undermined the broader human rights agenda within Bulgaria; and, most critically, has dramatically decreased the legitimacy of the Court as a counter-majoritarian body and as a guardian of human rights law (Smilova 2020: 197). By adopting anti-gender rhetoric as the basis for its decision, the Court has directly engaged in the misappropriation of rights and thus deepened the gap between domestic and European standards of human rights protection.

In 2023, the European Union acceded to the Istanbul Convention, representing a significant milestone in its efforts to combat gender-based violence and advance gender equality. The bumpy accession process was marked by heavy mobilization by anti-gender actors. In the EU context, however, opposition to the Convention was not limited to Central and Eastern European states; actors from Western Europe also raised objections, reflecting broader attempts to delegitimize the European Union and reinforce nationalist agendas. These critiques did not directly attack gender equality, making them more palatable in Western European public discourses. Instead, they were often framed within the colonial narrative that portrayed the IC as a tool through which the EU sought to illegitimately encroach upon member state sovereignty. Resistance was at times articulated via appeals to the principle of subsidiarity, enshrined in Article 5(3) of the Treaty on European Union (TEU), which stipulates that: "[i]n areas which do not fall within its exclusive competence, the Union shall act only if and in so far as the objectives of the proposed action cannot be sufficiently achieved by the Member States." For example, Nicolas Bay, former Secretary of France's Front National and current Member of the European Parliament, acknowledged the objectives of the IC as "laudable," yet argued that the European Union "has no diplomatic legitimacy to ratify such a convention, which it would impose on the Member States, who

[141] Ilcheva 2020.

should be the ones to decide." He further contended that "the European Union would once again be overstepping its rights and undermining the sovereignty of States."[142] A particularly troubling line of argumentation associated with this opposition invoked the purported failure of EU immigration policy as a source of violence against women. In such narratives, gender-based violence was attributed to the arrival of migrants, especially those from Muslim-majority countries, with responsibility ascribed to the EU for its allegedly lax border controls. A former British Member of the European Parliament, known for far-right, pro-Brexit views, stated bluntly: "[b]y letting millions of young migrant men with Muslim backgrounds into our countries, we have submitted our women to these attacks. It is a form of terrorism. No more coverups, no more mitigating circumstances, no more political correctness. Like President Trump, I would like more scrutiny of those you are letting in."[143]

The politicization of the Istanbul Convention, coupled with the fact that not all EU member states had ratified it, led the European Parliament to request an Opinion from the European Court of Justice (ECJ) to clarify the appropriate legal basis for the European Union's accession to the Convention. In 2021, the Court issued an Opinion,[144] stating that the EU could proceed with ratification without requiring unanimity or ratification by all member states. The Court affirmed that ratification could take place within the framework of the EU's competences in the areas of asylum, judicial cooperation in criminal matters, and the responsibilities of public institutions. However, the Court also emphasized that the Convention could not extend to areas falling under the exclusive competence of member states, such as education and family law. The ECJ's Opinion contributed to overcoming institutional objections related to so-called "gender ideology" and the principle of subsidiarity, thereby facilitating the legal pathway to ratification. Nonetheless, political resistance to the Convention persisted, as an example from Italy showcases.

Italy ratified the Istanbul Convention in 2013, under a center-left coalition government, with unanimous approval in the Chamber of Deputies. Public discourse on the Convention has been limited, particularly concerning "gender ideology." Notably, the right-wing populist, heavily anti-gender government led by Giorgia Meloni has carefully refrained from attempting to delegitimize the Convention at the domestic level. This restraint may reflect a strategic calculation, recognizing

[142] "Verbatim Report of Proceedings - EU Accession to the Istanbul Convention on Preventing and Combating Violence against Women (B8-1229/2016, B8-1235/2016) - Thursday, 24 November 2016," *European Parliament*, <www.europarl.europa.eu.www.europarl.europa.eu/doceo/document/CRE-8-2016-11-24-ITM-009-05_EN.html>, accessed October 1, 2025.

[143] "Verbatim Report of Proceedings - EU Accession to the Istanbul Convention on Preventing and Combating Violence against Women (Debate) - Wednesday, 23 November 2016," *European Parliament*, <www.europarl.europa.eu/doceo/document/CRE-8-2016-11-23-ITM-014_EN.html>, accessed October 1, 2025.

[144] Court of Justice of the European Union, "Press Release No. 176/21," October 6, 2021, available at <https://curia.europa.eu/jcms/upload/docs/application/pdf/2021-10/cp210176en.pdf>, accessed October 1, 2025.

that, unlike in several Central and Eastern European countries, Italian civil society may be less amenable to anti-gender mobilizations. However, during the European Parliament's vote on the European Union's accession to the Convention, two of the three parties comprising the governing coalition—the League and Brothers of Italy (Meloni's party)—chose to abstain. Their abstention was accompanied by statements expressing concern over what they described as the instrumentalization of the Convention for purposes related to gender and sexuality politics. In an official statement, the Brothers of Italy Head of Italian Delegation conceded that, consistent with the Opinion issued by the Court of Justice, "there is no possibility that the Convention could be used to impose specific regulations on national governments," but nevertheless maintained: "[w]e want to once again denounce the constant instrumentalization of the Convention by the rainbow left, who would like to use it as another Trojan horse to impose the LGBT agenda." This paradox underscores the political rather than legal nature of anti-gender objections, highlighting the strategic use of gender-related rhetoric to appeal to certain constituencies while navigating binding supranational legal frameworks.[145]

C. Concluding Remarks

Opposition to the Istanbul Convention represents a distinctive case in which an entire treaty has been misrepresented and instrumentalized by both governmental and non-governmental anti-gender actors—including religious institutions—to politicize gender equality and, concurrently, undermine the European Union integration process and disrupt the Council of Europe regime of protecting human rights. Comparative analysis across Central and Eastern European states reveals that, although the rhetoric employed to delegitimize the IC was largely similar across national contexts, the principal actors involved varied considerably. In countries such as Slovakia and Croatia, majority churches played a leading role in mobilizing opposition, whereas in Hungary, the anti-IC campaign was predominantly orchestrated by the illiberal government itself.

Across all cases, a common thread emerged: a clear association between anti-IC mobilization and broader trends of illiberalism and populism. This pattern persisted regardless of whether the primary actors were secular governmental authorities—such as Hungarian Prime Minister Viktor Orban—or religious institutions and affiliated NGOs, such as Ordo Iuris. The controversies surrounding the IC underscore the potent influence of misinformation and

[145] Fatto Quotidiano, "Lega e Fdi si sono astenuti sulla Convenzione di Istanbul contro la violenza sulle donne," *Il Fatto Quotidiano*, May 11, 2023, <www.ilfattoquotidiano.it/2023/05/10/lega-e-fdi-si-sono-astenuti-sulla-convenzione-di-istanbul-contro-la-violenza-sulle-donne/7157096/>, accessed October 1, 2025.

demonstrate how cultural anxieties can be strategically harnessed by illiberal and populist forces, particularly in moments of political opportunism, to erode human rights protections.

The Polish case stands out as particularly significant. The circulation of a proposed alternative to the Istanbul Convention among CEE highlights the seriousness of the threat posed by anti-gender mobilizations, which not only challenged the substantive content of established human rights norms but jeopardized the effective functioning of supranational human rights systems and institutions.

Conversely, the experiences of Romania, Moldova, Latvia, and Lithuania demonstrate that a strong, independent constitutional court can serve as a critical safeguard against anti-gender discourse. In each of these jurisdictions, constitutional courts have systematically dismantled anti-gender arguments, curtailed the influence of religious reasoning in constitutional interpretation, and upheld the treaty in line with its stated objectives and broader human rights frameworks. Notably, Moldova's Constitutional Court directly engaged with the Venice Commission, signaling its alignment with the Council of Europe's human rights standards. Similarly, in Romania, the Constitutional Court proactively affirmed the constitutionality of the IC even in a case not explicitly centered on the Convention.

The jurisprudence produced by these courts is of considerable significance. Their decisions are consistent with both EU law and the ECHR, and—as evidenced by the Lithuanian Court's citation of prior judgments—this body of case law may serve as a reference point for future adjudication. In contrast, the Bulgarian Constitutional Court's decision against the IC stands in marked opposition to this emerging regional trend. This divergence underscores the imperative to enhance both the independence and the quality of constitutional adjudication, particularly in political environments increasingly influenced by populist and illiberal forces.

The central role of independent courts is also highlighted in the case of the European Union. The CJEU's Opinion allowed the EU to move forward with ratifying the Istanbul Convention, in a context marked by lack of a common accord, and by a pernicious mobilization at misappropriating a human rights treaty. Indeed, the polymorphic opposition to the ratification of the IC by the European Union illustrates the convergence of nationalism, anti-Europeanism, racism, and misogyny that is characteristic of contemporary right-wing populism in Europe. It highlights how anti-gender polices transcend West–East boundaries and how anti-genderism serves as a platform for broader ideological attacks on both the EU and the fundamental values of pluralistic democracy and the rule of law it seeks to uphold.

7

Reinventing Traditions to Subvert Constitutional Law and the International Human Rights Regime

This chapter explores the ways in which narratives of tradition are invoked to justify the dismissal of international legal norms, reconfigure international relations, and reinterpret rights frameworks in a manner that legitimizes gender-based discrimination, suppresses freedom of expression, and facilitates the marginalization of minority groups. The chapter focuses on case studies from Russia, the United

Politicized Religion and the Reframing of Fundamental Rights. Susanna Mancini and Michel Rosenfeld, Oxford University Press. DOI: 10.1093/9780191982149.003.0009

States, and several African countries, demonstrating how different forms of traditionalism are employed as interpretive frameworks to justify the subordination of international law to imperialist policies and the reconfiguration of rights in conservative and religious terms.

In the Russian context, this phenomenon is shaped by a complex interplay of geopolitical theories, religious doctrines, and historical revisionism, which underscore narratives of national exceptionalism and imperial legacy. In the United States a similar dynamic emerges through the fusion of Christian theological principles—particularly dominion theology—with originalism as a method of constitutional interpretation. In certain African contexts, such as Uganda, US-based Christian organizations and other foreign actors exploit local theological traditions and demographic concerns, co-opting political leadership to reinstall colonial-era anti-homosexuality legislation, as a purportedly authentic expression of human rights aligned with African cultural values.

The comparative analysis will showcase that, despite these contextual differences, the invocation of traditionalism in all cases does not reflect an organic continuity with indigenous or historical traditions. Rather, it constitutes a deliberately constructed and ideologically driven form of conservatism, selectively engineered to serve authoritarian political and religious agendas.

A. Nothing New on the Eastern Front: The Reframing of International Law and Human Rights Through the Lenses of Traditional Values—The Case of Russia

(i) From Human Rights Enthusiast to Guardian of Traditional Values: Russia's Downward Trajectory After the Dissolution of the Soviet Union

Over the two decades following the dissolution of the Soviet Union, the Russian Federation underwent a profound transformation in its stance toward universal human rights. In the early 1990s, human rights discourse emerged as a powerful unifying framework for a broad pro-democracy movement, bridging ideological divides between former communists and dissidents. During this period, the language of rights not only replaced communism as a guiding utopian vision but also served to legitimize a series of decisive breaks from the Soviet past. Domestically, various legislative reforms and the establishment of institutions grounded in human rights principles testified to Russia's commitment to human rights. Internationally, the Russian Federation positioned itself as a vigorous advocate of universalist ideals (Horvath, 2016: 868). Riding the wave of enthusiasm, Russia acceded to the Council of Europe (CoE) in 1996 and ratified the European Convention on Human Rights (ECHR) in 1998. It did not, however, accept the jurisdiction of the European Court of Human Rights (ECtHR) until 2008, when the situation had already deteriorated. Shortly thereafter, indeed, Russia became the State Party with the highest number of judgments issued against it by the ECtHR.[1] Compliance with the Court's rulings remained persistently deficient in the following years, and violations of Convention rights were widespread and systematic. By May 2012, when Vladimir Putin began his third presidential term, the overall landscape had shifted dramatically. Domestically, democratic institutions had been hollowed out, functioning largely as formalities, while fundamental civil liberties—though still constitutionally guaranteed—were routinely disregarded in practice. Official discourse increasingly substituted the language of rights with an assertive form of anti-Western nationalism. Within public debates, the term "human rights defender" (*pravozashchitnik*) had acquired pejorative connotations, often associated with foreign influence and met with suspicion or hostility rooted in xenophobic sentiment (Horvath 2016: 868). Internationally, Russia's foreign policy and military behavior increasingly took a more assertive and often aggressive turn, signaling a shift toward a more imperialistic stance in several key regions. This shift has indeed disrupted international equilibria, particularly in Eastern Europe, in the Middle East, and in global security dynamics.

The CoE Parliamentary Assembly suspended Russia's voting rights on several occasions, such as in 2000–2001 following the Second Chechen War,[2] and in 2014 after the annexation of Crimea—which violated the 1994 Budapest Memorandum, in which Russia had guaranteed Ukraine's territorial integrity[3]—and the outbreak of armed conflict in the Donbas. These sanctions were reversed in 2019, despite ongoing opposition from Ukraine and Georgia and the continued occupation of Crimea and documented human rights abuses in Eastern Ukraine.[4]

Russia was not expelled from the CoE even after enacting constitutional amendments in 2020, which fundamentally reshaped the Constitution, with far-reaching implications for the country's political landscape and its relationship with the international community. The amendments effectively reset the clock on presidential term limits, allowing Putin to potentially serve two more six-year terms after the end of his term in 2024; they strengthened executive power control

[1] *See* European Court of Human Rights, "Annual Report 2019 of the European Court of Human Rights, Council of Europe," *Council of Europe*, 12 (2019) <www.echr.coe.int/Documents/Annual_report_2019_ENG.pdf>, accessed October 1, 2025.

[2] Russia's voting rights were reintroduced shortly thereafter based on Russia's assumed willingness to work for a solution "in conformity with the CoE's standards and values." Frank Judd, "Conflict in the Chechen Republic—Recent Developments: Report Doc 8929," *Parliamentary Assembly*, January 20, 2001, <https://pace.coe.int/en/files/9151>, accessed October 1, 2025.

[3] Memorandum on security assurances in connection with Ukraine's accession to the Treaty on the Non-Proliferation of Nuclear Weapons, 5 December 1994, <https://treaties.un.org/Pages/showDetails.aspx?objid = 0800000280401fbb>.

[4] European Court of Human Rights. *Grand Chamber Judgment: Multiple Violations in Case Brought by Ukraine Against Russia Concerning Crimea*, June 25, 2024.

over other branches of government; prohibited the transfer of Russian territory to other states, reinforcing the annexation of Crimea; and prioritized Russian law over international law, significantly undermining the country's obligations under the ECHR (Lauri 2021). The amendments, indeed, explicitly prohibited the implementation of ECtHR judgments deemed inconsistent with the Russian Constitution, and the Constitutional Court was empowered to prevent the enforcement of such judgments on the grounds of protecting the "foundations of public order."[5] Finally, the amendment includes, among the objectives of the Russian Federation, the "defense of the institution of marriage as a union of man and woman," and the "preservation of traditional family values." This move effectively enshrines traditional values conservativism within the constitutional framework, thereby providing a legal basis for further restrictions of the rights of women, children, and sexual minorities.

The Council of Europe's leniency toward Russia, despite the seriousness and ongoing nature of its violations, stemmed from concerns regarding the potential negative consequences that expulsion might have for Russian citizens. This was particularly salient given the exceptionally high volume of applications submitted against Russia to the ECtHR. Notably, Russia's continued participation in the CoE, notwithstanding instances of non-compliance, had contributed to the domestic mobilization around human rights issues within the country (Katz Miller 2024). As Dzehtsiarou and Coeffey (2019) note, however, Russia's membership in the CoE and recognition of the ECtHR's authority ultimately failed to forestall a broader regression in democratic governance, adherence to international law standards, and human rights protections.

Russia's controversial membership in the CoE finally came to an end on February 25, 2022, one day after the full-scale invasion of Ukraine,[6] marking the first expulsion in the organization's history. Following its expulsion, Russia's authoritarian trajectory has further accelerated, accompanied by an escalating disregard for international law and by a growing emphasis on the country's role as the "guardian of traditional values."

[5] Decree No. 445/2020 "Amendments to the 1993 Constitution of the Russian Federation Concerning International Law (2020)" (published online by Cambridge University Press in *International Legal Materials* 60, no. 2 (March 18, 2021): 341–46, <https://doi.org/10.1017/ilm.2021.10>).

[6] On that day, the Committee of Ministers suspended Russia's membership with immediate effect, invoking Article 8 of the Statute on the grounds of a "serious violation" of Article 3 obligations (Committee of Ministers, Council of Europe, *Consequences of the Aggression of the Russian Federation against Ukraine*, CM/Del/Dec(2022)1426ter/2.3, February 25, 2022, <https://search.coe.int/cm?i = 0900001680a5a360>). Subsequently, on March 15, 2022, Russia submitted a formal notification of withdrawal pursuant to Article 7. Nevertheless, on March 16, the Committee of Ministers, while taking note of Russia's withdrawal notification, determined—within the framework of the Article 8 procedure—that Russia had ceased to be a member of the CoE (Committee of Ministers, Council of Europe, *Resolution CM/Res(2022)2 on the cessation of the membership of the Russian Federation to the Council of Europe*, CM/Res(2022)2, March 16, 2022, <https://rm.coe.int/0900001680a5da51>).

In January 2023, President Vladimir Putin enacted a decree amending the *Basics of the State Cultural Policy*, a foundational document with legal authority. This revision asserts the concept of Russia's "cultural sovereignty," rooted in what are described as "spiritual and moral values," paving the way for Russian state propaganda to frame the conflict in Ukraine as a defensive effort to safeguard these values against threats posed by the "decadent and liberal" West.[7] The 2023 decree was just the tip of the iceberg in Putin's strategic construction of a narrative centered on "traditional values" to legitimize and promote his imperialistic ambitions, particularly in relation to Ukraine and other post-Soviet states. This traditional values discourse is framed in oppositional terms—defining Russian identity in contrast to the liberal West. In these narratives, Russia is presented as the defender of the moral order, often invoking conservative values—such as Orthodox Christianity, the sanctity of the "natural" family, national sovereignty, and heterosexual norms—as central to Russian identity. These are contrasted with what Russian propaganda depicts as the West's moral decay: LGBTQ+ rights, multiculturalism, secularism, and liberal individualism. This binary not only justifies Russia's internal authoritarianism but frames foreign interventions as civilizational battles, as showcased by Putin's justification of the annexation of Crimea in 2014: "[e]verything in Crimea speaks of our shared history and pride. This is the location of ancient Khersones, where Prince Vladimir was baptized. His spiritual feat of adopting Orthodoxy predetermined the overall basis of the culture, civilization, and human values that unite the peoples of Russia, Ukraine, and Belarus."[8]

The genesis of traditional values is complex and multifaceted, shaped by a unique blend of historical, cultural, religious, and geopolitical influences. The discourse of traditional values goes hand in hand with the rewriting of history, where narratives of historical continuity link Putin's rule to Peter the Great, Saint Prince Vladimir, and Joseph Stalin, to invoke millennia-old civilizational unity, especially over Ukraine and Belarus. The Putin administration pursues a deliberate strategy in shaping national memory of the Second World War, seeking to foster patriotism and national cohesion. Central to this effort is a selective reinterpretation of historical responsibility: while often crediting Stalin and the Communist Party, Putin has increasingly attributed the victory to the Russian people themselves. Through this reframing, the state attempts to cultivate a sense of collective identity grounded in shared sacrifice. Additionally, the memory of wartime suffering is mobilized to delineate a moral and historical boundary between Russia and the

[7] Cyril Hovorun, "'Traditional values' are Russia's geopolitical weapons," *Public Discourse*, July 26, 2023, <www.thepublicdiscourse.com/2023/07/90088/>, accessed October 1, 2025.

[8] Alexis Mrachek and Shane McCrum, "How Putin uses Russian Orthodoxy to grow his empire," *Heritage Found*, February 22, 2019, <www.heritage.org/europe/commentary/how-putin-uses-russian-orthodoxy-grow-his-empire> (quoting Vladimir Putin, "Address by the President of the Russian Federation to State Duma Deputies," *Kremlin*, March 18, 2014, <http://en.special.kremlin.ru/events/president/news/20603>, accessed October 1, 2025).

West—portraying the EU, NATO, and former Soviet satellite states, especially the Baltic countries and Ukraine, as ungrateful or even sympathetic to fascist elements (Reese 2018: 197–98). In some cases, as Stoeckl and Uzlaner explain, the Russian New Right frames the rehabilitation of Stalin within a broader opposition to gender-related liberalism. Within this narrative, Bolshevism is depicted as an alien intrusion imposed upon the Russian people. In contrast, Stalin is portrayed as the figure who preserved national integrity by suppressing the progressive, internationalist agenda of the Trotskyists and restoring patriarchal norms and nationalist sentiment. From this perspective, Stalin's actions are seen as having curtailed the revolutionary momentum, compelling Marxist thinkers to shift their ideological struggle to the West. The Frankfurt School's synthesis of Marxism and Freudian psychoanalysis, which is believed to have fueled the sexual revolution of the 1960s, is regarded as the principal culprit of Western decadence. In this ideological framework, Russia is cast as the contemporary bastion of traditional values, uniquely positioned to lead a global coalition of right-wing actors and thereby reassert its moral and ideological leadership on the international stage (Stoeckl & Uzlaner 2022: 73). Significantly, even within the Russian Orthodox Church, there exists a widespread—albeit unofficial—inclination toward a more favorable reassessment of Stalin's legacy. This revisionist historical narrative holds considerable appeal for Russian audiences, as it reconfigures national memory by positioning Russia as the ultimate victor of the Cold War. Within this framework, the dissolution of the Soviet Union is portrayed as a minor setback when contrasted with the enduring symbolic and moral triumph of victory in the Second World War. Consequently, Russia is depicted as being well-positioned to prevail in the contemporary global culture wars (Stoeckl & Uzlaner 2022: 74–75).

Narratives of traditional values are regarded as a fundamental component of contemporary Russian political and ideological conservatism, serving as a central element in the construction of national identity and functioning as regime legitimacy. From youth education to church–state collaboration, they provide a unifying ideology legitimizing both internal control and imperial foreign policy.

The following sections trace the ideological and religious roots of the narrative of traditional values, and its mobilization to alter the content of international law and human rights. Section ii focuses on the role of *Russkiy Mir* and neo-Eurasianism as alternatives to Western liberalism, used to justify domestic authoritarianism and non-compliance with international law and to reassert Russia's "civilizing mission" in neighboring countries. Section iii focuses on the contribution of the Russian Orthodox Church, in promoting the birth of a Russian Christian Right. Both analyses will demonstrate that the ideological and religious foundations of so-called traditional values in Russia are not rooted in original Russian thought but rather represent reconfigurations of Western right-wing intellectual history, Evangelical doctrines, and American religious propaganda.

(ii) *Russkiy Mir* and Eurasianism as Products of Right-Wing Western Intellectual History

To develop a comprehensive understanding of Russia's approach to human rights, international law, and international relations in the post-Soviet era, it is essential to engage with the concept of empire. The latter, indeed, occupies a central place in Russia's struggle with its identity and geography. As it has poignantly been pointed out, unlike Western powers, Russia did not *have* an empire—it *was* an empire. Loss of empire was, therefore, perceived as loss of itself (Hosking 1995: 27, quoted in Suslov 2014: 67). In the Russian context, the national imaginary is thus deeply infused with imperial themes. The dissolution of the Soviet Union marked the symbolic end of a world order widely perceived as imperial in nature, particularly given the stark contrast between the territorial scope of the USSR and that of contemporary Russia (Laruelle 2018). With the physical empire no longer existent, its revival occurs primarily in the discursive and ideological realm, through the construction of narratives and doctrines that envision an alternative, idealized version of Russia (Laruelle 2018). According to Laruelle, this imagined framework is structured around the symbolic rearticulation of three key dimensions traditionally associated with empire: territoriality, historical continuity, and religious legitimacy. The first dimension—geography—emphasizes territorial expansion as fundamental to Russia's claim to geopolitical significance. The second—history—draws upon an idealized lineage, invoking ancient and often Mediterranean sources of imperial authority, with the Roman Empire serving as a paradigmatic reference. The third—religious legitimacy—is rooted in Orthodoxy, particularly the concept of Moscow as the "Third Rome," which endows the Russian state with a sacral dimension that reinforces its imperial self-understanding (Laruelle 2018).

In this light, two concepts are at the core of the Russian attempt to reposition itself in the international arena, as an imperial power and the successor of the USSR: *Russkiy Mir* and Eurasianism.

Russkiy Mir ("Russian world") is an ambiguously defined concept, commonly employed to describe populations that maintain historical, cultural, or spiritual connections with Russia: ethnic Russians and Russophones in neighboring countries, as well as adherents of the Russian Orthodox Church. *Russkiy Mir* is actively shaped and propagated by the Kremlin for strategic and ideological purposes. Advocates of this notion portray Russia as a "distinct civilization" and a defender of "traditional values" and national conservatism. The concept is frequently associated with contemporary forms of Russian neo-imperialism, and with the idea that Russia extends beyond the borders of the Russian Federation and directly undermines "the efforts of neighboring states to develop independent civic identities and to separate their historical narratives from that of Russia" (Mankoff 2022: 25).

Another key framework informing Russian geopolitical thought is Eurasianism—an ideological paradigm that originated in the aftermath of the Tsarist Empire's collapse during the 1920s, among the Russian emigrant community of Western Europe (Backman 2020: 7). Eurasianism experienced a resurgence in the 1990s in the form of neo-Eurasianism, a radical Russian nationalist ideology that offers a distinct civilizational identity for Russia, positioning it as fundamentally different from both the Western and Eastern worlds. It is underpinned by a geographical and cultural determinism that asserts a unique path for Russia. As such, Eurasianism serves as a crucial lens through which to interpret Russia's geopolitical self-conception and identity formation. Neo-Eurasianism was most prominently theorized by Russian political theorist Aleksandr Dugin, whose interpretation is primarily rooted in the political and cultural philosophy of the European New Right. Neo-Eurasianism is grounded in a pseudo-geopolitical framework that contrasts the so-called "Atlanticist New World Order" with a Russia-centric "New Eurasian Order." The concept of Atlanticism functions as a geopolitical framework encompassing multiple interrelated dimensions. Historically and geographically, it signifies the Western sphere of global civilization. Politically, it refers to the collective identity and strategic alignment of NATO member states. In the realm of information, it denotes the interconnected media landscape dominated by Western outlets, which shapes global narratives and perceptions. Economically, Atlanticism is closely associated with the free market paradigm, liberal democratic governance, and the broader mechanisms of globalization (Pizzolo 2020). Atlanticism aspires to extend Western influence globally by promoting a normative model rooted in NATO-centric security arrangements and the dissemination of Western social, cultural, and economic values. From this perspective, Atlanticism is viewed not merely as a defensive alliance or ideological orientation, but as a project aimed at global hegemony through the universalization of Western institutional and normative frameworks (Pizzolo 2020).

Dugin portrays Russia as a quintessential land-based power, in opposition to the Anglo-American sea-powers. He overlays this geopolitical dichotomy with a series of civilizational binaries—such as Eastern Orthodoxy versus Western Christianity, ideocracy versus liberal democracy, collectivism versus individualism, and traditionalism versus modern dynamism—to delineate the profound ideological and cultural distinctions between the Eurasian and Atlantic worlds (Backman 2020: 9). According to Dugin, as a homogenizing force, the Atlanticist model undermines national and cultural plurality, which he views as central to Eurasian identity. From this perspective, Eurasia is portrayed as experiencing a profound ethnic, biological, and spiritual crisis, which necessitates an "organic cultural-ethnic regeneration" under Russian leadership. This regenerative process is envisioned as essential to preserving the cultural identities and traditions of Eurasian nations. Dugin imbues neo-Eurasianism with quasi-religious significance, elevating it to the status of a political religion that marks a departure from traditional ethnic nationalism toward an ethno-pluralist model aligned with the New Right (Shekhovtsov 2009). Moreover, and rather paradoxically, despite neo-Eurasianism emphasis on the inherently non-European nature of the Eurasian worldview, Eurasianist thinkers such as Dugin exhibited significant ideological affinities with various right-wing intellectual currents in Europe, particularly with proponents of the German "Conservative Revolution." These included a rejection of liberalism and globalism, a deep skepticism toward parliamentary democracy, critiques of capitalism, and a preference for collectivist conceptions of society that opposed the perceived fragmentation and individualism characteristic of modernity (Wiederkehr 2017 and Backman, 2020: 8, 4). Indeed, drawing on Schmitt's critique of Anglo-Saxon liberal internationalism (Schmitt 1950: 140ff) and on Heidegger's call for the reappropriation of (German) historical traditions (Heidegger 2000: 40–41, 29–30), neo-Eurasianism challenges the hegemony of Western liberalism and the universalistic and unipolar global world order, toward a multipolar world of profoundly different "civilizations" (Backman 2020: 3). This new world order will witness the erosion of conventional nation-state frameworks in favor of the formation of large-scale, civilizational entities, often referred to in Schmittian terms as "Great Spaces" (Schmitt 2011). These macro-regional constructs are intended to transcend national boundaries and consolidate cultural, historical, and geopolitical affinities into cohesive civilizational blocs. In this scheme, both Asia and Europe are destined to come under Russian Eurasian domination (Laruelle 2018: 43).

Alongside that of the German "Conservative Revolution," another conceptual framework originating in Western intellectual circles has influenced the construction of Russian civilizational exceptionalism: Samuel Huntington's "clash of civilizations" (Huntington 1996). Although Huntington himself did not designate Russia as a distinct civilization, Russian interpreters of his thesis have adapted it to support their own narratives. His civilizational paradigm provides a theoretical foundation for framing Russia as a unique cultural-historical entity. Particularly appealing to Russian theorists is Huntington's emphasis on religious traditions as core markers of civilizational identity. According to this adapted perspective, Russia is conceived not as a nation-state defined by ethnicity but as a supra-ethnic civilizational space encompassing multiple ethnic groups. What unites these groups, it is argued, is a shared cultural heritage, common language, and overlapping religious traditions.[9] In this light, Russia possesses a distinct civilizational "gravitational pull," exerting influence beyond its borders in a manner comparable only to a select few global powers, most notably the United States. These powers are likened to massive celestial bodies that not only attract but also absorb surrounding entities into their orbits.[10] From this cosmological metaphor emerges the belief, attributed to President Vladimir Putin and his ideological

[9] Hovorun, n 7.
[10] Ibid.

circle, that Western powers have disrupted Russia's rightful sphere of influence by drawing away territories historically considered integral to the Russian world—foremost among them, Ukraine, regarded as the most vital and symbolically significant component of this imagined geopolitical constellation.[11]

By the end of the 1990s, neo-Eurasianism had established a notable presence within multiple spheres of Russian society, including the political arena and academic institutions. It increasingly functioned as an ostensibly intellectual framework underpinning segments of the Russian state's rhetoric characterized by opposition to Western influence (Shekhovtsov 2009). In particular, Dugin's ideological framework has exerted a notable influence on key segments of Russia's political and military elite. From Dugin's perspective, the conflict in Ukraine represents a pivotal moment in the broader civilizational struggle between Atlanticist, liberal Western powers and the continental, traditionalist forces of Eurasianism. In his 1997 book *The Foundations of Geopolitics: The Geopolitical Future of Russia* (Dugin 1997), Dugin openly asserted that "Ukraine, as an independent state with certain territorial aspirations, constitutes a significant threat to the entirety of Eurasia, and without resolving the Ukrainian issue, any discussion of continental geopolitics is meaningless."[12] In this light, the 2022 invasion of Ukraine is by all means an extension of a long-standing Duginist vision aimed at destabilizing the liberal international order and reasserting Russia's role as a civilizational power.[13]

(iii) Importing the American Culture Wars

The Russian Orthodox Church has contributed to the legitimization of Russian military actions, including the annexation of Crimea and the invasion of Ukraine, through a framing of the latter in spiritual and civilizational terms, as a defense of Orthodox Christianity and Russian culture against Western corruption. The Russian Orthodox Church (ROC) and the ideological doctrine of neo-Eurasianism, though rooted respectively in religious and geopolitical domains, exhibit a significant degree of convergence within the broader framework of contemporary Russian nationalism and strategic statecraft. Both contribute to a unified civilizational narrative that constructs Russia as a distinctive sociocultural entity, imbued with a spiritual vocation and positioned in opposition to Western liberalism, secularism, and modernity. It is no coincidence that Aleksandr Dugin has strategically fostered relationships with influential factions within the ROC.

[11] Ibid.
[12] Benjamin Young, "Putin has a grimly absolute vision of the 'Russian World': The Ukraine war is fueled by a delusion of civilizational necessity," *Foreign Policy*, March 6, 2022, <https://foreignpolicy.com/2022/03/06/russia-putin-civilization/>, accessed October 1, 2025.
[13] Ibid.

In the vacuum that followed the collapse of the USSR, the ROC emerged as a source of national identity, tradition, and moral guidance—especially as it had been suppressed under Soviet rule. Many Russians, disoriented by the collapse of Soviet identity, turned to Orthodoxy to rediscover a sense of cultural and moral continuity. The ROC, however, lacked the conceptual and institutional resources necessary to adequately address the challenges posed by modernity (Stoeckl 2014). This deficiency necessitated comprehensive development across nearly all areas of pastoral practice and social teaching. Initially, the church articulated a critical stance toward the concept of human rights in its foundational document, *The Bases of the Social Concept of the Russian Orthodox Church* (2000). In this text, human rights are portrayed as a product of Western secular legal positivism—an ideological framework increasingly influential in post-Soviet Russia—that is deemed fundamentally incompatible with the country's historical legal traditions and cultural ethos (Stoeckl 2014).

The church's capacity to assert its renewed socio-political role evolved incrementally. A significant milestone in this process was the publication of *The Russian Orthodox Church's Teaching on Human Dignity, Freedom and Rights* in 2008. As Kristina Stoeckl (2014) notes, this document marked a transition from the church's earlier rejection of human rights discourse toward a more nuanced and conditional endorsement. Importantly, this shift did not invoke theological language per se but instead reinterpreted human rights through references to national cultural traditions and normative understandings rooted in Russian historical experience. In articulating this more restrictive conceptualization, the Moscow Patriarchate strategically engaged with the rhetorical and legal framework of the Universal Declaration of Human Rights, seeking to align its position with international discourse while simultaneously redefining its terms in accordance with a culturally specific vision of moral order. This vision is reflected in the "Orthodox Declaration of Human Rights. Declaration on Human Rights and Dignity," adopted in 2006 by the Tenth World Russian People's Council, an NGO with consultative status at the UN, headed by the Patriarch of Moscow. The Declaration opens by asserting the existence of a "unique Russian civilization," on whose behalf the document is proclaimed.[14] It subsequently engages with the concept of human dignity, which it identifies as the foundational basis for human rights, and proceeds to advance the following claim: "[i]t is by doing good [things] that the human being gains dignity. Thus, we distinguish between human worth and dignity. Worth is given, while dignity is acquired."[15] Human rights are thus inextricably linked to moral values; the concept of dignity cannot be coherently sustained in the absence of a moral

[14] The Tenth World Russian People's Council, "The Orthodox declaration of human rights: Declaration on human rights and dignity," *Pravoslavieto*, April 6, 2006, <www.pravoslavieto.com/docs/human_rights/declaration_ru_en.htm>, accessed October 1, 2025.

[15] Ibid.

foundation. The document further underscores this position by stating: "There are values no smaller than human rights. These are faith, morality, the sacred, motherland. Whenever these values come into conflict with the implementation of human rights, the task of the society, state and law is to bring both to harmony."[16] In this light, dignity constitutes a limit to autonomy and self-determination: "the freedom of choice becomes valuable and the person gains dignity inasmuch as the chosen alternative is good. Conversely, the freedom of choice leads to self-destruction and loss of human dignity when the choice is evil."[17]

Stoeckl attributes the changed attitude of the ROC regarding human rights to three main factors. In the first place, she holds that the leadership of the church had come to recognize that international human rights law was increasingly likely to encroach upon its internal governance—especially given the (then) pending ecclesiastical jurisdiction cases before the European Court of Human Rights—and that disengagement from the human rights arena was no longer a viable option. Second, church authorities were prepared to align with the expectations of the Russian government, which favored a religious institution capable of engaging with international discourses and developments, rather than one isolated within a self-referential Orthodox traditionalist framework. Third, and most importantly, Stoeckl holds that the ROC had become familiar with the rhetoric and tactical frameworks of rights-based advocacy, drawing notably on the experiences and strategies of moral conservative movements in the West, particularly those associated with the American Christian Right (Stoeckl 2023).

The ROC progressively intensified its engagement with international conservative non-governmental organizations, including through partnerships with Evangelical Christian networks in the United States and right-wing political parties across Europe. Domestically, the ROC established solid relations with Orthodox lay figures, such as Konstantin Malofeev, an oligarch closely associated to Dugin, who has become central to his public visibility and financial backing. A prominent financier and ideological supporter of the ROC, Malofeev—who has been on the EU sanctions' list since 2014[18]—openly espouses monarchist views. He established the Saint Basil the Great Charitable Foundation, which supports numerous initiatives promoting conservative family values (including anti-abortion campaigns), Orthodox religious education, and the preservation and development of Orthodox churches and monastic institutions (Laruelle 2018:120). Malofeev has cultivated strong ties with a diverse array of international right-wing actors, ranging from anti-gender activists and far-right political parties—such as France's Rassemblement National and Austria's Freedom Party—to Spanish

[16] Ibid.
[17] Ibid.
[18] European Parliament, "Russia's war on Ukraine: The Kremlin's use of religion as a foreign policy instrument," *European Parliamentary Research Service*, May 2022, <www.europarl.europa.eu/RegData/etudes/ATAG/2022/729430/EPRS_ATA(2022)729430_EN.pdf>, accessed October 1, 2025.

monarchists and conservative religious organizations (Laruelle 2018: 204). To this end, Malofeev's foundation has supported, inter alia, the activities of the World Congress of Families (WCF), a transnational non-governmental pro-"natural" family organization. The WCF was born in the mid 1990s, thanks to the combined effort of American religious pro-family activists and Russian demographs, concerned by the dramatic decrease in birthrate following the end of the USSR (Stoeckl 2020a). Through its yearly congresses across Europe, the United States, and the former Soviet Union, the WCF has provided the perfect learning environment for the new Russian Religious Right, which has adopted strategies and rhetorical frameworks from its American counterpart, incorporating their techniques and discursive models into domestic and international moral and political advocacy (Stoeckl 2020a).

The strategic alignment of the ROC with segments of the Western Christian Right has yielded significant and tangible consequences. Key themes of the US culture wars—particularly opposition to sexual and reproductive rights and efforts to expand the privileges of religious majorities—have been transposed into the Russian context, as will be explored in the following Section. This partnership has also bolstered the ROC's international influence, affording it new opportunities to exercise soft power on the global stage. The internalization of culture war dynamics, moreover, has reinforced the reciprocal interdependence between the ROC and the state. As a result, alternative theological and social perspectives—especially those of a more liberal orientation—have been increasingly marginalized or suppressed (Stoeckl & Uzlaner 2022: 12).

(iv) Reshaping Human Rights, at Home and Abroad

The convergence of interests between the Russian political leadership and the ROC has been responsible for shaping the country's human rights agenda according to traditional values, as an alternative discourse, conflicting with secular liberal human rights interpretation. Domestically, this dynamic has resulted, inter alia, in altering the scope and significance of religious freedom to secure the ROC's privileged position; and in preventing any liberalizing influence of international human rights on family law and in the sphere of sexual and reproductive rights. Internationally, by foregrounding traditional values and positioning itself as a global actor in culture wars over gender, sexuality, and family, the ROC has emerged as both a religious institution and a strategic normative actor in international affairs.

iv.1. From religious freedom to religious majoritarianism

As it has emerged in the previous discussion, the ROC has been critical in the conceptualization, legitimization, and mobilization of the narrative of traditional values and of its infusion in human rights. Thanks to its being widely regarded by the broader public as a key source of moral authority, the ROC has assumed a central role in defining and upholding moral and ethical norms within Russian society (Stepanova 2023). By the same token, religion has been enlisted by President Putin as a crucial element of Russia's foreign policy through the mobilization of a form of nationalism that combines religious and authoritarian elements. It is no coincidence that the period of Russia's disengagement from European norms, which culminated in its expulsion from the CoE, has also witnessed a dramatic reshaping of church–state relations. Under Putin, the ROC has received extensive state support—financial, legal, and symbolic. It plays a prominent role in national holidays, educational curricula, military chaplaincies, and even foreign policy discourses. This convergence has blurred the constitutionally enshrined separation between religious institutions and the state. The ROC's privileged status has led to the emergence of a system of religious majoritarianism, in which alternative or non-traditional religious groups face heightened scrutiny, legal restrictions, and downright persecution.

While the Russian trajectory regarding religious freedom can hardly be compared to that of any non-communist country, there is a parallel between the Russian progression to religious majoritarianism and similar tendencies in Western countries. As the analysis in Chapters 5 has shown, religions have regained a central position as sources of integration of the polity in many democratic states. In this respect, the emphasis is often placed not on the transcendent nature of religion but, rather, on its cultural dimension. Thus, religion undergoes a process of secularization and semantic disarticulation, and it becomes an implicit mainstay engrained in the secular nation's tradition and culture. This process fosters the return of Christian culture and tradition in the public sphere, challenging the principle of separation between church and state. The premise is that states must recognize that the national religious inheritance is not just one among other denominations but rather an element of civic cohesion. What follows is that the historical national religion should enjoy a preferential treatment, while other denominations should simply be tolerated. Secularism, thus, turns into 'semi-secularism' that represents what remains of the old dream of the 'Christian Republic' and is based on the opposite of the Westphalian principle: *cuius religio, eius et regio*. The result is, on the one hand, a new form of alliance between religion and public power, where the ethical force of the first one upholds the political force of the latter and vice versa. On the other hand, the culturalization of religion facilitates the othering and the marginalization of minority religious cultures, thus lowering the protection of religious freedom (Mancini 2014). This trajectory is exemplified in Europe by the *Lautsi* case, discussed in Chapter 5, which was reversed thanks to the support of US-based law organizations, that built on their country's decades old experience in strategic litigation aimed at advancing Christianity at the detriment of minority religions. Recent cases testifying to this tendency in the United States include decisions legitimizing various forms of public prayers;[19] public funding of fundamentalist Christian schools;[20] religiously based exemptions to the application of general laws and policies;[21] discrimination in the entry of immigrants, non-immigrants, and asylum-seekers based on religion;[22] as well as frontal attacks on minority religions, particularly those of Native Americans (McNally 2020).

These dynamics have been dramatically accelerated in Russia by the failure of the democratizing process and the rapid emergence of authoritarianism under Putin. During the Soviet period, religious expression was systematically suppressed while state-sponsored atheism was actively propagated. A significant shift toward the acknowledgment of religious freedoms occurred in 1990, during the period of Perestroika,[23] with the introduction of legislation that prohibited the establishment of a state religion and restricted government interference in religious matters. Under this legal framework, religious institutions were granted the autonomy to conduct worship services and missionary work, establish educational institutions such as schools and seminaries, possess property, and disseminate religious publications—without the obligation to register with the state (Davis 1997). This development was met with concern by the ROC, which perceived the law as a threat to its traditional dominance, particularly in light of increasing competition from newer, especially Protestant, denominations (Curanović 2015: 5).

The Moscow Patriarchate of the ROC aligned itself with the state in an effort to safeguard and strengthen its privileged status. Facing a crisis of legitimacy, the politically compromised Russian elites identified strategic value in endorsing the ROC—an institution that retained widespread public approval (Curanović 2015). This convergence laid the groundwork for a renewed form of symbiosis between religious authority and political power, wherein the moral legitimacy of the former served to reinforce the authority of the latter, and, reciprocally, the political establishment bolstered the institutional influence of the church.

The new Law on the Freedom of Conscience and Religious Associations[24] was enacted in 1997, reducing the scope of religious pluralism and conferring a "special role" on the ROC. It recognized the special role of Russian Orthodoxy in the country's "history and the formation and development of its spirituality and culture," as well as the existence of four "traditional" religions in the Russian Federation—Christianity, Islam, Buddhism, and Judaism. This effectively

[19] *Town of Greece v Galloway*, 572 U.S. 565 (2014); *Kennedy v Bremerton School District* 597 U.S. 507 (2022).

[20] *Carson v Makin* 596 U.S. 767 (2022).

[21] *Burwell v Hobby Lobby Stores, Inc.*, 573 U.S. 682 (2014), *Little Sisters of the Poor Saints Peter and Paul Home v Pennsylvania*, 591 U.S. (2020); *Masterpiece Cakeshop v Colorado Civil Rights Commission*, 584 U.S. 617 (2018).

[22] *Trump v Hawaii*, 585 U.S. 667 (2018).

[23] *See* McTernan 1990: 20–21.

[24] Federal'nyi Zakon RF o Svobodye Sovesti i o Religioznykh Ob"edinenyakh [Federal Law on the Freedom of Conscience and Religious Associations], *Rossiiskaia Gazeta* [*Russian Gazette*], September 26, 1997.

excluded from official recognition all religious communities that had been established in Russia following the collapse of the Soviet Union (Stoeckl 2020b: 243–44), thereby delivering a significant setback to the most formidable rivals of the ROC. This marked the initial step in a broader legislative trajectory that fundamentally reshaped the secular nature of the state and undermined the principle of equality among religious denominations as enshrined in the 1993 Constitution.[25] The law conferred upon the government the authority to impose restrictions on religious freedoms in the name of the constitutional structure and security of the government; the morality, health, rights, and legal interests of persons; or the defense of the country.[26]

Starting in 2016, anti-extremism legislation further restricted the religious freedom of minority faiths.[27] Indeed, this legislative framework grants state authorities the discretion to prohibit the activities of religious associations on broad grounds, including alleged violations of public order or involvement in so-called "extremist activity," and criminalized a wide range of behaviors, while failing to offer a clear legal definition of "extremism."[28] A law enacted in 2022 requires certain organizations, including religious groups and individuals, to publicly identify themselves as foreign agents, with the obvious objective to discredit them.[29] These provisions have legitimized the systematic repression of several religious minorities. A 2017 Supreme Court ruling declared the Jehovah's Witnesses Administrative Center to be an extremist organization, closed the organization on those grounds, and banned all Jehovah's Witnesses activities, including the organization's website and all its regional branches.[30] Starting in the early 2000s, the Supreme Court has also banned the activities of several Islamic organizations on the grounds of extremism.[31] Religious groups and non-governmental organizations were systematically reported. Authorities investigated, detained, imprisoned, tortured, and physically abused persons and seized their property because of their religious belief or affiliation or membership in groups designated "extremist," "terrorist," or "undesirable."[32]

[25] The 1993 Constitution declares the state is secular and guarantees freedom of religion, equal rights irrespective of religious belief, and the right to worship and profess one's religion.

[26] US Department of State, "Report on International Religious Freedom: Russia (2019)," <www.state.gov/wp-content/uploads/2020/05/RUSSIA-2019-INTERNATIONAL-RELIGIOUS-FREEDOM-REPORT.pdf>, accessed October 2, 2025.

[27] US Department of State, "Report on International Religious Freedom: Russia (2016)," <www.state.gov/wp-content/uploads/2019/01/Russia-3.pdf>, accessed October 2, 2025.

[28] US Department of State, Russia 2019 Report, n 26, 4.

[29] US Department of State, "Report on International Religious Freedom: Russia (2023)," <www.state.gov/reports/2023-report-on-international-religious-freedom/russia/>, accessed October 2, 2025.

[30] Tom O'Connor, "Religion in Russia: Jehovah's Witnesses declared 'extremist organization' by Russian justice ministry," *Newsweek*, March 17, 2017, <www.newsweek.com/russia-religion-jehovah-witnesses-declare-extremist-organization-569953>, accessed October 1, 2025.

[31] Ibid; US Department of State, Russia 2019 Report, n 26, 5.

[32] US Department of State, Russia 2023 Report, n 29.

iv.2. The assault on reproductive rights

The regulation of abortion in post-Soviet Russia has been influenced by a complex combination of the ROC's doctrine and of American Evangelical anti-abortion arguments and technics, which have been adapted to the unique Russian context.[33] In 1920, under the Bolsheviks, the Soviet Union became the first modern state to provide women with access to abortion services upon request within a medical framework. This policy was reversed in 1936 when abortion was recriminalized under Stalin, motivated primarily by demographic considerations, only to be decriminalized again in 1954. In the decades that followed, abortion became the primary method of birth control, largely due to the limited availability of contraceptives and the absence of comprehensive sexual education (Avdeev, Blum & Troitskaya 1995: 39–66 and 61–62).[34]

From the early 2000s onward, the Russian government has implemented a range of policies and initiatives aimed at curbing abortion rates while promoting fertility and population growth. These measures have taken both legal and non-legal forms—on the one hand, through the imposition of legislative restrictions on abortion access, and on the other, through public campaigns and programs designed to dissuade women from terminating pregnancies. As a result, Russia has transitioned from having one of the most liberal abortion regimes in the world to a regulatory framework more in line with that of many European countries, where comparatively restrictive abortion laws are in place. The current abortion legislation, which came into effect in 2012, emerged amid intense public and political debate that engaged three principal lines of argumentation simultaneously: the right to life of the fetus, the dangers posed by abortion to women's health and well-being, and the broader societal interest to increase birthrate (Mancini & Stoeckl 2018). These three narratives, which have developed concurrently in Russia and have coalesced into a unified rhetorical framework, are rooted in American anti-abortion movements.

In the aftermath of *Roe v Wade*, the pro-life movement persistently opposed abortion rights by invoking the inherent value of prenatal life. Central to this opposition was the claim that the fetus constitutes a human person endowed with a right to life. This framing relied on the construction of a rights-based conflict between women and fetuses, wherein the rights of the latter were posited as paramount. However, this fetus-centered approach ultimately failed to generate widespread public support. On the contrary, it alienated large segments of the American population—particularly women—who perceived such rhetoric as dismissive of their own rights and autonomy. The advent of the Reagan administration, which adopted a staunchly anti-choice stance, created new political opportunities for the

[33] Parts of this section draw on Mancini & Stoeckl 2018.

[34] *See* Avdeev, Blum & Troitskaya 1995: 39–66 and 61–62; Popov 1990: 5–7; Popov, Visser & Ketting 1993: 227–35; Sakevich & Denisov 2014: 1–25.

pro-life movement. Within this context, a strategic discursive shift emerged. Rather than foregrounding the fetus as a moral subject, the movement began to reorient its rhetoric toward women's health and rights. This new discourse appropriated feminist language, human rights frameworks, and scientific-medical terminology in an attempt to reframe the abortion debate and eliminate the perceived conflict between maternal and fetal rights. Instead of employing graphic imagery or overtly condemning women for terminating pregnancies, the movement began to portray women as victims of abortion. As Siegel (2008: 1655) observes, the emerging anti-abortion narrative contended that abortion harms women—physically, socially, psychologically, and emotionally—and undermines their rights to motherhood and to relationships with their children. Within this framework, the concept of "choice" was rendered illusory: abortion was redefined not as an exercise of autonomy but as a coerced or misguided act from which women needed protection. Accordingly, the restriction—or outright prohibition—of abortion was recast as a means of safeguarding women's well-being and reinforcing traditional gender roles. This rhetorical inversion transformed the "right to choose" into a "right not to choose," framed as a feminist achievement. Similarly, the "right to health" was deployed to justify limitations on reproductive autonomy, thereby subordinating women's control over their reproductive lives to a vision of protection grounded in conservative ideals of womanhood. Pseudoscientific claims have played a pivotal role in facilitating this rhetorical and strategic shift within the anti-abortion movement. Early efforts included the promotion of a purported link between abortion and breast cancer,[35] as well as the fabrication of "Post-Abortion Syndrome" (PAS)—a condition lacking recognition by any major medical or psychological association.[36] These initial assertions were soon accompanied by the widespread circulation of similarly unsubstantiated claims regarding the alleged physical and psychological dangers of both surgical and medical abortions. Such narratives stand in direct contradiction to the robust body of scientific evidence, which consistently affirms that abortion is among the safest medical procedures when performed in accordance with established clinical guidelines.[37] Finally, a more recent new generation of anti-abortion arguments has increasingly drawn upon replacement theories and demographic anxieties, framing abortion not merely as

[35] On the inexistence of a correlation between abortion and breast cancer *see, e.g.*: "Abortion, Miscarriage, and Breast Cancer Risk: 2003 Workshop," *National Cancer Institute*, January 12, 2010, <www.cancer.gov/types/breast/abortion-miscarriage-risk>, accessed October 1, 2025. On abortion and mental health *see*: APA Task Force on Mental Health and Abortion, *Report of the APA Task Force on Mental Health and Abortion*, <www.apa.org/pi/women/programs/abortion/mental-health.pdf>, accessed October 2, 2025.

[36] APA Task Force on Mental Health and Abortion, *Report of the APA Task Force.*

[37] National Academies of Sciences, Engineering, and Medicine, *The Safety and Quality of Abortion Care in the United States: 2018*, *<www.nationalacademies.org/projects/IOM-BPH-15-11/publication/24950>*, accessed January 24, 2026.

a moral or medical issue but as a threat to national identity and population stability. These discourses often invoke fears of declining birth rates among certain populations—typically white or "native-born" groups—while implicitly or explicitly situating reproductive control within broader narratives of racialized demographic decline and cultural displacement (Murillo 2025).

These narratives were effectively transposed into the Russian context, where their significance must be interpreted through the lens of post-Soviet social and cultural conditions. As Luehrmann (2011: 116) suggests, PAS in Russia functions as a form of "collective affliction," shaped by Orthodox religious teachings and the lingering effects of collective trauma. Within this framework, the existence of PAS is largely taken for granted and is frequently employed by anti-abortion activists as a scientific rationale for why women who have undergone abortions must actively participate in the anti-abortion struggle (Luehrmann 2011: 112). In post-Soviet Russia, many women who became involved in religious practice experienced a traumatic "discovery" that their past abortions constituted a grave sin. Consequently, anti-abortion activism acquired redemptive significance, framed as both a personal act of repentance and a collective mission to protect future generations of women and children. Russian activists interpret PAS through religious teachings that emphasize the moral consequences of sinful and virtuous actions (Luehrmann 2011: 113). In contrast to Western contexts—where PAS is instrumentalized to depoliticize anti-abortion rhetoric and emphasize individual psychological harm—Russian anti-abortion discourse imbues the trauma of abortion with deep moral and spiritual significance. Unborn children are framed not only as victims of a personal or medical tragedy but as symbolic representations of the collective sins of the Soviet past. Simultaneously, they become emblems of hope for a moral and demographic renewal of Russian society. These unborn victims are particularly potent symbols as they are easier to mourn than other victims of the Soviet regime "because they pose no threat to the political elites" (Luehrmann 2011: 116), which also explains the success of combining fetus-protective and women-protective anti-abortion arguments in Russia. Finally, likewise in US and European right-wing circles, in post-Soviet Russia, anti-abortion discourse has increasingly intersected with replacement theory narratives and demographic anxieties, particularly those centered on national decline and ethnic continuity. The sharp decline in birth rates following the collapse of the Soviet Union catalyzed a moral panic over the perceived disappearance of the "Russian people," which state institutions, the Orthodox Church, and nationalist movements have variously interpreted as a civilizational threat. Within this framework, abortion is not merely a moral or religious transgression but a demographic danger contributing to the erosion of the ethnic Russian population. As a result, anti-abortion rhetoric in Russia often converges with pronatalist policies, Orthodox Christian values, and ethno-nationalist ideology, presenting abortion as a form of demographic sabotage. Women, especially ethnic Russian women, are thus positioned as reproducers of the nation, whose reproductive choices are framed not only as personal decisions but as matters of national survival.

Within this broader cultural and political context, the ROC addressed the issue of abortion in a comprehensive manner in its *Social Doctrine* of 2000. The document articulated not only theological objections to abortion but also demographic concerns, particularly emphasizing the severe population decline following the dissolution of the Soviet Union. In response, the ROC advanced a two-pronged strategy aimed at reshaping abortion legislation in Russia. First, it called for the broad institutionalization of conscientious objection—not only for medical professionals but also for Orthodox Christian taxpayers, who, it argued, should not be compelled to support abortion through public funding. Second, the church positioned itself as a moral partner of the state, proposing collaboration on measures to "align" public morality with Orthodox teachings. In the years that followed, the positions outlined in the *Social Doctrine* were further elaborated in public discourse and gained traction in political debates surrounding abortion. In several instances, elements of the ROC's stance were incorporated into legislative initiatives, reflecting a growing receptiveness on the part of the Russian government to both the church's demographic analysis and its proposed moral framework. Indeed, legislative efforts to restrict abortion access began around the year 2000. The 1993 law, *Fundamentals of the Health Care of Russian Citizens*, permitted abortion on request up to twelve weeks of gestation, and up to twenty-two weeks in cases involving specified "social reasons." However, the scope of what constituted acceptable social grounds for abortion underwent multiple revisions throughout the 1990s and 2000s. In 2003, the list of permissible social reasons for abortions beyond twelve weeks—excluding medical indications—was significantly curtailed, with lawmakers justifying the change on the basis of protecting women's health, particularly the risks associated with late-term procedures. By 2012, this list had been narrowed to a single exception: pregnancies resulting from rape. It was no coincidence that the previous year, the WCF had convened its first Demographic Summit in Moscow, bringing together influential American Evangelical leaders, senior figures of the ROC, and prominent Russian political actors. In its promotional materials, the WCF asserted that the summit had played a key role in facilitating the passage of what it described as "the first Russian laws restricting abortion in modern history."[38]

Among the legislative proposals subsequently submitted to the state Duma was a bill that introduced a series of restrictive measures. These included mandatory ultrasound viewing of the fetus, the requirement for women to listen to the fetal heartbeat, and a compulsory consultation with a psychologist tasked with

[38] Adam Federman, "How US evangelicals fueled the rise of Russia's 'pro-family' right," *The Nation*, January 7, 2014, <www.thenation.com/article/177823/how_us_evangelicals_ fueled_rise_russiaspro_ family_right>, accessed September 12, 2025.

informing the patient of her "right to refuse abortion" (Stella & Nartova 2015: 8). While such language and framing had previously been absent from the Russian legal tradition, they strongly echo discursive strategies and policy mechanisms prevalent in American pro-life advocacy, and similar requirements have been codified in the laws of several US states (Weber 2009).

In 2010, the Russian state Duma established the Committee on Women, Family, and Children's Issues, which notably included participation from representatives of the ROC. This committee is widely regarded as having had a significant influence on the formulation of the revised national health law enacted in 2012. The legislation, titled *On the Fundamental Health Care Principles in the Russian Federation* (Federal Law No. 232-FZ), introduced substantial changes to abortion access. Among its provisions were the imposition of a mandatory waiting period—or "week of silence"—ranging from forty-eight hours to seven days between the initial medical consultation and the procedure, depending on the stage of pregnancy (Article 36). Additionally, Article 70 granted physicians the right to refuse to perform an abortion if the pregnancy did not pose an immediate threat to the woman's life or to public health (Stella & Nartova 2015: 8–9).

Likewise in the United States, the successes of anti-abortion actors did not lead to a de-politicization of reproductive rights. To the opposite, they galvanized activists, which further heightened the threshold. Since 2023, several notable changes have been enacted: regional parliaments introduced local legislation prohibiting "coercion to abortion," while at the federal level, a law was adopted criminalizing the "propaganda of refusal to bear children," enforceable through fines and potential arrests. In certain regions of Russia, financial incentives are now being offered to school-aged girls who carry pregnancies to term.[39] This policy, implemented in 2025 across ten regions, represents an expansion of Russia's broader demographic strategy. Initially introduced in March 2025 and limited to adult women, the initiative has since been extended to minors in response to the country's ongoing demographic crisis. In this context, the unborn child becomes both a symbol of moral renewal and a bulwark against perceived cultural and ethnic decline.

iv.3. The ROC's partnership with the state to subvert the international and European human rights regime

In a speech delivered in 2022, President Putin maintained that: "The dictatorship of the Western elites is directed against all societies, including the peoples of the Western countries themselves. This is a challenge to all. This is a complete denial

[39] Jennifer Mathers, "Russia is paying schoolgirls to have babies: Why is pronatalism on the rise around the world?," *The Conversation*, July 4, 2025, <https://theconversation.com/russia-is-paying-schoolgirls-to-have-babies-why-is-pronatalism-on-the-rise-around-the-world-258979>, accessed October 1, 2025.

of humanity, the overthrow of faith and traditional values." Against this backdrop, Russia, he felt, would lead the resistance to this "outright Satanism."[40]

Indeed—especially post-2012—the alignment of the ROC with the Kremlin has paved the way for Russia to become a central node in a transnational conservative movement, actively participating in global efforts to resist liberal norms. By championing "traditional values" and engaging in international culture wars over gender, sexuality, and family, the ROC functions not only as a religious institution but also as a strategic normative actor in global affairs, supporting the efforts of the Russian leadership to regain a leading role in the international arena.

A particularly illustrative example of "traditional values-inspired" international activism is provided by the 2011 resolution adopted by the United Nations Human Rights Council, entitled "Promoting human rights and fundamental freedoms through a better understanding of traditional values of humankind."[41] The resolution was prompted by the Russian government, which gained the support of several states from the "Global South," including countries of the Arab League. The resolution echoes the position of the ROC concerning the foundations and scope of human rights (Stoeckl 2014: 111). It affirms that "dignity, freedom and responsibility are traditional values," and that family, community, society, and educational institutions have a fundamental role in maintaining and passing on such values. As McCrudden notices, in this construction "dignity is seen . . . as having the potential to rebalance international human rights back towards the local and the indigenous, weakening the pull of a homogenizing, universal, and liberal agenda" (McCrudden 2014). Tellingly, the EU immediately pointed to the "potential harm . . . posed by the concept of traditional values in undermining the universality and inalienability of human rights."[42] Hence the resolution was part and parcel part of an attempt by Russia to reaffirm the transcendent foundations of human rights and the role of "religious beliefs in the sphere of norm creation, interpretation and interpretation"[43] and as a strategy to further impose itself internationally as the "leader of the non-West," with a special role to play in the world's clash of civilizations.[44] It was a strategy to reframe the debate by challenging the conventional dichotomy between universalism—typically associated with liberal, egalitarian, and progressive values—and contextualism—often viewed as illiberal and relativistic. Rather than rejecting universalism, the initiative advanced a traditionalist agenda that positioned itself as a legitimate and equally universal alternative

[40] Extracts from Putin's speech at annexation ceremony, September 30, 2022, <www.reuters.com/world/extracts-putins-speech-annexation-ceremony-2022-09-30/>, accessed October 1, 2025.

[41] Human Rights Council Resolution 16/L.6, UN Doc A/HRC/16/L.6, *Promoting Human Rights and Fundamental Freedoms Through a Better Understanding of Traditional Values of Humankind* (March 24, 2011).

[42] *Contribution of the European Union: Traditional Values* (European Union Permanent Delegation to the United Nations Office & Other International Organizations in Geneva, February 15, 2013).

[43] McCrudden 2014: 12.

[44] Curanović 2015: 11.

to the liberal human rights framework endorsed by Western states and the UN apparatus (Stoeckl & Uzlaner 2022: 120).

Another strategy put forward by Russia to undermine the universality of human rights has been the adoption of legislation blatantly at odds with European standards, particularly in the field of LGTBQ + rights. As a general observation, the rights of sexual minorities have been dramatically impacted by the import of the culture wars in Russia. The ROC's teaching on homosexuality (Zorgdrager 2013: 227) is incorporated into the infamous Russian federal "anti-gay propaganda legislation" adopted in 2013, banning the so-called propaganda of non-traditional sexual relationships among minors.[45] Similar bills had been in place since the early 2000s at the regional level in many parts of Russia, including in its second largest city, St. Petersburg. The Constitutional Court upheld the constitutionality of these laws on the ground that "[t]he family, motherhood and childhood in the traditional interpretation, received from our ancestors, are the values that provide a continuous change of generations, and are conditions for the preservation and development of the multinational people of the Russian Federation, and therefore require a special state protection."[46]

When the "anti-gay propaganda laws" were enacted, Russia was still a member of the Council of Europe. In this light, the anti-gay legislation constituted a neat example of Russia's attempt to undermine the universality of European human rights by propagating the notion that they should be contingent upon "traditional values." Indeed, by enacting the "anti-gay propaganda laws," Russia refrained—as Justine De Kerf (2017) notes—from "flagrantly violat[ing] the ECHR by recriminalizing homosexuality . . . proving that Russia does not wish to alienate itself from the human rights debate, but rather convey a new human rights framework centered on traditional values,"[47] formally granting equal rights to homosexuals as long as

[45] The law introduced Article 6.21 to the Russian Code on Administrative Offences [Kodeks Rossiiskoi Federatsii RF ob Administrativnykh (KOAP RF)]:

> Propaganda of non-traditional sexual relations among minors
> Propaganda of non-traditional sexual relations among minors expressed in distribution of information that is aimed at the formation among minors of non-traditional sexual attitudes, attractiveness of non-traditional sexual relations, misperceptions of the social equivalence of traditional and non-traditional sexual relations, or enforcing information about non-traditional sexual relations that evokes interest to such relations, if these actions do not constitute a criminal offence, is punishable by an administrative fine for citizens in the amount of four thousand to five thousand rubles; for officials—forty thousand to fifty thousand rubles; for legal entities—from eight hundred thousand to one million rubles, or administrative suspension of activities for the period of up to ninety days.

For the above English translation, *see* De Kerf 2017: 40.

[46] Kseniya A. Kirichenko, *Study on Homophobia, Transphobia and Discrimination on Grounds of Sexual Orientation and Gender Identity—Legal Report: Russian Federation* (The Danish Institute for Human Rights), para 101, <www.coe.int/t/Commissioner/Source/LGBT/RussiaLegal_E.pdf> [https://perma.cc/XC45-UX24] (quoted by De Kerf 2017: 39); *see also* Konstitutsiaa Rossiiskoi Federatsii [Constitution], art 38(1) (Russ.).

[47] The criminalization of homosexual conducts is forbidden under the ECHR since the European Court of Human Rights' decision in *Dudgeon v United Kingdom* (1981) 45 ECtHR (ser. A), paras 61, 63, where the Court held that the existence in Northern Ireland of laws which had the effect of making

they do not manifest their identity in public, or, said differently, as long as they stay in the closet (De Kerf 2017: 40). In 2017, however, the Russian "anti-gay propaganda legislation" was adjudged to be in violation of the right to freedom of expression[48] and the prohibition against discrimination[49] by the ECtHR in the case of *Bayev and Others v Russia*.[50] In a "remarkably straightforward and strong-worded" decision,[51] the Court rejected the argument put forward by the Russian government that the provisions were justified to protect the morals, health, and rights of others, particularly minors. According to the Court, states are obliged to take into account developments in society such as the inclusion of same-sex relationships within the concept of "family-life"; that there is a clear European consensus about the recognition of individuals' rights to openly identify themselves as gay, lesbian, or any other sexual minority and to promote their own rights and freedoms; that public health would be better protected with the dissemination of education on single-sex relationships; and that by adopting the "anti-gay propaganda legislation," "the authorities reinforce[d] stigma and prejudice and encourage[d] homophobia, which is incompatible with the notions of equality, pluralism and tolerance in a democratic society."[52] Unsurprisingly, the Russian judge, Dmitrij Dedov, dissented, arguing that the relevant law should be considered a "positive discrimination . . . to protect the traditional values of Russian society," and calling on the Council of Europe to "respect family relationships as these are traditionally understood in Russia."[53]

Repression against sexual minorities intensified after Russia's expulsion from the CoE. In 2023, the state Duma enacted legislation that significantly restricted the rights of transgender individuals. This law displays similarities with the wave of legislation across various US states that has targeted LGBTQ+ rights since the second Trump administration, with a particular focus on transgender individuals.[54] The Russian law, indeed, prohibits access to gender-affirming

certain homosexual acts committed in private between consenting adult males criminal offenses constituted a breach of Article 8 of the Convention.

[48] ECHR, art 10.

[49] ECHR, art 14.

[50] *Bayev and Others v Russia* App Nos 67667/09, 44092/12, and 56717/12 (ECtHR, 2017) <http://hudoc.echr.coe.int/eng?i = 001-174422> [https://perma.cc/5V27-UQ8U].

[51] Pieter Cannoot, "ECtHR finds Russia's gay propaganda law discriminatory in strong-worded judgment," *Strasbourg Observers*, July 11, 2017, <https://strasbourgobservers.com/2017/07/11/ecthr-finds-russias-gay-propaganda-law-discriminatory-in-strong-worded-judgment/>.

[52] *Bayev*, n 50, para 83.

[53] Ibid, *Protection of the Traditional Family*, paras 2–3 (Dedov J, dissenting). Judge Dedov's dissenting opinion attracted widespread criticism for his shameful equation of homosexuality with pedophilia. *See* "*Laurens Lavrysen, Bayev and Others v Russia*: On Judge Dedov's outrageously homophobic dissent," *Strasbourg Observers*, July 13, 2017, https://strasbourgobservers.com/2017/07/13/bayev-and-others-v-russia-on-judge-dedovs-outrageously-homophobic-dissent> [https:// perma.cc/4WQM-Z6AM].

[54] <https://translegislation.com/>.

healthcare, bars the legal recognition of gender transitions through changes to official documents, and mandates the annulment of marriages involving transgender persons. Furthermore, it disqualifies transgender individuals from adopting children or serving as legal guardians.[55] The similarity between Russian and US anti-trans legislation underscores a deeper ideological alignment between ultra-conservative forces in both the West and the East. This convergence on the so-called "culture war" issues reveals the performative and selective nature of Russia's anti-Western rhetoric and its claim to represent a distinct "civilizational" alternative. Rather than standing in opposition to Western values, Russia is actively participating in and shaping a global far-right movement. In this context, Russia emerges not as a cultural outlier but as a central player in the transnational push against gender rights and liberal democratic norms.

Importantly, legislation targeting sexual minorities in Russia has had repercussions in Europe and in former Soviet states, serving as a source of inspiration for local illiberal political actors. Indeed, "exporting" legislation targeting sexual minorities has become a central element of Russia's broader strategy to undermine the European Union. This strategy operates on two fronts: first, by "contaminating" EU member states with legislation inspired by traditionalist, illiberal values. As discussed in Chapter 5, the Hungarian Parliament enacted Russian-style legislation in both 2021 and 2024. Comparable legal measures were adopted in Bulgaria in 2024. The Bulgarian Revival Party, which advocates for closer ties with Russia and was responsible for drafting the legislation, employed language that closely mirrors the wording found in the Russian and Hungarian laws.[56] In second place, the Russian strategy operates by obstructing the EU accession processes of candidate countries in regions historically within Russia's imperial sphere of influence—particularly the Caucasus and central Asia. A recent example is Georgia, an EU candidate state, which in 2024 adopted anti-gay propaganda legislation initiated by the ruling, pro-Russian Georgian Dream party.[57]

[55] "Russia: Supreme Court bans 'LGBT movement' as 'extremist,'" *Human Rights Watch*, November 30, 2023 <www.hrw.org/news/2023/11/30/russia-supreme-court-bans-lgbt-movement-extremist>, accessed October 1, 2025.

[56] "Press release: Bulgaria passes anti-LGBTI propaganda law," *ILGA Europe*, August 7, 2024, <www.ilga-europe.org/press-release/bulgaria-passes-anti-lgbti-propaganda-law/>, accessed October 1, 2025.

[57] The 2024 law on "family values and protection of minors" in Georgia contains provisions that present risks to a wide range of human rights. These include the rights to equality, non-discrimination, education, health, freedom of expression, and peaceful assembly and association, as well as privacy, liberty, and security. The text imposes discriminatory restrictions on education, public discussion, and gatherings related to sexual orientation and gender identity. It also contains vague formulations and perpetuates negative stereotypes about LGBTIQ+ people by, for example, creating a false equivalence between consensual same-sex relationships and incest. The law prohibits the legal recognition of same-sex couples and of transgender people. It also hinders their access to healthcare and negatively affects efforts to fight HIV/AIDS in Georgia. Office of the High Commissioner for Human Rights, *Georgia: call to rescind new anti-LGBTIQ+ law*, <www.ohchr.org/en/press-releases/2024/09/georgia-call-rescind-new-anti-lgbtiq-law>, accessed January 24, 2026.

Finally, as it will be further discussed in Section C, the partnership between Russia and the ROC in Africa and other Global South regions is part of a broader soft power strategy employed by the Kremlin. This partnership combines religious, cultural, and geopolitical tools to extend Russian influence in countries that are historically outside its sphere of influence—particularly in the geopolitical landscape following the invasion of Ukraine. While Russia's political and military influence in the Global South is more visible, the ROC plays a subtler role as the cultural-diplomatic arm of the state, a harbinger of Russia's civilizational identity, which can counter Western liberalism, secularism, and neo-colonialism.

B. The Ecumenism of Hate: American Christian Nationalism at Home and Abroad

(i) Christian Nationalism as Ecumenism of Hate

The historical foundations of Christian nationalism in the United States can be traced to the early colonial period, particularly among European settlers who viewed their colonizing efforts as divinely ordained. This perspective was encapsulated in the Puritan concept of a "city upon a hill," a phrase drawn from biblical scripture (Matthew 5:14) and popularized by John Winthrop in the seventeenth century, which framed the New World as a moral exemplar for all nations. Early colonists believed they were enacting God's will by establishing a society governed by Christian principles, intertwining religious conviction with emerging national identity. As the United States developed politically, socially, and culturally, this foundational ideology did not disappear but rather transformed in response to shifting historical contexts. It resurfaced in various forms—during periods of perceived moral decline, in reaction to secularization, and amid cultural and demographic changes—thereby maintaining a continuous, though evolving, influence on the American socio-political landscape. Christian nationalism thus persists not as a static doctrine but as a dynamic ideology that reconfigures itself to align with contemporary narratives of identity, governance, and divine purpose.

Whitehead and Perry (2020) understand Christian nationalism as a sociocultural and political ideology that merges a particular vision of Christianity with American national identity. It is not synonymous with Christianity in its broad theological sense, nor with specific traditions such as Evangelicalism or white conservative Protestantism, nor limited to a particular denomination or racial group, although it is more prevalent in some than in others. Traditionally, identifying as a white Evangelical in the United States is strongly associated with increased exposure to Christian nationalist ideology (Whitehead & Perry 2020: 154). More recently, however, as briefly mentioned in Chapter 6, an increasingly close alliance has developed between ultra-conservative Catholics and Evangelicals—an alliance in which the former, historically marginalized from mainstream political power, now provide cultural and philosophical support to a politically savvy yet traditionally anti-intellectual Evangelical right. This alliance, which poses acute challenges in the context of rights misappropriation, has elicited significant concern within the Vatican, as will be elaborated upon below.

Christian nationalism promotes a distinct cultural framework composed of myths, symbols, narratives, and values that advocate for a nation explicitly defined by a particular ethnoreligious identity. The "Christianity" in Christian nationalism is deeply intertwined with assumptions of nativism, white supremacy, patriarchy, heteronormativity, authoritarianism, and militarism, making it as much an ethnic and political project as a religious one (Whitehead & Perry 2020: 10). Its adherents assert that the United States was founded as a Christian nation and should remain so, with Christian identity shaping its history, values, public symbols, and policies. This ideology must be distinguished from the concept of American civil religion, which, though also drawing on religious language and symbolism, is rooted in a civic-republican tradition and Old Testament prophetic ethics focused on justice, mercy, and humility. In contrast, Christian nationalism interprets America's national mission through a lens more aligned with Old Testament Israel, viewing the nation as divinely chosen and entitled to divine favor or punishment based on national faithfulness (Whitehead & Perry 2020: 11ff).Christian nationalism also incorporates apocalyptic and eschatological frameworks, with divisions between postmillennialists—who seek to bring society under Christ's dominion as part of an unfolding divine kingdom—and premillennialists—who anticipate moral decline until Christ returns. Key thinkers like Abraham Kuyper and R.J. Rushdoony have significantly influenced the former, promoting the idea of societal "reconstruction" under Christian rule (Whitehead & Perry 2020: 11).

Reconstructionism is a form of dominionism, an umbrella term referring to right-wing Christian political ideologies (Diamond 1995). Dominionists holds that Christians have a biblical obligation to assert control over all sectors of secular society, interpreting Jesus' directive to "make disciples of all nations" as a mandate for comprehensive Christian influence in governance, culture, and public life (Diamond 1995). In the United States, Christian nationalists represent a form of dominionism, believing that the nation's divine purpose is threatened by liberal secularism, feminism, LGBTQ+ rights, and the legal acceptance of abortion. These adherents argue that such developments jeopardize the spiritual and moral foundation of the country, which they perceive as divinely chosen. Proponents of this ideology endorse a patriarchal social order, viewing men as divinely appointed leaders over society and within the family.[58] Despite internal disagreements

[58] Frederick Clarkson, "The rise of dominionism: Remaking America as a Christian nation," *Public Eye*, December 5, 2005, <www.publiceye.org/magazine/v19n3/clarkson_dominionism.html>, accessed October 2, 2025.

regarding eschatological beliefs (i.e., views on the second coming of Christ), dominionists are united in their conviction that Christians are called to control all domains of public and private life (Diamond 1995). Dominionists advocate for a form of Christian nationalism, grounded in the conviction that the United States was historically founded as a Christian nation and ought to return to that identity. This perspective effectively rejects the Enlightenment principles that underpin American democratic governance. They support a framework of religious superiority, as adherents often disregard the equal legitimacy of other faith traditions and even alternative expressions of Christianity.[59] The invocation of religious language and symbolism thus masks efforts to preserve cultural dominance and resist social changes that promote equality for marginalized groups, including women, racial and ethnic minorities, LGBTQ+ individuals, and non-Christians (Whitehead & Perry 2020: 153).

Christian nationalism merges religious and national identities, allowing political goals to be framed as expressions of divine will. By invoking the authority of the Christian God, it lends sacred legitimacy to its vision for the country, leaving little room for pluralism or compromise. This absolutist stance undermines democratic norms, as dissent is viewed not as legitimate disagreement but as opposition to divine truth. As a result, Christian nationalism often adopts a consequentialist ethic, where unethical tactics—including misinformation, authoritarianism, and exclusion—are justified in service of the perceived greater good: restoring or preserving a Christian nation (Whitehead & Perry 2020: 162).

As Christian nationalism declines demographically, and the nation becomes more secular and racially diverse, its supporters often react defensively, perceiving threats not only to their religious expression but to an entire social order they value. Their fear extends beyond spiritual marginalization to anxieties about losing cultural dominance. Christian nationalism, therefore, is less about theology and more about defending a hierarchical social vision—one that prioritizes native-born citizens, white Americans, men, and heterosexuals—against perceived encroachments by more inclusive and egalitarian social norms (Whitehead & Perry 2020: 5).

Gorsky and Perry maintain that contemporary advocates of white Christian nationalism often hold a complex and seemingly contradictory array of political and social views, encompassing issues such as racial inequality, religious liberty, government authority, social welfare, public health mandates, voting rights, and political violence. While these positions may appear inconsistent, they are unified by a distinct ideological framework rooted in a particular conception of freedom, social order, and the legitimization of violence. Within this framework, *freedom* is

[59] Ibid.

construed in libertarian terms as freedom from governmental constraints, *order* is understood hierarchically with white Christian men at the apex, and *violence* is regarded as a justified, even sacred, tool for preserving both. These interpretations are historically grounded in American ethno-traditionalist narratives, which elevate white Christian identity as central to the national character and morality (Gorski & Perry 2022: 6ff). This worldview aligns with authoritarian populism, particularly as demographic shifts threaten the numerical dominance of white Christians in the United States. Historically, limited pluralism was tolerated so long as white Christian norms remained dominant. However, the growing political influence of racial, religious, and cultural minorities has led Christian nationalists to perceive democracy itself as a threat to their cultural and political supremacy. Their reaction has been to frame democratic expansion—such as efforts to broaden voter access or promote multicultural inclusion—as existential threats. This has fostered an "us vs. them" mentality, often expressed through rhetoric of persecution and divine warfare, which justifies resistance to democratic norms in the name of preserving a divinely ordained social order. The worldview promoted by Christian nationalists is framed as a stark battleground between absolute good and absolute evil, leaving no space for ambiguity or compromise—after all, who would willingly negotiate with evil incarnate? This binary, absolutist moral framework is hardly a novel phenomenon. As Richard Hofstadter observed in his 1963 seminal work, *Anti-Intellectualism in American Life*, the fundamentalist mindset is inherently Manichaean, incapable of grasping that human society functions as a delicate balance sustained through ongoing compromise, and the pursuit of total partisan victory is not only unrealistic but also undesirable (Hofstadter 1963: 133–35). In this light, Christian nationalism presents a profound challenge to (American) democracy, as it attempts to merge theological exceptionalism with ethno-nationalist authoritarianism.

This challenge has been critically addressed in an article entitled "Evangelical Fundamentalism and Catholic Integralism: A Surprising Ecumenism" by two theologians from different traditions: Antonio Spadaro, a Jesuit, and and Marcelo Figueroa, a Presbitarian, both close collaborators of the late Pope Francis. Published in *La Civiltà Cattolica*, the article critiques the "fundamentalist ecumenism" emerging from the aforementioned alliance between Evangelical fundamentalists and Catholic integralists "unified by a mutual aspiration to exert religious influence over political life."[60] The article lucidly delineates the

[60] Antonio Spadaro and Marcelo Figueroa, "Fondamentalismo evangelicale e integralismo cattolico: Un sorprende ecumenismo," *La Civilità Cattolica*, July 17, 2017, <www.laciviltacattolica.it/articolo/fondamentalismo-evangelicale-e-integralismo-cattolico/>, accessed October 2, 2025.

profound challenges this ideological alignment poses to democratic governance, secular institutions, pluralistic society, and the safeguarding of human rights, while simultaneously emphasizing the disconnect between the ecumenism of Christian nationalism and the foundational doctrines and ethical teachings of Christianity.

Spadaro and Figueroa contend that the alliance between fundamentalist Evangelicals and Catholics is grounded in a dualistic, Manichaean worldview that conceptualizes social and political realities through the binary lens of absolute good versus absolute evil. Rejecting traditional ecumenical dialogue, this coalition instead embraces an "ecumenism of conflict" or even an "ecumenism of hate," wherein intolerance is valorized as a mark of spiritual purity. This ecumenism exhibits a xenophobic and Islamophobic orientation, marked by calls for physical and ideological barriers, including the construction of walls and the pursuit of "purifying" deportations. In this context, the term "ecumenism" becomes paradoxical, signaling division rather than unity.

Spadaro and Figueroa further identify this ecumenical phenomenon as deeply intertwined with a literalist hermeneutic and reductive exegetical method. Scriptural interpretation within this framework often entails a decontextualized appropriation of Old Testament texts, particularly those related to conquest and divine warfare. This approach lends theological justification to militarism, conflict, and the proliferation of arms, all of which stand in stark contrast to the message of peace, mercy, and reconciliation found in the Gospels.

Another dimension of Spadaro's and Figueroa's critique involves specifically the theological doctrine of dominionism, which promotes, inter alia, human supremacy over nature, fostering indifference toward environmental degradation and climate change, and interpreting ecological crises not as ethical imperatives for care and stewardship but as eschatological signs confirming a literal and deterministic reading of apocalyptic scripture.

Closely linked to this theological-political paradigm is a redefinition of "religious liberty," no longer understood as a principle of coexistence in a pluralistic society but rather seen as the unfettered imposition of religious doctrine upon public policy. According to Spadaro and Figueroa, this approach subverts the secular nature of the state and recasts religious freedom as a mechanism for ideological domination.

In conclusion, the authors emphasize that authentic Christian identity is not to be found in triumphalism or the assertion of cultural supremacy, but rather in a posture of humility, dialogue, and service. Echoing the ecclesiology of Pope Francis, they advocate for a Christianity grounded in the Gospel model of self-giving love, exemplified by Christ's act of washing the feet of others—a vision that resists conflating spiritual authority with temporal power and rejects the instrumentalization of religion for political ends.

(ii) Exporting Christian Nationalism to Subvert International Human Rights: The Commission on Unalienable Rights

As Spadaro and Figueroa point out, the "ecumenism of hate" poses a fundamental threat to constitutional and human rights, which it seeks to appropriate and redefine through an exclusionary theological framework. The contribution of integralist Catholics to rights appropriation is particularly significant. As discussed in Chapter 4, in contrast to fundamentalist Evangelicals, Catholics are often more intellectually equipped to articulate a reconciliation between faith and reason. A key figure exemplifying the Evangelical–Catholic right-wing alliance is Princeton Professor Robert P. George, previously introduced in Chapter 6 as a principal drafter of the *Manhattan Declaration*. Catholic thinkers such as George provide interpretive frameworks for constitutional law and human rights that advance Christian traditionalist nationalist agendas in ways that are often more intellectually coherent and publicly palatable. George, for instance, argues that moral truths are fully accessible through rational inquiry, drawing heavily on the philosophical legacy of Pope John Paul II, who famously stated: "Faith and reason are like two wings on which the human spirit rises to the contemplation of truth" (John Paul II 1998). This perspective is echoed in the writings of Pope Benedict XVI, who maintained that religion does not obstruct democratic lawmaking but rather constitutes a vital contribution to public discourse and the pursuit of a just legal and political order.[61] In line with the Catholic natural law tradition that George invokes, "the objective norms that govern just action are accessible to reason independently of revealed truths." In this light, for example, George holds that "[a]bortion is not only wrong from a moral or religious standpoint; it is philosophically wrong, based on the fundamental convictions of the nation, which believes in the inalienable rights of the human being, regardless of age or size."[62]

Arguments of this kind, framed in the language of constitutional law and human rights, serve to reinforce and legitimize appeals to conservative religious traditions, which are portrayed as authentic sources for interpreting rights. A particularly illustrative case of the appropriation of rights discourse through the conflation of appeals to tradition and secularized theological reasoning is exemplified by the Commission on Unalienable Rights, established in 2019 by then Secretary of State Mike Pompeo. This Commission represents a key moment in the convergence of US foreign policy, Christian nationalism, and human rights rhetoric.

[61] Joseph Ratzinger, "Meeting with the representatives of British society, including the diplomatic corps, politicians, academics and business leaders: Address of his Holiness Benedit XVI," *The Holy See*, September 17, 2010 <www.vatican.va/content/benedict-xvi/en/speeches/2010/september/documents/hf_ben-xvi_spe_20100917_societa-civile.html>, accessed October 2, 2025.

[62] Robert P. George, "Faith and reason: The appropriation of knowledge and truth," *Brigham Young University*, April 23, 2015, <https://speeches.byu.edu/talks/robert-p-george/faith-reason-appropriation-of-knowledge-truth/>, accessed October 2, 2025.

Framed as a return to the "founding principles" of American human rights, the Commission was composed largely of conservative scholars and religious figures, and lacked adequate representation from LGBTQ+, immigrant, indigenous, and disabled communities (Huckerby & Knuckey 2023). Moreover, certain appointees had a documented history of opposition to sexual and reproductive rights, including the Commission's chair, Mary Ann Glendon, whose support for the Vatican's stance on these issues has been analyzed in Chapter 6. Specifically, Glendon posited that "the post-World War II dream of universal human rights risks dissolving into scattered rights of personal autonomy. . . . a range of novel sexual liberties might one day become the bread and circuses of modern despots—consolation prizes for the loss of effective political and civil libertiea."[63] Against this backdrop, it is unsurprising that the Commission alluded to the "dampening effect on compromise and democratic decision-making" of "the overuse of rights language."[64]

The Commission's members engaged in rights misappropriation using three common strategies: appeal to natural law; hierarchization of rights; and selection of only certain documents as authentic sources of rights interpretation. In July 2020, the Commission released a draft report, which dwelled at length on the "transcendent foundations to unalienable rights, appealing to both philosophy and faith, reason and revelation," openly raising the questions: "To what extent do unalienable rights rest on the work of a creator Deity? Can faith in such rights be sustained without faith in God? Can unalienable rights be known by all through reason? In what ways are unalienable rights bound up with the laws of nature, which tend to revolve around individual freedom, examined by early modern philosophers?"[65]

The task of the Commission on Unalienable Rights was to introduce reforms of "human rights discourse where such discourse has departed from our nation's founding principles of natural law and natural rights."[66] In particular, the report identified the nation's founding principles in Protestantism, civic republicanism, and classical liberalism: "Protestant Christianity, widely practiced by the citizenry at the time, was infused with the beautiful Biblical teachings that every human being is imbued with dignity and bears responsibilities toward fellow human beings, because each is made in the image of God. The civic republican ideal, rooted in classical Rome, stressed that freedom and equality under law depend on an ethical citizenry that embraces the obligations of self-government. And classical

[63] Mary Ann Glendon, "Reclaim Human Rights," *First Things*, August/September 2016, <https://firstthings.com/reclaim-human-rights/>, accessed February14, 2026.

[64] Department of State, *Report of the Commission on Unalienable Rights*, <https://2017-2021.state.gov/wp-content/uploads/2020/08/Report-of-the-Commission-on-Unalienable-Rights.pdf>, accessed January 24, 2026, 6.

[65] Ibid, 10–11.

[66] Department of State Commission on Unalienable Rights, 84 Fed. Reg. 25,109 (May 30, 2019).

liberalism put at the front and center of politics the moral premise that human beings are by nature free and equal, which strengthened the political conviction that legitimate government derives from the consent of the governed."[67]

Within this frame, the draft report concluded, not all rights are equally fundamental. Property rights and religious liberty are supposedly "foremost" among human rights, while social and economic rights are not "compatible [with the American founding principles] when they induce dependence on the state, and when, by expanding state power, they curtail freedom—from the rights of property and religious liberty to those of individuals to form and maintain families and communities."[68]

According to the draft report, at the core of inalienable rights lies the concept of human dignity, upon which rests the UN Universal Declaration of 1948, which "is not created by political life or positive law but is prior to positive law and provides a moral standard for evaluating positive law."[69] The draft report admits that the UN Declaration "refrains from specifying the ultimate source of that dignity," but it asserts that in US constitutionalism, inalienable rights "were the form in which the American founders gave expression to the idea of an inherent human dignity."[70]

Notoriously, however, the framers of the US Constitution did not enshrine human dignity, and it is questionable, to say the least, whether the "inalienable rights" that were at that time monopolized by white, property-owning men could be seen as giving "expression to the idea of an inherent human dignity" in a constitutional system where slaves counted as three-fifths of a free individual for the purposes of determining congressional representation.[71] Significantly, the expression "human dignity" first appeared in the US Reports only in 1946 (Jackson 2004: 14). Since then, as Vicki Jackson explains, "[a]lthough some members of the U.S. Supreme Court in the postwar period have embraced human dignity as a motivating principle for the U.S. Bill of Rights, the role of the concept of 'human dignity' in the Court's jurisprudence is episodic and underdeveloped" (Jackson 2004: 16). Uncoincidentally, however, dignity has been appropriated by conservative Christians in debates concerning reproductive rights and the equality of sexual minorities (Siegel 2012 and 2013) and has increasingly appeared in US constitutional discourse and in US Supreme Court judicial decisions (Barak 2015).

Dignity, however, in human rights law, is one of the mainstays of reproductive rights. This concept of dignity encompasses autonomy and privacy, which are particularly salient in the context of reproductive decision-making. Human rights instruments and their interpretive bodies have made it clear that states may not impose reproductive obligations or constraints, as such interference violates

[67] Ibid, 8.
[68] Ibid, 12.
[69] Ibid, 31.
[70] Ibid, 31.
[71] US Const, art I, § 2, cl. 3.

rights to privacy, bodily autonomy, and human dignity. The indivisibility and interdependence of rights, a foundational principle of the Universal Declaration of Human Rights (UDHR), imply that reproductive rights cannot be isolated from or subordinated to other rights. The erosion of one right often undermines others, illustrating the necessity of a holistic human rights approach. Although international human rights law recognizes potential tensions between rights—such as between reproductive autonomy and freedom of religion—the International Covenant on Civil and Political Rights (ICCPR) permits limitations on the manifestation of religious beliefs (Article 18(3)) where necessary to protect the fundamental rights and freedoms of others. The Human Rights Committee's General Comment No. 22 affirms that, while belief itself is inviolable, its expression may be lawfully limited to safeguard competing rights.

Moreover, contrary to what the Pompeo Commission's draft report suggests, human dignity is directly implicated in the protection of social and economic rights. It is, in effect, "a core component of constitutional jurisprudence" in systems which also incorporate "obligations of social solidarity (and government support of positive welfare) not found in the U.S. Constitution" (Jackson 2004: 17). In this respect, human dignity actually sets limitations to economic freedoms, as clearly highlighted by post WWII constitutions, of which Article 41 of the Italian Constitution constitutes a paradigmatic example, when it states that "Private economic enterprise ... may not be carried out against the common good or in such a manner that could damage safety, liberty and human dignity."[72]

Finally, the Commission's dichotomy between unalienable and political rights contradicts the fundamental tenets of human rights law, that all rights are universal and equal, interdependent and interrelated. The Commission on Unalienable Rights deliberately structured its report to exclude the core international human rights treaties—including those ratified by the United States, such as the ICCPR, the Convention Against Torture, and the International Convention on the Elimination of All Forms of Racial Discrimination (CERD)—from its formal mandate. Instead of grounding its analysis in the established international human rights legal framework, the Commission shifted its focus toward what it characterized as US constitutional and political traditions as the primary source of legitimate rights. This repositioning signaled not only a retreat from the United States' binding treaty obligations but also a rejection of the international legal principle of the "progressive development" of human rights law, which underpins multilateral efforts to interpret and expand treaty protections in light of evolving norms and global consensus. By privileging a historically rooted, domestically defined conception of rights, the Commission marginalized international human rights institutions and jurisprudence, effectively endorsing a sovereigntist and

[72] Constitution of Italy, art 41.

exceptionalist orientation that views human rights primarily through the lens of American assumed founding principles rather than through international legal commitments or universal norms (Young 2025).

(iii) Judicializing Christian Nationalism: Religion, History, and Traditions in the *Dobbs* Decision

One of the distinctive doctrines of judicial interpretation in the United States is originalism. Originalism, in a nutshell, posits that interpreters are bound by the original meaning of constitutional provisions (Scalia 1997). A continuously growing body of scholarly literature is devoted to the theory of originalism, clarifying what it entails as a method of constitutional interpretation—its core commitments, variations, and implications. Modern originalists hold diverse views on several foundational issues: they differ over which aspect of the Constitution's original nature commands adherence—whether it is the framers' intent, the ratifiers' understanding, or the public meaning at the time of enactment; they also dispute the justification for such adherence; and they debate whether the duty to interpret the Constitution in this manner applies solely to judges or extends to citizens, legislators, and executive officials as well. However, on the question of how strongly originalist commitments should be applied, there is broad consensus among originalists: they generally maintain that once a relevant original feature of a constitutional provision is identifiable, it should be given precedence over competing interpretive approaches. In other words, if the original meaning or intent can be ascertained with sufficient clarity, it must be followed (Berman 2009).

This section does not seek to engage with the broader body of scholarship on originalism. Rather, its engagement with originalist theory is narrowly focused on highlighting a specific aspect relevant to the analysis of the misappropriation of rights within the framework of religious nationalism. Originalism facilitates the incorporation of religious nationalist narratives into constitutional interpretation by emphasizing appeals to history and tradition. The US Supreme Court's decision in *Dobbs* serves as a clear illustration of this dynamic.

Originalism, as a constitutional interpretive method, enjoys relatively limited appeal outside the United States, including in other common-law jurisdictions, and is, as one commentator observes, "remarkably unpopular," particularly when proposed as a mechanism for constraining judicial discretion (Greene 2009: 1). Its strong resonance in the United States may be attributed, at least in part, to the American religious tradition and to the fundamental role that religion plays in the US cultural and political spheres. Originalism theologically resonates with Evangelicalism. American constitutionalism is frequently described as a form of "civil religion," and originalism—especially in its more rigid forms—bears notable affinities with certain strands of American Evangelical Christianity. Specifically, the originalist emphasis on fidelity to the Constitution's original public meaning parallels the Evangelical commitment to the literal interpretation of the Bible, according to the text's original semantic intention (Greene 2009: 8 and 80). In this context, originalism functions not only as a legal methodology but also as a culturally inflected modality of restoration. It may be understood as a secular analogue to the theological concept of "the Fall" in Christian thought: the Founding Era is constructed as a prelapsarian moment of purity and legitimacy, while subsequent deviations—particularly by unelected judges—are framed as corruptions. Originalism thus promises a return to this idealized origin and a purification of constitutional law through disciplined interpretive fidelity (Greene 2009: 81).

Although it has been suggested that certain versions of originalism can be framed as analogous to a "veil of ignorance" approach to constitutional interpretation—emphasizing its potential for neutrality and its purported detachment from predetermined outcomes (Sunstein, 1674)—it has more commonly been associated with a distinctly conservative political agenda. Its modern institutionalization can be traced to the US Department of Justice during the Reagan Administration, where originalist rhetoric and strategy were deployed to support a broader ideological project centered on "family values." A central objective of this movement included overturning *Roe v Wade*, achieved in part through deliberate judicial appointments and appeals to a narrative of constitutional restoration. As Cass Sunstein observes, originalism during this period functioned as "a highly political weapon in a highly political war over the future direction of the Supreme Court" (Sunstein 2018: 1974). Whether justifiable or not, originalism provided a theoretical framework for critiquing the jurisprudence of the Warren Court and opposing landmark decisions such as *Roe*. In this sense, it offered intellectual legitimacy to conservative legal outcomes and, predictably, gained greater traction among those on the political right—within both academia and the judiciary—than among those on the political left (Sunstein 2018: 1674).

The US Supreme Court's decision in *Dobbs v Jackson Women's Health Organization* has been widely critiqued precisely for exemplifying a form of political originalism, particularly in the way it operationalizes historical narratives to justify contemporary legal change (Siegel 2023). In *Dobbs*, the Court considered the constitutionality of Mississippi's Gestational Age Act, which banned most abortions after fifteen weeks of pregnancy, allowing exceptions only in cases of medical emergency or severe fetal abnormality. In a sharply divided opinion, the Court upheld the Mississippi law and, in doing so, overturned *Roe v Wade* (1973) and *Planned Parenthood v Casey* (1992). Writing for the majority, Justice Alito concluded that abortion is not a constitutionally protected right, asserting that the Constitution makes no reference to abortion and that such a right is neither "deeply rooted in this Nation's history and tradition" nor "implicit in the concept of ordered liberty." As a result, regulatory authority over abortion was returned to state legislatures and other elected bodies.

The majority's reliance on a selective reading of historical materials has drawn criticism. Reva Siegel argues that the *Dobbs* Court invoked a narrow and ideologically charged version of history to support its conclusions. Specifically, the Court's invocation of the "history-and-tradition" test leaned heavily on nineteenth-century laws that criminalized abortion, while disregarding the broader common-law context in which abortion prior to "quickening" was not uniformly prohibited (Siegel 2023: 1206). Moreover, Siegel highlights the problematic reliance on legal sources from a period in which women lacked the right to vote or participate in the legislative processes that produced the laws now cited as authoritative. This raises a fundamental question: why should constitutional meaning be derived from a historical period in which half the population was excluded from the political community? (Siegel 2023).

Siegel contends that this selective historical methodology—what she terms a manipulation of "constitutional memory"—functions to legitimate regressive legal change under the guise of neutral, objective originalism. The majority's historical approach, including its so-called "state-counting" method (tallying how many states banned abortion in the nineteenth century), echoes the tactics used by defenders of racial segregation prior to *Brown v Board of Education*—namely, using numerical prevalence of discriminatory laws to justify their constitutionality. Such a strategy does not constrain judicial discretion but enables it by allowing judges to choose which historical sources count. In this way, *Dobbs* constructs a "memory game" that reframes subjective value judgments as though they were neutral legal facts (Siegel 2023: 1207ff). The historical appendix to the opinion, listing nineteenth-century abortion bans, becomes more than evidentiary—it becomes rhetorical, anchoring constitutional meaning in an exclusionary past shaped by misogynistic, racial, and nativist ideologies. This approach marginalizes the voices and experiences of women and other historically disenfranchised groups, preventing them from contributing to the ongoing development of constitutional meaning (Siegel 2023).

Beyond its immediate effect in eliminating constitutional protection for abortion, *Dobbs* has broader jurisprudential and normative implications. The decision reconfigures the very framework through which rights are recognized, raising fundamental questions about what constitutes a right, whose interests are protected, and the sources from which those rights derive. "Invented history may underwrite a contemporary drive to enshrine the principle of fetal personhood in constitutional law. The *Dobbs* Court's selective use of history goes beyond curbing access to abortion—it may lay the foundation for a reappraisal of the courts' role in protecting minority interests, including an interest in the fetus as a distinct, rights-bearing entity" (Murray 2024).

Moreover, *Dobbs* represents a marked departure from the international and comparative human rights norms that have informed reproductive rights discourse in other liberal democracies. Rather than grounding rights in international treaties, transnational agreements, or evolving standards of human dignity, *Dobbs* emphasizes national, religious, and natural law traditions, aligning with the philosophy underpinning the Pompeo Commission's report. This preference for a domestically rooted, tradition-based framework signals a retreat from global human rights paradigms and a reorientation toward a more insular constitutional order (Young 2025). Notably, the majority's opinion employs the language of rights—particularly in references to fetal life or fetal personhood—while advancing interpretations that conflict with international understandings of reproductive autonomy. In this sense, *Dobbs* rearticulates the concept of "human rights" to support divergent values, reshaping its meaning within the American legal context. According to Young, this shift reflects an emerging hierarchy of interests, where fetal life is increasingly prioritized at the expense of women's bodily autonomy. The decision thus narrows the scope for balancing competing rights claims, creating a rigid legal structure with limited room for compromise. In this respect, *Dobbs* exemplifies what Young describes as "social rights exceptionalism"—a jurisprudential stance in which the United States asserts its detachment from global human rights norms, particularly those pertaining to social and economic rights, including reproductive health. This exceptionalist posture manifests not only in domestic adjudication but also in the broader constitutional imagination, where international legal developments are increasingly dismissed as irrelevant to US constitutional interpretation Young, 2025: 993ff).

The historical and traditionalist framework adopted by the majority in *Dobbs v Jackson Women's Health Organization* obscures the religious motivation behind the political forces that significantly shaped the path to the decision. While the majority opinion in *Dobbs* is formally presented as an exercise in originalist constitutional interpretation, the moral assumptions embedded in the decision suggest otherwise. From the outset, the Court constructs abortion as a "profound moral issue," presupposing a singular, self-evident moral gravity that overrides the plurality of ethical and religious perspectives on abortion in American society. Justice Alito explicitly distinguishes abortion from other constitutionally protected rights, stating: "None of the other decisions cited by *Roe* and *Casey* . . . involved the critical moral question posed by abortion. They are therefore inapposite." This framing implicitly privileges a particular moral tradition—rooted in conservative Christian thought—while disregarding other moral, religious, and philosophical understandings of reproductive autonomy.

In doing so, the Court's reasoning not only assumes the universality of traditional Christian moral doctrine but also marginalizes alternative religious interpretations, thereby raising significant concerns regarding the principle of church–state separation. Numerous religious traditions—including branches of Judaism and Islam—permit or even require abortion under certain circumstances. Moreover, a broad coalition of progressive religious organizations, including mainline Protestant denominations and some Catholic groups, affirm reproductive choice as compatible with their theological commitments. By anchoring its decision in a framework that reflects conservative Christian morality, the Court effectively elevates one religious worldview to constitutional significance, while subordinating others.

The implications of *Dobbs* for religious freedom are therefore profound. In returning abortion regulation to the states, the decision enables state legislatures to enact total or near-total abortion bans without constitutional constraint. Consequently, individuals whose religious beliefs affirm the permissibility—or even necessity—of abortion may face legal penalties for acting in accordance with their faith. This has already triggered legal challenges across the United States, as religious minorities contest abortion restrictions on the grounds that they violate the First Amendment's guarantee of religious liberty. For instance, in Ohio, a Jewish congregation, represented by the American Civil Liberties Union, filed a lawsuit challenging the state's abortion ban, arguing that it imposes undue burdens on religious exercise. Similar lawsuits have emerged in Texas, Indiana, and Florida, including from the Satanic Temple—a non-theistic religious organization asserting its members' right to bodily autonomy as a matter of religious doctrine. In Florida, a coalition of religious leaders—including Reform rabbis, a Unitarian Universalist minister, a United Church of Christ reverend, an Episcopal priest, and a Buddhist lama—have brought suit against recently enacted abortion restrictions. They contend that such laws impose "substantial" burdens on their congregants' ability to practice their faith and create "potential" liabilities for clergy offering spiritual counsel. As one of the plaintiff rabbis emphasized, the current legal trajectory undermines foundational constitutional protections: "The First Amendment, which is the first one that they enacted, upon which all other freedoms are based, was designed to prevent the exact type of thing that we see now: the merger of a radical fundamentalist type of Christianity with the state . . . This law criminalizes the practice of Judaism."[73] In sum, *Dobbs* does more than overturn *Roe* and eliminate constitutional protection for abortion rights; it reconfigures the constitutional landscape in ways that elevate a specific religious morality, restrict pluralistic understandings of reproductive justice, and threaten the constitutional guarantee of religious freedom for those outside the dominant moral and theological framework embraced by the Court's majority.

[73] Madeleine Carlisle and Adelaide Abrams, "Does religious freedom protect a right to an abortion? One rabbi's mission to find out," *Time*, July 7, 2022, <https://time.com/6194804/abortion-religious-freedom-judaism-florida/>, accessed October 2, 2025.

C. Colonial Legacies and Postcolonial Continuities: The Politicization of Homophobia Across Africa

(i) Globalization and the Resurgence of Anti-homosexual Legislation Across Africa

The criminalization of same-sex relationships has long been a feature of legal systems in many African countries, largely due to the legacy of British colonial penal codes (Gupta 2008; Currier & Gogul 2020). While several African states have taken legislative and judicial steps toward the decriminalization of homosexuality in recent years (Bodjongo & Juliot 2024), the past decades have also witnessed a dramatic resurgence in anti-LGBTQ+ legislation across the continent. Unlike the colonial statutes that primarily penalized specific sexual acts, the recent wave of laws has expanded to criminalize identity, advocacy, association, and even expressions of support for LGBTQ+ individuals.

President Robert Mugabe of Zimbabwe was among the first African heads of state to strategically deploy homophobia as a key instrument of political rhetoric. His denunciation of the organization Gays and Lesbians of Zimbabwe during his address at the 1995 Zimbabwe International Book Fair—ironically themed "Human Rights and Freedom of Expression"—marked a pivotal moment in drawing international attention to the politicization of homophobia across the African continent (Gloppen & Rakner 2020). Soon after, Mugabe delivered his notorious Hero's Day speech, wherein he described gay people as "worse than dogs and pigs" and incited others to arrest and hand over to the police people parading themselves as lesbians and gays (Muparamoto 2020).

Since the turn of the millennium, legal developments have occurred in several countries, including Uganda, Nigeria, Ghana, Kenya, and Burkina Faso between 2019 and 2024. The first major legislative wave began in 2005. In Zambia that year, the 1931 anti-sodomy provision, which prohibits "carnal knowledge of any person against the order of nature," was amended to also cover lesbian sex.[74] In 2009 Uganda's infamous Anti-Homosexuality ("Kill the Gay") Bill,[75] which proposed the death penalty for "aggravated homosexuality," was introduced and it was then adopted in 2014. In Nigeria, the Same-Sex Marriage (Prohibition) Act was signed into law in 2013,[76] criminalizing not only same-sex unions but also LGBTQ+ advocacy and public displays of same-sex affection. Beginning in the late 2010s and gaining momentum in the early 2020s, a second and more aggressive wave of anti-homosexual laws emerged. This period is marked by the increasing severity of

[74] Penal Code Act (as amended by Act No. 15 of 2005), sections 155, 156.

[75] Bill n. 18/2009, <https://bills.parliament.ug/uploads/4620The_Anti_Homosexuality_Bill,_2009.pdf>.

[76] <https://archive.gazettes.africa/archive/ng/2014/ng-government-gazette-dated-2014-01-08-no-2.pdf>, accessed October 1, 2025.

legal sanctions and a broader scope of criminalization. In Uganda, after the 2014 law was annulled by the Constitutional Court on strictly procedural grounds,[77] the Anti-Homosexuality Act[78] was adopted in 2023. It reinstated many of the previous law's provisions but with added harshness, including the reintroduction of the death penalty for "aggravated homosexuality" (Section 3). In Ghana, the proposed "Promotion of Proper Human Sexual Rights and Ghanaian Family Values Bill," if approved, will criminalize mere identification as LGBTQ+, ban LGBTQ+ organizations, and mandate conversion therapy. Although the bill is still under consideration, the Supreme Court seemingly incorporated language from it in a 2024 decision upholding a colonial-era sodomy law.[79] Burkina Faso, which, unlike former British colonies, did not inherit from France any anti-homosexuality law, has experienced a dramatic conservative shift since Ibrahim Traoré assumed power following a military coup in September 2022. Traoré has adopted a markedly sovereigntist position, explicitly rejecting "Western values" and strengthening political and ideological alignments with countries such as Russia and Iran. In 2025, the country's unelected transitional parliament enacted a bill prohibiting homosexual acts, a year after a draft of an amended family code that criminalized homosexuality and accorded legal recognition to both religious and customary unions was approved by the nation's cabinet.[80] The new legislation, which was unanimously passed, stipulates penalties of up to five years' imprisonment for engaging in same-sex relations.

Today, it is estimated that thirty-one of the fifty-four African states criminalize same-sex sexual acts between consenting adults.[81] Criminalization often entails gross breaches of privacy—e.g. through AI systems claiming to detect sexual orientation, or the use of fake profiles on dating apps by law enforcement—and inhumane and degrading treatment, including forced medical examinations.[82]

[77] Constitutional Court of Uganda, *Oloka-Onyango & Ors. v Attorney General* [2014] UGCC 14.

[78] <www.parliament.go.ug/sites/default/files/The%20Anti-Homosexuality%20Act%2C%202023.pdf>, accessed October 1, 2025.

[79] *Dr Prince Obiri-Korang v Attorney General* (J1/18/2021) [2024] GHASC 21 (July 24, 2024) <https://ghalii.org/akn/gh/judgment/ghasc/2024/21/eng@2024-07-24>. Under section 104(1)(b) of Ghana's Criminal Offences Act of 1960 (Act 29), which is inherited from British colonial law, "whoever engages in unnatural carnal knowledge . . . of a person sixteen years or older, with their consent, is guilty of a misdemeanor." The term "unnatural carnal knowledge" is defined in section 104(1)(2) as "sexual intercourse with a person in an unnatural manner or with an animal." According to the ruling of the Supreme Court judges, "unnatural manner" is understood to also encompass the use of sex toys. This ruling effectively broadens the interpretation of section 104(1)(b), in line with the anti-LGBT Promotion of Proper Human Sexual Rights and Ghanaian Family Values Bill of 2021. Specifically, clause 4 of the Bill prohibits any individual from engaging in actions that undermine "proper human sexual rights and Ghanaian family values."

[80] Available on the Amnesty International website, <www.amnesty.org/en/location/africa/west-and-central-africa/burkina-faso/report-burkina-faso/>, accessed October 1, 2025.

[81] <https://database.ilga.org/criminalisation-consensual-same-sex-sexual-acts>.

[82] European Parliamentary Research Service, 'Briefing: LGBTIQ+. In Africa,' *European Parliament*, May 2025, <www.europarl.europa.eu/RegData/etudes/BRIE/2025/772863/EPRS_BRI(2025)772863_EN.pdf>, accessed October 1, 2025.

Driven by a combination of political populism, religious conservatism, and foreign interference, these waves of legislation reflect both local dynamics and global ideological battles. On the one hand, the increased visibility of LGBTQ+ communities, facilitated by social media, international advocacy, and local activism, has provoked backlash from conservative sectors (Kaoma 2017). Legal repression has been employed in response to the perceived rise in LGBTQ+ presence and influence by populist political actors, who leverage anti-LGBTQ+ rhetoric as a strategy to consolidate support among constituencies, positioning themselves as defenders of authentic "African values."

The conservative and often fundamentalist turn of religions is another factor behind the rise of anti-homosexuality legislation. Islam and Christianity—the two most widely practiced religions in Africa—both express doctrinal opposition to same-sex relationships. As a result, it is unsurprising that religious leaders from both faiths often publicly endorse the criminalization of homosexuality. Despite the tensions and conflicts among Muslims and Christians, both have appropriated the narrative of the Western homosexual agenda. As a result, across the African continent, religious rhetoric—both Christian and Islamic—commonly frames homosexuality as morally unacceptable or "ungodly." Numerous interpretations of the Bible and the Qur'an are invoked to justify and reinforce anti-LGBTQ+ positions (Amusan, Saka & Adekeye 2019: 49).

Sexual minorities are an easy target to scapegoat in times of economic recession, internal conflicts, and unrest (Maietta 2019: 3), as exemplified by the case of Uganda at the time of the "Kill the Gay" Bill, when "unprecedented rates of unemployment, below-average wages, high taxes, an extremely high cost of living, and the poor state of health care" translated in protests called by the opposition (Tamale 2013). Similarly, in Nigeria, the anti-homosexuality legislation was adopted to conveniently distract public opinion from corruptions scandals, and the insurgency of Boko Haram (Maietta 2019: 3).

Anti-homosexuality legislation, which is almost invariably drafted in very vague language, can also be weaponized against political opponents and to suppress civil society, beyond LGTBQ + groups and individuals (Maietta 2019: 4). This is exemplified by the conviction of Zimbabwe's former President Canaan Banana on various counts of sodomy and unnatural acts in 1999,[83] under the presidency of Robert Mugabe.

Narratives of cultural nationalism and post-colonialism are often also at play. Advocates of anti-homosexuality laws often argue that homosexuality is a foreign imposition, with LGBTQ+ rights perceived as a form of Western cultural imperialism. This narrative frames anti-LGBTQ+ legislation as acts of cultural preservation and national sovereignty. By framing anti-LGBTQ+ legislation within

[83] High Court of Zimbabwe, *S v Banana* 1999 (1) ZLR 50 (H), Judgment of 18 January 1999.

populist and moralistic anti-Western narratives, these leaders seek to bolster their political standing and consolidate support. In response, the international community has largely condemned such legislation, frequently linking foreign aid and diplomatic engagement to improvements in the treatment of sexual minorities. However, rather than encouraging liberalization, this external pressure has, in many cases, strengthened the position of authoritarian and populist leaders. These actors have countered international interventions with narratives emphasizing national sovereignty and cultural autonomy, portraying external demands as neo-imperial interference, and accusing international donors of undermining domestic self-determination through conditional funding mechanisms (Amusan, Saka & Adekeye 2019: 60).

Adopting anti-homosexuality legislation can also function as a strategic tool for reshaping regional geopolitics. For instance, Nigeria's enactment of anti-homosexuality legislation in 2014 came in contrast to South Africa's progressive stance on sexual minority rights, exemplified by its sponsorship of the 2011 United Nations Human Rights Council Resolution 17/19, titled "Human rights, sexual orientation and gender identity." South Africa's advocacy in this domain positioned it as a leading voice on the continent for LGBTQ+ rights. Nigeria's oppositional posture framed South Africa as aligned with the normative agendas of the Global North, in contrast with "authentic" African values, a perception often linked to the lingering influence of South Africa's apartheid-era entanglements with Western powers (Maietta 2019: 5).

While the politicization of homophobia in Africa is undeniably driven by strategic and ideological forces, it is also deeply intertwined with a broader and more complex struggle over the conceptualization and implementation of human rights on the continent. The challenge lies in reconciling the competing narratives between universal human rights frameworks and local cultural, social, and political realities. The 1981 African Charter on Human and Peoples' Rights exemplifies this tension: while it endorses the principles set forth in the UDHR, it also emphasizes the protection of collective rights, including the rights of communities to maintain their cultural identity and determine their social values. Consequently, many African states justify opposition to homosexuality as a defense of indigenous cultural and religious norms, whereas proponents of sexual rights frame their advocacy in terms of universal human rights protections (Kaoma 2017: 88).

Moreover, while in precolonial African societies in many cases sexual minorities and same-sex relations were valued and accepted (Murray & Roscoe 1998), and women held meaningful public roles (Sudarkasa 1986), LGBTQ+ rights in Africa are often discussed through a binary lens, shaped by Western ideals of individual rights and personal freedoms, which may not align with communal or collective values prevalent in the continent. The global narrative surrounding LGBTQ+ rights tends to prioritize individual autonomy and privacy, yet in many African cultures, issues related to gender and sexuality are intricately linked to broader social responsibilities, family structures, and community cohesion. Kapia Kaoma, who conducted extensive field research across the African continent, found that debates surrounding homosexuality in these contexts are predominantly framed through the lens of same-sex marriage, so that the notion of "gay rights" ends up by overlapping with that of egalitarian marriage. "Even local research assistants" he observes "found it hard to speak of gay rights in their own languages but explained it in the same-sex marriage frame" (Kaoma 2017: 87). Similarly, Massad observes how international pro-gay actors frame sexuality exclusively according to Western conceptions, emphasizing the homo/hetero dyad, which does not fully capture African standards (Massad 2002: 361).

Conversely, globalization has also played a significant role in facilitating the transnational circulation of conservative ideologies—particularly those originating i the United States—that actively oppose sexual and reproductive rights. These movements often coalesce around a discourse that emphasizes the protection of the so-called "traditional family," which is framed as being under threat from progressive agendas related to gender and sexual diversity. In many African contexts, however, the notion of the traditional family extends beyond the nuclear model to encompass extended kinship networks and communal affiliations, rendering direct comparisons with Western family structures problematic (Kaoma 2017: 88).

This complex predicament is further complicated by international activism. As it will further be analyzed in the following section, the African continent has become a battlefield, where a range of international organizations, some defending and some attacking the rights of sexual minorities, collaborate with African political figures, civil society actors, and NGOs to shape developments affecting sexual minorities. Foreign engagement in these efforts, as Kaoma explains, produces two contradictory outcomes. On one hand, it amplifies the struggles of sexual minorities within global discourses; on the other hand, it pressures African political leaders to adopt explicit positions, either in support of or in opposition to sexual rights (Kaoma 2017: 89).

(ii) Exporting the Culture Wars: Foreign Right-Wing Activism Fomenting Homophobia in Africa

In 2012 Kapya Kaoma, a Zambian progressive pastor and scholar, published a report entitled "Colonizing African Values. How the U.S. Christian Right is Transforming Sexual Politics in Africa" (Kaoma 2012). Kaoma exposed for the first time the ties between US right-wing Evangelicals and the rise of anti-LGBTQ legislation in various African countries. He traced how organizations such as the American Center for Law & Justice, Human Life International, and Family Watch International have been progressively extending the institutional and ideological reach of the US Christian Right across the African continent by establishing new organizations and launching targeted advocacy campaigns. These efforts are significantly influencing domestic political landscapes and contributing to the reformulation of legal frameworks in several countries, often drawing upon models and narratives rooted in American conservative Christian ideology. Evangelical Christian movements, many of which receive funding and ideological backing from American and European groups, have been instrumental in galvanizing anti-LGBTQ+ sentiment in several African countries. Indeed, a powerful network of faith-based NGOs, mainly led by US Evangelicals and other right-wing Christians, has become highly influential in constitution-making and in shaping legislation in several African countries, "colonizing African values," by expanding colonial-era proscriptions on sexual rights. These organizations capitalize on Christian theologies that resonate in sub-Saharan Africa due to shared theological frameworks and sociocultural values, such as dominionism (analyzed in the previous section) and prosperity gospel, which promises material success and well-being through faith (Kaoma 2012: 2–3). Moreover, the influence of the US Christian Right introduces a heightened homophobic discourse that reshapes existing African interpretations of same-sex attraction. In certain indigenous belief systems, same-sex orientation has historically been understood through spiritual lenses, such as being connected to revered ancestral spirits. However, under the influence of imported conservative Christian ideologies, such interpretations are increasingly displaced by narratives that pathologize or demonize non-heteronormative identities (Kaoma 2012: VII).

The cultural valorization of fertility and the centrality of reproduction in many African societies further create fertile ground for the promotion of conservative "family values." Within this context, childlessness is often viewed as a personal and social misfortune, and narratives that frame reproductive control or population policies as Western efforts to undermine African growth and development gain significant traction (Kaoma 2012: 15ff). Family Watch International—an Arizona-based an anti-choice, abstinence-only organization—has been particularly inclined to use alarmist rhetoric that the United Nation's population control strategy will destroy the African family, and that LGBT people are somehow to blame (Kaoma 2012: VII). In 2023, the organization's president, Sharon Slater, met with Uganda's first lady, Janet Museveni, and other government officials to encourage passage of the new anti-homosexuality law. Slater, a vociferous anti-LGBTQ activist, has been organizing annual "training sessions" for African politicians in Arizona on how to lobby for conservative causes at the United Nations and other multilateral fora (Cullinan 2025).[84]

[84] Kerry Cullinan, "Women's groups sound alarm over 'African Family' conferences headlined by US conservatives," *Health Policy Watch*, May 8, 2025, <https://healthpolicy-watch.news/womens-groups-sound-alarm-as-prominent-us-conservatives-headline-african-family-conferences/>, accessed October 1, 2025.

While the receptivity of African countries to the agendas of the US Christian Right varies, these groups have, on the whole, achieved notable success in advancing their ideological influence across the continent, also thanks to the magnitude of their financial investment in the continent. Since 2007, more than twenty US-based Christian organizations—known for their opposition to LGBTQ+ rights, safe abortion access, contraception, and comprehensive sexuality education—have collectively invested over $54 million across the African continent. These findings, revealed in a recent investigation by *openDemocracy*, provide the first comprehensive documentation of the scale and scope of such financial involvement. Among these actors, the Fellowship Foundation—a highly secretive US religious organization—emerges as the largest financial contributor. Closely linked to Ugandan politician David Bahati, the architect of the widely condemned "Kill the Gays" Bill, the Fellowship Foundation directed over $20 million to Uganda between 2008 and 2018, underscoring its central role in supporting anti-LGBTQ+ and socially conservative agendas in the region.[85]

Another prominent example is the American Center for Law and Justice (ACLJ), which strategically expanded its operations during the heated debates surrounding Uganda's Anti-Homosexuality Bill in 2009 and 2010. During this period, the ACLJ established two affiliated offices in Africa: the East African Center for Law and Justice (EACLJ) in Kenya and the African Center for Law and Justice (AfCLJ) in Zimbabwe. In both contexts, these organizations have leveraged relationships with influential Evangelical leaders to secure access to high-ranking political figures. In Zimbabwe, the AfCLJ has aligned itself with the regime of former President Robert Mugabe, notorious, as mentioned above, for his openly homophobic rhetoric and action, and authoritarian governance (Kaoma 2012: 12ff). In Kenya, the EACLJ played an active role during the 2010 constitutional reform process, engaging in what is often referred to as a "culture war strategy." While they failed to remove provisions ensuring equal protection under the law—which include protections that could extend to LGBTQ+ individuals—they succeeded in embedding language asserting that "life begins at conception" and promoting a narrow, heteronormative definition of marriage as exclusively between a man and a woman (Kaoma 2012: II). Their efforts, though only partially successful, reflect a deliberate attempt to shape national legal and moral codes in alignment with conservative Christian doctrines. Additionally, Catholic Human Rights International—another US-based organization—has allocated a significant portion of its resources to sub-Saharan Africa, reportedly dedicating one-quarter of its overseas budget to the region. The organization maintains affiliated offices in Kenya, Malawi, South Africa, Tanzania, and Zimbabwe, where it actively campaigns against contraception,

[85] Lydia Namubiru and Soita Khatondi Wepukhulu, "Exclusive: US Christian Right pours more than $50m into Africa," *openDemocracy*, October 29, 2020, <www.opendemocracy.net/en/5050/africa-us-christian-right-50m/>, accessed October 1, 2025.

a widely accepted practice across much of the continent. Echoing the rhetoric of anti-LGBTQ+ campaigns, it propagates the unfounded claim that birth control is a Western imposition designed to undermine African societies (Kaoma 2012: 43ff). In a particularly stark departure from prevailing cultural norms in many African societies—which often regard abortion-related offenses as private matters—Human Life International (HLI), a missionary organization affiliated with Catholic Human Rights International, has taken a more aggressive approach. In Uganda, HLI missionaries reportedly facilitated the legal prosecution of a clinician for performing an abortion, directly contravening local social conventions that typically treat such matters discreetly (Kaoma 2012: 7).

Together, these examples illustrate the strategic and often intrusive efforts of US Christian Right organizations to reshape African legal and moral landscapes in accordance with their conservative ideological frameworks. By embedding themselves within local religious institutions and political processes, these transnational actors exert significant influence, often with profound implications for sexual and reproductive health rights, gender equality, and the broader human rights environment across the continent.

Their aim is to bring about a new legal infrastructure in Africa that enshrines their Christian Right worldview. To this end, they campaign for constitutional reforms enshrining that life begins at conception, expanding colonial sodomy laws, blending church and state—an incendiary goal when the Christians share the continent with Muslims and traditional religions. They also advocate for legislative reforms banning same-sex marriage or adoption—which demonstrate an obvious American influence in countries where LGBTQ+ people have virtually no rights—and support more regressive action against abortion, even though it is both largely illegal and fairly common (Kaoma 2012: VI).

As the African continent increasingly emerges as a key battleground in the ongoing global culture wars, new actors and stakeholders have begun to assert their presence and influence within this contested ideological landscape. Far-right European organizations are increasingly engaging in efforts to undermine sexual and reproductive rights across the African continent. A notable example of this growing involvement was the recent Pan-African Conference on Family Values held in Nairobi, which featured the participation of ultra-conservative groups such as the Polish Ordo Iuris (referred to in Chapter 6), the French La Manif Pour Tous, and the UK Christian Voice. The inclusion of these actors reflects a broader intensification of transnational anti-gender movements' strategic interest in Africa as a site for ideological expansion.[86]

[86] Āryā J. Karijo, Haley McEwen, Joy Asasira, and Olabukunola Williams, "Guns and bibles: How US radicalisation threatens African states' security," *openDemocracy*, August 7, 2025, <www.opendemocracy.net/en/5050/guns-and-bibles-how-us-radicalisation-threatens-african-states-security/>, accessed October 2, 2025.

Another significant external actor contributing to the transnationalization of culture wars on the African continent is the Russian Federation, often operating in collaboration with the ROC. Since the full-scale invasion of Ukraine, the ROC has intensified its activities abroad, and particularly in Africa. In 2024, Metropolitan Constantine, a bishop of the ROC and Patriarchal Exarch of Africa, visited over twenty African countries, including Uganda, where he laid the foundation stone for a mega cathedral to be named after African saints.[87] This expansion builds upon a preexisting schism within global Orthodoxy that began in 2019, which the Moscow Patriarchate has strategically exploited to extend its influence. Supported by the Kremlin and major Russian state-owned enterprises, the ROC receives substantial support that enables costly operations on the African continent. These include not only establishing parallel ecclesiastical structures in competition with the historically dominant Patriarchate of Alexandria but also advancing broader ideological goals aligned with the Russian state's geopolitical agenda. Rather than being primarily motivated by Evangelical aims or the conversion of non-Christians, the church's expansion serves to project Russian influence through the medium of religious authority and moral conservatism—leveraging the soft power of Orthodoxy to enhance Russia's global image.[88] In Africa, indeed, the ROC actively participates in the dissemination of anti-Western narratives and seeks to forge alliances with conservative actors who endorse its vision of "traditional values." At the Russia–Africa Summit held on July 27, Patriarch Kirill explicitly appealed to this ideological alignment, telling African leaders: "We are united by adherence to traditional values, a conservative view of human nature, and rejection of the ideology of permissiveness and overconsumption."[89]

(iii) Global Agendas, Local Harm: The Costs of Foreign Anti-LGBTQ+ Activism in Uganda

The repercussions of right-wing Christian activism in Africa are profound and far-reaching. In addition to the direct criminalization of individuals, anti-homosexuality legislation has had a chilling effect on civil society. LGBTQ+ organizations have been forced to cease operations, health outreach programs (including those focused on HIV/AIDS prevention) have been significantly curtailed,

[87] Earnest Kivumbi Benjamin, "Russian Orthodox Church expands in Africa with new projects and leadership," *HICGI News Agency*, December 25, 2024, <https://hicginewsagency.com/2024/12/25/russian-orthodox-church-expands-in-africa-with-new-projects-and-leadership/>, accessed October 1, 2025.

[88] Ksenia Luchenko, "Propaganda in holy orders: Africa, Ukraine, and the Russian Orthodox Church," *European Council on Foreign Relations*, September 20, 2023, <https://ecfr.eu/article/propaganda-in-holy-orders-africa-ukraine-and-the-russian-orthodox-church/>, accessed October 1, 2025.

[89] "Address by His Holiness Patriarch Kirill at the 2nd Russia–Africa Summit," *The Russian Orthodox Church*, July 27, 2023, <https://mospat.ru/en/news/90568/>, accessed October 2, 2025.

and activists have faced arrest or been driven underground. In some instances, anti-gay mobilization has incited mob violence and extrajudicial targeting, as governments either implicitly or explicitly condone anti-LGBTQ+ persecution.

In 2018, in a remarkable decision, a US federal court explicitly recognized the substantial harm caused to sexual minorities by the actions of foreign anti-LGBTQ+ actors, and framed their conduct as a violation of international law.

The case was filed against Scott Lively—a prominent figure in global anti-LGBTQ+ activism. Since the early 1990s, Scott Lively, a US citizen, has been a leading figure in the dissemination of extreme anti-LGBTQ+ propaganda. He is most widely known for coauthoring the Holocaust revisionist book *The Pink Swastika: Homosexuality in the Nazi Party* (1995), which asserts that the Nazi Party was predominantly composed of homosexual men, whose purported "savagery" enabled them to perpetrate the atrocities of the Holocaust. In 2007, Lively co-founded *Watchmen on the Walls*, an organization noted for its aggressively anti-LGBTQ+ stance. Although it originated in the United States, the group has since shifted its primary focus to Eastern Europe, where it continues to promote its conservative agenda. Since at least 2002, Scott Lively has collaborated with Ugandan religious and political leaders on a concerted strategy aimed at systematically eroding the rights of Uganda's sexual minorities. Lively is widely credited with proposing and assisting in the implementation of a strategic framework, or "blueprint," that has informed the infamous "Kill the Gay" Bill. His advocacy has led to tangible consequences: fundamental rights—including freedom of expression, assembly, and association—have been severely curtailed for LGBTI individuals and activists, while many have faced threats to their physical safety, as well as arbitrary arrests and acts of cruel, inhuman, or degrading treatment.

In response to Lively's involvement in the drafting of the "Kill the Gay" Bill, Uganda's leading LGBTQ+ advocacy group, Sexual Minorities Uganda (SMUG), in collaboration with the Center for Constitutional Rights, filed a lawsuit against him in a US federal court. The case was grounded in the charge of "persecution," a crime under international law defined as the intentional and severe deprivation of fundamental rights on the basis of identity. The plaintiffs argued that the very existence of SMUG and its affiliated organizations had been criminalized, and that its members have been systematically targeted, thereby constituting a clear case of persecution as recognized under human rights norms.

In *Sexual Minorities Uganda v Lively*, the District Court of Massachusetts addressed whether an American citizen could be held liable in the US for his role in the persecution of LGBT people in Uganda.[90] The Court strongly condemned Lively's actions, employing unequivocal and forceful language to denounce his conduct: "[d]efendant Scott Lively is an American citizen who has aided and

[90] *Sexual Minorities Uganda v Lively*, No. 17-1593 (1st Cir. 2018).

abetted a vicious and frightening campaign of repression against LGBTI persons in Uganda . . . This crackpot bigotry could be brushed aside as pathetic, except for the terrible harm it can cause. The record in this case demonstrates that the Defendant has worked with elements in Uganda who share some of his views to try to repress freedom of expression by LGBTI people in Uganda, deprive them of the protection of the law, and render their very existence illegal."[91] And, while deciding that the case could not be tried in the US, as Lively's actions took place entirely in a foreign territory, Judge Ponsor forcefully maintained that Lively's actions violated international law: "[a]nyone reading this memorandum should make no mistake. The question before the court is not whether Defendant's actions in aiding and abetting efforts to demonize, intimidate, and injure LGBTI people in Uganda constitute violations of international law. They do."

Another significant consequence of the colonization of human rights discourse in Africa—manifested in the proliferation of anti-homosexuality legislation—is the resulting misalignment of national legal systems with international human rights standards. A striking illustration of this phenomenon is the 2024 decision by the Constitutional Court of Uganda, which upheld the controversial Anti-Homosexuality Act of 2023. The latter reinstates the death penalty for "aggravated homosexuality" (Section 3) and imposes a sentence of life imprisonment upon conviction for the offense of homosexuality (Section 2). It further criminalizes the "promotion of homosexuality" (Sections 2 and 11), mandates a "duty to report acts of homosexuality" (Section 14), and grants courts the authority to order the "rehabilitation" of individuals convicted under its provisions (Section 16).

In a landmark ruling, the Court affirmed the constitutionality of these provisions,[92] concluding that they do not infringe upon fundamental rights to equality and non-discrimination,[93] privacy,[94] freedom of expression,[95] or the right to work for LGBTQ+ individuals.[96]

This decision provides critical insight into the prevailing cultural and political climate underpinning the resurgence of sodomy laws and their broader global implications. Particularly telling is the Court's invocation of widespread "public outcry," media discourse, and testimonies from purported "victims of homosexuality," including emotive accounts of children and families experiencing psychological trauma allegedly resulting from coerced recruitment into homosexual

[91] Ibid.
[92] Constitutional Court of Uganda, *Hon. Fox Odoi & 21 Others v Attorney General & 3 Others* [2024] UGCC 10. The Court declared only four sections unconstitutional. The nullified sections had criminalized the letting of premises for use for homosexual purposes, the failure by anyone to report acts of homosexuality to the police for appropriate action, and the engagement in acts of homosexuality by anyone which results in the other persons contracting a terminal illness.
[93] Ibid, paras 282ff.
[94] Ibid, paras 341ff.
[95] Ibid, paras 372ff.
[96] Ibid, paras 464ff.

acts.[97] Such language reflects the transplantation of a global right-wing narrative that frames anti-homosexuality measures as necessary for the protection of minors—a rationale that has drawn extensive criticism from international human rights bodies. Notably, comparable legislation in Russia—the so-called "anti-gay propaganda laws"—has been found to violate the ECHR, as discussed in Section A. In Africa, these narratives simultaneously express deep-seated anxieties about social reproduction in the face of rapid urbanization and the rise of consumer capitalism As one commentator observes, "[b]y placing children at the center of discussions about homosexuality, as victims easily drawn to a 'foreign' way of life, pastors and others deftly link homosexuality to other contemporary anxieties about social forces which threaten hegemonic relationships and social hierarchies" (Boyd 2013: 712).

In its reasoning, the Constitutional Court of Uganda engaged extensively with the traditional themes of the global culture wars, importing discourses and normative frameworks not native to the region, while simultaneously "Africanizing" debates that have historically divided the Global North. The Court referred to the "overt super-imposition of homosexuality on Ugandan culture"[98] and emphasized the lack of global consensus on non-discrimination based on sexual orientation. It further highlighted what it perceived as a tension within international human rights law—namely, between the universalist aspirations of human rights and the imperative to respect cultural diversity and the autonomy of national traditions.[99]

However, the Court's treatment of the principle of universality was conceptually flawed and analytically weak. It cited parliamentary debates in which the notion of universality was questioned on the basis that if homosexuality were truly universal, no objection to it would exist. One parliamentarian reportedly stated, "[f]or anything which is universal, like the right to eat, nobody will complain . . . Nobody will complain about rights that are truly universal. When you raise an issue of a human right and it is contested, it means it is not universal."[100] This reasoning reflects a fundamental misunderstanding of the concept of universality, which does not presuppose unanimous acceptance, but rather the inherent entitlement of all human beings to certain rights regardless of cultural or societal approval.

The Court also positioned the rights of individuals—specifically those related to self-determination, self-perception, and bodily autonomy—against what it framed as the collective rights of the community to preserve social, political, and cultural self-determination.[101] In doing so, it invoked the concept of human dignity, as recognized under both the Ugandan Constitution[102] and the African Charter on

[97] Ibid, para 65.
[98] Ibid, para 242.
[99] Ibid.
[100] Ibid, para 243.
[101] Ibid.
[102] Constitution of the Republic of Uganda, art 24: "*Respect for human dignity and protection from inhuman treatment.* No person shall be subjected to any form of torture or cruel, inhuman or degrading

Human and Peoples' Rights (ACHPR).[103] The Court emphasized what it described as the "dual element of human dignity," asserting that dignity encompasses both an inherent individual right and a collective right of the Ugandan people to demand that the state promote values conducive to societal well-being.[104] According to the Court's logic, when individual and communal interests are in conflict, the notion of dignity may justify restricting individual autonomy in favor of broader societal values.[105]

Further, the Court asserted that judicial power should be exercised in the name of the Ugandan people and in accordance with "the law and with the values, norms, and aspirations of the people,"[106] concluding that "the practice of homosexuality is inimical to the aspirations, values and norms of Ugandan society," which are purportedly embodied in the national Constitution.[107]

In a passage emblematic of what has been described as a strategy of "rights colonization," the Court attempted to align its interpretation of human dignity with Article 22 of the UDHR "insofar as that provision acknowledges that an individual's dignity and personal development is anchored in the economic, social and cultural rights that accrue to him/her by virtue of belonging to a society/community."[108] However, this interpretation is legally and conceptually flawed. As Diller (2012) explains, Article 22 of the UDHR establishes the right to social security, encompassing the economic, social, and cultural rights essential to human dignity and the free development of one's personality. While the realization of these rights is indeed contingent on national efforts and international cooperation—adapted to the capacities of each state—this provision does not confer upon societal majorities the authority to curtail the fundamental rights of minorities. Rather, it underscores the indivisibility and interdependence of all human rights, including those protecting individual autonomy and identity.

A further notable aspect of the Constitutional Court's reasoning—characteristic of rights manipulation—is its reliance on pseudoscientific claims, a strategy frequently observed in the context of reproductive rights and broader human rights debates (Mancini 2021). The Court denied fundamental rights to LGBTQ+

treatment or punishment"; art 44: "*Prohibition of derogation from particular human rights and freedoms.* Notwithstanding anything in this Constitution, there shall be no derogation from the enjoyment of the following rights and freedoms."

[103] ACHPR, art 5: "Every individual shall have the right to the respect of the dignity inherent in a human being and to the recognition of his legal status. All forms of exploitation and degradation of man, particularly slavery, slave trade, torture, cruel, inhuman or degrading punishment and treatment shall be prohibited."

[104] Constitutional Court of Uganda, *Hon. Fox Odoi & 21 Others v Attorney General & 3 Others* [2024] UGCC 10, para 232.

[105] Ibid, para 233.

[106] Ibid, para 234.

[107] Ibid, para 235.

[108] Ibid, para 237.

individuals by invoking the alleged absence of "scientific or medical evidence" to support the idea that homosexuality constitutes a natural or physiological aspect of human identity. Instead, the Court claimed that there is "proof of the luring of gullible Ugandans into homosexuality," asserting that some of these individuals, after undergoing counseling, later renounced same-sex practices. On this basis, the Court concluded that such outcomes "unravel the proposition that homosexuality is an innate predisposition, as opposed to a personal choice in exercise of individual autonomy," reasoning that an innate characteristic would not require persuasion for its adoption.[109]

The Court further emphasized the alleged negative health consequences associated with homosexuality, particularly anal sex, which it claimed imposes a burden on the national health system and contributes to the spread of HIV. These arguments, grounded in scientifically unfounded generalizations and moralistic assumptions, stand in stark contrast to established international human rights jurisprudence.

In particular, the United Nations Human Rights Committee's 1994 *Toonen v Australia*[110] decision unequivocally held that the term "sex" under Article 26 of the ICCPR includes sexual orientation. The Committee affirmed that consensual same-sex conduct in private falls within the scope of the right to privacy (ICCPR, Article 17), and that criminalization of such conduct cannot be justified as a reasonable or proportionate means of addressing public health concerns, including the spread of HIV/AIDS. On the contrary, such laws have been shown to drive vulnerable communities underground, undermining public health efforts and education campaigns. Furthermore, the Committee rejected the notion that moral issues are matters of exclusive domestic concern, emphasizing that this view would effectively shield discriminatory legislation from international human rights scrutiny.

Against the backdrop of the increased of anti-homosexual legislation worldwide, the universal character of human rights protections relating to sexual orientation has been reaffirmed in recent instruments, most notably the 2024 report of the UN Independent Expert on protection against violence and discrimination based on sexual orientation and gender identity.[111] The report—explicitly referencing the Ugandan case[112]—underscored that the principle that all individuals should be free from violence and discrimination based on their sexual orientation or gender identity is not a regionally bounded concept but an established international norm. The report also identified a growing trend in which opposition to

[109] Ibid, para 244.

[110] *Toonen v Australia*, UNHRC Communication No. 488/1992, March 31, 1994.

[111] Human Rights Council fifty-third session, 19 June–14 July 2023, "Freedom of religion or belief and freedom from violence and discrimination based on sexual orientation and gender identity: Report of the Independent Expert on protection against violence and discrimination based on sexual orientation and gender identity," Victor Madrigal-Borloz, A/HRC/53/37, January 24, 2024, <https://docs.un.org/en/A/HRC/53/37>.

[112] Ibid, 5–6, 8.

LGBTQ+ rights is couched in the language of cultural or religious exceptionalism. It noted that arguments denying the universality of LGBTQ+ rights often claim that sexual orientation and gender identity are merely subjective and, therefore, not protected under international human rights law. In such narratives, conflicts with religious or cultural beliefs are resolved in favor of the latter, often under the guise of promoting "traditional values."[113]

Crucially, the report warned that appeals to "traditional values," "public morals," and "national values" are frequently used to justify discrimination against women, LGBTQ+ individuals, and religious or belief minorities. These discourses are often underpinned by religious norms and patriarchal constructs of gender and family, and they are increasingly intertwined with nationalism.[114] In contexts where same-sex intimacy is punishable by death, such as under Uganda's Anti-Homosexuality Act, state justifications for such extreme penalties are often grounded in religious doctrine, cultural essentialism, or appeals to collective morality—factors that do not absolve states of their obligations under international human rights law.

The Ugandan Constitutional Court's decision also exemplifies a growing trend in the strategic use of comparative law to legitimize illiberal interpretations of rights—a phenomenon increasingly observed across jurisdictions (Dixon & Landau 2021). In this context, the Court draws upon the reasoning in the US Supreme Court *Dobbs v Jackson Women's Health Organization* case, discussed earlier, to support its own restrictive interpretation of individual autonomy. The Ugandan Court characterizes *Dobbs* as emblematic of a broader judicial shift that privileges "the nation's history and tradition, as well as the dictates of democracy and rule of law," over expansive understandings of personal liberty.[115] It further asserts that the originalist methodology employed in *Dobbs* parallels the constitutional framework in Uganda, which requires courts to consider the nation's "sociocultural norms, values, and aspirations" in adjudicating legal disputes. The Court invokes the democratic legitimacy of the Anti-Homosexuality Act by emphasizing that it reflects "the sociocultural realities of Ugandan society" and was enacted by an overwhelming majority of democratically elected representatives. In doing so, the Court suggests an equivalence between the democratic justifications invoked in *Dobbs* and those underpinning its own decision.

However, this comparison is conceptually flawed. Ugandan courts do not operate under an originalist interpretive doctrine akin to that employed by certain factions of the US judiciary. Furthermore, unlike the federal structure of the United States, where legal and political debates over abortion post-*Dobbs* have been decentralized and are now unfolding within state legislatures, courts, executive branches, and mechanisms of direct democracy (Murray & Shaw 2024: 806–7),

[113] Ibid, 3.
[114] Ibid, 4.
[115] Ibid, para 266.

Uganda is a unitary state with a centralized legal system. As such, the legal and institutional context is fundamentally different.

Ironically, the only genuine analogy between the two judgments is their selective and historically reductive appeals to history and tradition. Just as in *Dobbs* the US Supreme Court conveniently misrepresents and misconstrues the history of reproductive rights in the United States, the Ugandan decision overlooks the colonial origins of Uganda's anti-homosexuality laws, instead recasting them as expressions of indigenous cultural values. This strategic reframing reflects a broader pattern in which colonial legal legacies are obscured in favor of narratives that seek to authenticate contemporary repressive laws as inherently African or traditional, thereby reinforcing illiberal interpretations of human rights under the guise of cultural sovereignty.

D. Concluding Remarks

The comparative analysis of the deployment of traditionalist narratives in Russia, the United States, and selected African countries—most notably Uganda—reveals striking parallels in how appeals to history, religion, and tradition are employed to reject international legal norms, reconfigure international and regional relations, and reinterpret human rights frameworks in regressive ways. These similarities persist despite the distinct political, historical, cultural, and legal contexts that characterize each setting. Across all cases examined, the invocation of traditionalism is not rooted in a genuine or organic continuity with indigenous or historically grounded cultural practices. Rather, it represents a consciously constructed and ideologically driven form of conservatism. This form of traditionalism is selectively engineered to advance authoritarian political and religious agendas, often under the guise of defending the constitution, sovereignty, or universal values. It draws heavily on a mixture of geopolitical theory, religious doctrine, and historical revisionism, all of which underpin narratives of national exceptionalism.

Crucially, these narratives are structured in opposition to perceived external or alternative traditions, creating a dichotomy between "authentic" national values and supposedly foreign or imposed norms. Ironically, in both the Russian and African contexts, anti-Western rhetoric underpins these traditionalist discourses, even though the ideological foundations of these narratives are deeply entangled with Western conservative thought. In Russia, the differentialist theory of tradition is indebted to the legacy of Western traditionalist and counter-Enlightenment ideologies. In several African contexts, traditionalist claims frequently conflate precolonial indigenous norms with elements of colonial legacies, resulting in a hybridized and often contradictory conceptualization of "African tradition." In all cases, the appeal to tradition serves strategic purposes: it enables the reframing of rights in ways that narrow their scope, restrict spaces for pluralism and diversity, and reinforce the dominance and privileges of majority groups—whether defined in ethnic, religious, or cultural terms. The institutionalization of these narratives—in political discourse, constitutional texts, legislative reforms, and judicial interpretations—correlates strongly with patterns of democratic backsliding and increasing divergence from international human rights standards.

Moreover, the invocation of tradition functions not only as an internal mechanism for consolidating authoritarian rule but also as an external strategy for reshaping international and regional legal and political equilibria. In all three contexts, traditionalist rhetoric is employed to challenge the universality of human rights and promote alternative visions of sovereignty and governance. Thus, tradition becomes both a domestic instrument of repression and an international tool for redefining norms and power structures.

Conclusion

Our recounting of the historical evolution of secularism demonstrates that modern constitutional democracies can neither fully set apart religion from the state, nor can they prevent religion from altogether partaking in political life. Given the persistent elusiveness of a clean divide, the relationship between religion and the state seems bound to operate along a spectrum shaped by historical, cultural, and constitutional contingencies. France and Iran exemplify opposing ends of this spectrum. France's model of militant secularism, grounded in *laïcité* and constitutionally entrenched, proclaims and seeks to enforce state neutrality toward religion. Yet, as analyzed in Chapter 5, this approach emerges in practice as anti-religious and as privileging the cultural norms of the majority denomination under the guise of neutrality. As discussed in Chapter 2, Iran, by contrast, maintains a democratic constitution that explicitly adopts a single interpretation of Shi'a Islam, granting limited tolerance to select non-Muslim minorities while prohibiting any meaningful pluralism within Islam itself. Iran's democratic legitimacy is further compromised by the supremacy of clerical authority, as ultimate power rests with the Supreme Jurist. Despite these deficiencies, Iran remains within the bounds of constitutional democracy, particularly when contrasted with Saudi Arabia, whose constitutional framework enshrines religious authority without providing for any democratic institutions.

As detailed throughout our inquiry, and as critically examined in Chapter 4, a central unresolved question is whether institutional secularism should continue figuring within the constitutional regimes of democracies or whether it should give way to protection of ideological secularism as one broadly based conception of the good among many within a pluralistic polity. In this context, as we have underscored, the repoliticization of religion has increasingly produced exclusionary reinterpretations of fundamental rights, and most of these have denigrated secularism in all its forms. Indeed, contemporary populist and authoritarian movements have mobilized religious narratives and arguments to curtail the rights of women, LGBTQ persons, and religious or irreligious minorities. These developments, well illustrated in Chapter 3 by the example of Hungary's Orban constant invocations of religion for exclusionary political purposes, differ qualitatively from earlier efforts to reintroduce religion into public life. They are more systematically and more overtly anti-pluralistic and they are rights-restrictive for those who do not share their intolerant views. At the same time, these populist and authoritarian proponents have often sought to expand the rights of fellow travelers—including the right to openly discriminate in the public sphere against their fellow citizens on the ground of conscience-based objections or proclaimed religious convictions.

Ironically, as retraced in Chapter 1, secularism's origins lie within the bounds of a single religion, namely Christianity. Early Christian theology distinguished between the "City of God" and the "City of Man," and the Church institutionalized a division between spiritual and temporal functions. At its inception, secularism had no connection to pluralism; it was a means of organizing religious life rather than accommodating religious diversity. Pluralism emerged only later, in response to the devastating wars between Catholics and Protestants in early modern Europe. Early pluralist arrangements, such as the Edict of Nantes proclaimed by France's King Henry IV, were limited in scope and confined entirely within Christianity. It was not until the Enlightenment and the political transformations initiated by the American and French Revolutions that pluralism expanded beyond Christian boundaries.

Philosophically, this expansion was facilitated by the Enlightenment separation of faith and reason, articulated by thinkers such as Spinoza and systematized by Kant. Kant's rationalist framework emphasized human autonomy and reason as the proper guides for managing worldly affairs. Constitutionally, these ideas were institutionalized through guarantees of religious freedom and state neutrality, most notably in the religion clauses of the US Constitution. Institutional secularism thus emerged both as an ideal and as the logical culmination of a historical process aimed at ensuring peaceful coexistence in religiously divided societies.

In spite of all the models of state and religion relationships committed to approximate its core mission, the ideal of institutional secularism remains unattainable. From fundamentalist religions that justify coercion or violence in pursuit of what they consider the only valid metaphysical truth, to secular radically anti-pluralist ideologies, such as Nazism or Stalinism—and many more religious and secular perspectives that fit somewhere between these two extremes—have stood in the way of realization of any truly comprehensive ideological coexistence. Moreover, secularism itself has frequently fallen short of its own aspirations.

These failures raise the question of whether institutional secularism should be abandoned altogether. We argue against such abandonment for two principal reasons. First, the core principles of institutional secularism—commitment to pluralism and the refusal to base law on contested metaphysical truths—are indispensable to the inclusionary protection of fundamental rights. Second, even as an unrealizable ideal, secularism performs a vital counterfactual function by providing a benchmark against which exclusionary practices can be identified and criticized.

Secularism is an essentially contested concept. Its meanings vary across philosophical traditions, political theories, constitutional frameworks, and judicial interpretations. As the book showcases, courts within the same legal system have reached divergent conclusions about the permissibility of religious symbols, practices, and state-sponsored religious expressions. These disagreements reveal the difficulty of determining whether particular accommodations or incorporations of religion are compatible with secularism or inherently exclusionary. It is important to distinguish between restrictive versus expansive interpretations of rights, on the one hand, and inclusionary versus exclusionary ones, on the other. Restrictiveness alone does not imply exclusion; exclusion occurs when rights are reframed in ways that systematically marginalize or subordinate particular groups. This distinction can be illustrated through comparative constitutional examples. Variations in free speech and religious freedom protections between the United States, Germany, and France reflect differing historical and cultural contexts rather than exclusionary constitutional approaches. By contrast, the US Supreme Court's decision in *Dobbs v Jackson Women's Health Organization,* analyzed in Chapter 7, represents an exclusionary shift, as it revoked a long-recognized constitutional right and relied heavily on contested moral positions rooted in religious tradition.

The role of religion in exclusionary transformations of fundamental rights is complex. In some cases, religious motivations are explicit, as in movements seeking to prohibit abortion on theological grounds. In others, religious arguments are intertwined with secular justifications or translated into ostensibly neutral public-reason discourse. Regardless of whether exclusionary policies are justified in religious or secular terms, their effects on pluralism and rights protection remain decisive. Religion becomes particularly salient when it reinforces otherwise weak secular arguments, as exemplified by contemporary campaigns against "gender ideology," comprehensively tackled in Chapter 6, which draw persuasive force from conservative Christian doctrine. Indeed, whereas a secular clamor to return to the days when the role of women was largely confined to the familial home would likely be summarily dismissed by large majorities; appeal to a divine ordinance to the same effect would require at least some presumptive respect as the expression of long held widely shared metaphysically grounded religious convictions.

In conclusion, we defend continued adherence to the core principles of secularism and to an analytical framework that prioritizes inclusionary over exclusionary approaches to fundamental rights. While gray areas and reasonable disagreements are inevitable, the greater danger lies in the strategic misuse of constitutional, secular, or religious language by populist and illiberal actors to disguise exclusionary agendas. In factually pluralistic societies, inclusionary pluralism remains preferable to conflict, authoritarianism, and systematic rights erosion. It is noteworthy that even some religions that assert an exclusive possession of the truth have, at times, demonstrated the capacity to coexist peacefully within pluralistic frameworks. These religions have done so by shifting their perspective and thus characterize competing religions as achieving partial truth—or at least earnestly seeking the truth—instead of vilifying them as enemies of the truth. In that same spirit, we advocate a presumptive commitment to an expansive pluralism grounded in our shared humanity, and recognizing this as the most auspicious path for contemporary constitutional democracies.

Bibliography

Abazović, Dino. 2015. "Religious Claims during the War and Post-War Bosnia and Herzegovina." *Borderlands e-Journal* 14, no. 1: 1–20.

Abdulaziz, Sachedina. 2001. "The Rule of the Religious Jurist in Iran." In *Iran at the Crossroads*, edited by John L. Esposito and R. K. Ramazani, 123–47. New York: Palgrave.

Ajami, Fouad. 1993. *The Arab Predicament: Arab Political Thought and Practice since 1967*. 2nd ed. Cambridge: Cambridge University Press.

Ahlstrom, Sydney E. 1972. *A Religious History of the American People*. New Haven: Yale University Press.

Albertazzi, Daniele, and Duncan McDonnell. 2015. *Populists in Power*. London: Routledge.

Alfieri, Fernanda. 2010. *Nella Camera degli sposi. Tomás Sánchez, il matrimonio, la sessualità (secoli XVI-XVII)*. Bologna: Il Mulino.

Alijeva, Lilija. 2017. "Left Behind? A Critical Study of the Russian-speaking Minority Rights to Citizenship and Language in the Post-Soviet Baltic States. Lessons from Nationalising Language Policies." *International Journal on Minority and Group Rights* 24, no. 4: 484–536.

Amusan, Lere, Luqman Saka, and O. Adekeye Muinat. 2019. "Gay Rights and the Politics of Anti-homosexual Legislation in Africa." *Journal of African Union Studies* 8, no. 2: 45–66.

Anderson, Benedict. 1983. *Imagined Communities*. London: Verso Books.

Anderson, Benedict. 2006. *Imagined Communities: Reflections on the Origin and Spread of Nationalism*. Rev. ed. London: Verso.

Andes, Stephen J. C. 2020. "Catholicism, Revolution, and Counter-Revolution in Twentieth-Century Latin America." In *Oxford Handbook of Latin-American Christianity*, edited by David Thomas Orique, 175–93. Oxford: Oxford University Press.

Andreescu, Liviu. 2008. "Romania's New Law on Religious Freedom and Religious Denominations." *Religion, State & Society* 36, no. 2: 139–61.

Annicchino, Pasquale. 2011. "Winning the Battle by Losing the War: The *Lautsi* Case and the Holy Alliance between American Conservative Evangelicals, the Russian Orthodox Church and the Vatican to Reshape European Identity." *Religion & Human Rights* 6, no. 3: 213–19.

Arat, Yesim. 2010. "Religion, Politics and Gender Equality in Turkey: Implications of a Democratic Paradox?" *Third World Quarterly* 31, no. 6: 869–84.

Araujo, Robert J. 1994. "Political Theory and Liberation Theology: The Intersection of Unger and Gutiérrez." *Journal of Law and Religion* 11, no. 1: 63–104.

Arts, Wil, and Loek Halman. 2005. "National Identity in Europe Today: What the People Feel and Think." *International Journal of Sociology* 35, no. 4: 69–93.

Asad, Talal. 1992. *Genealogies of Religion*. Baltimore: John Hopkins University Press.

Asad, Talal. 2003. *Formations of the Secular: Christianity, Islam, Modernity*. Palo Alto: Stanford University Press.

Augustine. 1958. *The City of God*, translated by Gerald G. Walsh, Demetrius B. Zema, Grace Monahan, and Daniel J. Honan. New York: Image Books/Doubleday.

Avdeev, Alexandre, Alain Blum, and Irina Troitskaya. 1995. "The History of Abortion Statistics in Russia and the USSR from 1900 to 1991." *Population: An English Selection* 7: 39–66.

Backman, Jussi. 2020. "A Russian Radical Conservative Challenge to the Liberal Global Order: Aleksandr Dugin." In *Contestations of Liberal Order: The West in Crisis?*, edited by Marko Lehti, Henna-Riika Pennanen, and Jukka Joukhi, 289–314. London: Palgrave Macmillan.

Bâli, Asli. 2016. "The Perils of Judicial Independence: Constitutional Transition and the Turkish Example." *Virginia Journal of International Law* 52, no. 2: 235–320.

Balibar, Étienne. 1998. *Spinoza and Politics*, translated by Peter Snowdon. London: Verso.

Balogh, Lídia. 2020. "The Ratification Status of the Council of Europe's Istanbul Convention among EU Member States." MTA Law Working Papers 2020/7, Hungarian Academy of Sciences, Budapest.

Barak, Aharon. 2015. *Human Dignity: The Constitutional Value and the Constitutional Right.* New York: Oxford University Press.

Beissinger, Mark R. 2009. "Nationalism and the Collapse of Soviet Communism." *Contemporary European History* 18, no. 3: 331–47.

Berman, Mitchell N. 2009. "Originalism is Bunk." *New York University Law Review* 84, no. 1 (April 2009): 1–96.

Birnbaum, Pierre. 1988. *Un mythe politique: la "République juive"*. Paris: Fayard.

Birnbaum, Pierre. 2014. "On the Secularization of the Public Square: Jews in France and in the United States." In *Constitutional Secularism in an Age of Religious Revival,* edited by Susanna Mancini and Michel Rosenfeld, 136–45. Oxford: Oxford University Press.

Benhabib, Seyla. 2002. "Transformations of Citizenship: The Case of Contemporary Europe." *Government and Opposition: An International Journal of Comparative Politics* 37, no. 4: 439–65.

Blech, Benjamin. 1992. *Understanding Judaism: The Basics of Deed and Creed.* Northvale, NJ: Jason Aronson.

Bhargava, Rajeev. 2007. "The Distinctiveness of Indian Securalism." In *The Future of Securalism,* edited by T.N. Srinivasa, 121–47. Oxford: Oxford University Press.

Blackstone, William. 1884. *Commentaries on the Laws of England.* 3rd rev. ed. Chicago: Callaghan and Company.

Bob, Clifford. 2012. *The Global Right Wing and the Clash of World Politics.* Cambridge: Cambridge University Press.

Bodjongo, Mpabe, and Mathieu Juliot. 2024. "Can the Decriminalization of Homosexuality Counter Religious and Traditional Homophobia in Africa?" *Review of Law & Economics* 20, no. 3: 357–401.

Borovalı, Murat. 2009. "Islamic Headscarves and Slippery Slopes." *Cardozo Law Review* 30, no. 6: 2739–70.

Boyd, L. 2013. "The Problem with Freedom: Homosexuality and Human Rights in Uganda." *Anthropological Quarterly* 86, no. 3 (Summer): 697–724.

Brems, Eva. 2014. *The Experience of Full-Face Veil Wearers in Europe and the Law.* Cambridge: Cambridge University Press.

Brodeală, Elena, and Georgiana Epure. 2021. "Nature versus Nurture: 'Sex' and 'Gender' before the Romanian Constitutional Court." *European Constitutional Law Review* 17, no. 4: 724–52.

Brown, J. F. 1988. *Poland since Martial Law.* Santa Monica: Rand Corp.

Brownfield, Ellen Yonts. 2007. "The First Amendment Implications of Teaching the Theory of Evolution and Creationism in Public Schools." *The Journal of Law and Education* 36, no. 1: 141–48.

Brubaker, Rogers. 1996. *Nationalism Reframed: Nationhood and the National Question in the New Europe.* Cambridge: Cambridge University Press.

Brubaker, Rogers. 2017. "Between Nationalism and Civilizationalism: The European Populist Moment in Comparative Perspective." *Ethnic & Racial Studies* 40, no. 8: 1191–226.

Butler, Jon. 1992. *The Huguenots in America: A Refugee People in New World Society.* Cambridge, MA: Harvard University Press.

Butler, Judith. 1990. *Gender Trouble: Feminism and the Subversion of Identity.* Abingdon, Routledge.

Cagaptay, Soner. 2004. "Race, Assimilation and Kemalism: Turkish Nationalism and the Minorities in the 1930s." *Middle Eastern Studies* 40, no. 3: 86–101.

Cartabia, Marta, and Andrea Simoncini. 2015. *Pope Benedict XVI's Legal Thought: A Dialogue on the Foundation of Law.* New York: Oxford University Press.

Cartabia, Marta, and Andrea Simoncini. 2015. "A Journey with Benedict XVI through the Spirit of Constitutionalism." In *Pope Benedict XVI's Legal Thought: A Dialogue on the Foundation of Law,* edited by Marta Cartabia and Andrea Simoncini, 3–9. Cambridge: Cambridge University Press.

Casanova, José. 1994. *Public Religions in the Modern World*. Chicago: University of Chicago Press.

Case, Mary Anne. 2019. "Trans Formations in the Vatican's War on Gender Ideology." *Signs: Journal of Women in Culture and Society* 44, no. 3: 639–64.

Cavina, Marco. 2011. *Nozze di sangue: Storia della violenza coniugale*. Roma-Bari: Laterza.

Cesari, Jocelyne. 2018. "Unexpected Convergences: Religious Nationalism in Israel and Turkey." *Religions* 9, no. 11: 334–54.

Chaves, Mark. 2015. *American Religion: Contemporary Trends*. 2nd ed. Princeton, NJ: Princeton University Press.

Çinar, Alev. 2005. *Modernity, Islam, and Secularism in Turkey: Bodies, Places, and Time*. Minneapolis: University of Minnesota Press.

Coates, Amy L., Peter S. Hill, Simon Rushton, and Julie Balen. 2014. "The Holy See on Sexual and Reproductive Health and Rights: Conservative in Position, Dynamic in Response." *Reproductive Health Matters* 22, no. 44: 114–24.

Collins, Michael, and Matthew A. Price. 2003. *The Story of Christianity*. 2nd ed. London: Dorling Kindersley.

Cord, Robert L. 1982. *Separation of Church and State: Historical Fact and Current Fiction*. New York: Lambeth Press.

Cossman, Brenda, and Ratna Kapur. 1997. "Secularism's Last Sigh?: The Hindu Right, the Courts, and India's Struggle for Democracy." *Harvard International Law Journal* 38, no. 1: 113–70.

Crouzet, François. 2008. *The First Industrialists: The Problem of Origins*. Reissue ed. Cambridge: Cambridge University Press.

Curanović, Alicja. 2015. *The Guardians of Traditional Values: Russia and the Russian Orthodox Church in the Quest for Status*. Washington: German Marshall Fund of the United States.

Currier, Ashley, and Keeley B. Gogul. 2020. "African Antisodomy Laws as Unwanted Colonial Inheritances." *Women's Studies Quarterly* 48, no. 1/2: 103–21.

Datta, Neil. 2018. *Restoring the Natural Order. The Religious Extremists' Vision to Mobilize European Societies against Human Rights on Sexuality and Reproduction*. Brussels: European Parliamentary Forum.

Datta, Neil. 2020. *Modern-day Crusaders in Europe, Tradition, Family and Property: Analysis of a Transnational, Ultra-conservative, Catholic-inspired Influence Network*. Brussels: European Parliamentary Forum.

Datta, Neil. 2021. *Tip of the Iceberg: Religious Extremist Funders against Human Rights for Sexuality & Reproductive Health in Europe*. Brussels: European Parliamentary Forum.

Davis, Derek H. 1997. "Russia's New Law on Religion: Progress or Regress?" *Journal of Church and State* 39, no. 4: 645–55.

De Búrca, Grainne, and Katharine G. Young. 2023. "The (mis)Appropriation of Human Rights by the New Global Right: An Introduction to the Symposium." *International Journal of Constitutional Law* 21, no. 1: 205–23.

De Kerf, Justine. 2017. "Anti-Gay Propaganda Laws: Time for the European Court of Human Rights to Overcome Her Fear of Commitment." *Journal of Diversity and Gender Studies* 4, no. 1: 35–48.

Diamond, Sara. 1995. *Roads to Dominion. Right Wing Movements and Political Power in the United States*. New York-London: The Guildford Press.

Dietler, Michael. 1994. "'Our Ancestors the Gauls': Archaeology, Ethnic Nationalism, and the Manipulation of Celtic Identity in Modern Europe." *American Journal of Archaeology* 96, no. 3: 584–93.

Diller, Janelle M. 2012. *Securing Dignity and Freedom through Human Rights: Article 22 of the Universal Declaration of Human Rights*. Leiden: Nijhoff/Brill.

Dixon, Rosalind, and David Landau. 2021. *Abusive Constitutional Borrowing: Legal Globalization & The Subversion of Liberal Democracy*. New York: Oxford University Press.

Dorsen, Norman, Michel Rosenfeld, András Sajó, Susanne Baer, and Susanna Mancini. 2022. *Comparative Constitutionalism: Cases and Materials*. 4th ed. St. Paul, MN: Thomson/West.

Dugin, Aleksandr. 1997. *The Foundations of Geopolitics: The Geopolitical Future of Russia*. Moscow: Arktogeja.

Durham, W.C. 2013. "State Reactions to Minority Religions: A Legal Overview." In *State Responses to Minority Religions*, edited by David M. Kirkham, 3–16. Abingdon: Routledge.

Dyzenhaus, David. 2020. "Schmitten in the USA." *Verfassungsblog: On Matters Constitutional*, April 4, 2020. <https://verfassungsblog.de/schmitten-in-the-usa/>, accessed October 1, 2025.

Dzehtsiarou, Kanstantsin, and Donal K. Coeffey. 2019. "Suspension and Expulsion of Members of the Council of Europe: Difficult Decisions in Troubled Times." *International and Comparative Law Quarterly* 68, no. 2: 443–76.

Fanon, Franz. 1965. "Algeria Unveiled." In *Decolonization: Perspectives from Now and Then*, edited by Prasenjit Duara, 42–55. New York: Routledge.

Fieschi, Catherine. 2019. *Populocracy: The Tyranny of Authenticity and the Rise of Populism*. New York: Columbia University Press.

Francis I. 2013. *Esortazione apostolica Evangelii Gaudium del Santo Padre Francesco ai vescovi ai presbiteri e ai diaconi alle Persone Consacrate e ai Fedeli laici sull'annuncio del Vangelo nel mondo attuale*. The Holy See: Tipografia Vaticana.

Franklin, Cary. 2010. "The Anti-Stereotyping Principle in Constitutional Sex Discrimination Law." *New York University Law Review* 85, no. 1: 83–173.

Ganshof, François-Louis. 1976. *Feudalism*. 3rd ed. London: Longman.

Garcia, Robert K., and Nathan L. King (eds.) 2009. *Is Goodness without God Good Enough? A Debate on Faith, Secularism, and Ethics*. Lanham: Rowman & Littlefield Publishers.

Garrard-Burnett, Virginia. 2016. *Terror in the Land of the Holy Spirit: Guatemala under General Efraín Ríos Montt, 1982–1983*. Oxford: Oxford University Press.

Gauthier, Mary L. 1998. "Church Elites and the Restoration of Civil Society in Communist Societies of Central Europe." *Journal of Church and State* 40, no. 2: 289–317.

Gellner, Ernest. 1983. *Nations and Nationalism*. Oxford: Blackwell.

Genc, Kaya. 2019. "Erdogan's Way: The Rise and Rule of Turkey's Islamist Shapeshifter." *Foreign Affairs* 98, no. 5: 26–35.

Ginsburg, Ruth Bader. 1985. "Some Thoughts on Autonomy and Equality in Relation to Roe v. Wade." *North Carolina Law Review* 63, no. 2: 375–86.

Gloppen, Siri. 2021. "Conceptualizing Abortion Lawfare." *Revista Direito GV* 17, no. 3: 1–19.

Gloppen, Siri, and Lise Rakner. 2020. "LGBT Rights in Africa." In *Research Handbook on Gender, Sexuality and the Law*, edited by Chris Ashford and Alexander Maine, 194–209. Cheltenham: Edward Elgar Publishers.

Goldberg, Michelle. 2006. *Kingdom Coming: The Rise of Christian Nationalism*. New York: W. W. Norton.

Gorski, Philip S., and Samuel L. Perry. 2022. *The Flag and the Cross: White Christian Nationalism and the Threat to American Democracy*. New York: Oxford University Press.

Graff, Agnieszka, Ratna Kapur, and Suzanna D. Walters. 2019. "Introduction: Gender and the Rise of the Global Right." *Signs: Journal of Women in Culture and Society* 44, no. 3: 541–60.

Grandjean, Michel, and Bernard Roussel. 1998. *Coexister dans l'intolérance: l'Édit de Nantes (1598)*. Geneva: Editions Labor et Fides.

Greenawalt, Kent. 2009. "Secularism, Religion, and Liberal Democracy in the United States." *Cardozo Law Review* 30, no. 6: 2383–400.

Greenhouse, Linda, and Reva B. Siegel. 2011. "Before (and After) Roe v. Wade: New Questions About Backlash." *Yale Law Journal* 120, no. 8: 2060–67.

Grimm, Dieter. 2014. "Conflicts Between General Laws and Religious Norms." In *Constitutional Secularism in an Age of Religious Revival*, edited by Susanna Mancini and Michel Rosenfeld, 3–13. Oxford: Oxford University Press.

Gupta, Alok. 2008. *This Alien Legacy: The Origins of 'Sodomy' Laws in British Colonialism*. New York: Human Rights Watch.

Habermas, Jürgen. 1990. *The Philosophical Discourse of Modernity: Twelve Lectures*, translated by Frederick G. Lawrence. Cambridge, MA: MIT Press.

Habermas, Jürgen. 1992. "Further Reflections on the Public Sphere." In *Habermas and the Public Sphere*, edited by Craig Calhoun, 421–61. Cambridge: MIT Press.

Habermas, Jürgen. 1999a. "Between Facts and Norms: An Author's Reflections." *Denver University Law Review* 76, no. 4: 937–42.

Habermas, Jürgen. 1999b. "Struggles for Recognition in the Democratic State." In *Inclusion of the Other: Studies in Political Theory*, edited by Ciaran P. Cronin and Pablo de Greiff, 203–36. Cambridge: Polity Press.
Habermas, Jürgen, and Joseph Ratzinger (Pope Benedict XVI). 2006. *The Dialectics of Secularization: On Reason and Religion*. San Francisco: Ignatius Press.
Hamilton, Marci A. 2004. "The Religious Freedom Restoration Act: Letting the Fox into the Henhouse." *Cardozo Law Review* 16, no. 2: 357–98.
Harless, Sarah M. 2003. "From the Bedroom to the Courtroom: The Impact of Domestic Violence Law on Marital Rape Victims." *Rutgers Law Journal* 35, no. 1: 305–44.
Hasday, Jill E. 2000. "Contest and Consent: A Legal History of Marital Rape." *California Law Review* 8, no. 5: 1373–505.
Heidegger, Martin. 2000 (orig. 1935). *Introduction to Metaphysics*, translated by Gregory Fried and Richard Polt. New Haven: Yale University Press.
Hennette-Vauchez, Stéphanie. 2024. "Can Religious Schools Discriminate on the Basis of Religion? A Comparative Law Approach." *Connecticut Journal of International Law* 39, no. 1: 83–124.
Hirschl, Ran, and Ayelet Shachar. 2018. "Religious Talk in Narratives of Membership." In *Constitutional Democracy in Crisis?*, edited by Mark A. Graber, Sanford Levinson, and Mark Tushnet, 515–31. Oxford: Oxford University Press.
Hofstadter, Richard. 1963. *Anti-Intellectualism in American Life*. New York: Alfred Knopf.
Holyoake, George Jacob. 1896. *The Origin and Nature of Secularism*. London: Watts & Co.
Horsfjord, Vebjørn L. 2024. "Patriarch and Patriot: History in Patriarch Kirill's Sermons in the First Year of the Full-Scale War in Ukraine." *Religion, State & Society* 52, no. 4: 367–82.
Horváth, Gizela, and Rozália Bakó. 2009. "Religious Icons in Romanian Schools: Text and Context." *Journal for the Study of Religions and Ideologies* 8, no. 24: 189–206.
Horváth, Robert. 2016. "The Reinvention of 'Traditional Values': Nataliya Narochnitskaya and Russia's Assault on Universal Human Rights." *Europe-Asia Studies* 68, no. 5: 868–92.
Hosking, Geoffrey. 1995. "The Freudian Frontier." *Times Literary Supplement*, no. 4797: 27.
Huckerby, Jayne, and Sarah Knuckey. 2023. "Appropriation and the Rewriting of Rights." *International Journal of Constitutional Law* 21, no. 1: 243–65.
Huntington, Samuel P. 1996. *The Clash of Civilizations and the Remaking of World Order*. New York: Simon and Schuster.
Ilcheva, Miriana. 2020. "Bulgaria and the Istanbul Convention – Law, Politics and Propaganda vs. the Rights of Victims of Gender-based Violence." *Open Journal for Legal Studies* 3, no. 1: 49–68.
Jackson, Vicki C. 2004. "Constitutional Dialogue and Human Dignity: States and Transnational Constitutional Discourse." *Montana Law Review* 65, no. 1/2: 15–40.
Jaffrelot, Christophe. 1998. *The Hindu Nationalist Movement in India*. New York: Columbia University Press.
Jaffrelot, Christophe. 2007. "Ayodhya, the Babri Masjid, and the Ramjanmabhumi Dispute." In *Hindu Nationalism: A Reader*, edited by Christophe Jaffrelot, 279–301. Princeton, NJ: Princeton University Press.
Jakobs, Gunther. 1985. "Kriminalisierung im Vorfeld einer Rechtsgutsverletzung." *Zeitschrift für die gesamte Strafrechtswissenschaft* 97, no. 4: 751–85.
John Paul II. 1988. *Apostolic Letter Mulieris Dignitatem*. The Holy See: Libreria Editrice Vaticana.
John Paul II. 1995. *Encyclical Letter Evangelicum Vitae*. The Holy See: Libreria Editrice Vaticana.
John Paul II. 1998. *Encyclical Letter Fides et Ratio*. The Holy See: Libreria Editrice Vaticana.
Joppke, Christian. 2010. "How Liberal Are Citizenship Tests?" In *How Liberal are Citizenship Tests?*, edited by Rainer Bauböck and Christian Koppke, 1–4. Fiesole: Robert Schuman for Advanced Studies.
Juchnevičiūtė, Evelina, Milda Ališauskienė, and Gintarė Pocė. 2023. "The Christian Right in Contemporary Lithuania Key Actors and Their Agendas." In *The Christian Right in Europe: Movements, Networks, and Denominations*, edited by Gionathan Lo Mascolo, 265–78. Bielefeld: Transcript Verlag.
Juergensmeyer, Mark. 2008. *Global Rebellion: Religious Challenges to the Secular State, from Christian Militias to al Qaeda*. Berkeley: The University of California Press.

Kaoma, Kapya. 2012. *Colonizing African Values: How the U.S. Christian Right is Transforming Sexual Politics in Africa*. Sommerville, MA: Political Research Associates.

Kaoma, Kapya. 2017. *Christianity, Globalization and Protective Homophobia: Democratic Contestation of Sexuality in Sub-Saharan Africa*. London: Palgrave Macmillan.

Kapur, Ratna. 2007. "The Citizen and the Migrant: Postcolonial Anxieties, Law, and the Politics of Exclusion/Inclusion." *Theoretical Inquiries in Law* 8, no. 2: 541–54.

Kapur, Ratna. 2014. "The 'Ayodhya' Case: Hindu Majoritarianism and the Right to Religious Liberty." *Maryland Journal of International Law* 29, no. 1: 305–65.

Kapur, Ratna. 2020. "Secularism's Others: The Legal Regulation of Religion and Hierarchy of Citizenship." In *Handbook on Constitutions and Religion*, edited by Susanna Mancini, 41–58. Cheltenham: Edward Elgar Publishers.

Katz Miller, Ariella. 2024. "Cost of Expulsion, Dissent and Human Rights in Russia." *Russian Politics* 9, no. 1: 100–120.

Kelly, Liz. 1988. *Surviving Sexual Violence*. Minneapolis: University of Minnesota Press.

Khatab, Sayed. 2004. "Arabism and Islamism in Sayyid Quṭb's Thought on Nationalism." *The Muslim World* 94, no. 2: 217–44.

Kierkegaard, Søren. 1992. *Concluding Unscientific Postscript to Philosophical Fragments*, edited and translated by Howard V. Hong and Edna H. Hong. Princeton, NJ: Princeton University Press.

Korac, Maja. 1998. "Ethnic Nationalism, Wars and the Patterns of Social, Political and Sexual Violence against Women: The Case of Post Yugoslav Countries." *Identities: Global Studies in Culture and Power* 5, no. 2: 153–81.

Korolczuk, Elzbieta, and Agnieszka Graff. 2018. "Gender as 'Ebola from Brussels': The Anticolonial Frame and the Rise of Illiberal Populism." *Signs: Journal of Women in Culture and Society* 43, no. 4: 797–821.

Kovács, Kriszta, and Gabor Tóth. 2011. "Hungary's Constitutional Transformation." *European Constitutional Law Review* 7, no. 2: 183–203.

Kováts, Eszter. 2021. "Anti-gender Politics in East-Central Europe: Right-wing Defiance to West-Eurocentrism." *Gender – Zeitschrift für Geschlecht, Kultur und Gesellschaft* 13, no. 1: 76–90.

Kraszewski, Gracjan. 2012. "Catalyst for Revolution: Pope John Paul II's 1979 Pilgrimage to Poland and Its Effects on Solidarity and the Fall of Communism." *The Polish Review* 57, no. 4: 27–46.

Krizsán, Andrea, and Conny Roggeband. 2021. *Politicizing Gender and Democracy in the Context of the Istanbul Convention*. Cham: Springer Nature.

Krizsán, Andrea, Conny Roggeband, and Michael C. Zeller. 2024. "Who is Afraid of the Istanbul Convention? Explaining Opposition to and Support for Gender Equality." *Comparative Political Studies* 58, no. 10: 2161–201.

Kuhar, Roman, and David Paternotte. 2017. *Anti-Gender Campaigns in Europe: Mobilizing against Equality*. Lanham: Rowman & Littlefield.

Kuru, Ahmet T. 2008. "Secularism in Turkey: Myths and Realities." *Insight Turkey* 10, no. 3: 101–10.

Kütük-Kuriş, Merve. 2022. "The Rise and Fall of Support for the Istanbul Convention: Understanding the case of KADEM." *Women's Studies International Forum* 93, no. 4: 1–14.

Laruelle Marlene. 2018. *Russian Nationalism Imaginaries, Doctrines, and Political Battlefields*. Abingdon: Routledge.

Lauri, Mälksoo. 2021. "International Law and the 2020 Amendments to the Russian Constitution." *American Journal of International Law* 115, no. 1: 78–93.

Lawford-Smith, Holly. 2022. *Gender-Critical Feminism*. New York: Oxford University Press.

Lecler, Joseph. 1951. *Histoire de la tolérance au siècle de la Réforme*. Paris: Aubier.

Levy, Leonard W. 1986. *The Establishment Clause: Religion and the First Amendment*. Chapel Hill: University of North Carolina Press.

Lombardi Vallauri, Luigi. 2005. "Simboli e realizzazione." In *Symbolon/Diabolon: Simboli, Religioni, Diritti nell'Europa multiculturale*, edited by Edoardo Dieni, Alessandro Ferrari, and Vincenzo Pacillo, 13–26. Bologna: Il Mulino.

Luehrmann, Sonja. 2011. "Innocence and Demographic Crisis: Transposing Post-Abortion Syndrome into a Russian Orthodox Key." In *A Fragmented Landscape*, edited by Silvia De Zordo, Joanna Mishtal, and Lorena Anton, 103–22. New York: Berghahn Books.

Mad'arová, Zuzana, and Pavol Hardoš. 2022. "In the Name of the Conservative People: Slovakia's Gendered Illiberal Transformation." *Politics and Governance* 10, no. 4: 95–107.

Mahmood, Saba. 2016. *Religious Difference in a Secular Age: A Minority Report*. Princeton, NJ: Princeton University Press.

Maietta, Michel. 2019. "The Geopolitics of Homophobia." *Alternatives Humanitaires / Humanitarian Alternatives* 11 (July): 104–15.

Mancini, Susanna. 2009. "The Power of Symbols and Symbols as Power: Secularism and Religion in the Public Square." *Cardozo Law Review* 30, no. 6: 2629–69.

Mancini, Susanna. 2012. "Patriarchy as the Exclusive Domain of the Other: The Veil Controversy, False Projection and Cultural Racism." *International Journal of Constitutional Law* 10, no. 2: 411–28.

Mancini, Susanna. 2014. "The Tempting of Europe, the Political Seduction of the Cross: A Schhmittian Reading of Christianity and Islam in European Constitutionalism." In *Constitutional Secularism in an Age of Religious Revival*, edited by Susanna Mancini and Michel Rosenfeld, 282–308. Oxford: Oxford University Press.

Mancini, Susanna. 2017. "Global Religion in a Post-Westphalia World." In *Handbook on Global Constitutionalism*, edited by Anthony F. Lang and Antje Wiener, 421–32. Cheltenham, UK: Edward Elgar Publishing.

Mancini, Susanna. 2020. "Introduction." In *Handbook on Constitutions and Religion*, edited by Susanna Mancini, 1–19. Cheltenham, UK: Edward Elgar Publishers.

Mancini, Susanna. 2021. "False Science and Misogyny: Trump's Assault on Reproductive Rights." *DPCE Online* 46, no. 1: 1087–104.

Mancini, Susanna. 2023. "Global Religion in a post-Westphalia World." In *Handbook of Global Constitutionalism*, edited by Anthony F. Lang and Antje Wiener, 2nd edn, 556–67. Cheltenham, UK: Edward Elgar Publishing.

Mancini, Susanna. 2025. "Religious Freedom in Italy and Europe." In *The Oxford Handbook of Comparative Human Rights Law*, edited by Neha Jain and Mila Versteeg. New York: Oxford University Press.

Mancini, Susanna, and Nausica Palazzo. 2021. "The Body of the Nation: Illiberalism and Gender." In *Routledge Handbook of Illiberalism*, edited by Stephen Holmes, András Sajó, and Renáta Uitz, 403–22. Abingdon: Routledge.

Mancini, Susanna, and Michel Rosenfeld. 2018a. *Conscience Wars: Rethinking the Balance between Religion, Identity, and Equality*. Cambridge: Cambridge University Press.

Mancini, Susanna, and Michel Rosenfeld. 2018b. "Introduction: The New Generaiton of Conscience Objections in Legal, Political, and Cultural Context." In *Conscience Wars: Rethinking the Balance between Religion, Identity, and Equality*, edited by Susanna Mancini and Michel Rosenfeld, 1–20. Cambridge: Cambridge University Press.

Mancini, Susanna, and Kristina Stoeckl. 2018. "Transatlantic Conversations. The Emergence of Society: Protective Anti-Abortion Arguments in the United States, Europe and Russia." In *Conscience Wars: Rethinking the Balance between Religion, Identity, and Equality*, edited by Susanna Mancini and Michel Rosenfeld, 220–57. Cambridge: Cambridge University Press.

Mankoff, Jeffrey. 2022. *Empires of Eurasia: How Imperial Legacies Shape International Security*. New Haven: Yale University Press.

March, Andrew F. 2014. "Are Secularism and Neutrality Attractive to Religious Minorities? Islamic Discussions of Western Secularism in the 'Jurisprudence of Muslim Minorities' (Fiqh Al-Aqalliyyat) Discourse." In *Constitutional Secularism in an Age of Religious Revival*, edited by Susanna Mancini and Michel Rosenfeld, 282–308. Oxford: Oxford University Press.

Marx, Karl. 1975. "Contribution to the Critique of Hegel's Philosophy of Right: Introduction." In *Early Writings*, translated by Rodney Livingstone and Gregor Benton, 170–77. Harmondsworth: Penguin.

Massad, Joseph A. 2002. "Re-Orienting Desire: The Gay International and the Arab World." *Public Culture* 14, no. 2: 361–85.

McCann, Charles, and Charles Bradlaugh. 1881. *The Principles of Secularism*. London: Austin & Co.

McClintock, Anne. 1993. "Family Feuds: Gender, Nationalism and the Family." *Feminist Review* 44, no. 1: 61–80.

McCrudden, Christopher. 2014. "Human Rights, Southern Voices, and 'Traditional Values' at the United Nations 12." *Univ. Mich. Pub. Law Research Paper Series*, Paper No. 419.

McCrudden, Christopher. 2015a. "Transnational Culture Wars." *International Journal of Constitutional Law* 13, no. 2: 434–62.

McCrudden, Christopher. 2015b. "Benedict's Legacy: Human Rights, Human Dignity, and the Possibility of Dialogue." In *Pope Benedict XVI's Legal Thought: A Dialogue on the Foundation of Law*, edited by Marta Cartabia and Andrea Simoncini, 165–84. Cambridge: Cambridge University Press.

McCrudden, Christopher. 2015c. "Faith-based Non-governmental Organizations in the Public Square." In *Changing Nature of Religious Rights under International Law*, edited by Malcolm Evans, Peter Petkoof, and Julian Rivers, 185–210. Cambridge: Cambridge University Press.

McCrudden, Christopher. 2018. "Marriage Registrars, Same-Sex Relationships, and Religious Discrimination in the European Court of Human Rights." In *Conscience Wars: Rethinking the Balance between Religion, Identity, and Equality*, edited by Susanna Mancini and Michel Rosenfeld, 414–62. Cambridge: Cambridge University Press.

McNally, Michael D. 2020. *Defend the Sacred: Native American Religious Freedom beyond the First Amendment*. Princeton, NJ: Princeton University Press.

McTernan, Oliver. 1990. "Religion and Perestroijka." *Studies: An Irish Quarterly Review* 79, no. 313: 18–26.

Mégret, Frédéric. 2022. "Human Rights Populism." *Humanity: An International Journal of Human Rights, Humanitarianism, and Development* 13, no. 2: 240–59.

Meurens, Nathalie *et al.* 2020. *Tackling Violence Against Women and Domestic Violence in Europe. The Added Value of the Istanbul Convention and Remaining Challenges*." Brussels: FEMM Committee of the European Parliament.

Michel, Patrick. 1991. *Politics and Religion in Eastern Europe: Catholicism in Hungary, Poland and Czechoslovakia*, translated by Alan Braley. Oxford: Polity.

Miskolci, Richard, and Maximiliano Campana. 2017. "'Ideologia de gênero': notas para a genealogia de um pânico moral contemporaneo." *Revista Sociedade e Estado* 32, no. 3 (September/December): 725–47.

Mousnier, Roland. 1973. *The Assassination of Henry IV: The Tyrannicide Problem and the Consolidation of the French Absolute Monarchy in the Early Seventeenth Century*, translated by Joan Spencer. London: Faber and Faber.

Müller, Jan-Werner. 2016. *What Is Populism?* Philadelphia: University of Pennsylvania Press.

Muparamoto, Nelson. 2020. "LGBT Individuals and the Struggle Against Robert Mugabe's Extirpation in Zimbabwe." *Africa Review* 13, no. 3: 1–16.

Murillo, Lina-Maria. 2025. "Fears of White Population Decline: The Politics of Race, Gender, Reproductive Justice, and White Supremacy in the US." *Journal of Gender Studies* 34, no. 5: 716–31.

Murray, Melissa. 2024. "Making History." *The Yale Law Journal Forum*, April 11, 2024: 990–1015.

Murray, Melissa, and Katherine Shaw. 2024. "Dobbs and Democracy." *Harvard Law Review* 3, no. 3: 730–807.

Murray, Stephen, and Will Roscoe. 1998. *Boy-Wives and Female-Husbands: Studies of African Homosexualities*. New York: St. Martin's Press.

National Academies of Sciences, Engineering, and Medicine. 2018. *The Safety and Quality of Abortion Care in the United States*. Washington, DC: The National Academies Press.

Neuhaus, Richard John. 1984. *The Naked Public Square: Religion and Democracy in America*. Grand Rapids, MI: Eerdmans.

Numbers, Ronald L. 1992. *The Creationists: The Evolution of Scientific Creationism*. New York: Alfred A. Knopf.

Očesášová, Zuzana. 2022. "Poison in the Juice: 'Gender Ideology' and the Istanbul Convention in Slovakia." *Politické vedy* 24, no. 4: 38–55.

Pankowski, Rafal, and Marcin Kormak. 2013. "Radical Nationalism in Poland: From Theory to Practice." In *Right-Wing Extremism in Europe*, edited by Ralf Melzer and Sebastian Serafin, 157–168. Berlin: Friedrich Ebert Stiftung.

Parla, Taha, and Andrew Davison. 2004. *Corporatist Ideology in Kemalist Turkey. Progress or Order?* Syracuse: Syracuse University Press.

Pateman, Carole. 1988. *The Sexual Contract.* Cambridge, UK: Polity Press.

Pető, Andrea. 2021. "Gendering and Illiberalism." In *Routledge Handbook of Illiberalism*, edited by Stephen Holmes, András Sajó, and Renáta Uitz, 403–22. Abingdon: Routledge.

Petto, Andrew J. 2015. "Evolution, Creationism, and Intelligent Design." In *Basics in Human Evolution*, edited by Michael P. Muehlenbein, 15–27. San Diego: Academic Press.

Pizzolo, Paolo. 2020. *Eurasianism: An Ideology for the Multipolar World.* London: Bloomsbury Academic.

Pocé, Gintare, and Ilva Skulte. 2023. "Religious Voices Against 'Gender Ideology' in the Discourse on the Ratification of the Istanbul Convention in Latvian and Lithuanian Media." *Religion and Society in Central and Eastern Europe* 16, no. 1: 39–60.

Popov, A. A. 1990. "Family Planning in the USSR: Sky-High Abortion Rates Reflect Dire Lack of Choice." *Entre Nous Cph Den.* 16 (September): 5–7.

Popov, A. A., A. P. Visser, and E. Ketting. 1993. "Contraceptive Knowledge, Attitudes and Practices in Russia during the 1980s." *Studies in Family Planning* 24, no. 4: 227–35.

Pūraitė-Andrikienė, Dovilė. 2025. "Conclusion on the Constitutionality of the Istanbul Convention of the Lithuanian Constitutional Court: Context, Reasoning, and Legal Consequences." *Access to Justice in Eastern Europe* 8, no. 1: 1–25.

Ratzinger, Joseph. 1997. *La sal de la tierra.* Madrid: Libros Palabra.

Rawls, John. 1996. *Political Liberalism.* New York: Columbia University Press.

Rawls, John. 2005. *Political Liberalism: Expanded Edition.* 2nd ed. New York: Columbia University Press.

Redlich, Norman, Bernard Schwartz, and John E. Attanasio. 2005. *Understanding Constitutional Law.* 3rd ed. New Providence, NJ: LexisNexis.

Reese, Roger R. 2018. "The Legacy of World War II for Putin's Russia." *South Central Review* 35, no. 1: 196–212.

Robinson, George. 2001. *Essential Judaism: A Complete Guide to Beliefs, Customs and Rituals.* New York: Atria Books.

Rosenfeld, Michel. 1998. *Just Interpretations: Law between Ethics and Politics.* Berkeley: University of California Press.

Rosenfeld, Michel. 2006. "Judicial Balancing in Times of Stress: Comparing the American, British and Israeli Approaches to the War on Terror." *Cardozo Law Review* 27, no. 5: 2079–150.

Rosenfeld, Michel. 2010. *The Identity of the Constitutional Subject: Selfhood, Citizenship, Culture, and Community.* New York: Routledge.

Rosenfeld, Michel. 2011. *Law, Justice, Democracy and the Clash of Cultures: A Pluralistic Account.* Cambridge: Cambridge University Press.

Rosenfeld, Michel. 2014. "Recasting Secularism as One Conception of the Good among Many." In *Constitutional Secularism in an Age of Religious Revival*, edited by Susanna Mancini and Michel Rosenfeld, 79–108. Oxford: Oxford University Press.

Rosenfeld, Michel. 2020. "Constitution and Secularism: A Western Account." In *Handbook on Constitutions and Religion*, edited by Susanna Mancini, 21–40. Cheltenham, UK: Edward Elgar Publishers.

Rosenfeld, Michel. 2022. *A Pluralist Theory of Constitutional Justice: Assessing Liberal Democracy in Times of Rising Populism and Illiberalism.* Oxford: Oxford University Press.

Rousseau, Jean-Jacques. 1968. (orig. 1762). *The Social Contract*, translated by Maurice Cranston. London: Penguin Books.

Sadursky, Wojciech. 2020. "Constitutional Design: Lessons from Poland's Democratic Backsliding." *Constitutional Studies* 6, no. 1: 59–80.

Sakevich, Victoria I., and Boris P. Denisov. 2014. "Birth Control in Russia: Overcoming the State System Resistance." *HSE Working papers*, WP BRP 42/SOC/2014.

Saktanber, Ayse, and Gül Corbacioglu. 2019. "Veiling and Headscarf-Skepticism in Turkey." *Social Politics: International Studies in Gender, State & Society* 15, no. 4: 514–38.

Sapir, Gideon, and Daniel Statman. 2014. "Religious Marriage and Divorce in Israel: Time for Change." In *Constitutional Secularism in an Age of Religious Revival*, edited by Susanna Mancini and Michel Rosenfeld, 269–86. New York: Oxford University Press.

Sapir, Gideon, and Daniel Statman. 2019. *State and Religion in Israel: A Philosophical-Legal Inquiry.* Cambridge: Cambridge University Press.

Scala, Jorge. 2010. *La ideología del género. OO el género como herramienta del poder.* Rosario: Ediciones Logos.

Scalia, Antonin. 1997. *A Matter of Interpretation: Federal Courts and the Law.* Princeton, NJ: Princeton University Press.

Schmitt, Carl. 1950. *The Nomos of the Earth in the International Law of the Jus Publicum Europaeum*, translated by G. L. Ulmen. New York: Telos Press.

Schmitt, Carl. 1985 (orig. 1923). *The Crisis of Parliamentary Democracy.* Cambridge, US: MIT Press.

Schmitt, Carl. 2005. *Political Theology: Four Chapters on the Concept of Sovereignty*, translated by George Schwab. Chicago: University of Chicago Press.

Schmitt, Carl. 2005 (orig. 1927). "Three Concept of the Political." In *Political Theology: Four Chapters on the Theory of Sovereignty*, translated by George Schwab. Chicago: University of Chicago Press.

Schmitt, Carl. 2011 (orig. 1941). *The Großraum Order of International Law with a Ban on Intervention for Spatially Foreign Powers*, translated in: *Writings on War*, edited and translated by Timothy Nunan. Cambridge: Polity Press.

Sen, Ronojoy. 2020. "Reforming Religion: The Indian Constitution, the Courts and Hinduism." In *Handbook on Constitutions and Religion*, edited by Susanna Mancini, 222–36. Cheltenham, UK: Edward Elgar Publishers.

Sharma, Jyotirmaya. 2011. *Hindutva: Exploring the Idea of Hindu Nationalism.* Rev. ed. London: Penguin Books.

Shekhovtsov, Anton. 2009. "Aleksandr Dugin's Neo-Eurasianism: The New Right *à la Russe.*" *Religion Compass* 3, no. 4: 697–716.

Siegel, Reva. 1996. "'The Rule of Love': Wife Beating as Prerogative and Privacy." *The Yale Law Journal* 105, no. 8: 2117–207.

Siegel, Reva. 2008. "The Rights' Reasons: Constitutional Conflict and the Spread of Woman – Protective Anti-Abortion Argument." *Duke Law Journal* 57, no. 6: 1641–92.

Siegel, Reva. 2012. "Dignity and Sexuality: Claims on Dignity in Transnational Debates over Abortion and Same-Sex Marriage." *International Journal of Constitutional Law* 10, no. 2: 355–79.

Siegel, Reva. 2013. "Dignity and the Duty to Protect Unborn Life." In *Understanding Human Dignity*, edited by Christopher McCrudden, 509–24. New York: Oxford University Press.

Siegel, Reva. 2023. "Memory Games: *Dobbs*'s Originalism as Anti-Democratic Living Constitutionalism—and Some Pathways for Resistance." *Texas Law Review* 101, no. 5: 1127–204.

Sieyès, Emmanuel-Joseph. 1963 (orig. 1789). *What is the Third Estate?*, translated by M. Blondel. New York: Praeger.

Smilova, Ruzha. 2020. "The Ideological Turn in Bulgarian Constitutional Discourse: The Rise Against 'Genders.'" In *Critical Essays on Human Rights Criticism*, edited by András Sajó and Renáta Uitz, 177–97. The Hague: Eleven Publishing International.

Smith, Anthony D. 1981. *The Ethnic Revival in the Modern World.* New York: Cambridge University Press.

Smith, Rogers. 1997. *Civic Ideals: Conflicting Visions of Citizenship in US History.* New Haven: Yale University Press.

Spinner-Halev, Jeff. 2005. "Hinduism, Toleration, and Liberalism." *Political Theory* 33, no. 5: 28–52.

Spinoza, Benedict de. 1951. *Theological-Political Treatise*, translated by R. H. M. Elwes. New York: Dover.

Stacie, Ruth, and Carrie Beth Stoelting. 2013. *United the USA: Discover the ABCs of Patriotism*. Bloomington, IN: WestBow Press.

Stella, Francesca, and Nadya Nartova. 2015. "Sexual Citizenship, Nationalism and Biopolitics in Putin's Russia." In *Sexuality, Citizenship and Belonging: Transnational and Intersectional Perspectives*, edited by Francesca Stella, Yvette Taylor, Tracey Reynolds, and Antoine Rogers, 24–42. New York: Routledge.

Stepanova, Elena A. 2023. "'Everything Good Against Everything Bad': Traditional Values in the Search for New Russian National Idea." *Zeitschrift für Religion, Gesellschaft und Politik* 7, no. 1: 97–118.

Stoeckl, Kristina. 2014. *The Russian Orthodox Church and Human Rights*. Abingdon: Routledge.

Stoeckl, Kristina. 2020a. "The Rise of the Russian Christian Right: The Case of the World Congress of Families." *Religion, State and Society* 48, no. 4: 223–38.

Stoeckl, Kristina. 2020b. "Three Models of Church–State Relations in Contemporary Russia." In *Handbook on Constitutions and Religion*, edited by Susanna Mancini, 237–51. Cheltenham, UK: Edward Elgar Publishers.

Stoeckl, Kristina. 2023. "Traditional Values, Family, Homeschooling: The Role of Russia and the Russian orthodox Church in Transnational Moal Conservative Networks and their Efforts at Reshaping Human Rights." *International Journal of Constitutional Law* 21, no. 1: 224–42.

Stoeckl, Kristina, and Dmitry Uzlner. 2022. *The Moralist International: Russia in the Global Culture Wars*. New York: Fordham University Press.

Stoelting, Carrie Beth, and Ruth Stacie. 2013. *Unite the USA*. Grand Rapids, MI: WestBow Press.

Stone, Suzanne L. 1993. "In Pursuit of the Counter-Text: The Turn to the Jewish Legal Model in Contemporary American Legal Theory." *Harvard Law Review* 106, no. 4: 813–94.

Stopler, Gila. 2013. "National Identity and Religion–State Relations: Israel in Comparative Perspective." In *Israeli Constitutional Law in the Making*, edited by Gideon Sapir, Daphne Barak-Erez, and Aharon Barak, 503–16. London: Bloomsbury Publishing.

Stopler, Gila. 2020. "Constitutionalism and Religion in a Jewish and Democratic State." In *Handbook on Constitutions and Religion*, edited by Susanna Mancini, 208–21. Cheltenham, UK: Edward Elgar Publishers.

Stopler, Gila. 2025. *Women's Rights in Liberal States*. Cambridge, UK: Cambridge University Press.

Sudarkasa, Niara. 1986. "'The Status of Women' in Indigenous African Societies." *Feminist Studies* 12, no. 1: 91–103.

Sunstein, Cass R. 2018. "Originalism." *Notre Dame Law Review* 93, no. 4: 1671–98.

Suslov, Mikhail D. 2014. "'Holy Rus': The Geopolitical Imagination in the Contemporary Russian Orthodox Church." *Russian Politics and Law* 52, no. 3: 67–86.

Szelewa, Dorota, and Dorottya Szikra. 2022. "Leave Policies in Populist and Illiberal Regimes: The Cases of Hungary and Poland." In *Research Handbook on Leave Policy*, edited by Ivana Dobrotić, Sonja Blum, and Alison Koslowski, 100–14. Cheltenham, UK: Edward Elgar Publishing.

Tamale, Sylvia. 2013. "Confronting the Politics of Nonconforming Sexualities in Africa." *African Studies Review* 56, no. 2: 31–45.

Taylor, Charles. 2007. *A Secular Age*. Cambridge, MA: Harvard University Press.

Tazbir, Janusz. 1977. "Poland and the Concept of Europe in the Sixteenth–Eighteenth Centuries." *European Studies Review* 7, no. 1: 29–45.

Tegler, Henrietta. 2024. "Gendered Advocacy Coalitions in Estonia and Lithuania: A Comparative Study about the (non-)Ratification of the Istanbul Convention." *LUP Department of Political Science*, STVK04 20232.

Touraine, Alain. 1994. *Qu'est-ce-que-la democracie*. Paris: Fayard.

Tranfić, Ivan. 2022. "Framing 'Gender Ideology': Religious Populism in the Croatian Catholic Church." *Identities: Global Studies in Culture and Power* 29, no. 4: 466–82.

Troper, Michel. 2009. "Sovereignty and Laïcité." *Cardozo Law Review* 30, no. 6: 2555–271.

Troper, Michel. 2014. "Sovereignty and Laïcité." In *Constitutional Secularism in an Age of Religious Revival*, edited by Susanna Mancini and Michel Rosenfeld, 146–59. Oxford: Oxford University Press.

Tushnet, Mark. 2018. "Comparing Right-Wing and Left-Wing Populism." In *Constitutional Democracy in Crisis?*, edited by Mark Graber, Sanford Levinson, and Mark Tushnet, 639–50. Oxford: Oxford University Press.

Udayakumar, S.P. 1997. "Historicizing Myth and Mythologizing History: The 'Ram Temple' Drama." *Social Scientist* 25, no. 7/8: 11–26.

Uitz, Renáta. 2025. "How Hungary's Pride Ban Tests the EU's Commitment to Democracy." *Verfassungsblog: On Matters Constitutional*, April 2, 2025. <https://verfassungsblog.de/how-hungarys-pride-ban-tests-the-eus-commitment-to-democracy/>, accessed October 1, 2025.

Unal, Didem. 2024. "The Variety of Anti-gender Alliances and Democratic Backsliding in Turkey: Fault Lines around Opposition to 'Gender Ideology' and their Political Implications." *International Feminist Journal of Politics* 26, no. 1: 6–30.

Vaggione, Juan M. 2012. "La 'cultura de la vida': desplazamientos estratégicos del activismo católico conservador frente a los derechos sexuales y reproductivos." *Religião & Sociedade* 32, no. 2: 57–80.

Vaggione, Juan M. 2017. "Francis and 'Gender Ideology': Heritage, Displacement and Continuities." *Religion and Gender* 6, no. 2: 302–7.

Vassileva, Radosveta. 2018. "Bulgaria's Constitutional Troubles with the Istanbul Convention." *Verfassungsblog: On Matters Constitutional*, August 2, 2018. <https://verfassungsblog.de/bulgarias-constitutional-troubles-with-the-istanbul-convention/>, accessed October 1, 2025.

Vazirani, Gulab, and Lal Advani. 1991. *The Man and his Mission*. London: Arnold Publishers.

Walker, Neil. 2017. "Constitutionalism and Pluralism." In *Handbook of Global Constitutionalism*, edited by Anthony F. Lang and Antje Wiener, 2nd edn, 568–79. Cheltenham, UK: Edward Elgar Publishing.

Wallace, Gregory. 2009. "Justifying Religious Freedom: The Western Tradition." *Penn State Law Review* 14, no. 2: 485–570.

Walzer, Michael. 1983. *Spheres of Justice: A Defense of Pluralism and Equality*. New York: Basic Books.

Weber, Max. 1946. "Religious Rejections of the World and Their Directions." In *From Max Weber: Essays in Sociology*, edited by Hans Heinrich Gerth and Charles Wright Mills, 323–59. New York: Oxford University Press.

Weber, Max. 2002. *The Protestant Ethic and the "Spirit" of Capitalism and Other Writings*, translated by Peter Baehr and Gordon C. Wells. London: Penguin Modern Classics.

Weber, Sarah E. 2009. "An Attempt to Legislate Morality: Forced Ultrasounds as the Newest Tactic in Anti-Abortion Legislation." *Tulsa Law Review* 45, no. 2: 359–84.

Weil, Patrick. 2014. "Headscarf versus Burqa: Two French Bans with Different Meanings." In *Constitutional Secularism in an Age of Religious Revival*, edited by Susanna Mancini and Michel Rosenfeld, 195–215. Oxford: Oxford University Press.

Whitehead, Andrew, and Christopher P. Scheitle. 2018. "We the (Christian) People: Christianity and American Identity from 1996 to 2014." *Social Currents* 5, no. 2: 157–62.

Whitehead, Andrew L., and Samuel L. Perry. 2020. *Taking America Back for God: Christian Nationalism in the United States*. New York: Oxford University Press.

Wiederkehr, Stefan. 2017. "Conservative Revolution *à la russe*? An Interpretation of Classic Eurasianism in a European Context." *Journal of Modern European History / Zeitschrift für moderne europäische Geschichte / Revue d'histoire européenne contemporaine* 15, no. 1: 72–84.

Yavuz, Hakan M., and Ahmet E. Öztürk. 2019. "Turkish Secularism and Islam under the Reign of Erdogan." *Southeast European and Black Sea Studies* 19, no. 1: 1–9.

Yilmaz, Ishan. 2021. *Creating the Desired Citizen: Ideology, State and Islam in Turkey*. Cambridge: Cambridge University Press.

Young, Katharine. 2022. "Human Rights Originalism." *Georgetown Law Journal* 110, no. 5: 1097–168.

Young, Katharine. 2025. "Human Rights in the Constitutional Era of *Dobbs*." *Columbia Human Rights Law Review* 56: 1–72.

Yuval-Davis, Nira. 1997. *Gender and Nation*. Thousand Oaks: SAGE Publications.

Zagrebelsky, Gustavo. 2014. "One Among Many? The Catholic Church Between Universalism and Pluralism." In *Constitutional Secularism in an Age of Religious Revival*, edited by Susanna Mancini and Michel Rosenfeld, 247–68. Oxford: Oxford University Press.

Zorgdrager, Heleen E. 2013. "Homosexuality and Hypermasculinity in the Public Discourse of the Russian Orthodox Church: An Affect Theoretical Approach." *International Journal of Philosophy & Theology* 74, no. 3: 214–39.

Zubrzycki, Geneviève. 2001. "'We, the Polish Nation': Ethnic and Civic Visions of Nationhood in Post-Communist Constitutional Debates." *Theory and Society* 30, no. 5: 629–68.

Zúquete, José Pedro. 2017. "Populism and Religion." In *The Oxford Handbook of Populism*, edited by Cristóbal Rovira Kalwasser, Paul Taggart, Paulina Ochoa Espejo, and Pierre Ostiguy, 445–66. Oxford: Oxford University Press.

Index

For the benefit of digital users, indexed terms that span two pages (e.g., 52–53) may, on occasion, appear on only one of those pages.